LAW AND DEVELOPMENT OF MIDDLE-INCOME COUNTRIES

In 1960, there were 101 middle-income countries. By 2008, only thirteen of these had become high-income countries. Why do so many middle-income countries fail to develop after a promising start, becoming mired in the so-called middle-income trap? This interdisciplinary volume addresses the special challenges that middle-income countries confront from both a theoretical and a practical perspective. It is the first volume that addresses law and development issues in middle-income countries from the perspective of political, administrative, and legal institutions and policies. The goal is to provide international development agencies and domestic policy makers with feasible recommendations to address the wide range of technically, politically, and socially complex issues that middle-income countries face.

Randall Peerenboom is a Professor of Law at La Trobe University and an Associate Fellow of the Oxford University Center for Socio-Legal Studies. He is a former Director of the Oxford Foundation for Law, Justice and Society Rule of Law in China Programme and was Professor at UCLA Law School from 1998 to 2007. He has been a consultant to the Asian Development Bank, Ford Foundation, EU-China, UN Development Programme, and other international organizations on legal reforms and rule of law in China and Asia, and he is the Co–Editor-in-Chief of *The Hague Journal of Rule of Law*. He is also a China International Economic and Trade Arbitration Commission arbitrator, and he frequently serves as an expert witness on People's Republic of China legal issues. Recent books include *The Dynamics of Rule of Law in an Era of International and Transnational Governance* (edited with Michael Zürn and André Noelkamper, Cambridge University Press 2012); *Judicial Independence in China* (edited, Cambridge University Press 2010); *Regulation in Asia: Pushing Back on Globalization* (edited with John Gillespie, 2009); and *China Modernizes – Threat to the West or Model for the Rest?* (2007).

Tom Ginsburg is the Leo Spitz Professor of International Law, Ludwig and Hilda Wolf Research Scholar, and Professor of Political Science at the University of Chicago, as well as Research Professor at the American Bar Foundation. He currently codirects the Comparative Constitutions Project, a National Science Foundation–funded data set cataloging the world's constitutions since 1789. His recent coauthored book, *The Endurance of National Constitutions* (2009), won the best book award from the Comparative Democratization Section of the American Political Science Association. His other books include *Judicial Review in New Democracies* (2003), *Administrative Law and Governance in Asia* (2008), *Rule by Law: The Politics of Courts in Authoritarian Regimes* (with Tamir Moustafa, 2008), and *Comparative Constitutional Law* (with Rosalind Dixon, 2011). Before entering law teaching, he served as a legal advisor at the Iran-U.S. Claims Tribunal, The Hague, Netherlands, and he has consulted with numerous international development agencies and governments on legal and constitutional reform.

Law and Development of Middle-Income Countries

AVOIDING THE MIDDLE-INCOME TRAP

Edited by

RANDALL PEERENBOOM
La Trobe University, Melbourne

TOM GINSBURG
University of Chicago

CAMBRIDGE
UNIVERSITY PRESS

CAMBRIDGE
UNIVERSITY PRESS

32 Avenue of the Americas, New York, NY 10013-2473, USA

Cambridge University Press is part of the University of Cambridge.

It furthers the University's mission by disseminating knowledge in the pursuit of education, learning, and research at the highest international levels of excellence.

www.cambridge.org
Information on this title: www.cambridge.org/9781107609198

First published 2014
Reprinted 2014

A catalog record for this publication is available from the British Library.

Library of Congress Cataloging in Publication Data
Law and development of middle-income countries : avoiding the middle-income trap / Randall Peerenboom, La Trobe University, Melbourne; Tom Ginsburg, University of Chicago.
pages cm.
Includes bibliographical references and index.
ISBN 978-1-107-02815-9 (hardback) – ISBN 978-1-107-60919-8 (paperback)
1. Law and economic development. 2. Developing countries – Economic policy.
I. Peerenboom, R. P. (Randall P.), 1958– editor of compilation. II. Ginsburg, Tom, editor of compilation.
K3820.L38 2013
338.9009172'4–dc23 2013027235

ISBN 978-1-107-02815-9 Hardback
ISBN 978-1-107-60919-8 Paperback

Contents

List of Contributors

Nicholas Booth is Policy Advisor for Governance, Human Rights and Access to Justice, UNDP Asia-Pacific Regional Centre.

Juan Carlos Botero is Executive Director, The World Justice Project.

Daniel M. Brinks is Associate Professor of Comparative Politics and Public Law, University of Texas at Austin.

Bojan Bugaric is Associate Professor of Law, University of Ljubljana, Slovenia.

Kevin E. Davis is the Beller Family Professor of Business Law, NYU School of Law.

William Forbath is Associate Dean of Research and Lloyd M. Bentsen Chair in Law, University of Texas at Austin School of Law.

John Gillespie is Professor of Law and Director of the Asia Pacific Business Regulation Group, Monash University.

Tom Ginsburg is the Leo Spitz Professor of International Law and Ludwig and Hilda Wolf Research Scholar, University of Chicago Law School; Research Professor at the American Bar Foundation; and Professor of Political Science at the University of Chicago.

Fernanda Gómez-Abán is a Research Assistant at CIDE.

William Hurst is Associate Professor of Political Science, Northwestern University.

Lesley K. McAllister is Professor of Law and Martin Luther King Jr. Hall Research Scholar, University of California Davis School of Law.

Randall Peerenboom is Professor of Law, La Trobe University, and Associate Fellow, Oxford University Centre for Socio-Legal Studies.

Julio Ríos-Figueroa is Professor of Political Studies, CIDE.

César Rodríguez-Garavito is Associate Professor and Director, Program on Global Justice and Human Rights, University of los Andes, Colombia.

Gregory Shaffer is the Melvin C. Steen Professor, University of Minnesota Law School.

Surain Subramaniam is Associate Professor of International and Asian Studies, University of North Carolina at Asheville.

Charles Sutton holds a JD degree from the University of Minnesota.

Benjamin van Rooij is the John S. and Marilyn Long Chair in US-China Business and Law, University of California, Irvine.

Peter K. Yu is the Kern Family Chair in Intellectual Property Law, Drake University Law School.

Acknowledgments

The editors would like to thank the University of Chicago Law School, the Hague Institute for the Internationalisation of Law, and La Trobe University for financial support, and Sonali Maulik, Robert Meyer, Kayla Ginsburg, and Taimoor Aziz for superb research assistance. Ginsburg would like to thank the Russell Baker Scholars Fund of the University of Chicago Law School.

1

Law and Development in Middle-Income Countries

Introduction

Randall Peerenboom

In 1960, there were 101 middle-income countries (MICs). By 2008, only thirteen had become high-income countries (HICs).[1] Why do so many MICs fail to develop after a promising start, becoming mired in the so-called middle-income trap?

This volume addresses the special challenges MICs confront from a theoretical and a practical perspective. These challenges include maintaining sustainable economic growth while curbing rising income inequality and environmental degradation; creating social safety nets to protect those disadvantaged by economic reforms and globalization; reducing financial volatility and avoiding the crises that have frequently followed in the wake of financial liberalization; combating corruption; meeting Millennium Development Goals (MDGs) such as adequate health care, free primary education, and poverty alleviation; building the institutional capacity required for effective governance and a market economy; and maintaining social and political stability in the face of rising expectations and demands on the state.[2]

This is the first volume on MICs that addresses law and development issues from the perspective of political, administrative, and legal institutions and policies. Most of the existing literature that specifically discusses MICs, including empirical studies that sort by levels of wealth and distinguish between low-income countries (LICs), MICs, and HICs, is by economists or development specialists. There are many articles, for example, on international trade, foreign investment, financing and the banking sector, fiscal policy and currency exchange, technology transfer, and taxation, as well as traditional development topics such as infrastructure, rural development, urban planning, the environment, social welfare systems, and health care. There has been very little work, however, by political

[1] World Bank, *China 2030: Building a Modern, Harmonious, and Creative High-Income Society*, 2012, 11, available at http://www.worldbank.org/en/news/2012/02/27/china-2030-executive-summary.

[2] See, generally, the World Bank reports cited in the following text, and Independent Evaluation Group (hereafter referred to as IEG), *Development Results in Middle-Income Countries: An Evaluation of World Bank Support*, 2007, available at http://siteresources.worldbank.org/EXTMIDINCCOU/Resources/MIC_evaluation.pdf.

scientists, sociologists, legal scholars, and regulatory theorists on political and administrative reforms, rule of law, and good governance in MICs as a separate category of analysis.[3] This volume begins to fill the gap. The goal is to provide international development agencies and domestic policy makers with feasible recommendations to address the wide range of technically, politically, and socially complex issues that MICs face.

OVERVIEW OF MIDDLE-INCOME COUNTRIES

There is a general consensus about the goals of law and development programs: sustainable economic growth, establishment of rule of law and good governance, and consolidation of some form of constitutional democracy that protects human rights. Nevertheless, despite billions of dollars and the best efforts of international and domestic actors, the results of law and development projects have been on the whole disappointing. The World Bank's ongoing study of good governance concludes that there is no evidence of "any significant improvement in governance worldwide, and if anything the evidence is suggestive of a deterioration, at the very least in key dimensions such as rule of law, control of corruption, political stability and government effectiveness."[4]

While there has been considerable attention to failed and transitional states and the obstacles they face, much less is known about the particular issues facing MICs or what they should do to increase their chances for success. This is unfortunate, as 70 percent of the world's population, and one-third of the world's poor, live in

[3] There is a large literature on regime types by political scientists and the relationship between regime type and economic growth, rule of law, good governance and human rights, as well as many books and articles on democratic transition and consolidation, authoritarian resilience, etc. There is also a large literature on rule of law, good governance, and law and development by legal scholars, legal practitioners, and development specialists in the rule-of-law promotion industry. See, e.g., Thomas Carothers, ed., *Promoting the Rule of Law Abroad: In Search of Knowledge* (Endowment for International Peace, 2006); David Trubek and Alvaro Santos, *The New Law and Economic Development: A Critical Appraisal* (Cambridge University Press, 2006); Michael Trebilcock and Ronald Daniels, *Rule of Law Reform and Development: Charting the Fragile Path of Progress* (Edward Elgar, 2008); Linn Hammergren, *Envisioning Reform: Improving Judicial Performance in Latin America* (Pennsylvania State University Press, 2007). There are also various works on particular issues or topics related to rule of law – including several works on rule of law in authoritarian countries (e.g., Tom Ginsburg and Tamir Moustafa, ed., *Rule by Law* [Cambridge University Press, 2008]); rule of law in particular country contexts or regions (e.g., Randall Peerenboom, ed., *Asian Discourses of Rule of Law* [Routledge, 2004]); or particular institutions, usually the judiciary. However, on the whole, most of the literature does not distinguish between rule of law and good governance challenges in LICs, MICs, and HICs, or address the specific challenges of MICs.

[4] Daniel Kaufmann, et al., *Governance Matters*, 2005, 6, available at http://www.worldbank.org/wbi/governance/pdf/govmatters3.pdf. See also Wolfgang Merkel, "Measuring the Quality of Rule of Law: Virtues, Perils, Results," in *The Dynamics of Rule of Law in an Era of International and Transnational Governance*, ed. Michael Zurn, Andre Noelkamper, and Randall Peerenboom (Cambridge University Press, 2012), 21–47.

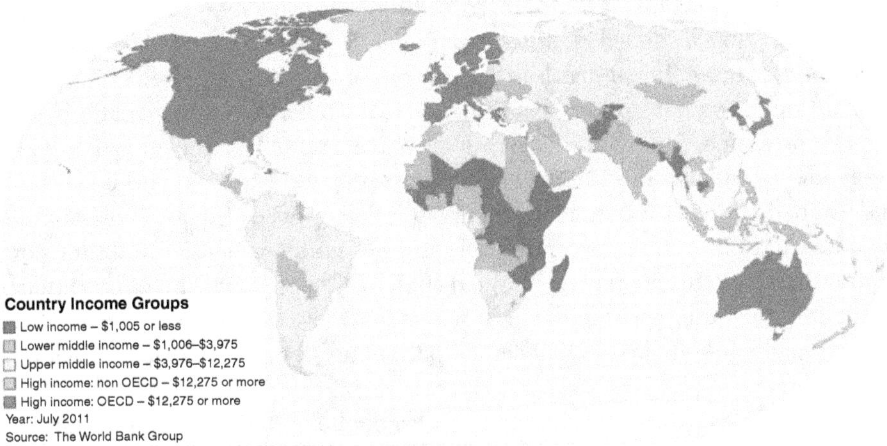

FIGURE 1.1. A global map of MICs.

MICs.[5] The World Bank considers countries with gross national income (GNI) per capita from $1,026 to $12,475 to be MICs.[6] There are currently 108 MICs (see Appendix).

As the Figure 1.1 indicates,[7] most countries in Asia and Latin America are MICs. There are also many MICs in Central and Eastern Europe (CEE) and the Middle East. In recent years, the number of African MICs has risen, though most of Africa remains in LIC status.

A World Bank study found that while MICs have grown at an average rate of 3.7 percent since 1995, they have not been able to achieve sustainable high-quality growth. Income inequality rose in more than half of the MICs, with regional disparities particularly pronounced in some countries. Aggregate growth has also come at a cost of serious environmental degradation, including rising carbon dioxide emissions, deforestation, and severe air and water pollution. Moreover, while MICs have been relatively more successful in reducing poverty than LICs, poverty remains a serious problem in many countries. MICs also confront critical health challenges. HIV/AIDS remains a grave, and in some countries worsening, problem. Some 70 percent of MICs are failing to meet their MDG of reducing child mortality by two-thirds.[8]

5 IEG, *Development Results in MICs*, supra.

6 More specifically, the World Bank classifies countries with GNI per capita of $1,025 or less as LICs, $1,026–$4,035 as LMICs, $4,036–$12,475 as UMICs, and $12,476 or more as HICs. 2011 GNI per capita is calculated using the World Bank Atlas method. See http://data.worldbank.org/about/country-classifications.

7 *Country Income Groups (World Bank Classification)*, available at http://chartsbin.com/view/2438. On the website, the names of the country are displayed when the cursor moves over them.

8 IEG, *Development Results in MICs*, supra.

Although some MICs have improved institutional capacity, institutions remain weak relative to developed countries, particularly in transitional states or states undergoing major political instability. Three out of four MICs showed no improvement in combating corruption. Ten MICs are in the bottom 10 percent of the World Bank's corruption index, and two out of three are below the global average (Appendix). Judicial corruption has undermined public trust in the courts and undermined efforts to implement rule of law.[9] Programs to increase judicial independence have proven disappointing.[10] Litigation is often expensive and time consuming. Access to justice remains limited (Botero, Chapter 10). These institutional constraints, including those in the legal system, may severely constrain the ability of MICs to make sound choices that can help them break though to more developed status.

In sum, MICs must address many complex challenges, while being limited by resource constraints and weak institutions. Moreover, MICs have had to face these challenges without much guidance from international development agencies and law and development scholars. International development agencies are only now beginning to focus on the special challenges facing MICs (Booth, Chapter 15). The World Bank, for instance, issued a new strategy paper for MICs in 2006, but the strategy is so new that it has yet be fully evaluated. That this is the World Bank's third strategy paper in six years reflects the difficulty that the World Bank has had grappling with the complex issues confronting MICs.[11]

To be fair, attempts to address the problems of MICs face significant challenges, including the wide diversity of MICs and the lack of clear models.

MICs are a varied group, socially, culturally, economically, and politically. They range in population size from 1.4 billion in China to small islands such as Palau with a population of just twenty thousand. The per capita income of the wealthiest MIC is twelve times that of the lowest. In ten MICs, 40 percent of the population lives in poverty; in ten others, less than 5 percent does. Prior to the HIC-created global financial crisis, two out of three MICs had growth rates of more than 2 percent, with some enjoying growth rates of more than 6 percent; conversely, ten were suffering from negative growth rates. The nature of the economies differ in terms of the relative importance of rural agriculture versus urban industry; amount and mix of

[9] Transparency International, "Global Corruption Report: Corruption and Judicial System," 2007, available at http://www.transparency.org/publications/gcr/download_gcr#download.

[10] IFES/USAID, "Guidance for Promoting Judicial Independence and Impartiality," 2002, 6, available at http://www.usaid.gov/our_work/democracy_and_governance/publications/pdfs/pnacm007.pdf; Carlos Santiso, "The Elusive Quest for the Rule of Law: Promoting Judicial Reform in Latin America," *Revista de Economia Politica/Brazilian Journal of Political Economy* 23, no. 3 (2003), 112–34; Randall Peerenboom, ed., *Judicial Independence in China* (Cambridge University Press, 2010).

[11] World Bank, "Strengthening Bank Group Engagement on Governance and Anticorruption," in *Development Results in Middle-Income Countries*, 2006; World Bank, *Enhancing World Bank Support to Middle Income Countries – Management Action Plan*, April 2004; World Bank, *Report of the Task Force on the World Bank Group and the Middle-Income Countries*, April 2001.

imports and exports; reliance on natural resources; openness to foreign investment and trade; financial and service sector liberalization; and access to global capital markets. They also vary widely in institutional capacity. A few are in the top quartile of the rule-of-law index; others are in the bottom quartile (see Appendix). Some are theocracies; others are atheistic. Some are democratic, or undergoing democratic transition; others are authoritarian or undergoing reversion to authoritarianism. Coming up with uniform advice for this diverse set of countries is likely to be impossible, and there are no one-size-fits-all solutions.

Another reason so little is known about how to address the problems encountered by MICs is that so few have managed to break into the exclusive club of wealthy states that enjoy rule of law, good governance, and adequate protection of human rights. The thirteen countries that graduated from MIC to HIC status between 1960 and 2008 are Spain, Greece, Portugal, Ireland, Israel, Japan, Hong Kong, Singapore, Taiwan, South Korea, Mauritius, Puerto Rico, and Equatorial Guinea.[12] In recent years, several CEE countries have also joined the upper ranks. Slovenia, Croatia, Slovak Republic, Czech Republic, Poland, and Hungary are now all HICs by World Bank standards, albeit all, with the exception of Slovenia, in the 12,480 to 18,500 GNI per capita range. There are also a number of oil-rich countries, such as Saudi Arabia, Kuwait, Oman, Bahrain, United Arab Emirates, and Qatar, as well as a number of small countries, often island states whose economies rely heavily on tourism and the provision of financial services to companies looking for tax havens, such as the Isle of Man, Cayman Islands, Barbados, and the Bahamas, or revenue from casinos and gaming (Monaco and Macau) (Appendix).

THE RESEARCH AGENDA: SALIENT ISSUES AND TOPICS

The preceding overview highlights several topics for more in-depth research and analysis, which we will begin to address in this volume and return to in the conclusion.

First, given the diversity among MICs, is "middle-income country" a useful analytical category? The World Bank further divides MICs into upper middle-income countries (UMICs) and lower middle-income countries (LMICs). Does that distinction provide additional analytical leverage? Do certain issue areas require additional subcategories or another basis for classifying MICs other than GNI per capita?

Second, is there a single middle-income trap? Alternatively, are there several or many middle-income traps? Or, is it just a myth that will be dispelled over the coming decades as more and more MICs become HICs? What are the obstacles (political, legal, economic, cultural, and institutional) to achieving sustained growth

[12] World Bank, *China 2030*, 11.

and establishing a legal system and governance institutions that would compare favorably with those in HICs?

Third, apart from wealth, what, if anything, do the countries that have successfully negotiated the transition from MIC to HIC status share? Are there any discernible patterns among the successful MICs with respect to politics, legal systems, cultural characteristics, institutions, colonial history, population size, or ethnic diversity? What distinguishes successful countries from the less successful countries, particularly those in the same region? Are there particular strategies that are within the control of policy makers that the successes share?

Fourth, why have East Asian countries been so successful? Many attribute their success to the developmental state (Subramaniam, Chapter 3), or more broadly to a particular sequencing of economic, political, and legal reforms that define the East Asian Model.[13] Are there background conditions that have enabled high growth? Is the East Asian export-led model sustainable in the postcrisis global economic order where rich countries must rein in consumption and increase savings to reduce debt? What challenges are Malaysia and China facing as they seek to move beyond MIC status, and what challenges are HIC Japan and Singapore now facing? What, if anything, can countries in other regions learn from successful East Asian states? Are there other models for MICs to follow? Does the recent ascension of several Eastern European MICs to HIC status provide an alternative to the East Asian Model? If so, what are the relative advantages of each approach? Has the Washington Consensus been thoroughly discredited? Is there a new Post-Washington Consensus (PWC) consensus? Should MICs be abandoning the neoliberal minimalist state in favor of a more interventionist New Developmental State (Bugaric, Chapter 7), and what exactly does that entail?

Fifth, what is the relationship between politics and development in MICs? Successful East Asian states experienced long periods of rapid growth under authoritarian regimes, were relatively stable, and democratized, if at all, at relatively high levels of wealth. In contrast, Latin American countries have a long history of regime change and instability. Yet for every successful authoritarian regime, there are numerous gross failures. And while many democracies seem to be trapped in transition – caught in a stable but bleak state of poverty, government malfeasance, and despair – most HICs are democratic, and democracy promotion remains the aim of many bilateral and multilateral programs. Accordingly, regime type alone does not explain MIC success or failure. Nevertheless, different regime types may face different traps or challenges, or give rise to different pathologies that inhibit growth, good governance, or the rule of law. Are there discernable general patterns? Beyond regime types, what types of political reforms and institutions are necessary or best suited to overcoming the challenges facing MICs?

[13] Randall Peerenboom, *China Modernizes: Threat to the West or Model for the Rest?* (Oxford University Press, 2007).

Sixth, in recent decades, MICs have had the benefit of a supportive global environment, including "relatively open trade, rising flows of foreign direct investment, steady growth in the world's major markets, sharply declining transport costs, increased intraindustry trade, and the introduction and spread of information and communications technology."[14] By contrast, MICs also face new challenges arising from globalization and an international trade regime that have led to greater global inequality and limited the ability of MIC governments to set and pursue certain policies in their national interest – including some policies pursued by now developed countries during their high growth periods (Shaffer and Sutton, Chapter 4; Yu, Chapter 5). With the World Trade Organization (WTO) and Trade-Related Aspects of Intellectual Property Rights, the rules are more extensive, detailed, and subject to coercive enforcement. How have MICs adapted to the new international economic order? Have some MICs been more successful than others in adapting to the new rules of the game? Much has been made of the rise of Brazil, Russia, India, China, and South Africa (the BRICS), and their role in the failed Doha Round of negotiations. Will divisions arise among the BRICS or between the larger MICs and smaller MICs? Will differences in interests on the part of LICs, MICs, and HICs undermine global trade agreements, accelerating the recent trend toward bilateral and regional trade agreements?

Seventh, although there is a close relationship between wealth and rule of law and good governance (Peerenboom, Chapter 16), debates continue about the direction of causality.[15] Moreover, even if wealth is closely related to rule of law and good governance, what are the implications for policy makers? The existing empirical studies do not shed enough light on how to achieve economic development, or the particular institutional arrangements necessary for rule of law or good governance. Nor do they shed much light on the path or sequencing of reforms. How have international donor agencies such as the World Bank and the UN Development Programme (UNDP) sought to address the special challenges for MICs? What policies and programs have they developed or should they develop to target MIC issues? Conversely, how do MICs take advantage of donor assistance to adopt and adapt the many "lessons learned" from decades of efforts to promote rule of law and good governance?

Eighth, MICs face a series of pressing socioeconomic issues from education to health care to labor rights to the environment. Socioeconomic issues are particularly problematic in MICs because citizen demands rise exponentially, and yet the government lacks the resources to meet all legitimate demands and institutions

[14] World Bank, *China* 2030, 6.

[15] Alberto Chang and Cesar Calderon, "Causality and Feedback between Institutional Measures and Economic Growth," *Economics and Politics* 12 (2000): 69; Roberto Rigobon and Dani Rodrik, "Rule of Law, Democracy, Openness, and Income," *Economics of Transition* 13 (2005): 533; Daniel Kaufmann, et al., *Governance Matters III: Governance Indicators for* 1996–2004, 2005, available at http://www.worldbank.org/wbi/governance/pdf/govmatters3.pdf.

are still relatively weak compared to institutions in HICs. How many of the limited resources available to MICs should be allocated to the provision of these key public goods? What are the implications for long-term growth of allocating funds to these goods rather than to infrastructure or the development of key industries? How should the fiscal burden and the operational tasks of providing these public goods and services be allocated among the government, markets and the private sector, nongovernmental organizations, and family networks? Should disputes over economic and social rights (ESR) be tried in the courts or resolved through political and administrative channels? Are state-centered formal dispute-resolution mechanisms effective only if supported by broader social movements?

METHODOLOGY

The volume is interdisciplinary. There are contributions from legal scholars, political scientists, and sociologists. Some of the chapters are quantitative while others are qualitative. Some address theoretical issues while others focus more on practical issues and implementation. Some chapters focus on the state while others focus on civil society and nonstate actors and institutions. Most chapters are explicitly comparative, with authors drawing on the experiences of countries in Europe, Latin America, and Asia, while others are case studies of one or two countries.

Given the broad nature of the topic and the variation within MICs, no single volume can address all of the important topics or cover all regions, much less all countries. We have focused on Latin America, Asia, and CEE because these are regions dominated by MICs. Although the Middle East is considered in some of the broader quantitative studies, we have not included individual chapters on the Middle East because of space limitations, and, more importantly, because the Middle East is currently very unstable and unpredictable. It may be the case that the "Arab Spring" and subsequent events will lead to radical changes in the political, economic, and legal systems in many countries in the region – or it might not. Furthermore, the close relationship between oil and wealth in the Middle East makes the policy and institutional environment rather sui generis relative to other regions.

Although we have not been able to cover everything everywhere, we believe the topics covered are of great importance for MICs. We hope the lessons learned will be of use to policy makers and donor agencies working in the area, and the questions raised will provide scholars the impetus for further research.

LAYOUT OF THE VOLUME AND CHAPTER SYNOPSES

The volume is divided into five parts. Part I examines politics and constitutional developments in MICs, and the choice of different development models. Part II addresses the role of MICs in a global economy, and focuses on the regulatory, legal, and political-economy dimensions of trade by examining the WTO and intellectual property (IP) rights. Part III discusses governance and legal issues, including civil service sector reforms; the relation between the judiciary and the military; anticorruption efforts; and access to justice. Part IV takes up socioeconomic issues, focusing on the role of the courts and other institutions in addressing labor, environmental, and health challenges. Part V explores the evolving strategies of international donor agencies for MICs in light of lessons learned about legal transplants from previous decades of law and development projects. Chapter 16 summarizes key findings and identifies areas for future research.

Part I. The Politics of Development in Middle-Income Countries

In Chapter 2, Tom Ginsburg captures in a nutshell the crux of "the middle-income trap": institutions suitable for growth at the early stages of development may no longer work for later stages. Yet the ruling regime may stick with the strategies and institutions that have worked to date because those strategies generated the economic growth that underpins regime legitimacy, as well as political returns that lock in particular structures. The problem is, therefore, one of path dependency, and ultimately a political challenge as much as an economic or technical challenge. He notes that one of the key differences between HICs and most MICs is that the former enjoy a relatively more autonomous legal system. Courts must be given sufficient autonomy over a wide enough range of issues to avoid political and economic commitment problems; encourage investment and innovation; and facilitate commerce. He then discusses the need to overcome the "legal middle-income trap" in which courts lack sufficient autonomy or scope, arguing that a successful resolution requires both the right political conditions and institutional underpinnings. He turns to Malaysia to illustrate what happens when the institutional underpinnings of judicial empowerment are present but favorable political conditions are lacking; the Maldives to illustrate what happens when favorable political conditions exist but the requisite institutional underpinnings are absent; and South Korea to show what can happen when both the right political conditions and the requisite institutional underpinnings are present.

In Chapter 3, Surain Subramaniam draws on the political economy and comparative politics literatures to explore the impact of politics on development in HIC Singapore and MIC Malaysia. In both countries, the development model was based on a developmental state that limited political freedom in exchange for delivering rapid economic growth, improved governance, and higher standards of living. Subramaniam attributes the greater success of Singapore to political economy factors. In Malaysia, the development model locked in quotas for majoritarian ethnic Malays as a political response to conflicts arising from a divided society. As a result of this strategy, growth has stalled, and the transition toward legal autonomy has been undermined, as described by Ginsburg. Thus Malaysia has become mired in both an economic and legal middle-income trap, leading to political opposition and a social backlash.

At the same time, Singapore's development model is also under pressure, with citizens clamoring for political liberalization. In a test of modernization theory, Subramaniam examines whether structural changes resulting from having achieved advanced economy status are facilitating gradual institutionalization of political liberalization, thereby moving the developmental state model beyond performance legitimacy toward a more liberal democratic model. Both Singapore and Malaysia illustrate the complex ways in which state-led modernization and economic growth and development intersect with pluralistic understandings of modernities; political and cultural identities; and democratic aspirations at the societal level to influence the trajectories of economic and political development.

Part II. Middle-Income Countries in a Globalized Economy

In Chapter 4, Gregory Shaffer and Charles Sutton note that while the WTO was designed to serve the interests of Europe and America, larger MICs have adapted to the rules of the game and become more adept in using the legalized trade regime and trade negotiations to advance their own interests. During the failed Doha Round, the G20 coalition, led by Brazil and India, resisted U.S. and European Union demands, and fought to protect their domestic policy space, including the ability to use industrial policies to develop their manufacturing sector and protect infant industries. Large MICs such as Brazil and more recently China have also developed the capacity to utilize WTO dispute settlement to defend their trading and domestic policy interests. They have likewise become more active in negotiating bilateral and plurilateral trade agreements, with HICs and with other MICs. Shaffer and Sutton emphasize that size matters: countries with large economies measured by aggregate GNI, such as China and India, exercise much greater power than countries with smaller economies, such as the Maldives, even though the Maldives has a higher GNI per capita than both India and China. Nevertheless, smaller MICs may sometimes benefit in trade negotiations or dispute settlement by piggybacking on other countries, including larger MICs, when they share common interests.

In Chapter 5, Peter Yu points out that the global IP regime already incorporates income categories similar to HIC (developed), MIC (developing), and LIC (least developed), with duties of assistance imposed on developed countries and favorable policies extended to developing and least developed countries. However, in discussing the politics of the IP regime, Yu, like Shaffer and Sutton, cautions that aggregate GNI is more significant than GNI per capita. Thus he develops a theory of middle intellectual property powers (MIPPs) based on six characteristics: a fast-growing and large aggregate economy; increased technological and innovative capabilities; emergence of local stakeholders; presence of alternative forms of innovation; uneven developments and internal tensions; and continuing piracy and counterfeiting problems. Yu suggests that MIPPs will play a greater role in the IP policy-making process than in the past. Policy areas in which the impact of MIPPs is likely to be felt include current issues such as enforcement of IP rights, protection of genetic resources, traditional knowledge and traditional cultural expressions, access to essential medicines, and telecommunications standards, as well as new and emerging issues, such as global climate change, the promotion of alternative innovation models, special and differential treatment for developing countries, solutions to address uneven economic and technological developments, and abuse of rights and restraints on trade. Nevertheless, Yu does not believe the rise of MIPPs constitutes a radical game changer. Rather, MIPPs are likely to favor middle-of-the-road policies that balance the interests of developed and developing countries. Moreover, given the differences among MIPPs and between MIPPs and other MICs and LICs, the policy agenda of MIPPs is likely to be characterized by a high level of inconsistency and incoherence.

As Figure 1.1 indicates, there are distinct regional patterns to income distribution. The recent addition of CEE countries to the ranks of HICs highlights the regional effect, while the patch of blue in Asia calls attention to rise of the bloc of East Asian Tigers. The success of East Asian countries has been much discussed and attributed to many factors: the developmental state, pragmatic policy making by technocratic leaders, high savings rates, demographic factors, and so on. In Chapter 6, John Gillespie adds another piece to the puzzle, arguing that intra-Asian transnational production regimes (TPRs) have driven firm innovation and industrial growth in East Asian MICs. TPRs are structured around supply chain and investment networks that transfer goods, capital, and knowledge among firms in HICs and MICs. TPRs transfer both technical know-how and regulatory knowledge, largely bypassing domestic laws and legal institutions. Gillespie argues that Asian TPRs differ from their Euro-American counterparts in ways that are significant for the international economic order and law and development agencies seeking to promote global standards for trade, IP, and rule of law. Euro-American TPRs are dominated by lawyers and accountants who organize transactions around hierarchical policies based on international and domestic regulations for corporate governance, IP, and transparency. Asian TPRs are less legalistic, emphasizing relationships and informal rules and norms rather than formal rules and law. Asian TPRs also place more emphasis on collaborative governance and responsive regulations than the top-down, state-centered command-and-control regulatory regime promoted by the Euro-American developing agencies and international development agencies such as the World Bank, International Labor Organization, and International Standards Organization. Whether the distinct regulatory patterns identified by Gillespie will continue as Asian MICs become HICs remains an open question. Gillespie finds some evidence that they will in the resistance in HIC Japan to recent regulatory reforms seeking to introduce a more command-and-control type regime with greater reliance on formal administrative law rather than informal administrative guidance.

Part III. Good Governance and the Rule of Law in Middle-Income Countries

MICs face not only economic or political challenges, but also challenges in delivering basic government services. The next four chapters focus on good governance and rule of law in MICs. They once again call attention to the diversity within MICs, and how historical trajectories produce different pathologies or path dependencies. This complicates the legal transplantation process and militates against one-size-fits-all solutions. Although the lawyer-dominated rule-of-law promotion industry has emphasized judicial reforms, these chapters highlight how good governance and rule of law require much more than reforms of the courts, including administrative restructuring and civil service reforms, police reforms,[16] and a coordinated response among all branches of government to curb corruption and meet citizen expectations for social justice.

In Chapter 7, Bojan Bugaric uses civil service reforms and innovation policies in CEE countries to highlight shortcomings in the Washington Consensus and to argue in favor of a PWC and the New Development State (NDS) model of development. He notes that regulatory structures in CEE were built during the age of the Washington Consensus, which had a strong antistatist bias. More attention was paid to courts and judges, and less to core administrative agencies needed to implement interventionist policies of the state. As a result, CEE faced the global recession with regulatory structures ill-equipped to respond to the major challenges caused by the crisis. The civil service sector has been prone to politicization and corruption, the public sector (education and health care) needs modernizing, and various regulatory bodies and structures, such as anticorruption commissions and audit committees, lack independence and credibility. The PWC and the NDS model recast the role of the state. In contrast to the invisible hand of the neoliberal state is the visible hand of a more interventionist government that steers investment; coordinates projects and provides information especially in projects with multiple inputs and long-term payoffs; facilitates extensive collaboration and communication between the public and private sectors; and promotes entrepreneurship, innovation, and new product development. Bugaric emphasizes that one of the key features of the new development model is experimentation and learning. Echoing the findings of Gillespie, he argues that MICs need to be more flexible, more adaptive, more pragmatic, more responsive, and less top-down and obsessed with producing formal rules, many of which are never implemented. Most fundamentally, they need to take

16 See Mariana Mota Prado, Michael Trebilcock, and Patrick Hartford, "Police Reform in Violent Democracies in Latin America," *The Hague Journal on Rule of Law* 4, no. 2 (2012): 252–85.

control over their own destinies and adopt a more proactive role in charting their futures.

Balance-of-power issues in MICs are often particularly salient. Many MICs undergo regime change from authoritarianism to democracy and frequently back to authoritarianism; even in new democracies that do not slide back into authoritarianism, consolidation remains a distant goal.[17] The polity and constitutional order remain in flux, with different state organs competing for power, while the concentration of wealth may lead to a form of political capitalism, in which private interests capture state organs, undermine the courts, and block reforms that would benefit the general public.

Latin America stands out for its history of military coups. In Chapter 8, Julio Ríos-Figueroa and Fernanda Gómez-Abán use reforms to military justice in Colombia and Mexico to explore how constitutional jurisprudence helps or hinders bargaining between the civilian government and military officers. They show that constitutional debates that are based on values and principles but also take into account political realities can be a fundamental resource for the improvement of conflictive political relations such as that between civilians and military officers. Moreover, the judiciary, and constitutional courts in particular, may play a positive role in addressing such delicate balance-of-power issues even during emergencies and times of crisis. However, much depends on context, as the differing results in Colombia and Mexico demonstrate.

In Chapter 9, Kevin Davis notes that all countries struggle with corruption but MICs face particular challenges and opportunities. Global surveys show corruption is generally more severe in MICs than HICs, and takes different forms. Yet MICs have more resources available to tackle corruption than many LICs. Drawing on a taxonomy developed by Michael Johnston, Davis explores three distinct forms of corruption prevalent in MICs: "Elite Cartel" corruption, which is centralized, organized, and relatively predictable; "Oligarchs and Clans" corruption, which involves participants who are not members of stable elites, and may include wealthy businessmen or criminal organizations; and "Official Moguls" corruption, which refers to powerful government officials that can divert state resources with impunity. Davis explores the extent to which these various forms of corruption can be curtailed through anticorruption laws or other methods. Given the diversity of forms of corruption and differences in state capacity and local contexts, he rejects the push toward convergence on a single global model of anticorruption law, and is skeptical about the ability of foreign parties to use legal tools for instrumental purposes, such as curbing corruption in other countries. He is generally cautious about the ability of law and the legal system to address corruption, although he does note that anticorruption commissions have worked in some countries. He concludes that

[17] Thomas Carothers, *Critical Mission: Essays on Democracy Promotion* (Carnegie Endowment for International Peace, 2004); Larry Diamond, *The Spirit of Democracy* (Henry Holt and Company, 2008).

anticorruption law may play a role in improving governance in MICs, but is most effective when combined with more fundamental economic, political, and cultural changes.[18]

In Chapter 10, Juan Botero presents a new metric for justice delivery that measures the accessibility, fairness, and efficiency of civil law, criminal law, and private arbitration. He finds that MICs lag behind HICs in all aspects of the delivery of justice. Moreover, he notes that the gap between HICs and MICs is greater than the gap between MICs and LICs. Botero also finds significant differences within HICs based on legal family origin. Courts in common-law HICs are more efficient, in keeping with the generalization that the common-law system emphasizes procedural justice whereas the civil law system emphasizes substantive law and a more accessible, protective, and "equalizing" justice. Interestingly, however, the statistically significant differences based on legal families disappear in MICs. This may be because legal systems in MICs tend to be hybrids, or because the economic conditions of MICs overwhelm the effect of legal families. What does emerge as a statistically significant determinant of justice outcomes in MICs is the general level of corruption. In addition, other factors that contribute to the problems MICs experience in delivering accessible, impartial, and efficient justice include "cultural and language barriers, overly-complex procedures and cumbersome legal requirements, financial limitations, mistrust of institutions derived from a colonial past, and radically different views on the nature and role of justice in society" (see p. 195, Chapter 10).

Part IV. Socioeconomic Challenges in Middle-Income Countries

The four chapters in this part examine in more detail why socioeconomic issues are so pressing in MICs and what can be done to address them.

In Chapter 11, Daniel Brinks and William Forbath locate the struggle to make good on the promise of ESR in MICs in the broader historical context of constitutional developments in Latin America and the impact of neoliberalism on welfare systems globally. As in many countries, including many MICs that recently democratized and amended or passed new constitutions, most Latin American countries have incorporated ESR in their constitutions. In keeping with global trends, they have also adopted institutional reforms to strengthen the role of courts in resolving ESR claims. They find that the judicialization of ESR cases can pay dividends, but courts are no panacea. These issues are best addressed when litigation is part of a multipronged strategy supported by broad social movements, and courts adopt a

[18] An Organisation for Economic Co-operation and Development study found that while the number of anticorruption institutions worldwide is growing, there is no strong evidence that they help reduce corruption, and there are more failures than successes. Organisation for Economic Co-operation and Development, "Specialised Anti-Corruption Institutions – Review of Models," 2007, available at http://www.eldis.org/cf/rdr/?doc=38569%em=061108%sub=gov.

more collaborative, policy-oriented approach that facilitates discussion between different state and nonstate actors. Brinks and Forbath note that MICs are at the forefront of judicialization of ESR. In contrast, LICs lack the wealth and institutions to support robust ESR claims, whereas HICs have been more reluctant to constitutionalize ESR and more wary of empowering the courts to decide ESR cases. They also suggests that courts in MICs may be forced into a more central position because other policy-making and monitoring institutions are weaker in MICs than in HICs.

In Chapter 12, César Rodríguez-Garavito uses an in-depth case study of Colombia to shed light on the causes and consequences of judicializing health care in democratic upper middle-income countries such as Brazil, Costa Rica, Argentina, and South Africa. These countries share certain features: health systems that do not meet the demands of citizens; easy access to courts and an activist judiciary keen to protect ESR; and civil society actors that have turned to the courts en masse to enforce the right to health. Rodríguez-Garavito finds that while the courts have been reasonably effective in protecting the right to health, judicialization of health care disputes has had negative effects as well, including inefficiencies from trying numerous individual cases over similar issues; strategic behavior on the part of patients, doctors, hospitals, pharmaceutical companies, and insurance companies leading to corruption; a sharp rise in health care costs to the state; and growing concerns over separation-of-power issues and the need to rein in an activist judiciary. These problems led to attempts by the judiciary, legislature, and executive to dejudicialize health care disputes by limiting access to the courts and issuing structural injunctions to avoid litigating the same type of case repeatedly; steering disputes to arbitration committees or other administrative channels; and limiting remedies. When that failed to satisfy citizen demands, the courts were forced to reevaluate and reengage. Like Brinks and Forbath, Rodríguez-Garavito argues that successful resolution of ESR cases in MICs requires collaboration among the executive, the legislature, the judiciary, and civil society. He recommends a dialogic approach in which courts focus not just on deciding individual cases but on addressing structural policy and institutional flaws and setting procedural standards for a public conversation. This approach avoids the inequities and inefficiencies of the indiscriminate judicialization of health, preserves a key role for the courts, and promotes citizen participation in the complex decision-making process about health care issues.

In Chapter 13, William Hurst continues the exploration of the strengths and weaknesses of courts relative to other institutions in protecting ESR by examining the struggle to judicialize labor rights in Indonesia and China. He suggests that whereas Indonesia created new institutions, in particular the Industrial Relations Courts, to facilitate the adjudication of labor rights, China enacted new laws and regulations to specify and strengthen labor protections. To be sure, Indonesia has passed numerous laws and regulations relating to labor. Conversely, there have been numerous institutional developments in China, including reforms of the letter and petition system; changes to the labor mediation and arbitration processes; and more recently the development of "grand mediation," which involves a collaborative approach on the part of various government and party agencies, the judiciary, labor organizations, citizens, and social organizations.[19] Despite their differences, Hurst finds that labor disputes continue to be a source of tension in China and Indonesia. The courts are not able to adequately resolve all disputes. As a result, workers engage in forum shopping or take to the streets in protest, particularly in China. Hurst concludes by suggesting that judicializing disputes may not be the best approach in MICs. Rather, labor may be better served by passing legislation to enact welfare, health care, and pension programs; by strengthening the institutional capacity of administrative agencies so that they are better able to enforce minimum wages provisions, workplace safety rules, and limits on overtime; and by permitting and nurturing strong independent unions or other worker organizations with at least some collective bargaining and strike rights.

In Chapter 14, Benjamin van Rooij and Lesley K. McAllister look at how different MICs have responded to environmental concerns. They note that industrializing MICs (IMICs) face particular challenges because significant industrial pollution problems are often accompanied by low levels of regulatory capacity and environmental awareness, and economic interests trump environmental interests, resulting in low compliance with environmental laws and undermining various forms of legal, political, and social action against polluting firms. They examine five innovations: enforcement campaigns in China; efforts to enhance environmental awareness and involve citizens and civil society organizations in monitoring and reporting violations of environmental laws in China; the use of prosecutors as environmental enforcement catalysts in Brazil; public disclosure of self-reported compliance data in Indonesia; and the delegation of compliance monitoring to private auditors in Mexico. In all cases, the innovations sought to enhance the regulatory capacity of the primary agency responsible for enforcing pollution law by creating enforcement alliances with other actors, including other government entities, citizens, and civil society organizations as well as the regulated entities. While the different approaches affected different actors in different ways, and the overall results varied, they all increased regulatory capacity and, somewhat counter-intuitively, some even increased the autonomy of the primary agency. Van Rooij and McAllister caution, however, that the incorporation of regulated entities into the alliance in a form of self-regulation or self-governance is riskier in MICs than in HICs, where the primary agency enjoys greater regulatory enforcement capacity. Accordingly, they recommend that IMIC governments sequence reforms to the extent possible, first strengthening enforcement capacity and then expanding the enforcement alliance to include a more active role for the regulated entities.

19 Keith Hand, "Resolving Constitutional Disputes in Contemporary China," *University of Pennsylvania East Asia Law Review* 7, no. 1 (2011).

Part V. International Donor Strategies for Middle-Income Countries

In Chapter 15, Nick Booth examines the evolving strategies of the UNDP for providing development assistance to MICs. He observes that the United Nations' focus on MDGs has proved a useful framework for LICs but is less relevant for MICs. The key development challenges for MICs include rising income equality, which is greater in MICs than in either LICs or HICs, and governance issues, which were not part of the MDGs. The United Nations has identified three basic principles for dealing with MICs, including leveraging the United Nations' comparative advantages of wide name recognition, global reach, deep knowledge base, and worldwide network of experts; adhering to the United Nations' normative mission of supporting the most vulnerable members of society; and developing policies that are more country specific. Unfortunately, little progress has been made in translating these broad principles into concrete policies. Booth draws on his experience as the UNDP Policy Advisor for Rule of Law and Access to Justice in Vietnam to argue that a dedicated in-house policy advisory is better able to respond to the more political and multistakeholder governance challenges that confront MICs. He suggests that a similar approach should work in other MICs, as it responds to key features shared by MICs: governance problems are complex and context specific; increased pluralism gives rise to competing interest groups; growing financial autonomy makes MICs less dependent on donors for advice and less willing to accept conditionalities; and improvements in governance take a long time, and require sustained engagement on the part of donors. Nevertheless, Booth calls for improvement to the United Nations' knowledge management system, more engagement outside the UNDP, more investment in research, and more flexible programming and procurement modalities.

CONCLUSION

MICs not only present challenges to donors and policy makers, but also to scholars. It is our hope that the chapters in this book can begin to address some of the conceptual issues. Together, the chapters cover a wide array of contexts in which the MICs face a distinct set of regulatory and legal challenges. The stark trade-offs among competing goals, and the challenges of implementation, require complex institutional responses. Much depends on the ability to identify these responses, and it is our hope that the reader will find the efforts herein an engaging step in that direction.

PART I

The Politics of Development in Middle-Income Countries

2

The Politics of Law and Development in Middle-Income Countries

Tom Ginsburg

INTRODUCTION

Middle-income countries (MICs) are a diverse group of economies. The category includes tiny island states like Kiribati and Tuvalu along with giants such as Russia, Nigeria, and Pakistan. It includes some economies nearly entirely dependent on oil exports (South Sudan), and others reliant on agriculture (Uzbekistan), tourism (Maldives), hydropower (Lao PDR), and a few fully industrialized economies (Latvia). The category also includes countries in every region, with every sort of religious and cultural background.

Politically, as well, the category is a diverse one. It includes established democracies (Jamaica), dictatorships (Turkmenistan), monarchies (Jordan), republics (Fiji), and theocracies (Iran). It includes leftist Bolivarian Regimes (Ecuador and Venezuela), those governed by the political right (Rumania), and those governed by madmen (Qadafi's Libya). Is it possible to make any generalizations about such a diverse group?

My thesis is that it is possible and that MICs face a particular set of challenges that are, ultimately, political rather than technical or purely economic in nature. The basic problem is one of path dependency. Institutions that are suitable for growth at the early stages of development may not be able to work for later stages. Instead, the regime that gets the country to middle-income status may stick with the strategies and institutions that have worked to date. After all, early-stage economic growth underpins regime legitimacy, and may generate increasing political returns that lock in particular structures.

The challenge for the political leadership in MICs is how to reform the political and institutional bases of growth at the right time to avoid what the economists call a "local maximum." It is an extraordinarily difficult challenge, but one that is essential to overcoming development barriers. It is also helpful, in some cases at least, for political survival. Developmental regimes that manage to transform their political bases and economic institutions to fit the changing environment may survive. Those that do not may be cast aside in favor of a new coalition. Alternatively, the regime may survive but keep the country stuck in middle-income status, or even witness dedevelopment or stagnation.

Law and legal institutions, I argue, are also part of the story. The Washington Consensus view that the rule of law and judicial independence are essential for economic growth may have been too simple and insufficiently contextualized in many cases. But there is some truth to the notion that a shift to a more autonomous set of legal institutions seems to be an essential step that characterizes countries at the high end of the development spectrum. A greater role for an autonomous legal system is surely one of the distinctions between high-income countries (HICs) and MICs. Law can play an important role in helping countries to avoid political and economic commitment problems, encourage investment and innovation, and facilitate commerce.

The politics of managing this legal transition is our central concern. We argue that legal institutions in HICs tend to be inclusive and autonomous. Legal institutions in MICs tend to have more limited scope, and in many cases lack autonomy from politics. There seems, then, to be a necessary condition that, at some point, courts be empowered to a particular degree in order to overcome what we might call the "legal middle-income trap" in which courts lack autonomy and scope. To effectuate this empowerment, in turn, requires a proper set of political conditions. But politics are not enough. To make sure that empowered courts can actually perform the role that they are required to necessitates institutional underpinnings. The courts must have the capacity and propensity to play the role they will be asked to in higher-income societies, and must be able to maintain a sufficient degree of autonomy. This requires some attention to the endowment of the legal system – its history and the capacity of actors to take on the added responsibility that seems characteristic of legal systems in HICs.

My argument proceeds as follows. We first survey some of the political factors that will effect judicial empowerment in developing countries. We then examine the politics of institutional transformation, which is a slightly different concept. We focus in particular on the legal and constitutional challenges that such demands entail, and the need for the alignment of institutional and political factors to effectuate transformation of the legal system.

We then turn to a series of case studies to illustrate the argument: Malaysia, in which the institutional underpinnings of judicial empowerment were present but without favorable political conditions; the Maldives, in which the politics were present but not the institutional underpinnings; and South Korea in the 1980s and 1990s, in which both political and institutional factors were aligned. In doing so, we thus draw not only on the experience of MICs but also of the small handful of countries that have, in recent years, jettisoned that status to become fully industrialized countries.

THE POLITICS OF LAW IN LOW-INCOME COUNTRIES

Let us begin with a paradigmatic lower-income country (LIC). The country's poverty may be due to a variety of factors, such as geographic isolation (e.g.,

Nepal), willful economic mismanagement (Zimbabwe), kleptocracy (the Congo), economic structure (Zambia), or external shock (Albania). Mobilizing a political coalition for development is a challenge in any environment and many countries do not do so. One needs to have agreement on a strategy that produces the public goods needed for growth, and the political will and power to pull it off.

Note that democracy and autocracy, perhaps the central analytic distinction in comparative political science, is not the central issue here. Very few LICs are democratic, either because they have exploitative leadership or perhaps because pressures for redistribution may hinder the process of capital formation and deployment. The key distinction is not between democracy and autocracy but between what are sometimes called developmental authoritarian regimes and kleptocratic ones. The former model, exemplified by the East Asian Newly Industrialized Countries, as they were known in the 1980s, involved the provision of public goods and relatively broad governing coalitions. The kleptocratic model, exemplified by countries like Burma and some Latin American economies, did not. Instead, leaders in kleptocracies fear the extension of economic power beyond the very narrow governing group. The freedom to make day-to-day management decisions in an apolitical way is beyond such regimes, for it would provide an autonomous space in which threats to authority can emerge.

Note that my discussion of kleptocracy echoes the recent account of Darin Acemoglu and James Robinson, who contrast inclusive and extractive institutions as the unicausal explanation for growth.[1] But my emphasis on insulated technocratic decision making is different. Their definition of inclusion is quite vague and a bit ad hoc, but it is hard to see how it would incorporate the regime of, for example, Park Chung Hee in South Korea or Chiang Kai-Shek in Taiwan. Both of these regimes excluded major elements of their societies from decision making and both repressed labor. Similarly, Acemoglu and Robinson underemphasize the possibilities of a developmental authoritarian model that has worked for so many of the HICs, which was by its nature neither inclusive nor extractive. It relied on insulated technocratic decision making, and this was crucial to its success.[2] I also follow the Weberian approach of emphasizing law and legal institutions, which are crucial underpinnings for growth, but don't really receive much emphasis in the Acemoglu and Robinson account.

In terms of legal institutions, specifically, a key variable is "what are the endowments of the country?" Some countries have what Jens Meierhenrich calls "Legacies of Law."[3] Meierhenrich's account of South African law from its inception, through the creation of the authoritarian apartheid regime (1948–61), and eventually through democratization in the 1990s shows how a tradition of law can provide a crucial resource to facilitate political transformation. In the nineteenth century, law played a role in liberal constraint of the state, and legal positivism served as a force for state

1 Darin Acemoglu and James Robinson, *Why Nations Fail: The Origins of Power, Prosperity and Poverty* (Crown Business, 2012).

2 See Shaffer and Sutton, Chapter 4 in this volume.

3 Jens Meierhenrich, *Legacies of Law* (Cambridge University Press, 2008).

building in the early twentieth century. As apartheid emerged in full force in the middle of the twentieth century, the regime relied extensively on law to effectuate oppressive practices, even as courts continued to constrain the government at its outer edges. For example, the regime responded to adverse rulings by the appellate division of the Supreme Court by packing the bench and limiting its jurisdiction. When it became clear that the apartheid regime could not be maintained, the National Party shifted views and began to promote a bill of rights designed not only to preserve the rights of prospective minority in the face of near certain electoral loss but also, crucially, to preserve the economic leverage of the elite.[4] There would be inevitable pressures for redistribution after the new majority took over. Drafting a new constitution securing property rights, and establishing a new constitutional court to monitor violations, was a way of entrenching the power and wealth of the old elite.

Crucially, the existence of a tradition of autonomous law that had operated even during apartheid made it possible for the African National Congress to make a credible commitment to the National Party. Without a tradition of law, the National Party might not have been willing to trust the new majority to uphold its promises. But the existence of courts that upheld the law in the authoritarian phase, even when it conflicted with the regime's demands, made law a viable solution for the post-authoritarian commitment problem. The new Constitutional Court oversaw the transition, even demanding changes in the final draft constitution to meet the requirements of the Interim Constitution. To be sure, the Constitutional Court has played many other roles in democratic transition, helping to define the new order and to incorporate global human rights discourse into the country.[5] In this sense, it has also been a vehicle of democratic consolidation. But it would arguably not have been created without its ability to serve as a downstream guarantor of the bargain ending apartheid. The core elements of this bargain – democratic rule in exchange for security of property rights and limited transitional justice – have remained intact against great political pressure, and the country's autonomous courts have been part of the reason.

What of countries that lack such a tradition of autonomous law? Here the task is to try to build it. In contrast with those who argue that "legal origins" are fixed,[6] we have many examples in history of authoritarian regimes building autonomous legal (and bureaucratic) institutions. Meiji Japan provides one example, as does early Chile. In each case, the rationale was only partly based in local politics, but also involved signaling to external actors. In other classic cases, such as Bismarck's Prussia, the rationale had to do with state building. Moustafa lists a number of reasons why authoritarians might empower courts, including controlling lower-level agents and

4 Ibid., 203–4.

5 Heinz Klug, *Constituting Democracy* (Cambridge University Press, 2003).

6 Rafael La Porta, Florencio Lopez-de-Silanes, Andrei Shleifer, and Robert W. Vishny, "Law and Finance," *Journal of Political Economy* 106 (1998): 1113–55.

external signaling.[7] When law is part of the developmental strategy, it provides an important resource to help overcome the middle-income trap. But when it becomes politicized, it cannot play this function.

What is needed, then, is a constellation of institutional underpinnings and political incentives to empower courts. Such coexistence at the right stage of development cannot be taken for granted. Nor can it always be engineered. But a common feature of the HICs is that they followed one of two alternative trajectories out of MIC-ness: either they invested in autonomous institutions, including courts, that then provided the necessary underpinnings for growth, and in most cases for democratic transition; or they had democratic politics, which encouraged investment in autonomous courts, which in turn underpinned growth. We do not see HICs that did not, at some point in the process, experience the political incentives to build autonomous courts with a significant degree of autonomy, particularly in areas that allow the regime to make credible commitments in the economic sphere.

I have argued elsewhere that a central condition for judicial empowerment in democracies is sufficient political uncertainty that various forces believe they may be out of power in a future period.[8] In such an instance, all will prefer to have a set of independent courts that can protect their policies from reversal and persons from retaliation. (The argument may apply to bureaucracies as well.) This same set of institutions can provide for secure property rights and neutral contract enforcement.[9] Should these neutral institutions manage and contribute to continued economic growth, the country will not experience a middle-income trap. This is the argument of MIC evolution to HIC status from democracy through law.

The alternative trajectory is from autocracy. Some autocracies also decide to invest in neutral, insulated judicial (and bureaucratic) institutions for a variety of reasons.[10] One set of motives is economic growth. By insulating property from expropriation, and economic activity from arbitrary action, authoritarian empowerment of insulated courts can facilitate growth. These institutions can, in turn, facilitate autocratic departure should pressures arise for democratization by securing the economic gains of the dictators and facilitating credible commitments not to expropriate them. This is the argument of MIC evolution to HIC status from autocracy through law to democracy. While autonomous legal institutions are hardly sufficient for such economic growth, they can play a useful role.

7 Tamir Moustafa, *The Struggle for Constitutional Power* (Cambridge University Press, 2007).

8 Tom Ginsburg, *Judicial Review in New Democracies* (Cambridge University Press, 2003). See also J. Mark Ramseyer, "The Puzzling (In)Dependence of Courts," *Journal of Legal Studies* 23 (1994): 721.

9 Douglass North and Barry Weingast, "Constitution and Commitment: The Evolution of Institutional Governing Public Choice in Seventeenth-Century England," *The Journal of Economic History* 49, no. 4 (1989): 803–32.

10 See Tamir Moustafa and Tom Ginsburg, "Introduction," in *The Politics of Courts in Authoritarian Regimes*, ed.Tom Ginsburg and Tamir Moustafa (Cambridge University Press, 2008) for a catalog.

Having identified two alternative trajectories, we can also theorize several barriers to completion of either path. The politics of autonomy may fail, as political coalitions may seek to gain particular benefits from the courts and thus erode insulation. Alternatively, the bases for insulation may not exist at all, or may fail to evolve for technical reasons. Distributional concerns matter as well. A growth coalition can become so comfortable with their particular benefits that they impede institutions for shared growth.

We now consider three case studies that exemplify the various patterns: Malaysia, the poster child for the middle-income trap, which had a legacy of some autonomous courts but failed to sustain it for internal political reasons, contributing to its institutional stagnation; the Maldives, which had no legacy of autonomy at the moment of democratization, threatening the democratic transition a few years later; and South Korea, a paradigm case of MIC evolution through autocracy.

MALAYSIA

A half century after independence, Malaysia has made tremendous strides toward the ambitious goal, set by developmentalist leader Mahathir Mohamed, of becoming a fully developed country by the year 2020. Today just 4 percent of Malaysians live in poverty, as compared with half the population fifty years ago. It has transformed its economic structure from a poor, colonial plantation economy into that of a modern, diversified, upper middle-income country. It has managed, though not resolved, significant ethnic tensions.

Despite these strong points, Malaysia is sometimes considered the epitome of a country in the middle-income trap. Unlike Singapore, its much smaller neighbor and erstwhile component state, Malaysia has not managed to develop a world-class educational system. Its economic structure has not been as dynamic. And, especially important for present purposes, its legal system has suffered from politicization at crucial junctures. This politicization, which has involved crude court packing, is greater in degree than in neighboring Singapore. While the country inherited a functioning set of common-law courts from Britain, and thus had the potential institutional structures in place for an autonomous legal system, it lacked political incentives to insulate it.

In addition, the primary mechanism to deal with racial strife, the New Economic Policy (NEP), illustrates precisely the lock-in effect at the heart of a political analysis. The NEP, which was formally in place from 1970 to 1990 but endured for two decades thereafter, famously seeks to ensure ethnic Malay participation in the economy through a set of educational and equity quotes. But unlike affirmative action programs in advanced industrialized countries, which tend to focus on underrepresented minorities, this policy was majoritarian in nature. While it has done a decent job of improving the lot of a certain class of Malays, the policy has also had some distorting effects. It drove Malaysians of Indian and Chinese descent out of the system (in some cases out of Malaysia), and discouraged innovation and investment in human capital. And it led to an overregulated economy without the political incentives to shift.

In response to many of these criticisms, Prime Minister Najib Tun Razak announced the adoption of a New Economic Model in 2010. This plan was designed to address these issues and renew a period of rapid growth. The nominal goal is to shift from the explicit use of racial quotas toward more need-based approaches. But the concrete results of this policy have not yet been realized.

The legal system in Malaysia has never played much of a role in these allocational decisions. At independence, Malaysia inherited the same set of common-law institutions as Singapore, but while the courts have become a central part of Singapore's competitiveness, Malaysia's courts have been quiescent. This is a result of the interaction of institutional and political factors. The Constitution of Malaysia is rather easily amendable, and the dominance of the political coalition around the United Malays National Organization (UMNO) has meant that the courts' jurisdiction can be selectively manipulated at will. While the same is true in Singapore, the leaders there have been very subtle in their approach to interfere with judicial independence, ensuring that courts are staffed with high quality but loyal people.[11] Malaysia's courts, by contrast, have been subject to significant interference at several key junctures. For example, in 1988, Prime Minister Mohamad Mahathir fired the Lord President and a number of Supreme Court Justices after an assertion by the courts of constitutional supremacy. Thereafter the constitution was amended to remove references to the judicial power of the federation. Later, he relied on the courts to punish his arch-nemesis, Anwar Ibrahim. Broadly speaking, one can speak of a politicized decline in insulation during the period of UMNO rule.

The trajectory has followed neither the democratic nor authoritarian path out of MIC-ness. The concentration of political power in the governing coalition means there is no demand for the "insurance" of autonomous courts. Nor has the regime sought to rely on courts as the primary mechanism for making credible commitments, as in the authoritarian path. It has been able to induce foreigners to make long-term investments by providing a stable political environment, but law hasn't played much of a role.

Beyond insulation, the regime has not invested the same level of resources into the judiciary as has Singapore (whose judges are the highest paid in the world). Without a set of reliably neutral institutions, and with a politicized affirmative action regime governing investment, economic actors are steered toward a situation in which political arrangements play a role in decision making. The political logic is self-reinforcing: actors that benefit from the current arrangements are unwilling to give them up and so new entrants must either conform or go elsewhere. The result is

[11] Gordon Silverstein, "The Exception That Proves Rules Matter," in *Rule by Law: The Politics of Courts in Authoritarian Regimes* (Cambridge University Press, 2008).

a certain degree of institutional stagnation. Malaysia is a kind of intermediate country: middle income, with middling institutions, and middling quality of democracy that has been insufficient to push for transformation.

MALDIVES

Sometimes a focus on very small countries can help to illuminate the basic forces at work. The Maldives is a good case for examining the challenges of building autonomous law to facilitate further development and growth. It is a small Indian Ocean nation, whose economy is highly dependent on tourism. Until the tourism industry began in the early 1970s, it was poor and peripheral, dependent on fishing. Tourism is controlled by a small number of families, and so the economic base is quite narrow.

The country was ruled from 1978 to 2008 by President Maumoon Gayoom. Gayoom, an Islamic scholar trained in Egypt, was initially hailed as a modernizer but became increasingly repressive after a failed coup attempt in 1988. Systemic torture and the use of the law to repress opponents were common. The constitution allowed him to replace judges at will, and at one point Gayoom also served contemporaneously as Minister of Justice, which allowed him to interfere in particular cases quite easily. At the same time, a good deal of development occurred under his watch, with great strides in literacy and infant mortality. A large network of people were promoted by him and provided with higher education overseas, including many in the political class. The number of primary schools in the country expanded from four to more than two hundred during Gayoom's regime. (Secondary schools were limited and higher education nonexistent.)

The Gayoom regime benefited from international isolation, and it was difficult to learn much about the country from outside. To some degree this was deliberate government policy. Foreigners were not allowed to travel freely in the country, and tourists were physically isolated from the local population. The country had signed very few treaties, if any, and so was not subject to monitoring by international organizations and treaty bodies.

Unlike some other autocracies, law was not part of the developmental equation. This partly reflected trends in development thinking. When Gayoom came to power in 1978, education and health were seen as the key metrics of development, with legal institutions playing not much of a role in theory or policy. But it also reflected the country's isolation, and the lack of any need to attract foreign investment. In addition, the relatively simple economic structure, based on tourism and fishing, did not require particularly complex legal rules. There were few commercial cases, no financial markets, and little international trade.

The legal system, such as it was, was based on Islamic sharia. Judges were appointed for political loyalty. The legal system was a shambles. Many of the judges lacked even secondary education, and they were guided by very little formal law.

The country did not have, for example, laws on civil and criminal procedure. Punishment was based on the age-old tradition of banishment, and physical abuse, including torture, was widespread. Lacking formal law, the system seems close to the Weber's stereotypical "qadi justice," in which judicial decision making was inconsistent from case to case and was not based on the internal requirements of the law. But even Sharia gave out to political expediency. One 2004 interviewee of the National Democratic Institute noted that if a judge wanted to acquit someone in a case, he or she would need to gather approval from the Ministry of Justice.[12]

As in many other countries, the political institutions that accompanied the early phases of development were insufficient for sustaining the growth coalition. The literature in political economy on the resource curse is relevant to understanding the challenges that are posed by dependence on tourism. A long line of research has identified a set of problems common to countries with geographically concentrated natural resources such as oil or diamonds. The basic argument is that governments in such states can obtain sufficient revenue from controlling those resources so that they do not need to strike a fiscal bargain with their citizens.

Countries that lack such resources, however, have no choice but to conclude a bargain with the citizens, in which the government offers services in exchange for taxes. Historically, such bargains are the basis of the emergence of modern constitutionalism and democracy. Without such a bargain, government can dominate citizens; in addition, cycles of conflict may result as factions compete to control the concentrated resources. Resource curse countries also have a different state structure in terms of information – the metaphorical backroom deal is sufficient rather than publicly transparent processes amenable to outside review.

Tourism in the Maldives does not fit this story perfectly, but has some features in common. Like oil, tourism is geographically concentrated in specific limited locations, and sold to consumers abroad. In the Maldives, the ownership of these resources is controlled by a small number of people, ultimately dependent on government recognition of their property rights. The government did not need to conclude a fiscal bargain with its citizens so long as it had the support of those who controlled the tourism industry. This basic economic setup would seem to be less than ideal for democracy.

Crucially, however, tourism is not a commodity for export, but a service industry that requires the foreign consumers to come to the country to enjoy it. This puts an upper constraint on repression, as the Maldives "brand" competes with other tourism destinations around the world. Unlike oil, which can always be sold on the world market, tourism is highly sensitive both to external shocks outside the control of the Maldives and to internal disruptions. While the fiscal aspects of the resource curse seem to be relevant to the Maldives' situation, the peculiar nature of tourism

[12] National Democratic Institute for International Affairs, *Assessment of the Opportunities and the Challenges to the Development of Political Parties in the Maldives*, December 7, 2004, at 44.

requires some basic agreement among the population so as not to disrupt the golden goose.

Gayoom's increasing repression began to cost him internal support in the late 1990s. Several of the families that owned the tourism industry began to question his long-standing rule. In addition, the great developmental successes in education helped to play a role in undermining the regime. Much as in the countries of the Arab world, a great expansion in the population base and educational attainment, combined with weak employment prospects, meant that many young people channeled their energies into political activities.[13] Today, the young people of the country are quite plugged into the electronic media, and an internal culture of hyper-communication around Twitter has emerged.

The trigger for reform came in 2003 when a young man was tortured to death in police custody. Demonstrations on the streets of Male, the capital city, followed, and Gayoom announced a tentative set of reforms. A young charismatic journalist, Mohamad Nasheed, began to mobilize opposition, and formed a protopolitical party in defiance of the law. Arrests and repression followed, but the demonstrations continued. The 2004 tsunami also had a significant effect as the government was given an overwhelming amount of aid that it was unable to channel. Foreign donors tied reconstruction to political reform, and Gayoom announced a timetable for the establishment of multiparty democracy. A new constitution was written, and elections held in 2008, bringing Nasheed to power.

The politics of legal system reform were especially interesting. Like many constitutions of its era, the Maldives document features a wide transfer of authority to the judiciary. The judiciary plays the central role in upholding rights and is given the power of constitutional review. Whereas the earlier era had allowed the president to hire and fire judges as well, the 2008 Constitution set up a Judicial Services Commission (JSC) to protect and promote judicial independence. This heightened judicial power is consistent with many other countries in South Asia and around the world. It fulfills the logic of insurance, and one might anticipate that the country could pursue the path out of MIC-ness from democracy.

Unlike many of those countries, however, the Maldives in 2008 had no tradition of judicial independence, relatively little formal law, and very limited judicial capacity. The constitution contemplated an interim period during which judges would be screened by the JSC, and those without sufficient skill or qualification would be removed from office. Though appointments are for a life term to age seventy, the constitution also included a provision allowing for five-year terms for current judges, presumably to allow some transition from the old regime.

In the actual sequence of events, the JSC ended up being captured by the old forces. With a three-month period between the passage of the constitution and the

[13] Filipe R. Campante and Davin Chor, "Why Was the Arab World Poised for Revolution? Schooling, Economic Opportunities and the Arab Spring," *Journal of Economic Perspectives* 26, no. 2 (2012): 167–88.

election, President Gayoom appointed a new set of judges and an interim Supreme Court. Although only three of the eight seats on the JSC were constitutionally mandated to the judiciary, the courts were essentially able to capture the JSC to ensure that the old judiciary remained in place under the new constitutional order. The Supreme Court first declared that provisions of a statute giving the JSC control over judicial administration were unconstitutional. This ensured that the court would be able to control the material resources of the judiciary, including administrative jobs and contracts. It then used various techniques to take effective control of the commission. The JSC, which under Article 285 of the constitution was tasked with screening out judges for corruption or lack of credentials, never engaged in a serious attempt to do so. Instead of having an open process with hearings before the JSC, the chair and certain members did some of the screening "administratively," uniformly finding that the judges were sufficiently qualified. One dissident member of the JSC attempted to challenge some of these procedural techniques. The JSC held meetings without her. She was ultimately attacked with a box cutter on the streets of Male.[14]

Once the screening process was completed, the courts were able to become involved in many areas of governance. They developed an expansive view of their own jurisdiction, holding that the Human Rights Commission, for example, had no jurisdiction over cases involving the courts. The Supreme Court has held that it has certain "inherent powers" borrowing a notion from common-law systems. With power usually comes accountability. However, the Supreme Court has passed rules stating that lawyers and others could not criticize the courts without being found in contempt. The overall result is that the court, staffed with judges unencumbered by actual legal training, has set itself up as a very central actor in the Maldives political system. And it is one that is insulated from outside scrutiny. The court consistently decided against Nasheed's government until it was removed forcibly in February 2012.

All this empowerment of the judiciary reflects the confluence of international norms and the domestic logic of what I have elsewhere called *political insurance in constitutional design*. Ran Hirschl's notion of hegemonic preservation is also applicable: a departing power unsure that it will remain in office has a strong incentive to empower the judiciary so as to provide a forum to check the legislature. In contrast, where a constitution is made under the aegis of a strong political party that knows it will win postconstitutional elections, the judiciary will be much weaker.

Nevertheless, the story suggests that the institutional as opposed to political underpinnings of judicial empowerment were insufficient. The judiciary has a tradition of undisciplined decision making. How could it be otherwise, without codified laws to apply? Furthermore, the political logic of patronage, so effectively established and nurtured during the Gayoom regime, remains in place even in a democratic era. Tackling judicial corruption will require significant political

[14] Interview with Aishath Velezinee, August 8, 2013.

resources. This results in uneven decision making, which seems to be perceived as such by the population.

What are the consequences for the economy? For an industry such as tourism, courts may not be very important. But they are important for broader-based growth. The country's strategic location could make it ideal for oil transhipment or financial services; the educated young population has a reputation for computer programming innovation. But diversifying the economy in a significant way will require a much more sophisticated set of legal institutions. At the moment, the economy is in serious trouble as political democratization has increased the state sector, with parties passing out jobs to seek political support.

The country is now going through a very uneven process of state transformation, from a patronage-based system toward one based much more on transparent, rational decision making. But progress has been very limited, and the older political logic pervades many of the new institutions. Nor is it certain that effective transformation will continue. Institutional design for development is a probabilistic exercise rather than a mechanistic one, and there is no surefire recipe that will guarantee outcomes. But the fundamental point is that the legal system needs not only power and autonomy but capacity. Without that, the path out of MIC-ness seems fraught. And democratic politics alone, without legal underpinnings, is going to be insufficient to sustain growth.

SOUTH KOREA

South Korea represents the ideal type of a country that has transformed its way out of MIC-ness using the authoritarian pathway. Poorer than Egypt in 1950, South Korea is now an Organisation for Economic Co-operation and Development member with a seemingly endless capacity to reinvent its economic strategy as conditions change. It also has experienced major transformations in the political and legal spheres. It is thus a case that requires close scrutiny.

The legal system is a legacy of the Japanese colonial period. Unlike Meiji Japan, however, modern law was adopted in Korea not as an instrument to maintain independence in the face of Western colonialism, but as a tool to deprive Korea of independence in the interests of Japanese colonialism.[15] The motives of Koreans to absorb legal know-how were thus reduced. Then, in the postindependence period, Korea came under the U.S. security umbrella. However, a decade after the Korean War the country set up a system of political economy remarkably like that of its former colonial master. It relied heavily on state direction of the economy, with planning technocrats picking winners. A set of large conglomerates dominated the

[15] Still, there was some accommodation of Korean custom and complex politics between colonial and metropolitan authorities around legal transfers. See Marie Seong-hak Kim, *Law and Custom in Korea: Comparative Legal History* (Cambridge University Press, 2012).

economy. And it enjoyed spectacular growth under the developmentalist regime of Park Chung Hee.

In terms of law, Korea had what I have described elsewhere as the Northeast Asian Legal Complex, which had its origins in Japan's peculiar adoption of modern Western law in the nineteenth century.[16] The Northeast Asian Legal Complex had three main elements: a professional, hierarchically organized, somewhat competent court system; a small, cartelized private legal profession without much independent political influence; and administrative law regimes that insulated bureaucratic discretion exercised by developmental regimes. These institutions interacted in a particular way that was internally consistent and stable, and underpinned law's role in the political economy of the high-growth era.

Each element of the Northeast Asian Legal Complex interacted with the others to produce a set of stable and reinforcing institutions. The predictable courts minimized pressure for private litigation (at least when compared with American "adversarial legalism."[17] This allowed the state to maintain severe rationing of private legal services. A small private bar, in turn, minimized the possibility of social movement litigation challenging the insulated domains of policy makers.[18] Furthermore, the possibility of judicial and prosecutorial retirement to the bar in Korea (though not Japan) led to a comfortable conservatism in those countries among the majority of legal practitioners, particularly in government.

The basic configuration of administrative discretion exercised by elite bureaucrats and a restricted supply of legal professionals meant that law was relatively unimportant as a means of social ordering, particularly in interactions with the state. Regulated parties, lacking legal recourse, were forced to cultivate particularistic relationships with the state, reinforcing the image of bureaucratic dominance. Long-term relationships among bureaucrats and the large industrial firms provided the basic structure, reducing the need for general rules to govern arms-length transactions. The Northeast Asian Legal Complex restricted law to a narrow zone.

The key point for our analysis is that there was some legacy of autonomous law, precisely because it had not interfered with either political authority or bureaucratic discretion. This turned out to be a useful legacy for both political and economic transformation. By the 1980s, a large middle class had developed, and joined with student and labor activists to put pressure on the military regime. A handful of five or six human rights lawyers formed an informal association, which they called Chun Bo Pae (rights and law association). They treated this as a "kind of a secret organization" to avoid the gaze of the late authoritarian state, coordinating and assigning

16 Tom Ginsburg, "Law and the Liberal Transformation of the Northeast Asian Legal Complex in Korea and Taiwan," in *Fighting for Political Freedom: Comparative Studies of the Legal Complex and Political Liberalism*, ed. Terrence Halliday, Lucien Karpik, and Malcolm Feeley (Hart Publishing, 2007), 23–43.

17 Robert Kagan, *Adversarial Legalism* (Harvard University Press, 2002).

18 Frank Upham, *Law and Social Change in Postwar Japan* (Harvard University Press, 1987).

cases among themselves because of the heavy workload. After the mass demonstrations of 1986 led directly to Korea's democratization, these lawyers formalized their association as the Minbyeon, with fifty-six lawyers. This association became a kind of alternative bar association, and drew many activist lawyers with political agendas, eventually drawing hundreds of members.

The 1987 Constitution included a new Constitutional Court, which became a locus of litigation by activist groups, including the People's Solidarity for Participatory Democracy (PSPD). The PSPD launched a wide range of activities, including legislative campaigns, litigation strategies, organization of rallies, and generally working for social change. Corruption grew to be seen as an issue with the potential to transform Korean governance in profound ways. Explicitly drawing from foreign models of anticorruption legislation, including from Singapore, Taiwan, Hong Kong, and the Ethics in Government Act of the United States, the PSPD drafted a statute and initiated a lobbying effort at the National Assembly that was ultimately successful. Litigation was also a component of the reform program, hardly surprising given the dominance of lawyers among its leadership, and the courts obliged with decisions that promoted both political and economic liberalism. There was a coalition of economic reformers and legal liberals that came together to produce the transformation, and they were lucky to have autonomous courts that were responsive at the right time.

Beyond this individual litigation, PSPD-associated intellectuals and lawyers began to think about structural reform of the legal system. In 1996, the PSPD published a blueprint for more significant reforms. The topics included reform of the judiciary, prosecutors' office, the bar, corrections system, entry into the legal profession, legal education, legal aid, and lay participation. Within a decade, significant progress had been made in each of these areas. While the process of legal reforms took time, within a decade and a half most of these elements had been achieved. The legal system has become more autonomous and expanded in scope from the original narrow configuration of the Northeast Asian Legal Complex.

Economic transformation has proceeded apace. This began under the Kim Young Sam regime, who embraced globalization and a program of state restructuring in 1995. The major economic crisis of 1997 spurred a process of reforming the basis of the economy, and within a decade Korea had emerged as more dynamic and powerful than ever. The simultaneous transformation of the economic structure, the politics, and the legal system were partly conditioned on the authoritarian legacies and so Korea represents a paradigmatic story of the authoritarian pathway. It enjoyed some institutional legacy but was also able to produce the right political configuration at the right time to move up the development ladder.

One issue not directly addressed by this account is the factors that trigger the transformation from authoritarian regimes to democracy. There are many reasons why authoritarian regimes develop semiautonomous institutions, but at some point, they need to democratize to become HICs. At that point, they may be in a position to expand the scope of judicial activity, and the legacy of authoritarianism may provide a resource to manage this legal transition.

CONCLUSION

These three stories, though diverse in terms of their political history and economic structure, illustrate a generalizable lesson. MICs are at risk of stagnating politically, legally, and economically. To make it to high-income stage seems to require a transformation of all three systems. In each, the MIC institutions can create pressures for patronage and other logics that serve to reinforce the ruling coalition. Law that is too manipulable for political ends will not be able to sustain growth. But legal reform toward autonomy is ultimately a political process, requiring either the insurance logic of democratization, or a developmental regime that sees a benefit in insulation of the legal system within a limited zone of autonomy. This limited zone allows the judges and legal professions to develop capacities that are important and can be leveraged at higher levels of growth.

Development is a complicated process and it requires an alignment of political incentives, institutional capacities, and economic conditions. The politics of autonomous legal institutions are a central part of the story and necessary to overcome the MIC challenge. This chapter has identified a legal middle-income trap that occurs when legal institutions fail to develop sufficient insulation from political pressures. While semiautonomous legal institutions can be created in a wide variety of settings, both democratic and authoritarian, they will only flourish if accompanied by a coalition for political reform at the right time. Some countries may have the institutional underpinnings of judicial empowerment without the favorable political conditions; others have the political incentives but not the proper institutional infrastructure. Only when politics and legal institutions are aligned to incentivize fully autonomous legal institutions will countries break out of the trap.

3

When Does "Politics" Get in the Way of Development?

The Developmental State, Good Governance, and Liberal Democratic Change in Malaysia and Singapore

Surain Subramaniam

INTRODUCTION

The "developmental state model" is often used to describe the political economic model that led to modernization and economic development in postwar Japan, South Korea, and Taiwan, countries that have transitioned to high-income economies.[1] This chapter examines the role of the developmental state in two cases in Southeast Asia, Singapore (a high-income economy) and Malaysia (an upper middle-income economy). Using the analytical tool of the "developmental state," this chapter will discuss the complex ways in which development has been shaped by the role of the state and the "politics" of development in each of these cases, with implications for political liberalization in the direction of liberal democratization.

THE "DEVELOPMENTAL STATE MODEL"

The "developmental state"[2] has been identified as being "the distinctive East Asian contribution" to the field of international political economy.[3] Challenging the market

[1] Chalmers Johnson, *MITI and the Japanese Miracle: The Growth of Industrial Policy*, 1925–1975 (Stanford University Press, 1982); Alice H. Amsden, *Asia's Next Giant: South Korea and Late Industrialization* (Oxford University Press, 1989); Robert Wade, *Governing the Market: Economic Theory and the Role of Government in East Asian Industrialization* (Princeton University Press, 1990); Meredith Woo-Cummings, ed., *The Developmental State* (Cornell University Press, 1999). More recent works have challenged some of these earlier models; see Dae-oup Chang, *Capitalist Development in Korea: Labor, Capital, and the Myth of the Developmental State* (Routledge, 2009); and Megan J. Greene, *The Origins of the Developmental State in Taiwan: Science Policy and the Quest for Modernization* (Harvard University Press, 2008).

[2] The Asian developmental state model has also been labeled the East Asian Model (hereafter referred to as EAM). See Randall Peerenboom, *China Modernizes: Threat to the West or Model for the Rest?* (Oxford University Press, 2007), 31–2. Among its many features, EAM is characterized by a "strong (soft-authoritarian) ruling regime" that ensured economic growth and political stability (26). Peerenboom describes Singapore and Malaysia as "nonliberal democracies dominated by a single party" (33).

[3] Walden Bello, "States and Markets, States versus Markets: The Developmental State Debate as the Distinctive East Asian Contribution to International Political Economy," in *Routledge Handbook of International Political Economy (IPE): IPA as A Global Conversation*, ed. Mark Blyth (Routledge, 2009), 180–200.

fundamentalism associated with neoliberal economic policies (such as those attributed to the Washington Consensus), the developmental state model "brings the state back in" as "an active agent in economic development."[4] As one scholar succinctly put it, "[a]t its simplest, the developmental state has become a generic term to describe governments that try to actively 'intervene' in economic processes and direct the course of development, rather than relying on market forces."[5]

In his 1982 seminal work on the developmental state, Chalmers Johnson lists the following as being the "essential features of the Japanese developmental state":

> "the existence of a small, inexpensive, but elite bureaucracy staffed by the best managerial talent available in the system"[6] (this chapter interprets this feature to mean a meritocratic bureaucracy charged with the sole aim of developing the economy)
>
> "a political system in which the bureaucracy is given sufficient scope to take initiative and operate effectively"[7] (state autonomy)
>
> "the perfection of market-conforming methods of state intervention in the economy"[8] and
>
> "a pilot organization like MITI [Ministry of International Trade and Industry]."[9]

While these four attributes seek to define the scope of the developmental state, Johnson also noted that the developmental state is not a unitary actor; rather, it achieves its goal through "public-private cooperation."[10] Summarizing Johnson's interpretation of the "developmental state," one scholar writes, the developmental state is a state "preoccupied with economic development through the establishment of [an] elite economic bureaucracy to 'guide' the market. A developmental state tends to engage numerous institutions for consultation and coordination with the private sector, and these consultations are an essential part of the process of policy formulation and implementation."[11] Almost two decades after the publication of his seminal work on the developmental state, Johnson observed, "[t]here is no longer any question that the Japanese use of market mechanisms for developmental purposes has been successfully emulated in other countries. The most important examples, in descending order of their distance from the Japanese precedent, are South Korea, Taiwan, Singapore, and Hong Kong."[12]

4 Mark Blyth, "Introduction: International Political Economy as a Global Conversation," in Blyth, *Routledge Handbook of International Political Economy*, 12.

5 Mark Beeson, *Regionalism and Globalization in East Asia: Politics, Security and Economic Development* (Palgrave Macmillan, 2007), 141.

6 Johnson, *MITI and the Japanese Miracle*, 315.

7 Ibid.

8 Ibid., 317.

9 Ibid., 319.

10 Chalmers Johnson, "The Development State: Odyssey of a Concept," in *The Developmental State*, ed. Meredith Woo-Cumings (Cornell University Press 1999), 32–60.

11 Henry Wai-Chung Yeung, "The Rise of East Asia: An Emerging Challenge to the Study of International Political Economy," in Blyth, *Routledge Handbook of International Political Economy*, 205.

12 Johnson, "The Development State," 40.

Drawing from Johnson's study, there are at least four other insights that could be applied to our case studies of Singapore and Malaysia. First, the time frame it took the Japanese to build the developmental state. Johnson writes, "[C]redit for the postwar Japanese economic 'miracle' should go primarily to conscious and consistent governmental policies dating from at least the 1920s."[13] This has interesting implications for the role of the state in terms of continuously plugging away, if you will, at achieving economic growth and development. More important, the time-frame issue has added significance for the larger political question examined in this chapter, which is at what point and under which conditions does a strong developmental state transition to a liberal democratic one? Related to this is the question of whether the transition to a liberal democratic model is a consequence of modernization and development (modernization theory) or a societal reaction against the developmental state's lack of success in achieving its goal? Both of these questions will be explored in this chapter. Second, in Johnson's discussion of industrial policy, we again see both parallels and contrasts between Singapore and Malaysia.[14] Government policies in Singapore that have incentivized Multinational Corporations' (MNCs) foreign direct investments are consistent with Johnson's interpretation of the role of the development state in managing industrial policy, that is, by "[a]ltering market incentives, reducing risks, offering entrepreneurial visions, and managing conflict."[15] By contrast, Johnson provides the counterexample of industrial policy, whereby, rather than the developmental state using industrial policy "to achieve national development," the state uses industrial policy "to protect vested interests" or "enrich itself and its friends at the expense of consumers, good jobs, and development,"[16] establishing, for this chapter, the contrast between Singapore and Malaysia. Third, is the relationship among authoritarianism, democracy, and the developmental state. Johnson writes that while there is no necessary connection between authoritarianism and the developmental state, he does concede that authoritarianism can sometimes inadvertently solve the main political problem of economic development using market forces – namely, how to mobilize the overwhelming majority of the population to work and sacrifice for developmental projects.

> An authoritarian government can achieve this mobilization artificially and temporarily, but it is also likely to misuse such mobilization, thereby making it harder in the future. In the true developmental state, on the other hand, the bureaucratic rulers possess a particular kind of legitimacy that allows them to be more experimental and undoctrinaire than in the typical authoritarian regime. This is the legitimacy that comes from devotion to a widely believed-in revolutionary project.... The leaders of a

[13] Ibid., 37.

[14] Within the context of the developmental state, industrial policy is defined as "what the state does when it intentionally alters incentives within markets in order to influence the behavior of civilian producers, consumers, and investors." Ibid., 48.

[15] Ibid.

[16] Ibid.

> developmental state do not enjoy legitimacy in the sense of a mandate bestowed on them by civil society. . . . The legitimacy of developmental states cannot be explained using the usual state-society categories of Anglo-American civics. The successful capitalist developmental states have been quasirevolutionary regimes, in which whatever legitimacy their rulers possessed did not come from external sanctification or some formal rules whereby they gained office but from the overarching social projects their societies endorsed and they carried out.[17]

The ideas evoked in the preceding text, pragmatism and performance legitimacy, have both been explicitly used by the People's Action Party (PAP) government in Singapore to legitimize its rule.[18] The pragmatic, nonideological, and outcome-oriented legitimacy that the PAP government claims for its model of governance is in contrast to the process-driven legitimacy on which liberal democracies are based.[19] Johnson states that legitimacy in a developmental state can be linked to "revolutionary authority" defined as "the authority of a people committed to the transformation of their social, political, or economic order. Legitimacy occurs from the state's achievements, not from the way it came to power."[20] Paradoxically, Johnson argues that "[s]uch legitimacy based on projects or goals is, of course, fragile in that it normally cannot withstand failure. Equally serious, *it cannot adjust to victory and the loss of mission*."[21] In short, the legitimacy of a developmental state is "akin to those of revolutionary mass movements."[22] Linking the "model" back to the Japanese example, Johnson writes, "[t]he postwar bureaucratically led movement to enrich Japan was a *revolutionary project*, one that enjoyed legitimacy among the Japanese people for what it promised rather than for how its leaders got there."[23] The fourth insight from Johnson is his idea of situational nationalism. He clarifies the unique conditions that gave rise to the developmental state in Japan when he writes,

> It may be possible for another state to adopt Japan's priorities and its high-growth system without duplicating Japan's history, but the dangers of institutional

[17] Ibid., 52.

[18] Surain Subramaniam, "The Dual Narrative of 'Good Governance': Lessons for Understanding Political and Cultural Change in Malaysia and Singapore," *Contemporary Southeast Asia: A Journal of Strategic and International Affairs* 23, no. 1 (April 2001): 65–80.

[19] Surain Subramaniam, "The Asian Values Debate: Implications for the Spread of Liberal Democracy," *Asian Affairs: An American Review* 27, no. 1 (Spring 2000): 19–35.

[20] Johnson, "The Development State," 53.

[21] Ibid., emphasis mine.

[22] Ibid.

[23] Ibid., 54, emphasis mine. Tied to this is the fervor with which the developmental state pursues this goal, as reflected here when Johnson writes, "The Japanese case is actually one of an economy mobilized for war but never demobilized during peacetime." Ibid., 41. The "war" metaphor is particularly instructive when one compares it to the ways in which the PAP government in Singapore has evoked political, economic, and security vulnerabilities to justify its approach to governance. Not surprisingly, Johnson references the Singapore case when identifying examples of societies that have been united behind pursuing the "one overriding objective" of economic development, and the specific time period he identifies is the period after Singapore's expulsion from Malaysia. Ibid., 53.

> abstraction are as great as the potential advantages. For one thing, it was the history of poverty and war in Japan that established and legitimized Japan's priorities among the people in the first place. The famous Japanese consensus, that is, the broad popular support and a willingness to work hard for economic development that have characterized the Japanese during the 1950s and 1960s, is not so much a cultural trait as a matter of hard experience and of the mobilization of a large majority of the population to support economic goals. The willingness of the Japanese to subordinate the desires of the individual to those of the group is markedly weakening as generations come on the scene who have no experience of poverty, war, and occupation.[24]

He uses the term *situational imperatives* to explain the reasons behind the broad-based support among Japanese in the 1950s and 1960s that formed the legitimacy of the developmental state. Johnson states, "These situational imperatives include late development, a lack of natural resources, a large population, the need to trade, and the constraints of the international balance of payments. It may be possible to borrow Japan's priorities and institutions, but the situational nationalism of its people during the 1950's and 1960's is something another people would have to develop, not borrow."[25]

To summarize, in Johnson's understanding of the developmental state, it is a time-limited model of state-led development in the sense that the revolutionary culture that forms the basis of its legitimacy at the societal level is quite unlikely to last in perpetuity, thereby undermining its viability as an alternative model to democratic capitalism. As one scholar succinctly put it, Johnson was not "oblivious to the fact that his MITI book covered only the period 1925–1975 and that events and predispositions change."[26] Drawing from this, the argument made in this chapter is that a culture of development has shaped the background understandings of Singaporeans with regard to the government's role in achieving economic development, as well as justifying (albeit for a specific time period) a nonliberal model of democracy. The question that arises is, how sustainable is this model in the long-term for Singapore?[27]

LINKING THE DEVELOPMENTAL STATE TO THE SINGAPORE CASE

There are parallels between the pathway adopted by the Singaporean government in achieving economic growth and development and the attributes of the developmental state in Japan discussed previously. Adrian Leftwich's study draws out many of the characteristics that could be applied to the Singapore case:

[24] Johnson, *MITI and the Japanese Miracle*, 307.
[25] Ibid.
[26] T. J. Pempel, "The Legacy of Chalmers Johnson," *The Pacific Review* 24, no. 1 (March 2011): 12.
[27] Johnson conceded the unique and contingent nature of the "developmental state" when he concluded that it "is not an easy combination to put together, but when it is done properly, it can produce miracles of economic development." See Johnson, "The Development State," 60.

A determined developmental elite
Relative state autonomy
A powerful, competent, and insulated state bureaucracy
A weak and subordinated civil society
The effective management of nonstate economic interests
Repression, legitimacy, performance[28]

Consistent with the model discussed previously, the developmental state in Singapore is able to achieve sustained economic growth because of its firm or genuine commitment to economic development as a national goal.[29] It does this by mobilizing private sector investment through state-private sector cooperation to promote economic growth.[30] The next section examines the extent to which the developmental state model could explain the economic growth and development in Singapore based on (1) the governing philosophy of the PAP government, and (2) selected policy approaches adopted by the government.

People's Action Party's Governing Philosophy

In *Public Administration Singapore Style*, Jon Quah writes that "the PAP government's twin goals are: to maintain Singapore's political stability; and to maximize its economic growth so that Singaporeans can attain the 'good life.'"[31] To this end, Quah identifies nine "strategies for intervention" by the PAP government in achieving these goals: (1) "meeting the basic needs of the population"; (2) "maintaining the tradition of meritocracy"; (3) "minimizing corruption to ensure clean government"; (4) "investing in education to enhance the population"; (5) "minimizing the potential for racial and/or religious conflict"; (6) "preventing internal subversion by relying on the Internal Security Act"; (7) "learning from other countries' experiences in solving problems"; (8) "rejecting the idea of the welfare state"; and (9) "adopting a proactive and interventionist leadership style."[32] Quah suggests that, on balance, the PAP government's approach to governance has yielded positive outcomes. Although the "price of success" (as identified by critics) may be that Singaporeans have sacrificed some of their freedoms for economic success, Quah justifies this in the following terms: "it is obviously better for Singapore to pay the price of success than the price of failure."[33] He also concedes that "those from the low-income households have not benefitted as much from Singapore's economic affluence," thereby identifying at least one area in which the PAP government may not have been as

[28] Adrian Leftwich, "Bringing Politics Back In: Towards a Model of the Developmental State," *Journal of Development Studies* 31, no. 3 (1995): 405. Quoted from W. G. Huff, "Turning the Corner in Singapore's Developmental State?," *Asian Survey* 39, no. 2 (March/April 1999): 216.

[29] Huff, "Turning the Corner in Singapore's Developmental State?," 214–42.

[30] Ibid.

[31] Jon S. T. Quah, *Public Administration Singapore Style* (Talisman, 2010), 201.

[32] Ibid., 209.

[33] Ibid., 231.

successful as in others.[34] On the face of it, the developmental state in Singapore appears to have been successful when evaluated against Johnson's "first and consistent priority of the state," economic development.[35]

People's Action Party's Government's Policy Outcomes

Linda Low makes the case that in small economies such as Singapore, "constructive government intervention" in the economy makes for "good governance."[36] Characterizing the Singapore case as a "government-made development model," Low labels the developmental state in Singapore, "Singapore, Inc," in which there is "no sharp dichotomy of state and society."[37] Thomas Bellows provides another defense of the Singapore developmental state, describing it as "a strong, honest, effective, and interventionist government that has committed itself to forward planning since coming to power in 1959," and that "countries that are going to pluralize politically, first must have a coherent and functioning government."[38] Other scholars who have examined the Singapore case have argued that while some cases of developmental states such as South Korea and Taiwan have pluralized beyond the statist models, Singapore continues to resemble the developmental state model as the government continues to play the dominant role in the economy, vis-à-vis the domestic capitalist class and the working class. The state has continued to intervene in response to economic challenges from exogenous forces such as globalization by adopting economic strategies that have been largely conceived by state government ministers and bureaucratic and civil service elites or technocrats.[39]

There are numerous examples of this throughout the economic history of the city-state, and scholars have examined the ways in which state action has yielded favorable outcomes in terms of successful responses to endogenous and exogenous challenges. Some of these examples include the government's responses to the economic effects in Singapore from the 1997 Asian Financial Crisis,[40] and from

[34] Ibid., 234.

[35] This view of PAP rule, however, is not without its critics. Some authors have raised significant questions about the outcomes of the twin governing principles of the PAP government, multiracialism and meritocracy. See Michael D. Barr and Zlatko Skrbis, *Constructing Singapore: Elitism, Ethnicity and the Nation-Building Project* (NIAS Press, 2008).

[36] Linda Low, *The Political Economy of a City-State: Government-made Singapore* (Oxford University Press, 1998), 1–2.

[37] Linda Low, "The Singapore Development State in the New Economy and Polity," *The Pacific Review* 14, no. 3 (2001): 433.

[38] Thomas J. Bellow, "Economic Challenges and Political Innovation: The Case of Singapore," *Asian Affairs: An American Review* 32, no. 4 (2006): 232.

[39] Alexius A Pereira, "Whither the Developmental State? Explaining Singapore's Continued Developmentalism," *Third World Quarterly* 29, no. 6 (2008): 1189–1203.

[40] Alan Chong, "Singapore's Political Economy, 1997–2007: Strategizing Economic Assurance for Globalization," *Asian Survey* 47, no. 6 (2007): 952–76.

the 2008 financial crisis triggered by the collapse of some major Wall Street firms.[41] Other examples of the dynamism of Singapore's developmental state in coming up with strategic responses to increasing competition from the global economy can be found in the ways in which its sovereign wealth funds have been repositioned from their early role as contributors to "domestic national development" to vehicles of "economic diplomacy" in the area of global finance, the aim here being to "secure the economic future of Singapore."[42] Not only has the global economic environment become more competitive with the "rise of the rest," it is also characterized now by a higher level of uncertainty, perhaps requiring more in the way of strategic actions by the developmental state. For example, in early 2009, Singapore's economy registered its worst performance since independence as a consequence of the 2008 global financial crises; at one point it seemed as though the financial crisis would threaten to "disrupt the global linkages which Singapore had painstakingly built up over the decades" through the policies enacted by the developmental state.[43]

In this age of globalization, then, a case could be made in favor of the actions attributed to the developmental state, as opposed to the alternative neoliberal models of development.[44] One observes a veritable lexicon of terms that have been used by state officials and/or scholars in Singapore to capture policies, both in the forms of immediate short-term tactical responses to "crises," and long-term strategic approaches in achieving economic growth and development in Singapore. I will illustrate this point with two cases: first, the government's recent initiatives in continuing to move Singapore's economy in the direction of transforming it into a "knowledge-based economy" by developing the biomedical industry cluster,[45] and second, (revisiting Johnson's point about the role of the developmental state in industrial policy) the example of the dynamic way in which the Singapore government is seeking to redefine private sector development policy, including recent government initiatives that have involved the creation of networks of partnerships among state economic development agencies, and between these agencies and the

[41] Faizal bin Yahya, "Singapore in 2010: Rebounding from Economic Slump, Managing Tensions between a Global City and a Fledging Nation State," in *Southeast Asian Affairs* 2011, ed. Daljit Singh (Institute of Southeast Asian Studies), 257.

[42] Henry Wai-chung Yeung, "From National Development to Economic Diplomacy? Governing Singapore's Sovereign Wealth Funds," *The Pacific Review* 24, no. 5 (December 2011): 625–52.

[43] Yahya, "Singapore in 2010," 257.

[44] This point is supported by recent studies that have assessed the developmental state in the wake of the financial crises of 2007, see Richard Stubbs, "The East Asian Developmental State and the Great Recession: Evolving Contesting Coalitions," *Contemporary Politics*, 17, no. 2 (2011): 151–66.

[45] Yong-Sook Lee and Ying-Chian Tee, "Reprising the Role of the Development State in Cluster Development: The Biomedical Industry in Singapore," *Singapore Journal of Tropical Geography* 30 (2009): 86–97. For a critical assessment of the role of the developmental state in Singapore's biotech industries, see Joseph Wong, *Betting on Biotech: Innovation and the Limits of Asia's Developmental State* (Cornell University Press, 2011).

private sector actors in business and organized labor, thereby creating "integral policy stakeholders."[46]

The preliminary conclusion that could be drawn from these examples is that through its actions the developmental state in Singapore reflects a level of dynamism. Specifically, it identifies challenges that could potentially derail continued economic growth, and then demonstrates a willingness to use hybrid (and pragmatic) approaches in responding to these challenges. Nevertheless, there are some areas in which the developmental state in Singapore, either by being ill-equipped politically, or by virtue of the imperatives of continuous economic development, has been less successful in achieving the desired outcomes of its policy initiatives. The often-cited example of this is the role of the state in "developing" the arts in which the Singapore government appears to be responding to the need for "democratic space" in the arts by, paradoxically, directing its creation, top down, much like it has engineered the economic growth of the country.[47] Another example that illustrates the deficiencies of a developmental state-centric approach involves issues surrounding some of the costs to nature conservation from an exclusively "economistic" conception of development.[48]

SHAPING THE "DEVELOPMENT" CULTURE IN SINGAPORE

This chapter argues that a *culture of development* lies at the core of the policies of the Singapore developmental state. One scholar has written that the Singapore government could be viewed as "a reflective dynamic group – a group capable of reconstructing values against the background of a unique cultural milieu and using the product of this reconstruction to regulate its own behavior in guiding the country's industrialization and post-industrial development."[49] The government's role in transforming the economy, society, and culture is grounded in a set of "state values," a hybridized version of Western and "Oriental" values that have been referred to as "a Singaporean type of state culture."[50] I would argue that a more accurate assessment of these "state values" would be that the developmental state in Singapore has created a political culture of developmentalism or a culture of development, which has become one of the platforms upon which the legitimacy

[46] Charles Conteh, "Network Governance of Private Sector Development Policy Implementation in Singapore," *Asian Journal of Political Science* 17, no. 1 (April 2009): 71–88.

[47] Ooi Can-Seng, "Political Pragmatism and the Creative Economy: Singapore as a City for the Arts," *International Journal of Cultural Policy* 16, no. 4 (November 2010): 403–17.

[48] Harvey Neo, "Challenging the Developmental State: Nature Conservation in Singapore," *Asia Pacific Viewpoint* 48, no. 2 (August 2007): 186–99.

[49] Johannes Han-Yin Chang, "Culture, State and Economic Development in Singapore," *Journal of Contemporary Asia* 33, no. 1 (2003): 87.

[50] The hybrid list of "state values" consists of "neo-social Darwinism, connectionism, Golden-Means seeking rationalism, pragmatism, communitarianism, conservative liberalism, and elitism." Ibid., 101.

of the PAP government is built.[51] Some of the criticisms that have been leveled against this culture of development are that its directed, top-down nature leads to deficiencies in creativity and entrepreneurship that could only emanate from the bottom up (or at the societal level), and that the attendant forms of political control exerted by the state as part of managing this culture of development sometimes leads to political alienation, tension, and reactions that are "inconsistent with the need of Singapore's development."[52]

Nevertheless, there is an unmistakable role that the developmental state has played in building this culture of development, and it is constantly being reinforced by the state using various strategies. For example, Terence Chong discusses one of the dominant narratives of the PAP, in which it is "the centerpiece of the Singapore success story." It has been framed along the lines of "a narrative of success," materially and ideologically, whereby "success" is defined materially in terms of overcoming daunting obstacles in achieving economic development, and ideologically, in terms of society prevailing over ascriptive social identities to embrace a pragmatic multiculturalism.[53] In this example, the "success story narrative" plays the role of "a national culture."[54]

"MANAGING" ETHNIC RELATIONS

The developmental state's role in shaping the culture of development in Singapore includes the ways in which it has "managed" ethnic relations among the Chinese, Malays, and Indians.[55] The term *manage* is a term of choice commonly deployed by government officials and scholars in reference to state policies that deal with economic and ethnic/racial issues in Singapore.[56] In the view of the PAP government, social stability is a prerequisite for economic development. Consequently, among the government's "developmental" roles is ensuring social and political stability, largely to facilitate continued foreign investments by MNCs in Singapore's economy. Social and political stability then are viewed by the government as interlinked conditions that facilitate continued economic development. To this end, "managing" the relations between the ethnic groups in Singapore is seen as equally important as maintaining political order. Critics of the government's strategy

[51] I discuss a similar role played by "Asian values" and "good governance," respectively, in Subramaniam, "The Asian Values Debate" and Subramaniam, "The Dual Narrative of 'Good Governance.'"

[52] Chang, "Culture, State and Economic Development in Singapore," 102.

[53] Terence Chong, "Introduction: The Role of Success in Singapore's National Identity," in *Management of Success: Singapore Revisited*, ed. Terence Chong (ISEAS, 2010), 1–20.

[54] Ibid., 4–9.

[55] Ooi Giok Ling, "The Role of the Developmental State and Interethnic Relations in Singapore," *Asian Ethnicity* 6, no. 2 (June 2005): 109–20.

[56] See section on "Managing Diversity" in *Singapore: Re-Engineering Success*, ed. Arun Mahizhnan and Lee Tsao Yuan (Institute of Policy Studies, 1998), 50–79. The term *re-engineering* in the title of this edited volume is also illustrative of the lexicon used in building the culture of development in Singapore.

of "managing" ethnic relations in Singapore have pointed out that among the effects of these policies are not only that issues of ethnicity have been "depoliticized," but so have "virtually all aspects of government," creating an "apolitical culture."[57] By defining ethnic relations as narrowly as has been done, whereby they are seen as being "inherently conflictual," the government has precluded other, more open and democratic ways of achieving racial harmony.[58] In a very tangible way, this criticism raises one of the paradoxes of ethnic pluralism in Singapore; it is both an important part of Singapore's identity as a society and a potential threat to national identity.[59] And the approach adopted by the government to get around this conundrum has been to use state intervention to diffuse any likelihood of ethnic issues negatively affecting social stability and, by extension, economic development. Consequently, while the state has been "successful in containing ethnic tensions and racial violence, Singapore remains a stratified and classified society."[60]

POLITICAL DIMENSIONS OF THE "DEVELOPMENTAL STATE" IN SINGAPORE

In describing the complex ways in which the PAP government has consolidated political power in Singapore, Ho Khai Leong writes,

> After more than four decades of independence, the Singapore political system has been transformed into a centralized structure characterized by the overlapping of party/government/state institutions. They are interrelated in astonishingly vast areas, with one helping the others to grow, resulting in the shoring and entrenchment of power.... The Singapore state, in essence, is represented by a diverse range of institutions: executive, legislature, courts, paramilitary, regulatory authorities, bureaucracies, statutory boards and community councils.... The widespread co-option of elites into the government and state, not necessarily recruitment as party members, has resulted in a symbiotic and collaborative relationship between the state apparatus and the government. At the same time, the PAP's dominance in Parliament has made alternative policy decisions almost impossible.[61]

The idea that a strong (even authoritarian) state would be necessary in achieving economic growth and development is implicit in the understanding of the developmental state, and this is certainly supported by the Singapore example. (We even

[57] Stephanie Lawson, "Sanitizing Ethnicity: The Creation of Singapore's Apolitical Culture," *Nationalism & Ethnic Politics* 7, no. 1 (Spring 2001): 63.

[58] Ibid.

[59] Nicole Tarulevicz, "Hidden in Plain View: Singapore's Race and Ethnicity Policies," in *The State, Development, and Identity in Multi-Ethnic Societies: Ethnicity, Equity and the Nation*, ed. Nicholas Tarling and Edmund Terence Gomez (Routledge, 2008), 148.

[60] Ibid.

[61] Ho Khai Leong, "Political Consolidation in Singapore: Connecting the Party, the Government and the Expanding State," in *Management of Success: Singapore Revisited*, ed. Terence Chong (ISEAS, 2010), 76.

see its tacit acceptance in Johnson's interpretation of the "developmental state model" in the preceding text.) However, this political economic compromise sits uneasily with the dominant global trend toward liberal democratization, especially in the last two decades since the end of the Cold War.[62]

The Adaptive State: *Evolving with Changing State-Society Perspectives*

From a comparative politics perspective, earlier scholarly works have raised at least two critiques of "statist" perspectives; first by "conceptualizing the state as an overpowering Leviathan" we could be obscuring "the myriad patterns in which state and society interact, overlap, and lead to unexpected, contingent outcomes."[63] And second, drawing from the work of Peter Evans, scholars have proposed a "second-generation" view of the state, whereby the state and society are seen as "mutually empowering," and that continued "economic development could emerge not so much from state power alone but from the synergy between state and society."[64] The question then arises, to what extent is this gradually being reflected in the Singapore case.

When we connect these theoretical insights to the Singapore case, we begin to recognize that societal forces have a contributing role in the continued development of Singapore, while acknowledging the primary role played by the state. Using the framework of "an evolving social compact" between state and society, scholars have repeatedly raised the prospect of broadening the parameters of citizen participation. Eugene K. B. Tan writes,

> Shared economic growth as the substratum of Singapore's success will remain a cardinal principle of governance and success. But Singapore's success will be more meaningful and sustainable if the hard-nosed pragmatism is accompanied by a deeply felt passion for Singapore by its stakeholder-citizens.... In responding to the clarion calls and the growing expectations for success to be repeated, the social compact has to be reconceptualized not only as a vertical bond between the government and the citizens, but also as one embracing and nurturing the horizontal bonds between citizens. Ultimately, the social compact must embrace and invigorate these mutual bonds of belonging between the state and citizens, and among citizens in an ever increasingly diverse Singapore.[65]

[62] Larry Diamond, *The Spirit of Democracy: The Struggle to Build Free Societies throughout the World* (Times Books, 2008).

[63] Erik Martinez Kuhonta, "Studying States in Southeast Asia," in *Southeast Asia in Political Science: Theory, Region, and Qualitative Analysis*, ed. Erik Martinez Kuhonta, et al. (Stanford University Press, 2008), 31.

[64] Ibid.

[65] Eugene K. B. Tan, "The Evolving Social Compact and the Transformation of Singapore: Going Beyond *Quid Pro Quo* in Governance," in *Management of Success: Singapore Revisited*, ed. Terence Chong (ISEAS, 2010), 95.

This takes us in the direction of imagining a new understanding of the "developmental state," one that this chapter would term the *adaptive state*, in that it is defined not only in terms of the primacy of the state, but also in the state's relationships with society's "multiple stakeholders." Not surprisingly, much like every other new challenge or new circumstance confronted by the state, this too has elicited an "official" response from the government. Tommy Koh has suggested that in seeking to address some of the challenges facing Singapore today such as raising the standard of living of the bottom 40 percent of the social pyramid (referencing the growing income and economic disparity and social stratification in Singapore), a credible way forward may be to engage in efforts "driven by multiple stakeholders with the government playing the role of the lead stakeholder."[66] Contrasting this to earlier periods in which "campaigns were driven singly by the government," Koh shares the view that "those days are over," because "we now live in a new world, a less hierarchical world, a world in which the government is still very important, but so are the people. I think that in future campaigns, the new wisdom is that all campaigns ought to be driven by multiple stakeholders."[67]

Democratic Culture and the Developmental State: Two Views on the Future of the "Developmental State"

Looking forward, to the extent that the developmental state in Singapore continues to respond to growing pressures for liberal democratic change by adapting to the challenges that arise by successfully maintaining economic growth, it may well continue to act in the mode of an adaptive state. To this end, it would appear to provide for some an alternative to the neoliberal, American-style democratic capitalist model, especially in terms of a successful model of state-managed economic development, without liberal democratic political liberalization. To quote Chua Beng Huat:

> ... Singapore demonstrates that political liberalism is not a necessary condition for national economic success in neo-liberal capitalism.... The apparent sustainability of the Singapore political system stands as a disruption in the universalizing ambitions of liberal democracy, particularly the version that is aggressively promoted by the United States and its home grown liberal agencies. This disruption would have to be taken more seriously if it becomes a loose "model" for the People's Republic of China (PRC) and other post-communist nations in Asia..... In the end, what the PRC, and other post-communist states in Asia, are looking for is precisely this: an incorrupt single-party state that delivers high economic growth, thus erasing mass poverty and raising the standard of living of the population – but

[66] Tommy Koh, "Closing Remarks," in *Singapore Perspectives 2010: Home, Heart, Horizon*, ed. Tan Tarn How (Institute of Policy Studies, 2010), 130.
[67] Ibid.

which does so without having to share political power and lose any governmental and administrative capacity.[68]

Other scholars are also less hopeful of the prospect of the Singapore developmental state transitioning in the direction of liberal democratic change. While there is growing "political consciousness among the younger and better educated citizenry," which is accompanied by demands for greater participation, pluralism, and openness, the PAP government is hesitant to put in place a "road map" to reach this goal; rather, there appears to be "no signs that the present Singapore conservative political model, together with the practice of co-option and the systematic centralization of power, will be abandoned for a liberal democracy."[69]

To state the obvious then, what is lacking in Singapore's developmental state model is what Mark Robinson and Gordon White have termed a "democratic developmental state," whereby the "political and institutional basis" of the "new form of developmental state" would allow it to "simultaneously carry forward a development project founded on growth and equality, and which rests on democratic political foundations" beyond those of electoral democracy.[70]

This alternative vision would involve moving away from the binary discussion of the necessary authoritarianism of the strong developmental state, on the one hand, and the notion that democratic politics are "considered to be a barrier to sustained development since unbridled political competition could generate demands which could not be accommodated within existing political institutions and prevailing resource constraints,"[71] on the other hand. The view posited here is that "democracy and development are not only compatible, but mutually reinforcing."[72] Robinson and White term this the case for compatibility or the "compatibility argument."[73] Drawing upon the preceding definition of the "democratic developmental state," it presumes expanded economic and political parameters for development, such that, development is redefined to be more broad based and sustainable, including addressing poor and socially marginalized groups that may not have benefitted equally under state developmental plans.[74] Correspondingly, the type of democracy that accompanies development is of the "legitimate and inclusive" sort, going well beyond the expectations associated with performance legitimacy.[75] To expand on this alternative view of the development state, Robinson and White write,

[68] Chua Beng Huat, "The Cultural Logic of a Capitalist Single-Party State, Singapore," *Postcolonial Studies* 13, no. 4 (2010): 348–9.

[69] Ho Khai Leong, "Political Consolidation in Singapore," 76–7.

[70] Mark Robinson and Gordon White, "Introduction," in *The Democratic Developmental State: Politics and Institutional Design*, ed. Mark Robinson and Gordon White (Oxford University Press, 1998), 4–5.

[71] Ibid., 1.

[72] Ibid., 2.

[73] Ibid., 2–3.

[74] Ibid., 4.

[75] Ibid.

> Our argument also rests on a broader conception of processes of democracy (more pervasive and participatory) and development (more redistributive and inclusive) which can be mutually reinforcing. In other words, greater mass participation and popular pressure, and increased political representation by women and other disadvantaged groups, can help make democratic regimes more sensitive to issues of poverty, social welfare, and forms of discrimination based on gender, ethnicity, and the like and impel them to take appropriate remedial action through policy commitments. . . . [T]he notion of the democratic development state has affinities with the basic tenets of social democracy, in which equitable and sustained development outcomes are achieved through the creation of durable and inclusive political institutions. . . . In ethical terms, a strong argument can be made that the well-being of the vast majority of the population of developing societies can better be achieved under the aegis of social democracy which seeks to combine economic growth with social justice than under a cramped and etiolated notion of liberal democracy which tolerates widespread exploitation and allows inequalities to grow. It is our contention that, if a "model" of democracy is needed to guide the political evolution of developing societies, it should be social rather than liberal democracy.[76]

Some have argued that we may be witnessing the early signs of this second view of the developmental state, the democratic developmental state, emerging ever so tentatively in Singapore, especially if some of the societal-level pressures for a great political voice seen during the 2011 general election were to continue to grow.[77]

THE MALAYSIAN CASE

To offer a contrast to our discussion thus far on the relationship between "politics" and the developmental state, this chapter will now turn to the second case study, Malaysia, to provide a comparative framework against which to assess the "developmental state model" in an upper middle-income economy. The Malaysian government is considered to be one of the "more interventionist" in the East Asia region, although "much of the government's interventionism is also about managing ethnicity."[78] The developmental state in Malaysia is unique in that its developmental goals include explicit social and economic policies designed to redistribute

[76] Ibid., 5–7.

[77] For a critique of some of the economic policies that have been adopted by the PAP government, that may have led to a "two-speed dual economy characterized by falling productivity and a widening income gap," see Tan Meng Wah, "Singapore's Rising Income Inequality and a Strategy to Address It," *ASEAN Economic Bulletin* 29, no. 2 (2012): 128–45. For early accounts of the significance of the 2011 general election on Singapore's future democratic trajectory see Derek da Cunha, *Breakthrough: Roadmap for Singapore's Political Future* (Straits Times Press, 2012); Kevin Y. L. Tan and Terence Lee, eds., *Voting in Change* (Ethos Books, 2011); Tan Jee Say, ed., *A Nation Awakes: Frontline Reflections* (Ethos Books, 2011); and Catherine Lim, *A Watershed Election: Singapore's GE 2011* (Marshall Cavendish, 2011).

[78] Hans C. Blomqvist, "The Developmental State of Malaysia: Efficiency versus Management of Ethnicity," *Asian Profile* 39, no. 4 (August 2011): 308.

wealth along ethnic/racial lines.[79] Beginning in 1971, Malaysia introduced the New Economic Policy (NEP), which included specific affirmative action policies for the Malays.[80] Ironically, while the aim of the NEP was "to eliminate poverty irrespective of race, and restructure society so that race would not be identified with economic function,"[81] perhaps no other policy enacted by the government has reified race/communal politics in Malaysia's politics, economics, society, and culture as much as the NEP.[82] On the significance of the NEP on Malaysia's developmental path, one scholar writes,

> [The NEP] also set a target of at least 30 percent *bumiputra* [Malays and other indigenous races] ownership of commercial and business activities. Government intervention in the economy expanded enormously, with numerous bodies set up to pursue business opportunities "in trust" for *bumiputra*, and to plan and monitor policies and regulations to meet NEP goals. Existing foreign companies were urged to restructure in accordance with these guidelines, and in several cases were bought out by state-linked Malaysian companies.[83]

Scholars have identified the period after 1981, which coincided with the Prime Ministership of Mahathir Mohamad, as being the point when Malaysia pivoted in the direction of "a developmental state in the Northeast Asian mould."[84] The highly publicized (and symbolic, for the purposes of this chapter) "Look East" policy introduced by Mahathir, launched industrial policy that was focused on state-run joint ventures with foreign (mostly Japanese and South Korean) heavy industries in the areas of automobile and motorcycle manufacturing, as well as steel and cement production.[85] Another distinguishing feature of the developmental state in Malaysia (and one that has been alluded to previously) is that its "bureaucracy has never been sharply separated from politics."[86] Unlike the state objectives discussed in Johnson's concept of the developmental state, the "politics" referenced here is *party politics*, specifically, policies favoring the United Malays National Organization (UMNO),

79 Hwok-Aun Lee, "Affirmative Action in Malaysia: Education and Employment Outcomes since the 1990s," *Journal of Contemporary Asia* 42, no. 2 (April 2012): 230–54.

80 In 1990, the NEP was replaced by the National Development Policy (hereafter referred to as NDP). The redistributive goals defined along ethnic lines, with affirmative action policies for Malays, continued with the NDP, the inclusive-sounding policy titles notwithstanding.

81 John Funston, "Malaysia: Developmental State Challenged," in *Government and Politics in Southeast Asia*, ed. John Funston (ISEAS, 2001), 168.

82 For an assessment of the effects of the NEP on the ethnic Chinese support for the Barisan Nasional ruling coalition, see James Chin, "The Malaysian Chinese Dilemma: The Never Ending Policy (NEP)," *Chinese Southern Diaspora Studies* 3 (2009): 167–81.

83 Funston, "Malaysia: Developmental State Challenged,"168. Tied to this, at least one "prime goal of the NEP was the creation of a Malay commercial and industrial community, or Malay capitalists." Peter Searle, *The Riddle of Malaysian Capitalism: Rent-seekers or Real Capitalists?* (Allen and Unwin, 1999), 242.

84 Funston, "Malaysia: Developmental State Challenged," 198.

85 Ibid., 170.

86 Ibid., 175.

which is the dominant political party in the ruling multiparty coalition and also considered to be the guardian of Malay preferential policies.[87] In the words of one scholar, "[s]enior bureaucrats were expected to be sympathetic to UMNO objectives, and the prohibition on political party activism was not rigidly enforced."[88] He later adds,

> The executive's role increased dramatically from the launch of the NEP in 1971, with the bureaucracy given major responsibilities to support the growth of the new *bumiputra* commercial and professional class, and to intervene directly in business activities as a proxy for *bumiputra*. Increased emphasis on privatization in the mid-1980s may have led to some decline in public sector employment, but the executive ... played a key role in determining privatization arrangements. The awarding of privatization contracts without open tendering, or any other form of transparent arrangements, enhanced executive power.[89]

Clearly, structural conditions, specifically the state's race-based preferential policies in favor of the Malays at the expense of the Chinese, Indian, and other races complicates the extent to which the "developmental state model" could be applied without qualifiers to the Malaysian case.[90] One scholar even claims that "[n]o other developing country can match Malaysia for its deliberate and consistent commitment to redistribution since 1970."[91] For example, one view of Malaysia's developmental state is that it uses industrial policy to achieve the "dual goals of economic development and pro-Malay redistribution."[92] And yet, to the extent that the developmental state (to draw from Johnson) is defined by its "one overriding objective," that of economic development, the Malaysian case would need to be qualified, as both these goals (development and redistribution) may well have worked at cross-purposes with each another.[93] Scholars have noted that the "obsession with redistribution may have cost the country dearly in terms of a sustainable manufacturing

[87] Edmund Terence Gomez and K. S. Jomo, *Malaysia's Political Economy: Politics, Patronage and Profits* (Cambridge University Press, 1999). Also see Edmund Terence Gomez, "The State, Governance, and Corruption in Malaysia," in *Corruption and Good Governance in Asia*, ed. Nicholas Tarling (Routledge, 2005), 214–44.

[88] Funston, "Malaysia: Developmental State Challenged," 175.

[89] Ibid., 176–7.

[90] Paul M. Lubeck, "Malaysian Industrialization, Ethnic Divisions, and the NIC Model: The Limits of Replication," in *States and Development in the Asian Pacific Rim*, ed. Richard P. Appelbaum and Jeffrey Henderson (Sage Publications, 1992), 176–98.

[91] Hal Hill, "Malaysian Economic Development: Looking Backward and Forward," in *Malaysia's Development Challenges: Graduating from the Middle*, ed. Hal Hill, et al. (Routledge, 2012), 40.

[92] Blomqvist, "The Developmental State of Malaysia," 314.

[93] As one of Malaysia's foremost political economists states, "In Malaysia, state intervention has been especially pronounced, particularly from the 1970s up to the mid-1980s, but much of it has been motivated or compromised by the priority given to interethnic economic redistribution exacerbated by rent-seeking activity of the politically influential." K. S. Jomo, "Rethinking the Role of Government Policy in Southeast Asia," in *Rethinking the East Asia Miracle*," ed. Joseph E. Stiglitz and Shahid Yusuf (The World Bank and Oxford University Press, 2001), 472.

sector and domestic technological and entrepreneurial ability."[94] It is claimed that "in Malaysia, even the term 'industrial policy' has negative connotations among the non-Malay part of the population because it has been so closely connected to the government's redistributive ambitions."[95] Partly as a consequence of path dependency, there is pessimism as to whether the developmental state in Malaysia would be able to extricate itself from the political interests that manifests in the affirmative action socioeconomic policies: "the problem is that the policy of 'special rights' is so deeply entrenched in the country that it is now hard to dismantle."[96] Ironically, scholars have raised serious misgivings about the record of the NEP, especially in terms of the uneven distribution of its beneficiaries.[97] Describing a patronage system that is characterized by "the deep entrenchment of ethnicization in the field of economy, where significant actors not only are linked with the government in possibly corrupt ways, but also foster the creation of a support base that is founded on ethnicized affiliations,"[98] another scholar writes, "The economic system in this respect does not merely mirror the political system; rather both reinforce each other in a two-way flow of ethnicization: State intervention in the economy based upon ethnicized affirmative action creates over time an impression among the 'clients' that certain privileges are seen as a natural right. This in turn secures support for ethnicized policies, economic and other, and protects and promotes the 'patron' who is most vocal about these 'rights.'"[99]

Looking ahead, the assessment of Malaysia's developmental state has moved in the direction of a paradigm shift away from the status quo socioeconomic arrangements that have sought to "embed" ethnic politics in developmental goals, to one where "Malaysia's democratic foundations" are strengthened, to achieve more broad-based developmental goals.[100] It is precisely the "patronage resources" that have been channeled in the direction of UMNO beneficiaries that have begun to alienate the population, not only among the non-Malays (the poor showing by the *Barisan Nasional* coalition parties in the last general election of 2008 was largely attributable to Chinese and Indian discontent with patronage politics masquerading

[94] Blomqvist, "The Developmental State of Malaysia," 317.

[95] Ibid.

[96] Ibid.

[97] Mohamed Ariff writes that the "growing income disparity within the Bumiputera community reflects the extremely uneven distribution of the benefits of the New Economic Policy. Arguably, all Bumiputeras have benefitted in one way or another, but it is clear that the bulk, if not the lion's share, of the benefits have accrued to the politically well-connected elites at the top." See Mohamed Ariff, "Preface: Development Strategy under Scrutiny," in Hill, et al., *Malaysia's Development Challenges* (Routledge, 2012), xix.

[98] Frederik Holst, *Ethnicization and Identity Construction in Malaysia* (Routledge, 2012), 88.

[99] Ibid.

[100] Vejai Balasubramaniam, "Embedding Ethnic Politics in Malaysia: Economic Growth, Its Ramifications and Political Popularity," *Asian Journal of Political Science* 14, no. 1 (September 2006): 23–39.

as developmental policies),[101] but also among some Malays who feel that government policies that were ostensibly aimed at uplifting all Malays have disproportionately benefitted politically well-connected Malays. When states are perceived to have "failed" in their developmental goals, the idea of performance legitimacy begins to lose its resonance. An alternative basis for legitimacy, democratic legitimacy, begins to take root, where legitimacy is based increasing on political processes and procedures and less on policy outcomes and political allegiances.[102] And, in the case of Malaysia, opposition political voices, cognizant of the fading legitimacy of the state, have begun to propose alternative models of achieving economic growth and development.[103]

CONCLUSION

This chapter will conclude by identifying some of the main differences between the varying roles played by the developmental state in Singapore and Malaysia, respectively, and offer some assessment in terms of change in the direction of political liberalization. In the case of Singapore, the challenge for the developmental state appears to be one of managing to maintain a sufficiently strong sense of "situational nationalism" (to borrow a phrase from Johnson) among the population that is increasingly less enamored by the idea that the "good life" should continue to be defined almost exclusively in terms of a culture of development; it would appear that some among the younger generations of Singaporeans (and even among the ranks of the older generation) are just as interested in being engaged citizens in the political process, thereby building the foundation for political legitimacy based on political pluralism and liberalization as well as economic performance. The full manifestation of a stakeholder society presumes that the state and society are seen as "mutually empowering." Rather than being mutually exclusive, economic development and political pluralism are synergically linked, invoking the idea of economic development as a common good between the state and society.[104] With regard to the relationship between the "politics" of race/ethnic identity and development, as discussed previously, in the case of Singapore, the developmental state has "managed" ethnic politics much like it has done with politics generally, subordinating it to the goals of development.

101 Surain Subramaniam, "Assessing Political Dynamics in Contemporary Malaysia: Implications for Democratic Change," *ASIANetwork Exchange: A Journal for Asian Studies in the Liberal Arts* 19, no. 1 (Fall 2011): 42–52.

102 William Case, "Political Legitimacy in Malaysia: Historical Roots and Contemporary Deficits," *Politics & Policy* 38, no. 3 (2010): 497.

103 Tony Pua, *The Tiger That Lost Its Roar: A Tale of Malaysia's Political Economy* (Democratic Action Party, 2011).

104 For a discussion of how the idea of a "common good" between the regime (state) and the people (society) could be fractured by focusing much too narrowly on instrumental rationality and elitism, and consequently eroding the legitimacy of the regime, see Benjamin Wong and Xunming Huang, "Political Legitimacy in Singapore," *Politics & Policy* 38, no. 3 (2010): 523–43.

In the case of Malaysia, rather than developmental goals trumping ethnic cleavages and the political process, the former is defined by the overriding goals of the NEP (1971) and its successor policies, whereby state-led developmental policies are conceived as much by their ability to yield favorable outcomes for Malays, as they are in achieving general societywide developmental goals. And yet, political trends (some of which were being signaled by the 2008 general election results) appear to be moving in the direction of more political liberalization, precisely because the government's record of delivering developmental goals has been perceived by many to be uneven. Unlike the Singapore case, the "situational nationalism" in Malaysia has always been fragmented by overriding racial and communal interests. A reasonable argument could be made that the developmental state in Malaysia has always been of a hybridized variant. At this juncture of its political economic development, legitimacy to the system is being sought more from the anticipated benefits of political liberalization than from the maintenance of the status quo.

PART II

Middle-Income Countries in a Globalized Economy

4

The Rise of Middle-Income Countries in the International Trading System

Gregory Shaffer and Charles Sutton

With the collapse of the Doha Round in December 2011, and the rise of middle-income countries (MICs) in the global economy, it is an opportune time to assess the place, role, and strategies of the MICs in the international trading system. Over the past twenty years, there has been a shift in relative global economic influence, one that has become more salient since the financial crisis besetting the United States and Europe in 2008. This chapter assesses how MICs have engaged with the international trading system over time, what strategies they advance, and what are the implications for going forward, focusing on the negotiation and enforcement of the rules of the World Trade Organization (WTO). A central goal of MICs is to transform themselves into high-income countries (HICs) and to use trade policy as a tool for doing so.

Scholars of various persuasions have found that the WTO system has been structured to benefit the interests of the United States and Europe. Yet MICs, and the larger MICs in particular, have learned to adapt to the legalized system of trade relations and become more adept in using it to advance their interests, whether to open foreign markets or to defend domestic policy. They also have increased their bargaining leverage, which has made trade negotiations more difficult given their differentiated trading interests, and in particular their demands for "policy space" for a greater role of the state in economic development. By policy space, we refer to the ability of a government to intervene to support particular economic development policies, whether through state-owned enterprises or government support of infant industries and particular strategic sectors. In many ways, the collapse of the Doha Round can be explained by the rise of the MICs in light of their distinct interests, their increased ability to advance them, and their increased rivalry with, and relevance to, HICs, which have correspondingly, but so far unsuccessfully, demanded additional concessions from them.

Since the collapse of the Doha Round, the efficacy of trade negotiations under the WTO has been called into question. The WTO dispute-settlement mechanism

All data on dispute settlement in this chapter is as of April 5, 2012, unless otherwise noted.

(DSM) has thus become of even greater salience for upholding existing trade rules, determining how they apply in new and different contexts, and maintaining global economic stability. The global financial crisis that erupted in 2008 has put considerable pressure on the international trading system. Although the WTO system has had some success in handling protectionist pressures arising from the crisis, the system continues to face significant challenges.

This chapter is in six sections. The first section assesses the extent to which analysis of trade and trade policy can and should meaningfully treat MICs as a distinct category. It sets forth and analyzes a theory of MIC trading interests that calls for greater policy space for economic development. The second section provides a descriptive background of changes in the economic power and trading patterns of MICs that have implications for future trade negotiations and dispute settlement. The third, fourth, and fifth sections, respectively, examine the experiences of MICs in multilateral trade negotiations, regional and bilateral trade agreements, and multilateral dispute settlement. The sixth section concludes regarding MIC trading strategies and their global implications.

MIDDLE-INCOME COUNTRIES' TRADE AND DEVELOPMENT STRATEGIES: THE ISSUE OF POLICY SPACE

Most of the existing literature on trade law and policy focuses on a binary division between developed and developing countries, while noting great variation within the category of developing countries. This chapter, as the larger book project in which it is contained, focuses on MICs as a distinct category. The term *MIC* refers to the World Bank criteria of countries that vary in terms of their per capita gross national income (GNI) from $1,006 to $12,275. The question arises whether it makes sense to do so in relation to international trade strategy. The argument is that it does, subject to some important caveats involving both the common challenges faced by all countries (MICs and non-MICs), and differentiation within the category of MICs in terms of their economic size. The chapter thus further breaks down MICs into those that have larger and smaller aggregate GNIs.

We live in a world in which context, and in our case economic development context, matters. From a legal realist perspective, law should be adapted to context. Assessing the distinct situation of MICs can thus be fruitful. Dani Rodrik and Joseph Stiglitz have been two economists at the forefront of contending that one size does not fit all for trade policy so that multilateral rules should provide flexibility for developing countries to tailor strategies and sequence reforms.[1] They contend that there are strong reasons for developing countries to retain policy space to build

[1] See, e.g., Joseph Stiglitz and Andrew Charlton, *Fair Trade for All: How Trade Can Promote Development* (Oxford University Press, 2005) (noting the role of the state and unorthodox trade policies in economic development); Dani Rodrik, *The Globalization Paradox: Democracy and the Future of the Global Economy* (W. W. Norton and Company, 2011) (noting the role of government intervention and policy space in economic development); and Dani Rodrik, *One Economics, Many Recipes:*

comparative advantage in particular sectors and thereby facilitate dynamic economic growth. As they and others write, HICs used a wide range of interventionist trade policy strategies that would not comply with current WTO rules.[2]

One theorist who has aimed to develop a theoretical grounding for proposing a distinct trade strategy for MICs is Roberto Unger in his book *Free Trade Reimagined*.[3] Unger builds from existing economic theory for departing from free trade policy, while implicitly tailoring it to the situation of MICs. Even though he does not explicitly write in terms of MICs, the policies he proposes are certainly pertinent for them, including for his own country, Brazil, where he briefly served as a senior minister, dubbed the Minister of Ideas, under the second Lula administration.

Unger, like Rodrik and Stiglitz, recognizes the importance of trade, as well as the political challenges of tailoring government intervention for development purposes. Yet he maintains that to spur growth, an across-the-board free trade policy is not the appropriate strategy for countries that are only "relatively backward" and have industries within "striking distance" of those in the most advanced economies (aka the MICs). At the same time, he contends that free trade is a more appropriate strategy for countries of the same level of development (such as among HICs) and for countries with large development gaps (such as among HICs and low-income countries, or LICs).

Unger labels this situation one of "relative advantage" in that the more advanced economy (in our case a HIC) has advantages in terms of human capital and economies of scale that can be overcome through emulation by a country within striking distance (a MIC), but not by one at a radically different level of development (a LIC). For such a MIC, it must counterbalance the static losses arising from trade protection against the potential dynamic gains of economic growth spurred by strategic investment. Trade protection will result in the loss of static gains in aggregate national welfare provided by specialization, per neoclassical free trade theory. Yet it also can permit a country to move up the production chain through emulation and innovation, provided that the right government interventions are made.

Unger's theory has similarities with conventional trade theory regarding the potential long-term gains from government support for "infant industries" and strategic economic sectors implicated by increasing returns. These theories contend that, in limited circumstances, a country can benefit from trade intervention.[4] In

Globalization, Institutions and Economic Growth (Princeton University Press, 2008) (arguing against a universal set of rules and for policies tailored to local contexts).

2 See, e.g., Ha-Joon Chang, *Kicking Away the Ladder: Development Strategy from a Historical Perspective* (Anthem Press, 2003); Ha-Joon Chang, *Bad Samaritans: The Myth of Free Trade and the Secret History of Capitalism* (Bloomsbury Press, 2008).

3 Roberto Unger, *Free Trade Reimagined* (Princeton University Press, 2007).

4 Unger has been critiqued for not adequately acknowledging the earlier work of other economic theorists from which he builds. See, e.g., Francisco Rodriguez, "Review of Free Trade Reimagined: The World Division of Law and the Method of Economics," *Journal of Economic Literature* 46 (2008): 1004 (in an otherwise generally favorable review).

particular, in sectors involving technological know-how, dynamic learning, economies of scale, and increasing returns from production, comparative advantage can be manufactured and become entrenched, whether because of more favorable access to capital markets, or through strategic government policy. Unger focuses on the unique context of MICs by emphasizing the unique situation of "a relatively backward economy" (a MIC) as opposed to "a relatively advanced economy" (a HIC) because it is easier for human capital and technologies to migrate between sectors in a relatively advanced economy.[5] Thus it is more likely for a MIC to get trapped at a certain development level unless its government takes a more active role in selectively restraining trade in key sectors. Unger proposes that the trading system should provide for sufficient flexibility for these countries to adapt pragmatic, experimentalist development policies to move up the economic chain of production and become HICs.

Unger's theory of relative advantage as applied to MICs is attractive because it has some empirical support in the historical policies of many of today's HICs, including the United States, Germany, Japan, and Korea.[6] Yet the theory is also subject to a number of significant caveats. First, MICs face common challenges with HICs and LICs regarding government interventionist trade policies. As Unger recognizes, all countries face similar internal political economy challenges when it comes to trade policy, because their government leaders will be subject to demands of favoritism from particular economic sectors, whether for demanding protection from imports or government support for exports. Thus selecting areas for appropriate government intervention is always a fraught one. Unger contends that a "radically democratic" government subject to "sustained popular engagement in politics" will experiment successfully to advance economic development and growth, when balancing successes against inevitable failures.[7] The condition of domestic politics, however, and the empirical reality of both successful and failed government interventions in the past raise concerns with his optimism.

Second, in a globalized world, one country's trade measures have external effects on others. In particular, when one country demands policy space to support a particular industry, it will adversely affect the prospects of an industry in another country, creating trade frictions. If these trade frictions are not managed, they can lead to adverse protectionist outcomes for both countries, especially in the context of a financial crisis, as witnessed by the Great Depression of the 1930s.

5 Unger, *Free Trade Reimagined*, 118.

6 See Chang, *Kicking Away the Ladder*. But cf. Douglas Irwin, *Book Review of Kicking Away the Ladder: Development Strategy in Historical Perspective*, EH.net (April 25, 2004); and William Easterly, "The Anarchy of Success," *New York Review of Books* 56 (October 8, 2009) (both reviews critiquing the book for its selective examples and thus the lack of any proven causation between infant industry policies and superior economic growth).

7 Unger, *Free Trade Reimagined*, 138–50.

Third, Unger's policy recommendations are unlikely to be attractive to HICs, nor industries within them, given the recent rise in economic power of the MICs, and in particular of China. HICs will demand reciprocity if they are to forego trade intervention and retain open markets for MIC exports. The United States opened its borders to imports from Japan, Korea, and the other "Asian Tigers" in the context of the Cold War. Whether it will do so when its relative economic power has declined against China and other MICs seems less likely. Moreover, the key sectors identified by Unger are those experiencing increasing returns, as modeled in strategic trade theory. Large HICs generally have particular advantages over MICs in supporting these sectors in light of the greater amount of government resources and human capital available so that MICs should be interested in legal constraints on subsidies that affect all WTO members, HICs and MICs. Thus, while there is theoretical logic to Unger's argument and policy proposals, adopting them will create challenges in the international trading system. The WTO exists not just to facilitate trade liberalization, but (also importantly) to manage stable trade relations so that governments do not mutually erect escalating, tit-for-tat trade barriers that harm each other. Because MICs depend on access to HIC markets, they will need to manage trade relations with HICs in order to maintain market access.

Fourth, by demanding "policy space" to move up the economic production chain, MICs will confront the trade interests not only of HICs, but also of other MICs. Under Unger's theory, other MICs have relatively comparable levels of development to each other so that free trade policies should apply between them. They should thus sign preferential free trade agreements with each other to enhance each other's competitiveness and the benefits of specialization. Yet their respective trade interventions to promote particular sectors in global context should also raise trade tensions between them that they will again have to manage.

Fifth, Unger's analysis does not explicitly address the relationship of MICs and LICs, but implicitly pertains to it as well. Applying his theory, MICs should adopt free trade policies with LICs while permitting LICs to engage in interventionist polices in sectors in which MICs currently specialize in order for LICs to compete with them and become MICs. Whether MICs will permit such asymmetric trade relations favoring LICs is another question.

Sixth and finally, MICs exhibit significant variation so that generalizing about them is problematic. MICs differ from each other, in particular, in terms of economic size. The term *middle-income country* encompasses a broad range of countries, exhibiting great variation in terms of aggregate and per capita GNI. This measure of per capita income, however, does not capture the impact of a country on the international trading system or its ability to resist unilateral pressure from an economic power. Rather, aggregate GNI matters most in the international trading system from a political economy perspective. As a result, China and India exercise much greater bargaining power in international trade negotiations than, say, the Maldives, even though the Maldives has a higher GNI per capita than both of them.[8] They also exercise much greater leverage than smaller HICs, such as New Zealand and Norway, even though Norway is the wealthiest country in the world in per capita terms. In complement, the larger MICs benefit from economies of scale in developing capacity for experimenting with industrial policy, trade bargaining, and dispute settlement. Large MICs thus exercise greater leverage in trade negotiations and trade dispute settlement, which permits them to have relatively greater autonomy for their domestic policies. In contrast, small MICs are more dependent on piggybacking on others with whom they have common trade interests in trade bargaining and dispute settlement. In complement, they may be more likely to develop liberal trade policies because they lack domestic economies of scale and depend on foreign export markets. Such tendencies are historically reflected in the trade policies of such smaller countries as the Netherlands, Singapore, and Hong Kong, all of which are now HICs.

What are the implications of the theory and this long list of caveats? We believe there are two. First, in light of ongoing uncertainty regarding the empirical relation of trade policy and economic development, and the very different contexts that developing countries face, it is hubristic to maintain that one size fits all. Thus the trade system should be careful not to constrain developing country experimentation in trade and development policy too much. Chile may wish to adopt a more free trade– and free market–oriented trade and development policy than Brazil, for example, and the two countries can and should learn from comparing the results. Second, however, if constraints are too weak, developing countries can engage in trade policies that have considerable negative externalities on others, including on each other. Thus management of these relations is required, which is facilitated by the WTO as a centralized international institution. This management of trade relations gives rise to reciprocal bargaining to constrain policies with adverse external trade effects, such as terms-of-trade effects as theorized by others.[9] The significant moral hazards raised in our series of caveats to Unger's theorizing support the critical need for an institution such as the WTO that provides core rules on nondiscrimination to support bargaining, and that monitors and enforces the commitments made. The result is a system of managed liberalism, providing greater predictability and transparency for international trade, which is the way the WTO system should be viewed. The management of trade relations, nonetheless, will be more difficult on account of the decline of U.S. economic hegemony and the rise of the MICs, as we address next.

8 In 2010, China had a GNI of almost $6 trillion, whereas Maldives had a total GNI of just less than $2 billion. Similarly, a relatively poor country, like India (GNI per capita $1,330) has significant power in the global trading system given the size of its economy (GNI $1.7 trillion). World Bank Data, available at http://databank.worldbank.org/ddp/home.do?Step=12&id=4&CNO=2.

9 See Kyle Bagwell and Robert Staiger, *The Economics of the World Trading System* (MIT Press, 2002), 5.

SHIFT IN ECONOMIC POWER, TRADE PATTERNS, AND THEIR IMPLICATIONS: THE RISE OF THE MIDDLE-INCOME COUNTRIES

Power in the international trading system roughly corresponds to the size of a country's market – measured in terms of the ability of a country to exercise leverage by offering market access, or threatening to withdraw access, for foreign goods and services. The United States emerged from World War II as the preeminent world economic power, and it was central to the creation of the General Agreement on Tariffs and Trade (GATT) in 1948, which consisted of only twenty-three members, most of which were developed countries. It was in the U.S. interest for other market economies to develop rapidly after the devastation of World War II, especially in the context of the Cold War, and those countries were accordingly granted relative autonomy in developing their economic and trade policies.[10]

European economies gradually recovered from the devastation of World War II and, with the creation and expansion of the European Union (EU), the EU economy became approximately the same size as the U.S. economy by the mid-1990s. In 1995, at the time of the creation of the WTO, the combined gross domestic product (GDP) of the United States and EU consisted of approximately 50 percent of global GDP. Not surprisingly, the United States and EU were the dominant players in the development of global trading rules under the WTO and their use in early WTO dispute settlement.

During the GATT years, the United States and EU were by far the largest trading partners of today's MICs, although trading values were much less significant, especially in the GATT's first two decades.[11] MICs generally exported raw materials and low value-added products, such as textiles, produced by cheap labor. In return, they imported higher value-added goods, such as more advanced manufacturing products. As Ian Little writes, in a leading book from the early 1980s on economic development, developing countries "never expected to be able to export manufactures to the industrialised countries."[12]

Many developing countries, particularly in Latin America, tried to protect their manufacturing sectors by engaging in "import substitution" policies.[13] East Asian

10 Robert Gilpin, *Global Political Economy: Understanding the International Economic Order* (Princeton University Press, 2001).

11 Richard Baldwin, "Multilateralizing Regionalism: Spaghetti Bowls as Building Blocks on the Path to Global Free Trade," *The World Economy* 29 (2006): 1451, 1454–6 ("in 1963 there were two 'hubs' – North America and Western Europe. A large fraction of world trade was either within or between these two hubs. The flows between the hubs and the various 'spokes' – Latin America, Africa, the Middle East, Asia and Japan – were small; there was no significant trade among the spokes").

12 Ian M. D. Little, *Economic Development: Theory, Policy, and International Relations* (Basic Books, 1982), 61.

13 Kathryn Sikkink, *Ideas and Institutions: Developmentalism in Brazil and Argentina* (Cornell University Press, 1991), 75–9. Import substitution industrialization refers to a development policy advocating local production of higher value goods and services over importation. Such local production is facilitated through trade protection and government subsidies. The Argentine economist Raul Prebisch, director of the UN Economic Commission for Latin America, was a major proponent of such policies.

countries, by contrast, focused increasingly on production for global markets by the 1980s, and less on production for domestic and regional markets. As a result, their companies had to invest more in technological development to stay competitive. The export-led growth model of the four "Asian Tigers" (Korea, Taiwan, Hong Kong, and Singapore) was spectacularly successful in the 1980s and caught policy makers' attention.

Attracted by this East Asian Model, developing countries reoriented their economic policies during the 1990s to become more integrated into the global economy. The fall of the Berlin Wall and the discrediting of the Soviet model further facilitated a shift in economic policy as MICs became more interested in exploring the opportunities provided by global economic integration and liberalization policies. During the last twenty years, the amount of MIC trade (exports plus imports) in relation to domestic GDP has grown dramatically. For all MICs, trade has grown from 20 percent of GDP in 1970, to 38 percent in 1990, to 56 percent in 2010. In China, it grew from 5 percent in 1970, to 55 percent in 2010, and in India, from 8 percent in 1970, to 46 percent in 2010. In Thailand, it skyrocketed, with the value of trade reaching 135 percent of GDP in 2010.[14] In Brazil, it grew much slower, but nonetheless rose from 14 percent in 1970, to 23 percent in 2010. In broad terms, the economic policies of today's MICs shifted from a focus on insulating the economy from international trade pressures to a greater focus on integrating into the global economy through enhancing trade, while still aiming to retain (for many countries) the ability to use industrial policies to develop the manufacturing sector.

The rise of MICs in the last decade has challenged U.S. and EU dominance in the trading system, as the combined GDP (in terms of purchasing power parity, or PPP) of the United States and the EU as a share of global GDP has declined by around 12 percent. In 1990, the U.S. and EU economies constituted 49.7 percent of global GDP, which remained at about 48.3 percent in 2000. However, by 2010 this amount had plunged to 37.8 percent of global GDP, with the difference largely taken up by the BRICs (Brazil, Russia, India, and China).[15] At the end of 2010, the BRICs constituted approximately 18 percent of the global economy in terms of GDP, compared to 8.3 percent in 2000, and 8 percent in 1990.[16] Between 2001 and 2009, China doubled its share of world manufacturing trade in major import markets.[17] Commentators project that its market-based GDP will almost equal that of the United States by 2030 and its GDP (PPP adjusted) will surpass the United States', even if China grows at a rate under 7 percent per year.[18]

14 World Bank Data, available at http://databank.worldbank.org/ddp/home.do?Step=12&id=4&CNO=2.

15 Ibid.

16 Id.

17 See Aaditya Mattoo and Arvind Subramaniam, "China and the World Trading System," *Policy Research Working Paper* 5897 4 (2011); see also Aaditya Mattoo and Arvind Subramaniam, "A China Round of Multilateral Trade Negotiations," Working Paper Series 11–22 (2011).

18 See, e.g., Arvind Subramaniam, *Eclipse: Living in the Shadow of China's Economic Dominance* (Peterson Institute for International Economics, 2011), 80, 87 (see Tables 4.2 and 4.7).

In recent years, the larger MICs have gained a greater power of autonomy in relation to the creation and application of global trading rules. Benjamin Cohen writes of power of autonomy in these terms: "[i]n this case, power does not mean influencing others; rather, it means not allowing others to influence you."[19] Although MICs do not currently have the power to shape decision making by the United States and EU on trade policy, they have become relatively more autonomous and less influenced by U.S. and EU demands.

During the last decade, China has become a critical trading partner for many MICs. In 2010, China was the top destination for Brazilian exports (receiving 15 percent by value), and was second as a source of Brazilian imports (14 percent by value, after the United States).[20] It was the top source of Indian imports (12 percent by value), and the third-largest destination for Indian exports (6 percent by value). It was also the top destination of Thai exports (11 percent by value), and the second-largest source of Thai imports (13 percent by value, after Japan).[21]

Production in MICs today is increasingly part of global supply chains involving multinational companies. MICs and other developing countries compete with each other to attract investment to be part of these supply chains, and, in particular, for production for HICs, such as the United States, EU, and Japan. China has become a hub in Asia for exports globally, with its exports roughly equally divided between developed and developing countries in 2010.[22] This development has helped spur the signature of a web of preferential trade agreements examined in section 4.

Nonetheless, China's trading relationship with other MICs has been characterized as "neocolonial" in that China imports largely raw materials from the other MICs and exports manufacturing goods to them.[23] For example, 75 percent of Brazilian exports to China in 2010 were classified as "inedible crude materials (except fuels)" and "animal and vegetable oils fats and waxes" (sections 2 and 4 of Standard International Trade Classification, SITC), and 56.5 percent of Indian exports fell into these two categories. In contrast, 55.9 percent of Chinese exports to Brazil were classified as "machinery and transport equipment," and 97.6 percent

19 Benjamin J. Cohen, "The Macrofoundation of Monetary Power" in *International Monetary Power*, ed. David M. Andrews (Cornell University Press, 2006), 32.

20 In each case, we are referencing data in terms of the value of imports and exports, respectively. 2010 International Trade Statistics Yearbook, Annex I, UN COMTRADE.

21 Ibid.

22 Exports measured in terms of value. See, generally, Peter K. Schott, "The Relative Sophistication of Chinese Exports," *Economic Policy* 23, no. 5 (2008): 24 (finding that from 1972–2005 China's export similarity with the Organisation for Economic Co-operation and Development increased substantially).

23 Interview of Paulo Sotero, Director of the Brazil Institute of the Woodrow Wilson International Center, November 1, 2012, with Sofia News Agency, available at http://www.novinite.com/view_news.php?id=121707 (noting "some people have complained that the economic relationship between Brazil and China risks [becoming] a kind of neocolonial relationship").

of its exports were manufactured goods.[24] Similarly, 50 percent of Chinese exports to India in 2010 were classified as "machinery and transport equipment" (SITC section 7), 20.69 percent as "manufactured goods classified chiefly by materials" (SITC section 6), and 19.35 percent as "chemicals and related products" (SITC section 5).[25] These trading patterns have raised consternation within industries in many MICs. The BRICs have so far been able to manage these tensions in public, but the underlying pressure will remain.

MULTILATERAL TRADE NEGOTIATIONS AND MIDDLE-INCOME COUNTRIES

Most of today's MICs were not original members of the 1948 GATT, the majority of which were developed countries. Over time, developing countries joined the organization and constituted the majority of GATT members by the beginning of the 1970s, but they were not active ones.[26] Until the Uruguay Round of trade negotiations launched in 1986, developing countries were generally not pressed to engage in reciprocal trade negotiations, in part because the United States and EU did not feel under significant economic threat from them, and in part because of U.S. policies during the Cold War that granted developing countries greater trade policy autonomy at that time.

GATT members added a Part IV to the agreement in 1966 at the end of the Kennedy round of negotiations, which provided that developed countries did not expect reciprocity for tariff reductions or the elimination of other trade barriers. In 1971, GATT members granted a waiver that permitted them to abrogate the most-favored-nation (MFN) obligation in providing developing countries with nonreciprocal tariff preferences under the General System of Preferences.[27] This waiver became a permanent component of the GATT system with members' adoption of the Enabling Clause in 1979.[28] Because developing countries did not have to engage in reciprocal bargaining, they were able to retain flexibility regarding their tariff levels and their use of nontariff barriers. This carve-out of reciprocity expectations made GATT negotiations simpler, because they largely involved negotiations among the larger HICs, and in particular the United States and EU. It also meant,

[24] Manufactured goods were made up of SITC categories 5–8. John Whalley and Dana Medianu, "The Deepening China Brazil Economic Relationship," CESifo Working Paper no. 3289, Category 8: Trade Policy (December 2010).

[25] 2010 International Trade Statistics Yearbook, UN COMTRADE. Moreover, India had an $89.6 billion trade deficit in 2009, of which $20.2 billion was with China. Id. Annex 1.

[26] Robert E. Hudec, *Developing Countries in the GATT Legal System* (Cambridge University Press, 2011), 39–40 (originally published 1987).

[27] Id. Developed countries agreed to these provisions in response to developing countries' push for creating an institutional alternative to the GATT within the United Nations through the creation of the UN Commission on Trade and Development formed in 1964.

[28] Differential and More Favourable Treatment Reciprocity and Fuller Participation of Developing Countries, Decision of November 28, 1979 (L/4903) (Enabling Clause).

however, that barriers of interest to many of today's MICs, such as textiles and agriculture products, were generally not covered by GATT rules.[29]

The years leading to the Uruguay Round and its completion with the WTO's creation in 1995 coincided with changes in the policy strategies and trade negotiation priorities of today's MICs, as discussed previously. As the economies of MICs became more competitive, and as the competitive advantage of the United States and EU shifted toward knowledge-producing industries and services, the United States and EU, in turn, used their leverage to press for the inclusion of new commitments from developing countries, both in terms of tariff bindings and new rules covering services and intellectual property.[30]

The conclusion of the Uruguay Round resulted in a number of important changes for MICs. Tariff levels for goods were reduced, curtailing or eliminating many of the preferential trade advantages benefitting MICs under the General System of Preferences. New disciplines on nontariff barriers applied, constraining MICs' options for industrial policy, at least formally. New affirmative obligations were added, such as the protection of intellectual property. And the dispute-settlement system was made automatic and compulsory. All MICs who became members of the WTO were required to sign and make commitments under all WTO-covered agreements as part of a "single undertaking," which raised the stakes. Many analysts consider that, collectively, MICs made greater trade commitments in the Uruguay Round than did HICs, although the level of bound tariffs in HICs remains much lower.[31] The United States and EU made even greater demands on MICs acceding to the WTO after its creation, such as China and Russia.

Trade negotiations are organized around "modalities" that create formulas (and exceptions to them) for different types of concessions, such as cuts in tariffs and limits on subsidies. Constructing these modalities requires sophisticated econometric analysis of a country's relative trade position and future prospects in relation to its trading partners. The United States and EU, followed by other HICs, such as Japan and Canada, traditionally were the primary producers of these modalities, in

[29] Hudec maintained that the focus on special and differential treatment in negotiations and refusal to engage in reciprocal exchange hurt developing countries, because it did not put the required pressure on HICs to liberalize in areas of interest to them, like agriculture and textiles, and prevented them from gaining experience and building up successful institutions to deal with reciprocal trade negotiations. Hudec, *Developing Countries in the GATT Legal System.*

[30] Richard H. Steinberg, "In the Shadow of Law or Power? Consensus-Based Bargaining and Outcomes in the GATT/WTO," *International Organization* 56 (World Bank, 2002): 339; Diana Tussie and Miguel F. Lengyel, "Developing Countries Turning Participation into Influence," in *Development, Trade, and the WTO: A Handbook*, ed. Bernard Hoekman, Aaditya Mattoo, and Philip English (2002), 486.

[31] John Barton, et al., *The Evolution of the Trade Regime: Politics, Law, and Economics of the GATT and the WTO* (Princeton University Press, 2006), 66; Will Martin and Alan L. Winters, eds., *The Uruguay Round and Developing Countries* (Cambridge University Press, 1996); J. Michael Finger and Ludger Schuknecht, "Market Access Advances and Retreats: The Uruguay Round and Beyond," Policy Research Working Paper Series 2232, World Bank (1999). Finger and Schuknecht argue that developing countries made deeper tariff cuts then the developed countries.

reflection of the fact that they were the world's major traders and were primarily affected by the reciprocal concessions made. These four countries constituted the "Quad" during the Uruguay Round, the most important countries in trade negotiations, with the United States and EU being predominant.

MICs' negotiation positions were often formed in response to U.S. and EU bargaining positions, rather than being proactive in advancing their own goals.[32] MICs typically did not coordinate with the affected private sector to develop negotiating positions and assess their implications. This lack of coordination meant that government officials lacked the information needed to support effective negotiations.

U.S. and EU demands for reciprocity during the Doha Round pressed MICs to develop greater capacity to create alternative modalities for trade negotiations and assess their impact. At the Cancun Ministerial Meeting, the larger MICs created a new coalition that upset the traditional negotiating dynamics within the system. Brazil and India were instrumental in creating a new G-20 negotiating group in response to a U.S.-EU proposal on agriculture.[33] That proposal took account of U.S. and EU interests, but failed to account for those of India and Brazil, even though, until then, India had interests that were more aligned to those of the EU, and Brazil with those of the United States, on agricultural trade liberalization. In response, India and Brazil created comprehensive new modalities that accounted for each other's interests, garnered the support of the new G-20 block, and reoriented the negotiations.

The G-20's proposed framework for agricultural negotiations was a critical step for MICs for many reasons. It set forth proactive demands and an alternative framework for negotiations, rather than limiting itself to blocking the U.S.-EU proposal. It formed and maintained a coalition of countries that had previously negotiated from conflicting positions on the issue of agriculture, resulting in a "Southern" agenda for agriculture that encompassed Brazil's and India's respective trade liberalization and development policy goals. And it received China's support, which had recently acceded to the WTO and had yet to join a particular coalition, so that the G-20 proposal came from countries representing a relatively large percentage of global trade (around 12 percent in 2003), and of global GDP (around 23 percent in terms of PPP), and these percentages were rising.[34] The need for the United States and EU to respond to the G-20 negotiating block gave rise to what some commentators called a new Quad, consisting of the United States, EU, Brazil, and India.[35]

32 Sheila Page, "Developing Countries in GATT/WTO Negotiations," Working Paper, Overseas Development Institute 20 (2002): 14.

33 Amrita Narlikar and Diana Tussie, "The G20 at the Cancun Ministerial: Developing Countries and Their Evolving Coalitions in the WTO," *World Economy* 27 (2004): 947.

34 World Bank Data, available at http://data.worldbank.org/.

35 David Deese, *World Trade Politics: Power, Principles and Leadership* (Routledge, 2007), 155: noting that in 2004, "the Brazilian and Indian ministers established themselves as co-leaders in the most contentious issue area, agriculture, because they were able to gradually press the US and EC for substantial agricultural reforms they would not offer on their own."

What was critical for Brazil and India in developing this framework was harnessing expertise, including that outside of government. Traditionally, developing country ministries were extremely guarded about trade negotiations. But Brazil and India increasingly realized that they needed to tap into broader-based expertise if they were to participate effectively in the Doha Round negotiations. The Brazilian think tank ICONE, supported by the Brazilian agribusiness sector, provided crucial support for the government as part of an internal Brazilian working group in which ICONE's director served as a special assistant to the Minister of Agriculture.[36] ICONE generated key econometric simulation analysis of the impact of different methodologies for tariff and subsidy reductions. The Indian government, in turn, worked with Indian-based think tanks in assessing the new agricultural modalities, such as the National Council for Applied Economic Research and a new Centre for WTO Studies created in 1999 (at the Indian Institute of Foreign Trade) that supports the Ministry of Commerce and Industry.[37] These analyses were instrumental for the development of the G-20's negotiating positions and they provided the analytic heft for the G-20 in the Doha Round agricultural negotiations.

Smaller MICs, however, have not developed the negotiating capacities of the BRICs. In particular, they have not invested significantly in developing the internal expertise to construct modalities and understand their impact on their stakeholders, in large part because the costs are fixed and the relative gains are smaller because of the smaller value of their trade. Moreover, the prospect of their being successful in negotiations is more limited because they exercise less leverage given the lesser importance of their markets.

MICs' ongoing growth prospects are dependent, in significant part, on continued access to the markets of the United States and EU. They thus will have to engage with the United States and EU to ensure that that they retain access to U.S. and EU markets. In future multilateral trade negotiations, negotiators will need to account for the positions of the larger MICs, but the MICs will also continue to be pressed to provide reciprocal concessions to HICs and each other.[38]

PREFERENTIAL TRADE AGREEMENTS AND MIDDLE-INCOME COUNTRIES

Since the creation of the WTO on January 1, 1995, WTO members have negotiated and signed an increasing number of bilateral and plurilateral preferential agreements, often referred to as regional trade agreements (RTAs), but that should more

[36] Gregory Shaffer, Michelle Ratton Sanchez, and Barbara Rosenberg, "Winning at the WTO: What Lies behind Brazil's Success," *Cornell International Law Journal* 41 (2008): 383–501.

[37] Cf. Shishar Priyadarsh, "Decision Making Process in India: The Case of Agriculture Negotiations," in *Managing the Challenges of WTO Participation: 45 Case Studies* (Cambridge University Press, 2005) (in respect of India's 2001 proposal on agriculture, also noting the roles of the Indian Council for Research on International Economic Relations and the Research and Information System for the Non-Aligned and Other Developing Countries).

[38] Mattoo and Subramaniam, "China and the World Trading System" (discussing the need to reorient trade negotiations around the new economic reality of Chinese trade power).

accurately be called preferential trade agreements (PTAs) because they are often not regional in scope. Originally relatively limited in number, PTAs now represent an important challenge to the core principle of nondiscrimination in the multilateral trading system. According to the WTO, there were 319 PTAs in force as of January 2012.[39] With the stalemate in multilateral negotiations, their importance should continue to grow.

Scholars have noted four important trends in PTAs relevant for MICs.[40] First, PTAs have become the focus for most countries' trade policy negotiations, deflecting resources from multilateral bargaining. Second, PTAs cover trade partners around the world, making the term *regional* in RTA a misnomer. Third, there has been an increase in north-south PTAs based on reciprocity, eroding the benefits of tariff preference regimes under the General System of Preferences. For example, MICs that previously had preferential trade agreements with the EU, such as the Africa-Caribbean-Pacific countries, have been forced to adjust to a system of reciprocal trade negotiations with the EU.[41] Fourth, the number of south-south PTAs has increased, although actual use by traders remains in question. While intra-Asian trade is growing so that intra-Asian PTAs should be of great interest to traders, a 2007–8 report of the Asian Development Bank finds that traders in Asia only use the PTA preferential tariff rate around one-quarter of the time, although the percentage appears to be growing. They do so primarily because they do not know of the benefits or because it is not worthwhile for them to seek the lower tariff because the difference with the applied MFN rate is small in light of the cost of complying with rule-of-origin and other customs requirements.[42] The proliferation of PTAs creates a complex web of trade agreements with different customs requirements that can be difficult for MIC officials and exporters to navigate if they lack the resources and incentives to do so.[43]

PTAs offer potential benefits and detriments for MICs, as for other countries, which have been extensively assessed in the literature.[44] Politically, larger MICs hope that PTAs will promote south-south trade and allow them to become hubs for

[39] See World Trade Organization, Regional Trade Agreements, available at http://www.wto.org/english/tratop_e/region_e/region_e.htm.

[40] Roberto V. Fiorentino, Luis Verdeja, and Christelle Toqueboeuf, "The Landscape of Regional Trade Agreements," in *Multilateralizing Regionalism*, ed. Richard Baldwin and Patrick Low (Cambridge University Press, 2009), 28–76.

[41] Jo-Ann Crawford and Roberto Fiorentino, "The Changing Landscapes of Regional Trade Agreements," WTO Discussion Paper no. 8, at 2, available at https://www.wto.org/english/res_e/booksp_e/discussion_papers8_e.pdf (2005).

[42] Masahiro Kawai and Ganeshan Wignaraja, "Free Trade Agreements in Asia: A Way Towards Liberalization?," ADB Briefs (June 2010); World Trade Organization, "World Trade Report," (2011), 8.

[43] See Crawford and Fiorentino, "The Changing Landscapes of Regional Trade Agreements."

[44] Cf. Jagdish Bhagwati, *Trading Blocs: Alternative Approaches to Analyzing Free Trade Agreements* (MIT Press, 1999); Robert Z. Lawrence, *Regionalism, Multilateralism, and Deeper Integration* (Brookings Institution, 1996); and "The WTO and Preferential Trade Agreements: From Co-existence to Coherence," World Trade Report (2011).

smaller MICs.[45] MICs increasingly negotiate PTAs to be part of global supply chains, aiming to offer industries preferential access to as many countries as possible as part of such supply chains.[46] By increasing the amount of south-south trade through PTAs, MICs also can be less dependent on the markets of the United States and EU, potentially reducing the leverage that the United States and EU wield over them. Negotiating PTAs can also help MICs build experience that can later be beneficial in multilateral trade negotiations, and, over time, it can reduce the marginal cost of engaging in trade negotiations generally because of the negotiating experience that they now have on tap.[47]

Yet PTAs also raise risks for MICs. When a smaller MIC enters a PTA negotiation with a large country such as the United States or EU, it is in a weaker bargaining position, especially when it is competing for preferential access to that country's market with other MICs. MICs can be pressed to agree to terms that they otherwise would block in multilateral negotiations. For example, the United States and EU often include enhanced intellectual property protections, known as Trade-Related Aspects of Intellectual Property Rights plus provisions, in PTAs.[48] In addition, many PTAs between the United States or EU with MICs include a number of the "Singapore Issues," issues that were rejected by MICs at the Cancun ministerial meeting in 2003.[49] Once the United States signs a PTA with a MIC, others can feel pressure to sign one as well in order for their exporters to remain competitive. This dynamic may result in less economically powerful countries agreeing to less favorable terms.

MICs will likely increasingly engage in PTA negotiations with other MICs in order to expand ties, increase the diversity of export opportunities, and decrease dependence on U.S. and EU markets so that they enhance their relative autonomy. The result will be a further increase in the "spaghetti bowl" of PTAs, which has raised concerns for the multilateral system.[50] Nonetheless, despite the proliferation of PTAs, the multilateral trading system should remain relevant not only (potentially) for future negotiations, but also because of its trade monitoring and dispute-settlement systems, to which we now turn.

[45] See Crawford and Fiorentino, "The Changing Landscapes of Regional Trade Agreements."

[46] Jean-Pierre Chauffour and Jean-Christophe Maur, "Beyond Market Access," in *Preferential Trade Access Policies for Development*, ed. Jean Pierre Chauffour and Jean-Christopher Maur (World Bank, 2011).

[47] We thank Alejandro Jara, Deputy Director-General of the WTO and former Ambassador to the WTO from Chile, for this point.

[48] See, Carolyn Deere-Birkbeck, *The Implementation Game: Developing Countries and the Global Politics of Intellectual Property Reform in Developing Countries* (Oxford University Press, 2008) (discussing the negotiations and political pressure surrounding the Agreement on Trade Related Aspects of Intellectual Property Rights).

[49] Chauffour and Maur, "Beyond Market Access." The four issues placed on the WTO negotiating mandate at the Ministerial Meeting in Singapore in 1996, and thus known as the Singapore issues, are trade and investment, trade and competition, trade facilitation, and government procurement.

[50] See, e.g., Jagdish Bhagwati, *Termites in the Trading System: How Preferential Trade Agreements Undermine Free Trade* (Oxford University Press, 2008).

INTERNATIONAL TRADE DISPUTE SETTLEMENT AND MIDDLE-INCOME COUNTRIES

With the demise of the Doha Round and stalemate of the WTO political process for defining trade obligations, the WTO's DSM becomes even more salient. Although many plurilateral and bilateral trade agreements include dispute-settlement provisions, they generally are not used. The WTO's DSM is preferred because it places a greater spotlight on the trade measure at issue, enhancing the prospects of its removal. The multilateral forum is particularly preferable for smaller countries, such as in litigation between MICs and the United States and EU, because it provides them with greater bargaining leverage to use law to their advantage in light of the greater reputational concerns at stake in the multilateral context.[51]

Greater judicialization of international trade dispute settlement can benefit MICs as compared to bilateral bargaining because it reduces the role of market power. Yet judicialization does not come without costs. The WTO system has become much more complex and its jurisprudence proliferated, comprising more than seventy thousand pages of panel and appellate body decisions issued through mid-2012.[52] The demands on human resources have multiplied for WTO members wishing to use the DSM. Countries with larger economies are much better positioned.

In order to use the system successfully, a WTO member must develop cost-effective mechanisms to perceive injuries to its trading prospects, identify responsible parties, and mobilize resources to bring a legal claim or negotiate a favorable settlement.[53] In the domestic sociolegal literature, these stages of dispute settlement are referred to as "naming, blaming and claiming."[54] In the WTO context, a member's participation in the system will be, in part, a function of its ability to process knowledge of trade injuries, their causes, and their relation to WTO rights. The United States and EU have developed formal and informal legal mechanisms to identify foreign trade barriers, prioritize them according to their impact on markets, and mobilize resources for WTO complaints.[55] They mobilize resources

[51] Peter Drahos, "Weaving Webs of Influence: The United States, Free Trade Agreements and Dispute Resolution," *Journal of World Trade* 41 (2007): 191–210.

[52] This figure was calculated from the database at *WTO Dispute Settlement Reports* (Cambridge University Press) 1996–2010, available at http://www.cambridge.org/aus/series/sSeries.asp?code=DSR). Cf. Gregory Shaffer, "Developing Country Use of the WTO Dispute Settlement System: Why It Matters, the Barriers Posed, and Its Impact on Bargaining," in *Trade Disputes and the Dispute Settlement Understanding of the WTO: An Interdisciplinary Assessment*, ed. James Hartigan (Emerald, 2009) (citing WTO paper regarding "well over 30,000 pages" of WTO jurisprudence as of 2008) (just four years earlier).

[53] See Gregory Shaffer, "The Challenges of WTO Law: Strategies for Developing Country Adaption," *World Trade Review* 5 (2006): 177; Shaffer, "Developing Country Use."

[54] See William Felstiner, et al., "The Emergence and Transformation of Disputes: Naming, Blaming and Claiming," *Law and Society Review* 15 (1980–1): 631.

[55] See Gregory Shaffer, *Defending Interests: Public-Private Partnerships in WTO Litigation* (Brookings Institution Press, 2003).

through interagency coordination and networking with the private sector, which has in turn engaged private law firms. Although many larger MICs have taken significant steps in this direction, all MICs have had to confront considerable internal bureaucratic hurdles. These hurdles include a bureaucratic tradition of foreign affairs ministries assuming the lead on trade dispute matters in which they have limited background, a lack of support from home capitals, a lack of financial and informational support from the private sector, a lack of legal expertise, and language barriers.

Brazil was the first MIC to advance significantly in overcoming these challenges.[56] Brazil has developed what it terms a *three-pillar structure* involving a specialized WTO dispute-settlement unit in its capital Brasilia, coordination on WTO legal matters between Brazil's Geneva mission and the Brasilia unit, and organized relations with the private sector. As part of the third pillar, the Brazilian government has helped facilitate the training of young attorneys in Brazilian law firms in WTO dispute settlement in the hope that they can supplement constrained governmental resources. As one Brazilian representative notes, through creating internships in Brazil's WTO mission in Geneva, "we are trying to spread knowledge of the system in order to create a critical mass" of Brazilian lawyers trained in WTO dispute settlement.[57]

In recent years China has also made a concerted effort to build legal capacity to defend its interests in WTO dispute settlement.[58] In light of the continued key role of the state in its economy, it has done so by strengthening public-private cooperation through working in tandem with foreign and local Chinese law firms. China aims to build local WTO-related capacity, in particular, through requiring that international law firms work with local firms in helping the government with WTO disputes.

Aggregate trading stakes (the aggregate of a WTO member's exports and imports) is the best predictor of how frequently a WTO member will use the DSM.[59] The more that a member trades, the greater its aggregate stakes in the system, and the greater its incentives to advance its trading rights, including as a result of pressure from affected businesses. The more that a country trades, the more likely its exports will encounter some form of trade barrier. Private sector actors encountering these barriers will more likely encourage their government to bring a claim. Concomitantly, when a country with a large market applies a trade barrier, foreign

56 For a detailed study of Brazil, see Gregory Shaffer, Michelle Ratton Sanchez, and Barbara Rosenberg, "The Trials of Winning at the WTO: What Lies behind Brazil's Success," *Cornell International Law Journal* 41 (2008): 383–501.

57 Shaffer discussion with Brazil representative, February 1, 2005, Geneva.

58 Han Liyu and Henry Gao, "China's Experience and Challenges in Utilising the WTO Dispute Settlement Mechanism," in *Dispute Settlement at the WTO: The Developing Country Experience*, ed. Gregory Shaffer and Ricardo Ortiz-Meléndez (Cambridge University Press, 2010), 137–73.

59 See also Joseph Francois, Henrik Horn, and Niklas Kaunitz, "Trading Profiles and Developing Country Participation in the WTO Dispute Settlement System," ICTSD Issue Paper No. 6 (2008).

exporters are more likely affected, which makes them more likely to lobby their government to bring a WTO claim.

Studies show, however, that a complementary, but different, explanation for discrepancies in participation in the DSM lies in variation in members' mobilization of legal resources (known as legal capacity).[60] These two explanatory factors, aggregate trade stakes and legal capacity, are related because the larger a WTO member's economic stakes in the system, the more likely that it will invest in developing and mobilizing legal resources, including in coordination with its private sector and outside legal counsel.

By many measures, the legal system has worked well for the MICs, whose overall relative use of the legal system has increased significantly since the WTO's creation. From 1995 to 2004, MICs were complainants in 106 of the 324 disputes, comprising nearly one-third of complaints. Since January 1, 2005, MICs were complainants in 55 of the 111 disputes, almost one-half of all WTO complaints.[61] They have generally been as successful on the merits as HICs, and in obtaining compliance with rulings.[62]

When analyzed further, however, there are signs of significant disparity among MICs, which reflects variation in the size of their economies. Aggregate GNI, and not per capita GNI, is the best predictor of a member's engagement with the DSM. Larger MICs, such as Brazil, India, and China, have thus been much more active than smaller ones. A larger MIC like India may have relatively lower per capita income than others, but it nonetheless can more effectively defend its interests in WTO litigation than smaller MICs because of the scale and scope of its economy. In short, it has relatively high aggregate trading stakes.

In Figures 4.1 and 4.2, we look at the relationship between a MIC's aggregate GNI and its participation in WTO dispute settlement. Figure 4.1 depicts a strong relationship between a MIC's aggregate GNI[63] and the number of WTO disputes in which it has been a complainant or respondent per year (r-squared = 0.62). Figure 4.2 shows a similarly strong relationship between a MIC's aggregate GNI and its overall participation in the DSM, including as a third party in disputes (r-squared = 0.76). If we remove China, which joined the WTO only in 2001, the relationship remains

60 See, e.g., Marc Busch, Eric Reinhardt, and Gregory Shaffer, "Does Legal Capacity Matter? A Survey of WTO Members," *World Trade Review* 8 (2009): 559; and Andrew Guzman and Beth Simmons, "Power Plays & Capacity Constraints: The Selection of Defendants in WTO Disputes," *Journal of Legal Studies* 34 (2005): 557.

61 As of April 5, 2012.

62 See Bruce Wilson, "Compliance by WTO Members with Adverse WTO Dispute Settlement Rulings: The Record to Date," *Journal of International Economic Law* 10 (2007): 397 (referring to a 90 percent compliance rate); and Beth Simmons, "Treaty Compliance and Violation," *Annual Review of Political Science* (2010), 273–96 (discussing the success in getting both developing and developed countries to comply with rulings).

63 Atlas Method, 2010.

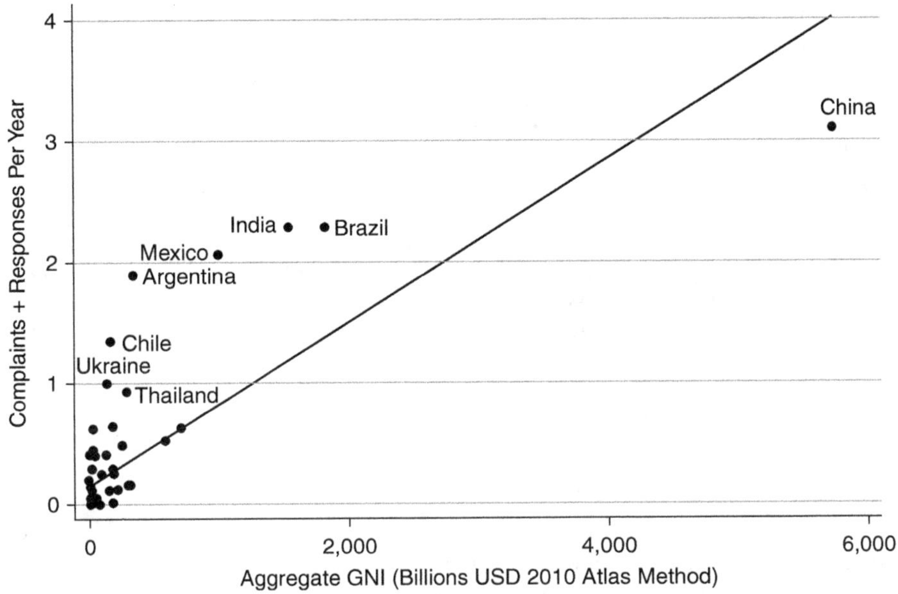

FIGURE 4.1. MICs as complainants + respondents per year/aggregate GNI (1995–2011).

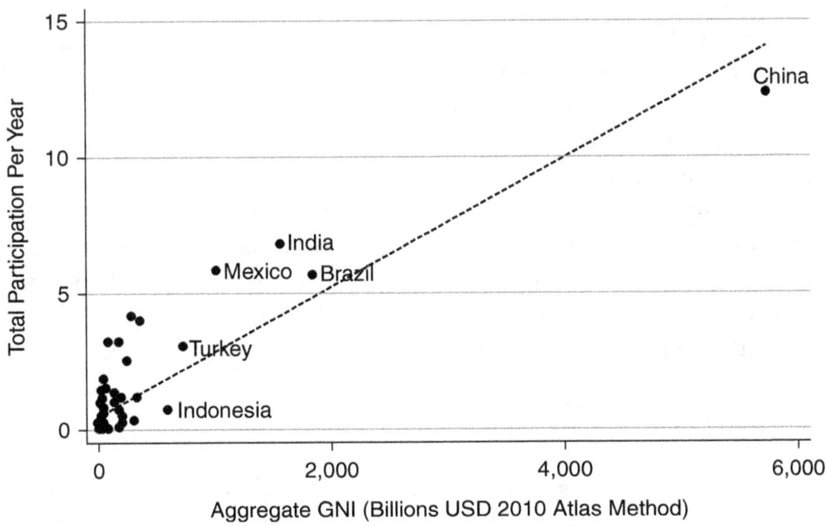

FIGURE 4.2. MICs total participation (including as third parties) per year/aggregate GNI (1995–2011).

TABLE 4.1. *MIC Participation in DSM (January 1, 1995–April 5, 2012)*

Country/Group	Complaints	Respondents	Complainants + Respondents	3rd Parties	Total
All MICs	177	167	344	742	1,086
China	8	26	34	89	123
India	20	21	41	74	115
Brazil	25	14	39	67	106
Mexico	21	14	35	64	99
Thailand	13	3	16	55	71
Argentina	15	17	32	36	68
Chile	10	13	23	31	54
Major Users	112	108	220	416	636
Major Users % of all MICs	63%	65%	64%	56%	59%

pronounced.[64] In contrast, there is only a very weak correlation between a MIC's per capita GNI and its participation in the DSM, suggesting that per capita wealth is not a good predictor of DSM use.[65] Larger MICs are more likely to be complainants because of the size and scope of their trade, and they are more likely to be respondents because of the importance of their markets. In many cases, U.S. and EU claims against MICs first spurred them to develop legal capacity for WTO dispute settlement.[66]

Table 4.1 breaks down participation in the DSM among the major MICs. It shows that the seven largest MIC users account for 63 percent of total MIC participation as complainants, 65 percent as respondents, and 56 percent as third parties. The latter figure suggests that smaller MICs have been slightly more comfortable participating in the DSM as a third party in which they can observe and learn, because third-party participation does not require significant resources. Smaller Latin American countries, in particular, have participated as third parties to gain a better understanding of the system. For example, El Salvador has participated once as a complainant, never as a respondent, and fourteen times as a third party, while Paraguay has never participated as a complainant or

64 When excluding China, the relationship in Figure 4.1 increases to an r-squared = 0.7 and Figure 4.2 decreases to an r-squared = 0.67. China skews the data because it has such a large economy and it originally did not participate in many DSM cases, except as a third party. All calculations are per the number of full years the country has been a member of the WTO, in order to account for later accessions. As indicated on the graph the results reflect participation from January 1, 1995–December 31, 2011.

65 The relationship between the per capita wealth level of a MIC (measured by GNI/per capita, Atlas Method 2010) and the number of WTO disputes in which it has been involved per year (from January 1, 1995–December 31, 2011) has an r-squared = 0.02, and has an r-squared = 0.01 when including participation as a third party.

66 Shaffer, et al., *The Trials of Winning at the WTO*; Gregory Shaffer and James Nedumpara, India and the WTO (work in progress).

TABLE 4.2. *HIC Participation in DSM (January 1, 1995–April 5, 2012)*

Country/Group	Complaints	Respondents	Complainants + Respondents	3rd Parties	Total
All HICs	285	268	553	729	1,282
United States	100	114	214	94	308
European Union	86	84	170	114	284
Japan	15	15	30	118	148
Canada	33	17	50	72	122
Korea	15	14	29	62	91
Australia	7	12	19	63	88
Major Users	256	256	512	523	1,035
Major Users % of all HICs	89.8%	95.5%	92.6%	71.7%	80.7%

respondent, but participated fifteen times as a third party. Similarly, before 2007, China first invested in participating as a third party in the DSM to learn the system, having appeared only once as a complainant, four times as a respondent, and sixty-three times as a third party. Since then, China has been a target of numerous complaints, particularly from the United States, and begun initiating its own, also predominantly against the United States.

Table 4.2 provides comparative data for the major users of the DSM among HICs, showing that a few large HICs likewise dominate HIC use of the DSM, even more so than is the case with the larger MICs in comparison with all MICs.[67] The United States, EU, Japan, and Canada have participated the most as complainants and respondents in the DSM, although China has already surpassed Canada when accounting for third-party participation.

Given the rise of the MICs and the shift in global trading patterns, one would expect to see growth in use of the DSM among MICs. MICs made few claims against each other during the WTO's first five years (only twelve claims from 1995 to 1999), but they filed considerably more claims against each other during the second five years (thirty claims from 2000 to 2004). The number of inter-MIC claims declined in aggregate terms since 2004 (twenty-two claims from 2005 to 2010, and only two in 2011), but the trend reflects a general decline in WTO dispute-settlement activity, arguably in part on account of members' focus on Doha Round

[67] In total, there are thirty-five high-income members of the WTO (all EU members who joined the EU after 2003 are counted separately; otherwise an EU member is not counted), seventy-five middle-income members, and twenty-eight low-income members. Only one LIC (Bangladesh) had brought a complaint, and it has a relatively larger economy in terms of aggregate GDP, ranked forty-fourth by CIA World Factbook, before many MICs, including Morocco, Ecuador, and Uruguay, e.g. Another LIC (Chad) participated as third party and was supported by nongovernmental organizations and the ACWL in the US-Cotton Subsidy dispute.

negotiations. In relative terms, inter-MIC complaints constituted around 30 percent of total disputes in which a MIC was a complainant from 1995 to 1999; 46 percent from 2000 to 2004; and 47 percent from 2005 to 2011. In total, MICs have been complainants in 161 disputes, sixty-nine of which have been against other MICs.[68]

Latin American countries have been particularly active users of the DSM, likely reflecting a legal culture that is more comfortable with litigation than is much of Asia. Latin American countries initiated forty-eight of the sixty-seven inter-MIC complaints, constituting 72 percent of the total. They initiated forty-two of these fifty complaints against other Latin American countries, constituting 84 percent of total Latin American complaints against MICs.

Given the growing importance of imports from China, which is now the largest trading partner of most MICs, it is interesting to note how infrequently MICs have initiated complaints against it – only five in total (including Mexico's complaint initiated in October 2012), constituting less than 7 percent of total inter-MIC complaints, and less than 3 percent of total MIC complaints. Among MICs, only Mexico and Guatemala have brought complaints against China, four times in the case of Mexico and once in the case of Guatemala. However, they have generally piggybacked on a U.S. complaint so that the United States took the lead. These figures likely reflect, in part, countries' political concerns over China's response that could affect their producers' market access. In addition, they reflect the fact that MICs primarily export to China raw materials or low-end processed goods as part of global supply chains that are subject to few barriers because China welcomes them. China also has been willing to remove trade barriers to maintain good diplomatic relations with other MICs.[69]

Interestingly, the BRICs have filed no WTO claims against each other since the launch of the Doha Round in 2001, and only once before then, an antidumping complaint that India brought against Brazil but did not pursue to the panel stage. One explanation for this pattern is a political one, given the desire of the BRICs to advance a common front against HICs on issues of global trade and economic governance. The other explanation, once more, lies in the nature of MICs' exports to China so that they do not confront trade barriers.

MICs, nonetheless, have used domestic import relief measures to protect their markets from Chinese competition. The Global Trade Alert found that China was the top country affected by protectionist measures in Argentina, Brazil, and India.[70] In a 2011 study of temporary trade barriers (TTBs), Chad Bown found that "the share

[68] Note: this number differs from that in Table 4.11 because some disputes have had multiple MIC complainants.

[69] Shaffer, interviews in Geneva, May 2012.

[70] Simon Evenett, *Trade Tensions Mount: The 10th GTA Report* (Global Trade Alert, 2011).

of China's exports to other developing countries is subject to more foreign-imposed TTBs than its share of exports to developed economies."[71]

Smaller MICs have participated less in the DSM because of the structural factors we have noted. However, the creation of an Advisory Centre on WTO Law (ACWL) in 2001 has enabled them to participate at subsidized rates, which represents an important development for them.[72] In practice, the ACWL has represented MICs almost exclusively (97.5 percent of seventy-nine cases), having only once advised a least developed country as a party (Bangladesh against India regarding an antidumping measure) and once as a third party (Chad in the US-Cotton Subsidy dispute). Asian and Latin American countries have used the ACWL relatively equally, and Thailand is its most frequent user (four times as complainant, once as a respondent, and three times as a third party). Over time, smaller MICs have increasingly used the ACWL to bring claims against each other. As the ACWL's 2011 annual report notes, "in eight of the first ten disputes in which the ACWL provided support, the respondent was a developed country," but "[i]n eight of the ten most recent disputes in which the ACWL assisted the complainant, the respondent was another developing country."[73]

With the global financial crisis, domestic producers have placed considerable pressure on countries to take protectionist measures, and MICs are no exception. Most recently, commentators have critiqued larger MICs for taking such measures. The Global Trade Alert found that Argentina placed third, India sixth, China seventh, and Brazil ninth, in a ranking of "number of (almost certainly) discriminatory measures imposed."[74] Similarly China was found to be the country whose discriminatory measures impacted the highest number of trading partners.[75] Brazil's measures appear to reflect, in large part, their attempts to protect its manufacturing sectors from Chinese imports.[76] MICs have repeatedly declared that they are committed to the rules-based WTO system. However, in light of some flagrant

[71] Chad P. Bown, "Taking Stock of Antidumping, Safeguards, and Countervailing Duties, 1990–2009," Policy Research Working Paper 5436 (2010). Bown nonetheless notes that these TTBs generally "played an important and perhaps even critical role during the 2008–9 crisis." Chad Bown, *The Great Recession and Import Protection: The Role of Temporary Trade Barriers* (Vox, 2011), 2.

[72] The larger MICs do not use the ACWL for bringing and defending WTO claims, although India used it in the ACWL's early years. Rather, the larger MICs use outside private law firms, and some of them (such as Brazil, China, and India) have invested in working with local firms whose lawyers often have studied or practiced in the United States or Europe. The ACWL is funded in part by an endowment created by HICs (notably excluding the United States and Japan), together with developing country membership fees (determined by a country's share of world trade and per capita income), and legal service fees (determined using the same criteria). Developing country membership fees form part of the endowment. See The Agreement Establishing the ACWL. See Gregory Shaffer, "Assessing the ACWL from a Broader Governance Perspective," in *The ACWL at Ten: Looking Back, Looking Forward*, ACWL (2011), available at http://www.acwl.ch/e/documents/reports/10th%20year%20Anniversary.pdf.

[73] Advisory Centre on WTO Law, Report on Operations, 12 (2011).

[74] *See* Evenett, *Trade Tensions Mount*, at Table 5.

[75] Id.

[76] "A Self-Made Siege," *The Economist*, September 24, 2011, available at http://www.economist.com/node/21530144.

breaches of the rules in 2011 and 2012,[77] there is evidence that some MICs may mean that they are committed to complying with WTO dispute-settlement rulings (second-order rules), which can take more than three years to complete, and not necessarily with the underlying substantive rules without a legal ruling (first-order rules).

In general, if a MIC is to participate meaningfully in the WTO dispute-settlement system, it will need to increase its institutional capacities and, in particular, develop coordinative mechanisms that include private stakeholders. Endeavors to build legal capacity will be most sustainable if they permeate broadly throughout institutions and include the private sector. Smaller MICs will also wish to harness the services of the subsidized ACWL. In addition, they should consider proposing the addition of a small claims procedure within the DSM in order to reduce litigation costs, the advantages of which Häkan Nordstrom and Shaffer have presented elsewhere.[78]

CONCLUSION

There has been a shift in relative economic power in the world with "the rise of the rest" over the last decade, and, in particular, of the largest MICs. China is now the world's second-largest economy, Brazil recently surpassed the United Kingdom as the world's sixth-largest economy, and Russia and India are respectively the ninth and tenth largest.[79] Collectively, the larger MICs have exercised a growing influence on the global trading system. This influence is reflected in their increased role and bargaining power in multilateral trade negotiations, their increased use of the DSM, and their increased negotiation of PTAs.

The rapid economic growth of MICs calls for assessment both of their impact on the trading system, and the strategies that MICs should adopt to cross the threshold to become HICs. There are strong theoretical and empirical grounds for MICs to retain policy space to favor the development of technologically advanced industries in a dynamically changing world, following in the footsteps of today's HICs such as Japan and Korea. The WTO constrains some of these policy options, such as granting industry-specific subsidies that affect trade, and conditioning foreign investment approvals on the use of domestically produced components. HICs will not wish to renegotiate these constraints. The MICs will thus have to find ways to advance their strategies within the constraints created by the WTO. It is possible for them to do so, in part through interpretation of the WTO agreements, and in part

77 See, e.g., Daniel Pruzin, "World Bank Cites Growing South-South Trade, Warns of Developing Country Protectionism," *International Trade Reporter* 28 (April 28, 2011): 689; Daniel Pruzin, "U.S., Others Slam Argentina's Protectionism; Cite Import License, Pre-Approval Measures," *International Trade Reporter* 29 (April 5, 2012): 540; Ed Taylor, "Brazil Exempts 18 Automakers from Excise Tax Aimed at Imports," *International Trade Reporter* 297 (February 9, 2012): 217.

78 See Häkan Nordstrom and Gregory Shaffer, "Access to Justice in the WTO: A Case for a Small Claims Procedure?," *World Trade Review* 7 (2008): 587 (proposing the addition of a small claims mechanism).

79 CIA, *The World Factbook*.

on account of the WTO's weak system of enforcement that permits for some de facto flexibility.[80] In aiming to do so, however, tensions will arise with HICs, as well as potentially among MICs. MICs' trade relations with China, for example, generally raise concerns for their manufacturing sectors. These tensions will have to be managed. The WTO can play an important role in helping countries do so, including through its committee system and its DSM, so that MICs will want to invest in building capacity to engage effectively with the WTO system. The WTO system provides not only a sword to challenge countries' policies, but also a shield to defend countries against unilateral pressure from those exercising market power.

Not all MICs are in the same position. MICs with large economies, regardless of their per capita wealth, have gained the experience and have the resources to participate in negotiations and dispute settlement in a way that can, at a minimum, block U.S. and EU initiatives and thus affect the system's future. Smaller MICs do not wield such influence. They need to form bloc-coalitions with larger MICs or with the United States or EU when their interests align. A country's economic size, as opposed to its per capita wealth, is the key factor in understanding power in the international trading system.

Despite their progress, MICs, especially smaller ones, still face many challenges. The maintenance of an institutionalized multilateral trading system is important for all MICs, but particularly smaller ones that rely on external trade more than on their internal market and exercise little leverage in bilateral relations with the economic powers. Given the rise of the MICs' economic importance, reflecting a diffusion of global economic power, how they engage in the international trading system, including how they work with each other, will determine whether or not the system remains a relatively open one, managed through a system of multilateral rules and institutions. The relative decline of U.S. and EU dominance in international economic relations means that the WTO as a centralized international institution becomes even more important for overseeing and supporting a liberal, predictable, and stable international trading order. It also means that the challenges facing the international trading system should increase.

80 WTO remedies are not retrospective, and WTO cases can take close to three years to complete, including appeals. This system of remedies can create an incentive for respondents to use the procedural system to create delays. The respondent is given around six months, on average, to comply with a decision after the WTO Dispute Settlement Body adopts it (the "implementation date"). The complainant may seek authorization to withdraw an equivalent amount of concessions only if the respondent does not comply by the implementation date. Once authorized, the complainant may withdraw such equivalent amount of concessions, but effective only as of the implementation date.

5

The Middle Intellectual Property Powers

Peter K. Yu

INTRODUCTION

Since a large group of developing countries joined the international intellectual property regime following the decolonization movement,[1] developed countries and their developing counterparts have engaged in a half-century-long debate over the appropriate standards for protecting and enforcing intellectual property rights. While developed countries complain about how the standards are insufficient to meet the needs of their growing intellectual property interests, developing countries are frustrated by how the very same standards have stifled access to essential medicines, knowledge, information and communication technologies, and other key development resources.[2]

As is typical of any debate involving the North-South divide, the international intellectual property debate is binary and highly polarized; it involves two sides that insist on their own positions while expecting the other side to change. In recent years, however, that debate began to slowly change following the emergence of a core group of middle-income countries (MICs). Although these countries continue to struggle with traditional Southern economic, technological, and development challenges, their high levels of technological proficiency and innovative capacity have allowed them to share some common interests with the developed North.

It is increasingly common for policy makers and commentators to remark on the special roles China, Brazil, and India play in the international intellectual property regime.[3] Only recently, this small group of countries has begun to team up with each

[1] Sam Ricketson and Jane C. Ginsburg, *International Copyright and Neighboring Rights: The Berne Convention and Beyond*, 2d ed. (Oxford University Press, 2005), 885.

[2] Peter K. Yu, "The Global Intellectual Property Order and Its Undetermined Future," *WIPO Journal* 1 (2009): 1.

[3] E.g., Robert C. Bird, "Defending Intellectual Property Rights in the BRIC Economies," *American Business Law Journal* 43 (2006): 317–63; Robert C. Bird and Daniel R. Cahoy, "The Emerging BRIC Economies: Lessons from Intellectual Property Negotiation and Enforcement," *Northwestern Journal of Technology and Intellectual Property* 5 (2007): 400–25; Amrita Narlikar, *New Powers: How to Become One and How to Manage Them* (Columbia University Press, 2010); Chidi Oguamanam, *Intellectual Property in Global Governance: A Development Question* (Routledge, 2012); Peter K. Yu, "Access to

other and with Russia and South Africa to form collaborative fora, such as the BRICS summit and the India–Brazil–South Africa (IBSA) Dialogue Forum.[4] The arrival of the "BRICS" and "BASIC" acronyms also has invited greater attention on developments in Brazil, China, India, Russia, and South Africa.[5]

This chapter focuses on a group of countries that have played or will play important roles in the international intellectual property regime, known collectively as the "middle intellectual property powers" (MIPPs). Like MICs, this group of emerging powers is open-ended. Unlike MICs, however, this group is much harder to define. Although the MIPPs clearly include Brazil, China, and India, the three uncontested leaders of the developing world, other MICs could easily fall into the group. Thus, instead of declaring in advance which country, other than Brazil, China, and India, should be considered as a MIPP, this chapter focuses on a set of specific characteristics. Based on these characteristics and the examples given, readers are encouraged to draw their own conclusions.

This chapter begins by noting the challenges in identifying intellectual property developments in MICs, due in large part to their divergent needs, interests, conditions, and priorities. It then contends that a smaller subset of this group, the MIPPs, will play important roles in the international intellectual property regime. Focusing on these emerging powers, this chapter identifies six common characteristics that are found within the group. It also examines the policy positions this group will take in the international intellectual property regime as well as the interactions they will have with other countries. The chapter concludes with four different lessons policy makers and commentators can draw from the experiences of the MIPPs.

THE CLASSIFICATION PROBLEM

World Trade Organization

The World Bank defined MICs as those having an average gross national income (GNI) per capita of more than U.S.$1,026 as of July 1, 2011. The groupings of high-income countries (HICs), MICs, and low-income countries (LICs) virtually coincide with those used by the World Trade Organization (WTO). The Agreement on Trade-Related Aspects of Intellectual Property Rights (TRIPs Agreement), for

Medicines, BRICS Alliances, and Collective Action," *American Journal of Law and Medicine* 34 (2008): 345–94.

4 Peter K. Yu, "ACTA and Its Complex Politics," *WIPO Journal* 3 (2011): 12.

5 "BRICs" refers to Brazil, Russia, India, and China. "BRICS," with a capital S, adds South Africa to the mix. "BASIC" refers to Brazil, South Africa, India, and China. For an up-to-date analysis of the BRICs and what Jim O'Neill now calls "growth markets," see Jim O'Neill, *The Growth Map: Economic Opportunity in the BRICs and Beyond* (Portfolio, 2011). Goldman Sachs' past literature on the BRICs is available at http://www.goldmansachs.com/our-thinking/brics/.

example, separates countries into three different tiers: developed, developing, and least developed. Articles 65 and 66 specifically allow developing and least developed countries to delay their implementation of the agreement until after the expiry of the specified transitional periods. Article 67 further requires developed countries to provide technical, legal, and financial assistance to developing and least developed countries.

For the purposes of the WTO and its TRIPs Agreement, least developed countries are defined based on the criteria the UN General Assembly established in 1971. As of this writing, the income threshold is U.S.$992, based on a three-year average estimate of GNI per capita, using the World Bank Atlas method.[6] Although only three countries (Botswana, Cape Verde, and Maldives) have ever graduated from this group, countries could do so by achieving the specified average GNI per capita by the time of the next triennial review – higher than U.S.$1,190 by 2012, for example. While the U.S.$992 figure is not identical to the U.S.$1,026 threshold used by the World Bank and in this volume, the two figures are very close. Mauritania is the only LIC that is not classified as a least developed country.

Once we go beyond the floor, however, the WTO classification scheme presents a much bigger problem. The WTO allows countries to determine for themselves whether they should be treated as a developed or developing country. To avoid abuse, the organization further allows other WTO members to "challenge the decision of a member to make use of provisions available to developing countries."[7] When China actively negotiated to join the WTO in the mid-1990s, one of the major challenges concerned whether the country could be designated as a developing country.[8] Such designation would entitle China to the benefits derived from transitional measures and special and differential treatment. To earn its admission ticket, the country eventually agreed to take on WTO-plus commitments beyond what is required of developing countries, even though it insisted on designating itself as a developing country.[9]

6 "Least Developed Countries: Criteria for Identification and Graduation of LDCs," available at http://www.unohrlls.org/en/ldc/164/.

7 "Who Are the Developing Countries in the WTO?," available at http://www.wto.org/english/tratop_e/devel_e/d1who_e.htm. On the designation of "developing countries," see Guglielmo Verdirame, "The Definition of Developing Countries under GATT and Other International Law," *German Yearbook of International Law* 39 (1996): 164–97.

8 Frederick M. Abbott, "Reflection Paper on China in the World Trading System: Defining the Principles of Engagement," in *China in the World Trading System: Defining the Principles of Engagement*, ed. Frederick M. Abbott (Kluwer Law International, 1998), 26–8; Jeffrey L. Gertler, "Negotiating China's Protocol of Accession," in *China and the Long March to Global Trade: The Accession of China to the World Trade Organization*, ed. Sylvia Ostry, Alan S. Alexandroff, and Rafael Gomez (Routledge, 2003), 28.

9 Samuel S. Kim, "China in World Politics," in *Does China Matter? A Reassessment: Essays in Memory of Gerald Segal*, ed. Barry Buzan and Rosemary Foot (Routledge, 2004), 49; Julia Ya Qin, "China, India and WTO Law," in *China, India and the International Economic Order*, ed. Muthucumaraswamy Sornarajah and Wang Jiangyu (Cambridge University Press, 2010), 173–5;

Over the years, commentators have cited additional problems concerning the "developing country" designation. For example, Bradly Condon and Tapen Sinha stated in the public health context: "The U.N. classification, based solely on per capita income, was developed for giving economic aid. It was not meant for handling a complex issue such as HIV/AIDS, which encompasses epidemiological issues (such as incidence of infection in the population)."[10] Shamnad Basheer and Annalisa Primi also pointed out that countries can be technologically proficient even though they may not be economically developed, especially on a per capita basis.[11] In addition, Daniel Benoliel and Bruno Salama noted the need to separate countries based on their bargaining power within the international intellectual property regime. As they observed: "[I]nnovation in intellectual property–sensitive technologies creates a paradoxical effect within the group of innovative Newly Industrialized Countries.... The paradox lies in that innovation weakens, rather than boosts, their bargaining power vis-à-vis the prospect of bargaining retaliations."[12]

PER CAPITA

While it is challenging to distinguish between developed and developing countries, the per capita basis used in defining MICs is especially unsuitable for evaluating intellectual property developments. Consider, for example, the widely criticized linkage between intellectual property protection and foreign direct investment (FDI). Although policy makers, industries, and commentators from developed countries have repeatedly extolled the benefits of strong intellectual property protection in attracting FDI, stronger intellectual property standards in developing countries have not always resulted in greater FDI flows. Considerable empirical literature has shown that the relationship between intellectual property protection and FDI is at best ambiguous. As noted economist Keith Maskus reminded us, if stronger intellectual property protection always led to more FDI, "recent FDI flows to developing economies would have gone largely to sub-Saharan Africa and Eastern Europe ... [rather than] China, Brazil, and other high-growth, large-market developing economies with weak [intellectual property rights]."[13]

Peter K. Yu, "The Middle Kingdom and the Intellectual Property World," *Oregon Review of International Law* 13 (2011): 224.

10 Bradly Condon and Tapen Sinha, "Global Diseases, Global Patents and Differential Treatment in WTO Law: Criteria for Suspending Patent Obligations in Developing Countries," *Northwestern Journal of International Law and Business* 26 (2005): 41.

11 Shamnad Basheer and Annalisa Primi, "The WIPO Development Agenda: Factoring in the 'Technologically Proficient' Developing Countries," in *Implementing the World Intellectual Property Organization's Development Agenda*, ed. Jeremy de Beer (Wilfred Laurier University Press, 2009), 100–17.

12 Daniel Benoliel and Bruno Salama, "Towards an Intellectual Property Bargaining Theory: The Post-WTO Era," *University of Pennsylvania Journal of International Law* 32 (2010): 271.

13 Keith E. Maskus, "The Role of Intellectual Property Rights in Encouraging Foreign Direct Investment and Technology Transfer," *Duke Journal of Comparative and International Law* 9 (1998): 129.

The positive correlation between intellectual property protection and FDI is generally explained as follows: because firms are reluctant to invest in a foreign country unless they are assured protection of their intellectual assets and financial investments, developing countries need to introduce strong intellectual property protection to attract FDI. While this explanation is generally valid, empirical research has shown that two additional conditions may be needed.[14] First, the country needs to have a strong capacity to imitate foreign products and technologies. If local competitors are unable to copy those products and technologies, the business interests of foreign firms are unlikely to be threatened, and intellectual property protection will be unnecessary. Second, the country needs to have a sufficiently large market to enable foreign firms to capture economies of scale or scope. In a country that lacks such a market, foreign firms are unlikely to find it advantageous to move productions abroad. Because per capita indicators do not speak to a country's imitative or innovative capacity, nor do they always correlate to the existence of a sufficiently large market, those indicators present challenging problems.

ONE SIZE FITS ALL

To complicate matters even further, the TRIPs Agreement has greatly curtailed a country's ability to tailor intellectual property policy to its local needs, national interests, technological capabilities, institutional capacities, and public health conditions.[15] Instead of providing the much-needed tailoring, the agreement imposes on all WTO members a one-size-fits-all model of intellectual property protection and enforcement. Because the language for most TRIPs provisions was taken from the developed countries' proposals,[16] the existing one-size-fits-all model has become a super-size-fits-all model. Due to mismatched conditions, that model has serious deleterious effects on both MICs and LICs.

Although the TRIPs Agreement includes safeguards, limitations, exceptions, ambiguities, and flexibilities, such as the transition periods discussed earlier,[17] its primary focus is to establish minimum standards for a large variety of intellectual property areas.[18] In addition to copyrights, patents, and trademarks, the three main branches of intellectual property, the agreement also covers geographical indications, industrial designs, plant variety protection, integrated circuit topographies, and protection of undisclosed information.

[14] Ibid., 129–33; Carlos A. Primo Braga and Carsten Fink, "The Relationship between Intellectual Property Rights and Foreign Direct Investment," *Duke Journal of Comparative and International Law* 9 (1998): 167–8.

[15] Peter K. Yu, "The International Enclosure Movement," *Indiana Law Journal* 82 (2007): 855–72.

[16] Daniel J. Gervais, "Intellectual Property, Trade & Development: The State of Play," *Fordham Law Review* 74 (2005): 507–8.

[17] Yu, "International Enclosure Movement," 863–6.

[18] Peter K. Yu, "International Enclosure, the Regime Complex, and Intellectual Property Schizophrenia," *Michigan State Law Review* (2007): 7.

Even worse for MICs and LICs, Article 64 requires that the mandatory WTO dispute-settlement process be used to settle all intellectual property disputes arising under the Agreement (see Shaffer and Sutton, Chapter 4). Through this process, developed countries have successfully induced developing countries to align their intellectual property laws with the super-size-fits-all standards laid down in the TRIPs Agreement.[19]

If these high standards are not problematic enough, the proliferation of TRIPs-plus bilateral, plurilateral, and regional trade and investment agreements have further tightened the policy space of MICs.[20] Examples of these agreements are the highly controversial Anti-Counterfeiting Trade Agreement and the still-under-negotiation Trans-Pacific Partnership Agreement. As a result of the TRIPs and TRIPs-plus agreements, the laws MICs have adopted largely mirror those found in HICs. There is not much meaningful distinction between the two, and a study of the intellectual property developments in MICs is largely futile.

THE MIDDLE INTELLECTUAL PROPERTY POWERS

Given the challenges in identifying intellectual property developments in MICs, this chapter focuses on developments in a smaller subset of these countries. Examples that immediately come to mind are the two historical leaders of the international intellectual property regime (Brazil and India) and the regime's rising star and newly minted leader (China). One could also add other countries such as Russia and South Africa (the two other BRICS countries), Indonesia (the world's fourth most populous country), and Thailand (an emerging economy in Southeast Asia and a sometime leader of the Association of Southeast Asian Nations, ASEAN).

Table 5.1 lists the top thirty economies outside of the Organisation for Economic Co-operation and Development (OECD) that have a GNI per capita of less than U.S.$15,000, based on the 2011 estimates of GNI using the World Bank Atlas method. In descending order, the top fifteen countries are China, Brazil, India, Russia, Indonesia, Argentina, South Africa, Venezuela, Thailand, Colombia, Malaysia, Egypt, the Philippines, Pakistan, and Nigeria. Out of these countries, China (1st), Brazil (6th), India (5th), Russia (8th), Indonesia (7th), Argentina (13th), South Africa (15th), Thailand (3rd), Malaysia (2nd), and the Philippines (4th) are among the top fifteen countries based on the estimates on high-technology exports in 2010 (the latest available year).

Although one would still need to factor in geopolitical power, bargaining leverage, and other social, economic, and technological factors, the list here provides a good starting point for a survey on the MIPPs. To facilitate comparison, Tables 5.2,

19 Peter K. Yu, "Are Developing Countries Playing a Better TRIPS Game?," *UCLA Journal of International Law and Foreign Affairs* 16 (2011): 332–5.

20 Yu, "International Enclosure Movement," 866–70.

TABLE 5.1. *Top Thirty Non-OECD Economies with GNI Per Capita below U.S.$15,000*

Top 1–10	Top 11–20	Top 21–30
China	Malaysia	Bangladesh
Brazil	Egypt	Vietnam
India	Philippines	Morocco
Russia	Pakistan	Iraq
Indonesia	Nigeria	Angola
Argentina	Romania	Croatia
South Africa	Peru	Ecuador
Venezuela	Algeria	Belarus
Thailand	Ukraine	Sri Lanka
Colombia	Kazakhstan	Dominican Republic

5.3, 5.5, and 5.6 include data for not only the ten countries surveyed in this chapter, but also the United States. In reviewing these data, it is important to remember that the MIPPs are not limited to only ten countries. For example, one could make a strong case for inclusion of such highly populous countries as Pakistan (6th), Nigeria (7th), Bangladesh (8th), Vietnam (13th), and Egypt (15th). One could also challenge the exclusion of OECD countries. For example, Turkey and Mexico, which have a GNI per capita of U.S.$10,410 and U.S.$9,240, respectively (similar to Argentina, Brazil, and Russia), are good candidates for being a MIPP. In addition, it is worth noting that the data used in these tables focus mostly on past achievements, not future potential. As MICs continue to develop economically and technologically, their status as a MIPP may change. This is particularly true considering the rapid and highly dynamic economic growth in these countries.

On a quick glance, the list of the MIPPs strongly resembles the combined lists of the BRICS and the N-11 (next eleven) countries. In October 2003, two Goldman Sachs global economists published a provocative study on Brazil, Russia, India, and China.[21] Building on Jim O'Neill's concept of the "BRICs" (Brazil, Russia, India, China, but not South Africa),[22] this study predicted that the economies of four fast-growing developing countries will likely overtake many existing developed economies by 2050.[23] Since then, Goldman Sachs analysts have expanded the analysis to cover other smaller but similarly situated economies, known as the N-11.[24] These countries included Bangladesh, Egypt, Indonesia, Iran, Mexico, Nigeria, Pakistan, the Philippines, South Korea, Turkey, and Vietnam.

[21] Dominic Wilson and Roopa Purushothaman, "Dreaming with BRICs: The Path to 2050," Goldman Sachs, Global Economics Paper No. 99, October 1, 2003.

[22] Jim O'Neill, "Building Better Global Economic BRICs," Goldman Sachs, Global Economics Paper No. 66, November 30, 2001.

[23] Wilson and Purushothaman, "Dreaming with BRICs," 4.

[24] Jim O'Neill, Dominic Wilson, Roopa Purushothaman, and Anna Stupnytska, "How Solid Are the BRICs?," Goldman Sachs, Global Economics Paper No. 134, December 1, 2005.

Although the BRICs concept has gained currency among academic commentators, policy makers, and diplomats, some commentators remain skeptical of this grouping, citing the wide differences between the group members. Thus, instead of focusing on the BRICs, this chapter uses only Brazil, China, and India, the three uncontested leaders of the developing world, as the starting point. Based on these countries, this chapter further identifies the common characteristics and policy positions of the MIPPs. While it is inherently subjective to identify these characteristics and policy positions, and the use of Brazil, China, and India as a starting point may ignore important developments in other parts of the world, the present approach does take into account objective evidence concerning past norm-setting activities in the international intellectual property regime.

To provide a glimpse of developments in the MIPPs, Table 5.2 lists the data from the World Intellectual Property Organization (WIPO) concerning the number of resident and nonresident patent applications, resident and nonresident patent grants, resident trademark applications, and resident industrial design applications. The table also includes the amount of payments of and receipts in royalty and licensing fees, drawn from World Bank data.[25] Because of its limited length and scope, this chapter focuses primarily on patents, similar to other economic literature in the field. Nevertheless, it is conscious of the differences between different forms of intellectual property rights. The data on trademark and industrial design applications in Table 5.2 seek to address this shortcoming.

SIX COMMON CHARACTERISTICS

Based on past research on intellectual property developments in Brazil, China, India, and other developing countries,[26] this chapter identifies six common characteristics that are found within the MIPPs: (1) a fast-growing and large aggregate economy; (2) increased technological and innovative capabilities; (3) emergence of local stakeholders; (4) the presence of alternative forms of innovation; (5) uneven developments and internal tensions; and (6) continuing piracy and counterfeiting problems.

Because the MIPPs have both strengths and weaknesses, the characteristics highlighted here seek to cover these contrasting sets of qualities and conditions. The first two characteristics draw on our earlier discussion about the two preconditions needed for an intellectual property system to have its intended effects. The next two characteristics cover factors that will help drive present and future intellectual property developments. The final two characteristics focus on the ongoing challenges confronting the MIPPs.

[25] All the WIPO data were taken from WIPO, 2011 *World Intellectual Property Indicators* (WIPO, 2012). All the World Bank data were taken from http://data.worldbank.org/indicator.

[26] Yu, "Access to Medicines," 345–94; Peter K. Yu, "Intellectual Property and Asian Values," *Marquette Intellectual Property Law Review* 16 (2012): 329–99.

TABLE 5.2. *Indicators on Intellectual Property Developments in 2010*

Countries	Resident Patent Application	Nonresident Patent Application	Resident Patent Grants	Nonresident Patent Grants	Resident Trademark Application	Resident Industrial Design Application	Royalty/Licensing Payments (U.S.$M)	Royalty/ Licensing Receipts (U.S.$M)
Argentina	1,107	3,610	N/A	N/A	53,635	1,441	1,540	118
Brazil	2,705	19,981	314	2,937	102,449	3,863	2,850	397
China	293,066	98,111	79,767	55,343	973,462	409,124	13,039	830
India	7,262	27,025	1,725	4,443	134,403	4,267	2,437	128
Indonesia	N/A	N/A	N/A	N/A	N/A	3,601	1,616	59
Malaysia	1,233	5,230	204	1,973	13,099	699	1,133[a]	265[a]
Philippines	166	3,223	8	346	8,855	435	445	4
Russia	28,722	13,778	21,627	8,695	32,735	1,981	5,066	625
South Africa	821	5,562	822	4,509	18,040	1,017	1,941	59
Thailand	1,214	723	306	466	24,781	3,276	3,084	153
United States	241,977	248,249	107,792	111,822	236,826	16,706	33,450	105,583

[a] 2009 data.

TABLE 5.3. *Indicators on Economic Developments in 2011*

Countries	GDP (U.S.$M)	GDP/ capita (U.S.$)	GDP growth	GNI (Atlas) (U.S.$M)	GNI (PPP$M)	GNI/ capita (U.S.$)	GNI/ capita (PPP$)	Total Population (thousand)
Argentina	445,988	10,941	8.9	397,189	703,278	9,740	17,250	40,764
Brazil	2,476,652	12,594	2.7	2,107,628	2,261,060	10,720	11,500	196,655
China	7,298,096	5,430	9.1	6,628,086	11,325,384	4,930	8,430	1,344,130
India	1,847,981	1,489	6.9	1,746,480	4,488,037	1,410	3,620	1,241,491
Indonesia	846,832	3,495	6.5	712,737	1,098,924	2,940	4,530	242,325
Malaysia	278,671	9,656	5.1	243,107	438,252	8,420	15,190	28,859
Philippines	224,753	2,370	3.7	209,449	394,937	2,210	4,160	94,852
Russia	1,857,769	13,089	4.3	1,476,085	2,845,251	10,400	20,050	141,930
South Africa	408,236	8,070	3.1	352,037	545,679	6,960	10,790	50,586
Thailand	345,649	4,972	0.1	307,129	583,284	4,420	8,390	69,518
United States	15,094,000	48,442	1.7	15,097,082	15,232,385	48,450	48,890	311,591

A Fast-Growing and Large Aggregate Economy

One of the reasons why Brazil, China, India, and other similarly situated countries have attracted a great deal of attention is the large size of their domestic market and overall economy and their high rate of economic growth. To illustrate these qualities, Table 5.3 provides data from the World Bank concerning the country's gross domestic product (GDP), GDP per capita, GDP growth, GNI, GNI based on purchasing power parity (PPP), GNI per capita, GNI per capita based on PPP, and total population. It is worth noting that sharp contrasts exist between the aggregate and per capita data. Those countries that have very high aggregate GDPs and GNIs (such as China and India) also have rather low GDPs and GNIs per capita. With a GDP per capita of U.S.$1,410 in 2011, India barely made the cut for MICs. These variations should be taken into account when evaluating the market for intellectual property–based goods and services.

Increased Technological and Innovative Capabilities

Technological and innovative capabilities are hard to measure; they depend on a large variety of factors, ranging from inventions to scientific research to innovation infrastructure. To illustrate these capabilities, Table 5.4 includes data from the World Bank concerning the volume of resident patent applications, the amount of research and development (R&D) expenditure (as a percentage of GDP), the volume of high-technology exports, the number of researchers in R&D, and the

TABLE 5.4. *Indicators on Technological and Innovative Capabilities in 2007*

Countries	Resident Patent Application	R&D Expenditure (% GDP)	High-tech Exports (U.S. $M)	Researchers in R&D (M)	Science and Technology Journal Articles	Tertiary Ed. Enrollment (% gross)	Global Innovation Index	Global Comp. Index
Argentina	937	0.51	1,139	983	3,364	67	34.4 (70)	3.87 (94)
Brazil	4,023	1.07	9,076	658	11,891	26[a]	36.6 (58)	4.40 (48)
China	153,060	1.40	302,773	1,077	56,811	22	45.4 (34)	4.83 (29)
India	6,296	0.76	5,997	136[a]	18,203	13	35.7 (64)	4.32 (59)
Indonesia	288[a]	N/A	5,356	N/A	198	17	28.1 (100)	4.40 (50)
Malaysia	670	0.63[b]	65,223	365[b]	808	33	45.9 (32)	5.06 (25)
Philippines	225	0.11	29,526	78	195	28[†]	29.0 (95)	4.23 (65)
Russia	27,505	1.12	4,108	3,274	13,954	73	37.9 (51)	4.20 (67)
South Africa	915	0.92	1,832	396	2,808	N/A	37.4 (54)	4.37 (52)
Thailand	945	0.21	30,321	316	1,728	47	36.9 (57)	4.52 (38)
United States	241,347	2.67	218,115	4,673	209,898	83	57.7 (10)	5.47 (7)

[a] 2006 data.
[b] 2005 data.

number of articles in science and technology journals. Although the table uses data from 2007, the latest year in which most of these data are available, it is worth noting that, in many countries surveyed in this chapter, technological and innovative capabilities have dramatically increased in the past few years. Table 5.4 also includes four additional indicators: the overall score and ranking in the 2012 Global Innovation Index published by INSEAD and WIPO;[27] and the overall score and ranking in the 2012–2013 Global Competitiveness Index published by the World Economic Forum in Davos.[28]

Emergence of Local Stakeholders

As I have noted in the past, the successful development of an intellectual property system depends on the presence of a critical mass of local stakeholders.[29] Because these stakeholders can provide the much-needed internal push for reforms, their presence will help sustain the future development of the intellectual property system.[30] History has shown that countries offered much weaker protection during their formative period of development.[31] As their economic and technological conditions improve, they began to offer greater protection, in line with their own economic and technological developments.

Consider China for example. The country is already among the top five countries filing patent applications through the Patent Cooperation Treaty (PCT).[32] In 2011, the number of these applications increased by 33.4 percent to 16,406, earning China the fourth spot, behind only the United States, Japan, and Germany. Among all the applicants, ZTE Corp. and Huawei Technologies have the largest and third-largest number of PCT applications. Commentators have also cited many notable achievements in China in space technology, biotechnology (including genomics and stem cell research), information technology, nanotechnology, and advanced energy technology.[33]

27 INSEAD and WIPO, *The Global Innovation Index 2012: Stronger Innovation Linkages for Global Growth* (INSEAD and WIPO, 2012).

28 World Economic Forum, *The Global Competitiveness Report 2012–2013* (World Economic Forum, 2012).

29 Peter K. Yu, "From Pirates to Partners (Episode II): Protecting Intellectual Property in Post-WTO China," *American University Law Review* 55 (2006): 958–9; Peter K. Yu, "The Copyright Divide," *Cardozo Law Review* 25 (2003): 431–3.

30 Peter K. Yu, "The TRIPS Enforcement Dispute," *Nebraska Law Review* 89 (2011): 1123.

31 Hiroyuki Odagiri, Akira Goto, Atsushi Sunami, and Richard R. Nelson, "Conclusion," in *Intellectual Property Rights, Development, and Catch-up: An International Comparative Study*, ed. Hiroyuki Odagiri, Akira Goto, Atsushi Sunami, and Richard R. Nelson (Oxford University Press, 2010), 424–6.

32 "International Patent Filings Set New Record in 2011," March 5, 2012, available at http://www.wipo.int/pressroom/en/articles/2012/article_0001.html.

33 John L. Orcutt and Shen Hong, *Shaping China's Innovation Future: University Technology Transfer in Transition* (Edward Elgar Publishing, 2010), vii–ix.

Similar developments can be found in India and Brazil, which have the second- and fourth-largest PCT applications among the MIPPs, respectively. The strength of the Indian software industry speaks for itself.[34] The Indian generic pharmaceutical industry, which features such companies as Ranbaxy and Dr. Reddy's Laboratories, is also considered one of the most important and sophisticated in the world.[35] In addition, "Indian biotech companies, like Biocon, Avesthagen and Bharat Serums & Vaccines, are starting to mature into respected global players."[36] Similarly, Brazil has world-class strengths in "aerospace, where Embraer has emerged as one of the world's technological leaders, and oil exploration and drilling, thanks to the rapid increase in the technological capabilities of the erstwhile national oil company, Petrobras [Petroleo Brasileiro]."[37]

Table 5.5 includes the top thirty R&D spenders from the MIPPs, along with rankings based on the Booz & Company Global Innovation 1,000 Database. It is interesting, but unsurprising, that all of these "spenders" are located in Brazil, China, or India – twenty from China, six from India, and four from Brazil. Because the list covers only publicly listed companies, the table does not include such large R&D spenders as Huawei Technologies, even though that firm had the third-largest number of PCT applications in the world in 2011.

The Presence of Alternative Forms of Innovation

Although the existing intellectual property system focuses primarily on pathbreaking creations and innovations, many MIPPs have embraced sequential and cumulative innovations. Utility models or petty patents remain an important feature of the intellectual property systems in many developing countries.[38] Out of all the ten countries surveyed in this chapter, only India does not offer such protection. As of this writing, even India is considering proposals to offer such protection.[39]

34 Suma S. Athreye, "The Indian Software Industry," in *From Underdogs to Tigers: The Rise and Growth of the Software Industry in Brazil, China, India, Ireland, and Israel*, ed. Ashish Arora and Alfonso Gambardella (Oxford University Press, 2006), 7–40; Bhaven N. Sampat, "The Accumulation of Capabilities in Indian Pharmaceuticals and Software: The Roles that Patents Did (and Did Not) Play," in Odagiri et al., eds., *Intellectual Property Rights, Development, and Catch-up*, 369–71.

35 Sudip Chaudhuri, *The WTO and India's Pharmaceuticals Industry: Patent Protection, TRIPS, and Developing Countries* (Oxford University Press, 2005), 180–221.

36 David Llewelyn, *Invisible Gold in Asia: Creating Wealth through Intellectual Property* (Marshall Cavendish Business, 2010), 194.

37 Roberto Mazzoleni and Luciano Martins Costa Póvoa, "Accumulation of Technological Capabilities and Economic Development: Did Brazil's IPR Regime Matter?," in Odagiri et al., eds., *Intellectual Property Rights, Development, and Catch-up*, 282.

38 Assafa Endeshaw, *Intellectual Property in Asian Emerging Economies* (Ashgate Publishing, 2010), 73; Yu, "Intellectual Property and Asian Values," 389–90. For a more skeptical view, see Mark D. Janis, "Second Tier Patent Protection," *Harvard International Law Journal* 40 (1999): 151–219.

39 Jane Denny, "India Moves towards a New Utility Model Regime," November 18, 2011, available at http://www.iam-magazine.com/blog/Detail.aspx?=9df68046%2D4324%2D465b-996a-5fbc85dadebd.

TABLE 5.5. *Top R&D Spenders in the MIPPs*

77 PetroChina Co. Ltd. (China)
102 Vale SA (Brazil)
123 ZTE Corp. (China)
139 China Railway Construction Corp. Ltd. (China)
150 Petroleo Brasileiro SA (Brazil)
186 China Petroleum & Chemical Corp. (China)
244 A-Power Energy Generation Systems Ltd. (China)
280 Dongfeng Motor Group Co. Ltd. (China)
324 China Communications Construction (China)
330 China South Locomotive and Rolling Stock Corp. (China)
355 Lenovo Group Ltd. (China)
357 Metallurgical Corp. of China Ltd. (China)
401 Byd Co. Ltd. (China)
426 Tencent Holdings Ltd. (China)
445 Shanghai Electric Group Co. Ltd. (China)
446 Semiconductor Manufacturing International Corp. (China)
517 Shanghai Zhenhua Heavy Industry (China)
523 China CNR Corp. Ltd. (China)
627 Tata Motors Ltd. (India)
683 China Railway Group Ltd. (China)
696 Dongfang Electric Corp. Ltd. (China)
699 Infosys Technologies Ltd. (India)
788 CPFL Energia SA (Brazil)
799 Dr. Reddys Laboratories Ltd. (India)
819 Lupin Ltd. (India)
846 Empresa Brasileira de Aeronautica (Brazil)
848 Reliance Industries Ltd. (India)
849 Sun Pharmaceutical Industries Ltd. (India)
906 Harbin Power Equipment Co. Ltd. (China)
921 China National Materials Co. Ltd. (China)

WIPO, 2011 *World Intellectual Property Report: The Changing Face of Innovation* (WIPO, 2011), 41.

In addition, there has been a growing consensus among countries in the developing world to push for greater protection of traditional knowledge and traditional cultural expressions – or what Michael Finger and Philip Schuler have termed "poor people's knowledge."[40] Since its establishment in September 2000, the WIPO Intergovernmental Committee on Intellectual Property and Genetic Resources, Traditional Knowledge and Folklore has worked hard to develop legal mechanisms and practical tools to address the misappropriation of genetic resources, traditional knowledge, and traditional cultural expressions.[41] In 2006, the MIPPs, along with their allies, also advanced the Article 29*bis* proposal to create an obligation within the WTO to require disclosure of the source of origin of the biological resources and traditional knowledge in patent applications.[42]

[40] J. Michael Finger and Philip Schuler, eds., *Poor People's Knowledge: Promoting Intellectual Property in Developing Countries* (Oxford University Press, 2004).

[41] Peter K. Yu, "Cultural Relics, Intellectual Property, and Intangible Heritage," *Temple Law Review* 81 (2008): 437.

[42] "Doha Work Programme – The Outstanding Implementation Issue on the Relationship between the TRIPS Agreement and the Convention on Biological Diversity: Communication from Brazil, China, Colombia, Cuba, India, Pakistan, Peru, Thailand and Tanzania," WT/GC/W/564/Rev.2, July 5, 2006.

Finally, burgeoning literature has focused on the development of new forms of innovation that sustain economic growth, including open source software and other open innovation models. Commentators have also identified "new concepts such as 'frugal', 'reverse' or 'trickle-up' innovation."[43] In the context of China, a growing number of commentators have paid attention to those new forms of innovation that are slowly emerging in the country. While Zeng Ming and Peter Williamson wrote about "cost innovation,"[44] Tan Yinglan discussed "process innovation."[45] In a recent book, Dan Breznitz and Michael Murphree also identified "China's innovation capabilities ... in the organization of production, manufacturing techniques and technologies, delivery, design, and second-generation innovation."[46]

Uneven Developments and Internal Tensions

Compared with developed countries, the MIPPs face continued, complex, and considerable challenges concerning highly uneven economic and technological developments. For example, in China, the economic and technological developments in the major cities, such as Beijing, Shanghai, Guangzhou, and the coastal regions far exceed those in the inner and rural areas.[47] Fareed Zakaria observed that "India might have several Silicon Valleys, but it also has three Nigerias within it – that is, more than 300 million people living on less than a dollar a day."[48] In his recent book, Nobel laureate Michael Spence also noted the "dual economy" in Brazil, which consists of "a relatively rich one whose growth is constrained by the normal forces that constrain the growth of relatively advanced economies, and a poor one where the early-stage growth dynamics ... just didn't start, owing to its separation from the modern domestic economy and the global economy."[49]

Table 5.3 already shows that the MIPPs all have large aggregate GDPs and GNIs but rather small GDPs and GNIs per capita. Although China has now overtaken Japan to become the world's second-largest economy on an aggregate basis, Japan still dominates China dramatically on a per capita basis – with a GDP per capita of 39,738 in 2009 over China's 3,744. Likewise, even though India is the

[43] WIPO, 2011 *World Intellectual Property Report*, 40.

[44] Zeng Ming and Peter J. Williamson, *Dragons at Your Door: How Chinese Cost Innovation Is Disrupting Global Competition* (Harvard Business School Press, 2007).

[45] Tan Yinglan, *Chinnovation: How Chinese Innovators Are Changing the World* (John Wiley and Sons, 2011), xii.

[46] Dan Breznitz and Michael Murphree, *Run of the Red Queen: Government, Innovation, Globalization, and Economic Growth in China* (Yale University Press, 2011), 4.

[47] Peter K. Yu, "Intellectual Property, Economic Development, and the China Puzzle," in *Intellectual Property, Trade and Development: Strategies to Optimize Economic Development in a TRIPS Plus Era*, ed. Daniel J. Gervais (Oxford University Press, 2007), 203.

[48] Fareed Zakaria, *The Post-American World* (W. W. Norton and Company, 2008), 133.

[49] Michael Spence, *The Next Convergence: The Future of Economic Growth in a Multispeed World* (Farrar, Straus and Giroux, 2011), 204.

TABLE 5.6. *USTR's Special 301 Actions*

Country	2001	2002	2003	2004	2005	2006	2007	2008	2009	2010	2011	2012
Argentina	PWL	PWL	PWL	PWL	PWL	PWL	PWL	PWL	PWL	PWL	PWL	PWL
Brazil	WL	PWL	PWL	PWL	PWL	PWL	WL	WL	WL	WL	WL	WL
China	306	306	306	306	OCR	PWL	PWL	PWL	PWL	PWL	PWL	PWL
India	PWL	PWL	PWL	PWL	PWL	PWL	PWL	PWL	PWL	PWL	PWL	PWL
Indonesia	PWL	PWL	PWL	PWL	PWL	PWL	WL	WL	PWL	PWL	PWL	PWL
Malaysia	PWL	WL	WL	WL	WL	WL	WL	WL	WL	WL	WL	
Philippines	PWL	PWL	PWL	PWL	PWL	WL	WL	WL	WL	WL	WL	WL
Russia	PWL	PWL	PWL	PWL	PWL	PWL	PWL	PWL	PWL	PWL	PWL	PWL
South Africa												
Thailand	WL	WL	WL	WL	WL	WL	PWL	PWL	PWL	PWL	PWL	PWL

WL = "Watch List"; PWL = "Priority Watch List"; 306 = Section 306 Review; OCR = Out-of-Cycle Review.

world's tenth-largest economy based on GNI, it is technically a lower MIC. Indonesia is also a lower MIC, despite having a top twenty economy.

Continuing Piracy and Counterfeiting Challenges

Another notable challenge for the MIPPs concerns their limited ability to protect and enforce intellectual property rights. There are no good, objective indicators for piracy and counterfeiting; most of the available data were supplied by trade groups and other self-interested parties. Nevertheless, the past Section 301 actions taken by the U.S. Trade Representative (USTR) may provide a good idea of what external pressures the MIPPs have faced in regard to their piracy and counterfeiting problems.

To be certain, the Section 301 process has been severely criticized by commentators, myself included.[50] Highly political in nature and heavily influenced by the intellectual property industries, the process at times reflects more about a country's trade deficit with the United States than the actual piracy and counterfeiting problems. Nevertheless, the external pressures generated by this external process have historically proven to result in developments in the intellectual property area, especially in the MICs.

Table 5.6 shows that the USTR has put nine of the ten countries surveyed in this chapter on either the Watch List or the Priority Watch List virtually every year since 2001. Out of these countries, only Malaysia succeeded in avoiding the list in 2012.

[50] Joe Karaganis and Sean Flynn, "Networked Governance and the USTR," in *Media Piracy in Emerging Economies*, ed. Joe Karaganis (Social Science Research Council, 2011), 75–98; Paul C. B. Liu, "U.S. Industry's Influence on Intellectual Property Negotiations and Special 301 Actions," *UCLA Pacific Basin Law Journal* 13 (1994): 87–117; Peter K. Yu, "From Pirates to Partners: Protecting Intellectual Property in China in the Twenty-First Century," *American University Law Review* 50 (2000): 138–54.

Interestingly, South Africa was excluded entirely during the surveyed period. This exclusion, however, has more to do with the concern about the political backlash from taking actions against a country struggling to respond to an HIV/AIDS crisis than to the country's success in addressing piracy and counterfeiting problems. In 2000, amid the pharmaceutical industry's highly unpopular lawsuit against Nelson Mandela's government, the Clinton administration adopted Executive Order 13155, which enables countries in sub-Saharan Africa to enhance access to HIV/AIDS medicines and related medical technologies without fear of trade retaliation.[51]

STATE OF PLAY

In light of these six common characteristics, it is fair to question whether the roles of the MIPPs in the international intellectual property regime would be different from those played by either developed countries or the rest of the developing world. If these emerging powers could mediate the interests and positions of these two groups, they are likely to play a critically important role in the international intellectual property regime.

POLICY POSITIONS

Although Brazil has been a member of the Paris Convention for the Protection of Industrial Property (Paris Convention) since its inception,[52] developing countries did not have meaningful input or participation in the international intellectual property regime until after the decolonization movement. With the arrival and support of a large number of newly independent countries, India and Brazil began assuming leadership on behalf of the developing world in the 1960s. Together, they created what I have described as the "Old Development Agenda."[53]

For example, India was instrumental in demanding special concessions in the international copyright system in light of the divergent economic, social, cultural, and technological conditions in the developing world.[54] Such demands eventually led to the establishment of the Stockholm Protocol Regarding Developing Countries to the Berne Convention for the Protection of Literary and Artistic Works (Berne Convention). A revision of this protocol has now become the Berne Appendix, which the TRIPs Agreement incorporated by reference.

In November 1961, Brazil also advanced before the UN General Assembly a highly influential draft resolution entitled "The Role of Patents in the Transfer

[51] Executive Order No. 13155, 65 *Federal Register* 30,521 (May 12, 2000).

[52] Peter K. Yu, "A Tale of Two Development Agendas," *Ohio Northern University Law Review* 35 (2009): 506.

[53] Ibid., 468–511.

[54] Ibid., 471–84.

of Technology to Under-Developed Countries."[55] That resolution expressed the developing countries' dissatisfaction with the existing international patent system. A drastically weakened version of that resolution was adopted a month later. Picking up the momentum generated by this draft resolution and the ensuing debate, both Brazil and India actively pushed for the drafting of the International Code of Conduct on the Transfer of Technology in the 1970s and the revision of the Paris Convention in the early 1980s.[56] These developments eventually led to the stalemate between developed and developing countries that precipitated the formation of the WTO (and its TRIPs Agreement).

In recent years, Brazil and India have been equally active in pushing for prodevelopment efforts in the international intellectual property regime, establishing what I have described as the "New Development Agenda."[57] For example, these two countries were major players in the access to essential medicines debate, which culminated in the adoption of the Doha Declaration on the TRIPs Agreement and Public Health and a protocol to amend the TRIPs Agreement.[58] If ratified, the proposed Article 31*bis* of the TRIPs Agreement will allow countries with insufficient or no manufacturing capacity to import generic versions of patented pharmaceuticals. At the 2004 WIPO General Assembly, Brazil, along with Argentina, also advanced a proposal to establish a development agenda within the organization.[59] Adopted three years later, this agenda includes forty-five recommendations for action ranging from technical assistance and capacity building to norm setting and public policy and from technology transfer to assessment, evaluation, and impact studies.[60]

Although China was not as active as Brazil and India in the international arena before joining the WTO in 2001 and has maintained a rather low profile in the first few years following its accession, the country has now become much more assertive in the international intellectual property regime. Today, China no longer serves only as a passive taker of international intellectual property norms; it has also slowly assumed the additional roles of both a shaker and a maker of these norms.[61] When countries proposed Article 29*bis* to require disclosure of genetic resources and traditional knowledge used in patent applications, China joined Brazil and India as the proposal's cosponsors. In the widely noted TRIPs Council meeting in June

55 Ibid., 505–6. On the 1961 draft resolution, see Andréa Koury Menescal, "Changing WIPO's Ways? The 2004 Development Agenda in Historical Perspective," *Journal of World Intellectual Property* 8 (2005): 764–72.

56 Yu, "Tale of Two Development Agendas," 493–511.

57 Ibid., 511–40.

58 Yu, "International Enclosure Movement," 872–86.

59 "Proposal by Argentina and Brazil for the Establishment of a Development Agenda for WIPO," WO/GA/31/11, August 27, 2004.

60 "The 45 Adopted Recommendations under the WIPO Development Agenda," available at http://www.wipo.int/ip-development/en/agenda/recommendations.html.

61 Yu, "Middle Kingdom," 237–58.

2010, China and India also made high-profile interventions criticizing the developed countries' effort to negotiate the Anti-Counterfeiting Trade Agreement and to create TRIPs-plus enforcement standards.[62]

In the future, the positions of Brazil, China, and India are likely to be very important to the development of the international intellectual property regime, especially when these positions are supported by other MIPPs. Based on past negotiations, these positions will include issues that are already on the international intellectual property policy agenda, such as enforcement of intellectual property rights; protection of genetic resources, traditional knowledge, and traditional cultural expressions; protection of geographical indications; access to essential medicines; and standards concerning the Internet and new communications technologies. The MIPPs' positions will also touch on new and emerging issues, such as global climate change, the promotion of alternative innovation models (including utility models), special and differential treatment for developing countries, solutions to address uneven economic and technological developments, and abuse of rights and restraints on trade.[63]

Notwithstanding the wide variety of issues that the MIPPs may negotiate, the outcome of their negotiation efforts may not be as dramatic and confrontational as one would expect. Because the MIPPs harbor concerns that are found in both developed and developing countries, the compromises they foster are likely to be much more moderate than those fostered by the other two groups. As a result, regardless of how strong the rhetoric they use on behalf of the developing world, the intellectual property standards the MIPPs help to shape are likely to fall somewhere between the positions taken by the developed world and those taken by the rest of the developing world.

At times, the positions these emerging powers take may also be quite inconsistent and incoherent, due in large part to their highly uneven economic and technological developments. As I have noted elsewhere, the combination of these developments and the presence of fast-growing sectors have led Brazil, China, India, and other large, complex developing countries to adopt policies that are somewhat "schizophrenic."[64] For example, while China may want to have stronger protection of entertainment, software, semiconductors, and selected areas of biotechnology, it may want much more limited protection of pharmaceuticals, chemicals, fertilizers, seeds, and foodstuffs, due to its huge population, continued economic dependence on agriculture, the government leaders' worries about public health matters, and their concerns about the people's overall well-being.

[62] Council on Trade-Related Aspects of Intellectual Property Rights, "Minutes of Meeting," IP/C/M/63, October 4, 2010, paras. 249–73.

[63] On the discussion of these issues, see Yu, "Intellectual Property and Asian Values," 379–97.

[64] Yu, "International Enclosure, the Regime Complex," 25–6.

TABLE 5.7. *Dual Relationships with the MIPPs*

	Cooperative	Confrontational
Among the MIPPs	Bonded Siblings	Rivaling Siblings
Between the MIPPs and developed countries	A Happy Family	A Feuding Family
Between the MIPPs and the rest of the developing world	Big Brothers	New Bullies

INTERACTIONS WITH OTHER GROUPS

In addition to policy positions, it is important to consider the interactions between the MIPPs and the other two groups of countries. Because of the uneven economic and technological developments and therefore incoherent policy positions, their interactions will be hard to predict. The outcome will depend on the issue areas, the sectors involved, the relevant national comparative advantages, the global economic climate, and changing domestic and global politics, among other factors. Thus, instead of identifying a certain outcome, this chapter advances a duality of outcomes depicting both the cooperative and confrontational aspects of interactions with the MIPPs (see Table 5.7).

Among the MIPPs, the interactions are likely to create either bonded siblings or rivaling siblings. To be certain, it makes good sense for these emerging powers to team up with each other by building a coalition that would help achieve a more powerful voice, greater political leverage and more desirable bargaining outcomes.[65] In previous works, I have noted the benefits of establishing an "intellectual property coalition for development," or IPC4D for short.[66] Nevertheless, it remains unclear whether these countries are ready to work with each other. Although they have established the BRICS summit and the IBSA Dialogue Forum, having a dialogue is very different from committing to common negotiating positions. There is a good chance these countries may refuse to collaborate not because of their differing positions on intellectual property law and policy, but because of intellectual property–irrelevant matters, such as historical conflicts, border disputes, economic rivalries, cultural differences, or spillover issues from other trade-related areas.

By comparison, the interactions between the MIPPs and developed countries are likely to be not so different from the interactions they have today. The present positions of these emerging powers are still quite far away from those of the developed world. Nonetheless, the rapid increase in technological proficiency and the internal reforms pushed by the fast-growing domestic industries may slowly tip

[65] Yu, "Access to Medicines," 370–87.

[66] Peter K. Yu, "Building Intellectual Property Coalitions for Development," in *Implementing the World Intellectual Property Organization's Development Agenda*, ed. Jeremy de Beer (Wilfred Laurier University Press, 2009), 79–99.

the policy balance toward the positions of the developed world. If such a scenario occurs, the positions of the MIPPs will slowly migrate from one end of the spectrum to the other end. Although the MIPPs and developed countries could start off as a feuding family, a gradual convergence of interests will move them slowly toward a much happier family.

Finally, the interactions between the MIPPs and the rest of the developing world could be quite complicated. To be certain, there are still many benefits for these emerging powers to side with their much poorer neighbors in the developing world. These benefits include the retention of historical leadership, increased political clout in a "one country, one vote" system, trade diversification, fear of domination by developed countries, and sympathy from the sizeable poor in the MIPPs.[67] Nevertheless, as these emerging countries continue to rise in power in the international economic system, they likely will become much more powerful vis-à-vis other countries in the developing world. It remains to be seen whether the MIPPs would become big brothers or just new bullies, similar to their developed counterparts. Commentators and policy makers in Africa, Latin America, and Southeast Asia have already noted their concern about the neocolonial threats posed by China and other emerging powers.[68]

LESSONS

While it is important to explore the roles the MIPPs will play in the international intellectual property regime and the interactions they will have with the two other groups of countries, one may wonder whether the emergence of these countries will provide any lesson for policy makers and commentators, especially those in the developing world. The study of intellectual property developments in the MIPPs can provide at least four important lessons.

First, it speaks to what Alexander Gerschenkron, Justin Lin, and other commentators have referred to as the "advantage of backwardness."[69] The important takeaway from this seemingly paradoxical concept is that countries do not need to progress in a linear fashion or a locked-step manner to play economic and technological catch-up. Given the right conditions and support, countries could easily

[67] Yu, "Access to Medicines," 388–9.

[68] Pádraig Risteard Carmody, *The New Scramble for Africa* (Polity, 2011); Fantu Cheru and Cyril Obi, "Introduction – Africa in the Twenty-First Century: Strategic and Development Challenges," in *The Rise of China and India in Africa: Challenges, Opportunities and Critical Interventions*, ed. Fantu Cheru and Cyril Obi (Zed Books, 2010), 1–9; Dot Keet, "The Role and Impact of Chinese Economic Operations in Africa," in *China's New Role in Africa and the South: A Search for a New Perspective*, ed. Dorothy-Grace Guerrero and Firoze Manji (Fahamu, 2008), 78–86; Peter K. Yu, "Sinic Trade Agreements," *U.C. Davis Law Review* 44 (2011): 953–1028.

[69] Alexander Gerschenkron, *Economic Backwardness in Historical Perspective* (Belknap Press of Harvard University Press, 1962), 169; Justin Yifu Lin, *The Quest for Prosperity: How Developing Economies Can Take Off* (Princeton University Press, 2012), 143.

leapfrog from underdevelopment and backwardness to economic strength and technological proficiency. While stronger intellectual property protection and enforcement will not always result in leapfrogging, they could benefit developing countries by enabling them to develop a larger market or to increase their imitative or innovative capacity. The developments in China and India in the past two decades were breathtaking, and the emergence of a robust and well-functioning intellectual property system certainly has played some role in facilitating these developments.[70] From the policy standpoint, the successful development of this system may also hold the key for these countries to avoid the so-called middle-income trap.

Second, it is important for countries to not only develop their innovative capacity, but also to innovate their innovation models. Countries need to adopt models that are specially tailored to their own needs, interest, conditions, and priorities. While the existing international intellectual property system was built upon a super-size-fits-all model that privileges pathbreaking creations and innovations, commentators have identified many new, alternative forms of innovation. Because the existing system does not prevent the adoption of new models, developing countries should explore how they could use these models to facilitate economic and technological catch-up.

Third, the international intellectual property system is highly path-dependent. The impact of such dependency becomes even greater when the path is broadened to cover coevolutionary developments with the international economic and trading systems. As shown by the developed countries' push for a super-size-fits-all model enshrined in the TRIPs Agreement, international standards tend to be shaped by those who have proven success in the existing system – whether it is developed countries today or developed countries and the MIPPs in the near future. To a large extent, the international intellectual property system is a system for winners; it has limited sensitivity to those struggling to catch up.

As Ha-joon Chang observed in his oft-cited book, developed countries have successfully used the international trading system, including international intellectual property standards, to "'kick away the ladder' by which they have climbed to the top."[71] These countries ignore the fact that developing countries are now merely using policies and institutions they themselves have used during their formative period of development. Thus developing countries need to be very skeptical of the moral and normative bases of existing international intellectual property standards. Many of these standards were adopted not because they had moral appeal or promoted economic efficiency, but because they were backed by political power

70 Yu, "Intellectual Property, Economic Development," 193.

71 Ha-joon Chang, *Kicking Away the Ladder: Development Strategy in Historical Perspective* (Anthem, 2002), 129.

and economic might as well as strong interest group lobbying within the developed world.[72]

Finally, there is a point where developing countries will cross over from the pirating side of the intellectual property divide to one that is respectful of intellectual property rights.[73] Such crossover happened with virtually all developed countries, including the United States, Germany, Japan, Singapore, and South Korea.[74] While the significant mismatch between the local conditions and the TRIPs and TRIPs-plus standards has made it difficult for developing countries to cross the intellectual property divide, the recent emergence of the MIPPs seems to suggest that China, India, Brazil, and other similarly situated countries can still successfully cross over this divide, following the footsteps of other once-developing countries.

Once these emerging powers have crossed over to the other side, however, it remains to be seen whether they will expect the same standards as in the existing international intellectual property system. As I noted earlier in the inaugural issue of *The WIPO Journal*: "[I]t is premature to assume that less-developed countries, once developed, will always want the existing international intellectual property system. There is a good chance that they may want or need something rather different!"[75] The six common characteristics highlighted in this chapter seem to suggest that the MIPPs may want standards that are more in line with their own historical traditions, cultural backgrounds, socioeconomic conditions, ideological values, and policy preferences.

CONCLUSION

Although it is challenging to examine intellectual property developments in MICs, a smaller subset of these countries, the MIPPs, do play very important roles in the ongoing and future development of the international intellectual property regime. Based on the characteristics of Brazil, China, India, and other similarly situated countries, this chapter identifies six common characteristics of the MIPPs as well as the interactions they will have with the developed world and the rest of the

[72] William P. Alford, "How Theory Does – and Does Not – Matter: American Approaches to Intellectual Property Law in East Asia," *UCLA Pacific Basin Law Journal* 13 (1994): 17; Rosemary J. Coombe, *The Cultural Life of Intellectual Properties: Authorship, Appropriation, and the Law* (Duke University Press, 1998), 247; Ruth L. Okediji, "The International Relations of Intellectual Property: Narratives of Developing Country Participation in the Global Intellectual Property System," *Singapore Journal of International and Comparative Law* 7 (2003): 320–5; Yu, "From Pirates to Partners," 235.

[73] Yu, "Global Intellectual Property Order," 10–15; Peter K. Yu, "The Rise and Decline of the Intellectual Property Powers," *Campbell Law Review* 34 (2012): 528–43.

[74] Assafa Endeshaw, *Intellectual Property Policy for Non-industrial Countries* (Dartmouth, 1996), 120; William Kingston, "An Agenda for Radical Intellectual Property Reform," in *International Public Goods and Transfer of Technology under a Globalized Intellectual Property Regime*, ed. Keith E. Maskus and Jerome H. Reichman (Cambridge University Press, 2005), 658; Yu, "Intellectual Property, Economic Development," 175.

[75] Yu, "Global Intellectual Property Order," 15.

developing world. The study of the MIPPs will not only help us better understand the state of play in the international intellectual property regime, but will also provide important lessons for policy makers and commentators in both the developed and developing worlds. What is going on in the MIPPs and how these emerging powers develop deserve our urgent attention.

6

Growing Wealth in East Asian Middle-Income Countries with Transnational Production Regimes

John Gillespie

INTRODUCTION

Since the 1960s, law and development theorists have prescribed law-based measures for stimulating economic development in East Asian middle-income countries (MICs).[1] During the last decade, a growing number of scholars from different disciplines claim that rapid economic growth in this region is taking place without fully functioning legal systems.[2] They argue that consistent and pragmatic state developmental policies, more than formal laws and legal institutions, are the main ingredients for economic growth.[3] This chapter provides a complementary explanation for economic growth in East Asia. It posits that transnational production regimes (TPRs) are responsible for generating much wealth creation in East Asian MICs over the last thirty years. TPRs are structured around supply chain and investment networks that transfer goods, capital, and knowledge among firms in high-income countries (HICs) and MICs.[4]

This chapter musters evidence that, over the last three decades, intra-Asian TPRs have incrementally displaced Euro-American TPRs as the main source of technical and regulatory knowledge in East Asian MICs. This transformation has three principle implications: first, knowledge transferred through TPRs largely bypasses domestic laws and legal institutions and directly influences East Asian firms; second, intra-Asian TPRs are more likely than Euro-American TPRs to convey the regulatory knowledge needed to innovate and upgrade into higher value-added activities in

1 See, generally, Michael Trebilcock and Ronald Daniels, *Rule of Law Reform and Development: Charting the Fragile Path of Progress* (Edward Elgar Publishing, 2008).

2 See Donald Clarke, "Economic Development and the Rights Hypothesis: The China Problem," *American Journal of Comparative Law* 51 (2003): 89; Frank Upham, "From Demsetz to Deng: Speculations on the Source," *New York University Journal of International Law and Politics* 41, no. 3 (2009): 522–602.

3 See Ronald Gilson and Curtis Milhaupt, "Economically Benevolent Dictators: Lessons for Developing Democracies," *American Journal of Comparative Law* 59 (2011): 277.

4 TPRs form networks, while legally autonomous organizations work together to achieve collective goal. See Keith Provan and Patrick Kenis, "Modes of Network Governance: Structure, Management, and Effectiveness," *Journal of Public Administration Research and Theory* 18, no. 2 (2008): 229–52, at 231.

world markets; and third intra-Asian TPRs are a key factor in generating wealth creation and raising the next wave of East Asian countries into the ranks of HICs.

This chapter brings three previous disconnected literatures – socioeconomic, institutional learning, and law and development – into communication. Read together, this literature provides new insights into the regulatory factors that influence wealth creation in MICs. One, the socioeconomic literature shows that, in conjunction with market access treaties and state-led industrial planning, firms in East Asian MICs rely on imported technical and regulatory knowledge to innovate and upgrade their competitiveness.[5] Studies show that knowledge transfers increase competitiveness in two distinct processes: direct knowledge transfers from firms in HICs to firms in East Asian MICs; and indirect knowledge flows among firms located within East Asian MICs. This latter process, known as knowledge spillover, is regarded as an important source of economic growth in this region. Critically for this study, the socioeconomic literature shows that it is not just technical know-how that increases competitiveness; regulatory practices, such as *kaizan* routines and decentralized flexible management also play a role.

Two, the institutional learning literature advances this study by explaining how firms in East Asia absorb and integrate imported regulatory knowledge.[6] It shows that the closely knit relational connections that bind intra-Asian networks are more likely to communicate new regulatory knowledge than the arms-length legalist relationships associated with Euro-American TPRs. It is this flow of knowledge that stimulates innovation and industrial upgrading in East Asian firms. When knowledge spills over from intra-Asian TPRs through worker mobility[7] and agglomeration effects take hold, the overall national competitiveness increases, raising national levels of wealth in East Asian MICs.

Three, the law and development literature presents a diverse range of explanations for economic development in East Asia. A unifying theme is that only formal legal systems, especially rights protection, can provide the commercial certainty and transactional efficacy required for the advanced industrial economies that underpin HICs.[8] But recent scholarship queries the connection between formal law and

5 The literature is vast, but see Timothy J. Sturgeon and Richard K. Lester, *The New Global Supply Base – New Challenges for Local Suppliers in East Asia* (Industrial Performance Centre, Massachusetts Institute of Technology, 2003); Fukunari Kimura, "International Production/Distribution Networks in Indonesia," *The Developing Economies* 43 (2005): 17–38; Beata Javorcik, "Can Survey Evidence Shed Light on Spillovers from Foreign Direct Investment?," *World Bank Research Observer* 23, no. 2 (2008): 139–59.

6 For an overview of this literature, see Mark Easterby-Smith and Marjorie A. Lyles, ed., *Handbook of Organizational Learning and Knowledge Management* (Wiley, 2011); L. Sproull and M. Cohen, *Organizational Learning* (Sage, 1996).

7 See Luiz De Mell, "Foreign Direct Investment in Developing Countries and Growth: A Selective Survey," *Journal of Development Studies* 34, no. 1 (1997): 1–34; Ari Kokko and Victoria Kravtsov, "Innovative Capability in MNC Subsidiaries: Evidence from Four European Transition Economies," *Post-Communist Economies* 20, no. 1 (2008): 57–75.

8 See, e.g., Michael Trebilcock, and Jing Leng, "The Role of Formal Contract Law and Enforcement in Economic Development," *Virginia Law Review* 92 (2006): 1517–80.

economic development, raising the question: Where do East Asia firms acquire the regulatory knowledge to innovate and compete on global markets?

The discussion in this chapter begins by using the three literatures to argue that intra-Asian TPRs are the main driver of innovation and wealth creation in East Asian MICs. Next it explores three case studies that illustrate differences in the absorption and integration of knowledge transferred through intra-Asian and Euro-American TPRs. The analysis of these case studies points to a type of collaborative regulation in intra-Asian networks that bypasses and displaces state-based laws and legal institutions. Finally, it is argued that there is a need to refocus law and development studies upon the interaction between domestic regulatory systems in East Asian MICs and the bottom-up regulation from intra-Asian TPRs.

DEVELOPING AN EAST ASIAN REGULATORY MODEL

If North East Asian firms are currently stimulating economic development in firms located in East Asian MICs, the question arises how did North East Asia develop in the first place? To answer this question, it is necessary to distinguish the regulatory conditions responsible for rapid economic growth in North East Asian countries (i.e., Japan, South Korea, and Taiwan) during the 1950s and 1960s from the current conditions influencing rapid development in East Asia MICs (i.e., China, Vietnam, and Indonesia).

From the 1950s to 1980s, countries in North East Asia used collaborative regulation to increase national competitiveness.[9] In Japan, for example, a form of collaborative capitalism developed during the high-growth period (1950s–80s) that commanded considerable prestige within North East Asia. Although its exact workings remain a matter of controversy, in essence the system consisted of an elite bureaucracy that worked closely with big business in developing regulatory policy.[10] The political system gave the bureaucracy sufficient scope to initiate and operate effectively. Representing the state, the Ministry of International Trade and Industry used formal and informal directives known as administrative guidance to guide industries in their investment decisions and marketing practices.

Precisely how administrative guidance shaped business outcomes in Japan is debated. What is clear is that state officials negotiated regulatory policies with business leaders to create a type of responsive regulation.[11] Both state and corporate Japan distrusted command-and-control regulation, which had been imposed during

[9] See Robert Wade, *Governing the Market: Economic Theory and the Role of Government in East Asian Industrialization* (Princeton University Press, 1990).

[10] Frank Upham, "Privatized Regulation: Japanese Regulatory Style in Comparative and International Perspective," *Fordham International Law Journal* 20 (1997): 396.

[11] See, generally, F. L. Hartman, "Japanese Foreign Investment Regulation: Semantics and Reality," *New York Law Forum* 18 (1972–3): 355; John Ohnesorge, "Law and Development Orthodoxies and the Northeast Asian Experience," in *Law and Development in Asia*, ed. Gerald McAlinn and Caslav Pejovic (Routledge, 2012), 7, 16–30.

the U.S. occupation.[12] Instead of arms-length, top-down, legalistic rules, they sought more fluid relational connections that changed the role of government from dictator of rules to facilitator of agreements with stakeholders. In this regulatory architecture, the state became one of many interest groups and exercised a determining judgment about economic development in concert with the leading corporations in each industrial sector.

Different versions of this responsive regulatory model evolved in Korea to reflect the dominance of the family-controlled *chaebols* and in Taiwan to accommodate the comparative lack of large firms and the corresponding reliance on small- and medium-sized firms.

Responsive regulation allowed Japanese and other North East Asian firms considerable latitude to develop their own self-regulatory networks. Japanese *keiretsu* and Korean *chaebol* business networks defused the traditionally adversarial relationship between buyers and suppliers. Patterns of cross-ownership gave members of these business networks access to information that inculcated a sense of mutual benefit. The complex interfirm networks infused the exchange of market information and technical know-how with rich social relations of a noneconomic character.[13] Studies show that *keiretsu* enhanced the performance of the network as a whole by realigning their members' prospects and resources. *Keiretsu* and *chaebol* networks avoided costs associated with formal regulation, such as legal and compliance imposts, by keeping contractual arrangements among members implicit and by using personal monitoring.[14] Rather than pricing transactions at what the market would bear, these networks set prices at what seemed appropriate given the identity of the members and the needs of the network as a whole. This type of responsive regulation aimed to strengthen personal ties among firms as a means of generating efficient and innovative outcomes.

Relatively easy access to technical know-how from American firms and preferential access to U.S. markets during the Cold War also contributed to economic growth in North East Asia.[15] During the 1970 and 1980s, when Japanese firms began to challenge U.S. market dominance, access to technology and domestic markets became restricted. By this time, Japanese firms had developed their own technical know-how and innovative modes of production in transport, electronics, machine parts, and many other types of manufacturing.

[12] See Chalmers Johnson, *MITI and the Japanese Miracle: The Growth of Industry Policy* (Stanford University Press, 1982).

[13] See James R. Lincoln, Michael L. Gerlach, and Christina L. Ahmadjian, "Keiretsu Networks and Corporate Performance in Japan," *American Sociological Review* 61, no. 1 (February 1996): 67–88.

[14] See James R. Lincoln and Michael L. Gerlach, *Japan's Network Economy: Structure, Persistence, and Change* (Cambridge University Press, 2004), 147–204.

[15] See Committee on Japan, *Maximizing U.S. Interests in Science and Technology Relations with Japan*, U.S. Office of International Affairs (1997), available at http://www.nap.edu/openbook.php?record_id=5850&page=1.

When North East Asian firms began to move offshore to find low-cost suppliers in East Asia during the 1970s and 1980s, they brought the *keiretsu* and *chaebol* networks with them. The networks have instilled certain core regulatory characteristics into most intra-Asian TPRs. They tend to deemphasize rule-based hierarchies in favor of tightly knit relational communities structured around nodes of production.[16] Japanese firms pioneered *kaizan* routines that enabled suppliers in East Asian MICs to design their own operational environments. This collaborative governance unconsciously steered and coordinated members of the production network.[17] Particularly now that the competitiveness of East Asian firms rests not only on labor and raw material costs, to remain competitive firms increasingly rely on flexible production that responds rapidly to shifting patterns of demand in the fragmented and protean Asian markets.[18] While many firms in East Asian MICs successfully used collaborative networks to compete on price, a select group managed to build up design competencies of their own and emerged as direct competitors to firms from Asian and Western HICs.[19]

There is mixed evidence that intra-Asian TPRs have changed to reflect regulatory reforms in East Asian HICs during the 1990s and 2000s.[20] Studies show that the *Keidanren*, representing major Japanese firms, successfully resisted reforms aiming to instill independent directors and more transparency into *keiretsu* networks. A recent study of Toyota[21] confirms deep resistance to rule-based governance among the leading Japanese firms targeted for reform. Meanwhile, reforms have entirely bypassed the majority of intra-Asian TPRs, which are structured around the small and medium firms that followed large companies into East Asian MICs.[22]

To summarize, intra-Asian TPRs developed a type of responsive regulation that reflected the regulatory conditions during the high-growth period in North East Asia.[23] As we shall see, this regulatory model is currently out-competing rival TPRs

16 See Victor Nee and Richard Swedberg, ed., *The Economic Sociology of Capitalism* (Princeton University Press, 2005); Chi-Nien Chung, "Beyond Guanxi: Network Contingencies in Taiwanese Business Groups," *Organisational Studies* 27, no. 4 (2005): 461–89.

17 See Masahiko Aoki, *Information, Incentives and Bargaining in the Japanese Economy* (Cambridge University Press, 1988); Masahiko Aoki, Gregory Jackson, and Hideaki Miyajima, ed., *Corporate Governance in Japan* (Oxford University Press, 2007), 370–98.

18 See Sven W. Arndt and Henryk Kierzkowski, *Fragmentation: New Production Patterns in World Economy* (Oxford University Press, 2001); Joshua Cohen and Charles Sabel, "Directly-Deliberative Polyarchy," *European Law Journal* 3, no. 4 (1997): 313–42.

19 Timothy J. Sturgeon and Richard K. Lester, *The New Global Supply Base-New Challenges for Local Suppliers in East Asia*, IPC Working Paper Series (October 2003), available at http://web.mit.edu/ipc/publications/pdf/03-006.pdf.

20 See John Luke Nottage, *Perspectives and Approaches Corporate Governance in the 21st Century: Japanese Gradual Transformation* (Edward Elgar, 2008), 21–52.

21 See Bruce Aronson, "Learning from Toyota's Troubles: The Debate on Board Oversight, Board Structure, and Director Independence in Japan," *Journal of Japanese Law* 15, no. 30 (2010): 67–87.

22 See Kwong-Chiu Fung, Hitomi Iizaka, and Alan Siu, "United States, Japanese, and Korean FDI and Intra-East Asian Trade," *Asian Economic Papers* 9, no. 3 (2010): 129–54.

23 Research shows that firms replicate the regulatory conditions found in their home jurisdiction. See Louis W. Pauly and Simon Reich, "National Structures and Multinational Corporate Behaviour," *International Organization* 51, no. 1 (1997): 1–30.

that use less flexible command-and-control regulation. It is possible that a combination of more rigorous domestic and extraterritorial enforcement of corporate governance standards might eventually compel North East Asian firms to formalize their responsive regulatory networks. In addition, naming and shaming by transnational nongovernmental organizations, such as the Fair Trade Alliance and Forest Stewardship Council, might create external lines of accountability for environmental and labor conditions that reshape intra-Asian TPRs in the future. As we shall see in the next section, in the meantime intra-Asian TPRs are a significant, if not the dominant, force shaping competitiveness and wealth creation in East Asian MICs.

KNOWLEDGE TRANSFERS INTO EAST ASIAN MIDDLE-INCOME COUNTRIES

Socioeconomic studies point to the three main factors responsible for industrial upgrading and growth in East Asian MICs. First, over the last three decades, multilateral treaties such as the World Trade Organization and Asean + 3 have reduced tariffs and other imposts on intra-Asian trade and investment.[24] Of equal importance, bilateral government compacts have smoothed the way for close interregional economic cooperation.[25] They perform several main functions such as laying administrative foundations for economic activity, promoting economic cooperation, and resolving trade tensions. East Asian MICs have also used free trade zones to link TPRs with domestic firms.

Second, there is strong evidence that stable macroeconomic policies and the targeting of specific sectors for development by many East Asian MICs facilitated the accumulation of skills required for industrial upgrading and growth. To a limited extent, government policies can ameliorate endogenous constraints to economic development, such as difficult physical geographies and knowledge and skills shortages. The most effective policies have not supported legal institutions, but rather mobilized "soft social resources" such as knowledge, social capital, and research and development to proactively advance the innovative capacities that are essential for sectoral upgrading into higher value-added activities in world markets.[26]

Third, a growing body of scholars identifies the interactive complementarities and coupling effects between local firms and translocal actors as the key factor propelling regional economic development in East Asian MICs.[27] Although acknowledging the

[24] See Kozo Kiyota, Yoko Sazanam, and Yu Ching Wong, "Intra-regional Trade in Asia: Dynamics of Production Sharing," unpublished paper, 2006.

[25] See, e.g., Minh Wan, *Sino-Japanese Relations: Interaction, Logic and Transformation* (Woodrow Wilson Center Press, 2006), 57–63.

[26] See Bob Jessop and Ngai-Ling Sum, *Beyond the Regulatory Approach* (Edward Elgar, 2006), 201–6.

[27] See Neil M. Coe, et al., "Globalizing Regional Development: A Global Production Networks Perspective," *Transactions of the Institute of British Geographers* 29, no. 4 (2004): 468–84.

role local institutions play in scaling up institutional capacities, this group of scholars argues that intraregional knowledge flows are the main driver of competiveness and wealth generation in this region. Henry Yeung has shown, for example, that endogenous factors alone cannot adequately account for economic growth in East Asia.[28] He wrote: "Asian firms have strategically disembedded from state apparatus and successfully reembedded themselves in the competitive dynamics of global production networks."[29] Other commentators show how intra-Asian TPRs generate efficiencies where they link geographically proximate regions with different location advantages such as design efficiencies and low labor costs.[30] Still other commentators make the claim that, since the 1990s, intra-Asian TPRs have become the main source of firm growth and competitiveness in East Asian MICs.[31]

Significantly for this study, the socioeconomic literature shows a dramatic shift from Euro-American to intra-Asian TPRs coincided with large increases in the per capita gross domestic product in East Asian MICs. Incomes rose from U.S.$1315 in 1980 when Euro-American TPRs dominated East Asian trade and investment to U.S.$8,322 in 2010 when intra-Asian TPRs dominated.[32] Most of this wealth was generated by manufacturing,[33] the industrial sector most closely associated with intra-Asian TPRs. This link between economic development and the change in the flows of regulatory knowledge into East Asia has been largely ignored by the law and development literature.

Before 1980, Western firms accounted for more than 50 percent of trade and investment in East Asia.[34] First Japan, then Korea, and now China[35] have used

[28] See Henry Wai-chung Yeung, "Regional Development and the Competitive Dynamics of Global Production Networks: An East Asian Perspective," *Regional Studies* 43, no. 3 (2009): 325–51.

[29] See Henry Wai-chung Yeung, "Globalizing Competition in Asia: An Evolutionary Perspective on Firm-State Relations in the Asian Newly Industrialized Economies," in *Competition, Regulation and Capitalism Lessons from Asia*, ed. Michael Dowdle, John Gillespie, and Imelda Maher (Cambridge University Press, forthcoming).

[30] See Kazunobu Hayakawa, J. Zheng JI, and Ayako Obashi, "Spatial Distribution of Industrial Production: A Comparison of East Asia and Europe," *The Developing Economies* 49, no. 4 (December 2011): 363–81.

[31] See Sturgeon and Lester, *The New Global Supply Base*, 4. See also M. Peng and J. Zhou, "How Network Strategies and Institutional Transitions Evolve," *Asia Pacific Journal of Management* 22 (2005): 321–36.

[32] See "United Nations Main Aggregates Data Base," available at http://unstats.un.org/unsd/snaama/selbasicFast.asp.

[33] "The Value Added by Economic Activity, Annual Average Rate of Growth – Percentage for East Asia" shows that manufacturing followed by transport were the fastest growing economic sectors from 1980 to 2010. See "United Nations Main Aggregates Data Base," available at http://unstats.un.org/unsd/snaama/selbasicFast.asp.

[34] E.g., in 2000, U.S. firms accounted for approximately 30 percent of trade with Asia, but currently they accounts for less than 14 percent. Over the same time frame, intra-Asian trade has increased from 30 percent to more than 60 percent, while intra-Asian investment has increased from around 16 percent in 1991 to more than 79 percent in 2005. See Paul Gruenwald and Masahiro Hori, "Intra-regional Trade Key to Asia's Export Boom," *IMF Survey Magazine* (2008), available at http://www.imf.org/external/pubs/ft/survey/so/2008/car02608a.htm; Durgesh K. Rai, "Asian Economic Integration and Cooperation – Challenges and Way Forward," *East Asia Forum* (2010), available at http://www.eastasiaforum.org/2010/07/01/asian-economic-integration-and-cooperation-challenges-and-way-forward/.

[35] See Tang Haiyan and Zhang Huiqing, "China Reshapes the East Asian Production Network," *China Economist* 4. no. 2 (2009), available at http://papers.ssrn.com/sol3/papers.cfm?abstract_id=1544327##.

foreign direct investment and production networks to become exporters of regulatory knowledge to East Asian MICs. By 2010, East Asian firms accounted for more than 70 percent of production networks and more than 80 percent of investment. Official data probably underestimates the full extent of intra-Asian trade and investment, because much investment is informal and not captured in official statistics. Surprisingly, the level of intraregional trade and investment in manufacturing is significantly higher in East Asia than in formally constituted trading blocs such as the European Union and the North Atlantic Free Trade Agreement.[36]

Before examining the implications of this transformation, it is necessary to understand the key regulatory differences between intra-Asian and Euro-American TPRs. A central question arises: Do these TPRs have different regulatory logics?

COMPARING INTRA-ASIAN AND EURO-AMERICAN TRANSNATIONAL PRODUCTION REGIMES

American trade officials dislike intra-Asian TPRs, claiming that they create preferential transactions that restrain trade. However neoliberal economists are the most vehement critics of these TPRs.[37] Intra-Asian TPRs obstinately refuse to conform to transaction cost theory, which predicts that as firms reach a particular size, rules-based transactions reduce the risk and the cost of doing business.[38] Another reason for their antipathy is that intra-Asian TPRs actively promote collectivism, a value that Fredrick Hayek[39] and other progenitors of neoliberal economics strongly opposed because of its association with the political extremism of Nazi Germany and Stalin's Soviet Union.[40]

Despite government and academic disapproval, some Euro-American transnational firms attempted to emulate the characteristics of *keiretsu* networks. Firms as diverse as Chrysler, Virgin Airways, and the Zara clothes chain developed TPRs that were loosely modeled on *keiretsu* networks.[41] Commentators have observed, however, that the Euro-American networks differed in one fundamental way from the Japanese model. Instead of making mutual cooperation the key objective, as in

36 See Kwong-Chiu Fung, Hitomi Iizaka, and Alan Siu, "United States, Japanese, and Korean FDI and Intra-East Asian Trade," *Asian Economic Papers* 9, no. 3 (2010): 129–54.

37 The East Asian Financial crisis was interpreted by neoliberal economists as vindication that collaborative capitalism has failed. See James R. Lincoln and Michael L. Gerlach, *Japan's Network Economy: Structure, Persistence, and Change* (Cambridge University Press, 2004), 295–300.

38 See James R. Lincoln and Michael L. Gerlach, *Japan's Network Economy: Structure, Persistence, and Change* (Cambridge University Press, 2004).

39 See F. A. Hayek, *The Road to Serfdom* (Routledge, 2005), 33–44.

40 For a discussion about neoliberalism and collectivism, see Christian List and Philip Pettit, *Group Agent: The Possibility of Design and the Status of Corporate Agents* (Oxford University Press, 2011), 131.

41 See, e.g., J. Dyer, "How Chrysler Created an American Keiretsu," *Harvard Business Review* 74, no. 4 (July–August, 1996): 42–52; Hugh Collins, "The Network Architecture of Supply Chains," in *Networks: Legal Issues of Multilateral Co-Operation*, ed. M. Amstutz and G. Teubner (Hart Publishing, 2009), 187–210.

intra-Asian TPRs, the Euro-American TPRs primarily used networks to relocate different parts of the production process to capture geographical comparative advantages. As a consequence, the Euro-American TPRs did not develop the responsive regulation that is a feature of intra-Asian TPRs.[42]

Typically, lawyers and accountants who run Euro-American TPRs organize transactions around hierarchical policies[43] based on global and domestic corporate governance, intellectual property, disclosure, and anticorruption rules. Further reinforcing rule-based hierarchies, shareholders use the extraterritorial reach of U.S. and European courts to monitor and enforce business standards in offshore subcontractors. In addition, norm-setting transnational organizations, such as the International Labor Organization and International Standards Organization, ensure that Euro-American TPRs adhere to corporate governance and labor and environmental standards.[44]

Hybrid networks combine intra-Asian and Euro-American TPRs. Research shows that hybrids are comprised of interlocking but regulatory-discrete TPRs. The production of Apple iPhones is a case in point.[45] As the main design and marketing innovator,[46] Apple shapes the regulatory character of the supplier networks with Foxconn, the Chinese-based assembler. Meanwhile, Toshiba in Japan and Samsun in Korea are the main computer chip innovators and suppliers to Foxconn. Their supplier networks are regulatorily distinct from the Apple networks.

What emerges from the socioeconomic literature is a regulatory continuum along which there are many points representing different types of TPRs. Rules-based Euro-American TPRs occupy one end of the continuum, while responsive intra-Asian TPRs are at the other end. The institutional learning literature considered in the next section, takes the discussion further by more precisely identifying the types of TPRs that are most likely to generate innovation and competitive upgrading in East Asia MICs.

[42] See Tetsuo Abo, "Hybridization of Japanese Production Systems in North America, Newly Industrialized Economies, South East Asia and Europe: Contrasting Configurations," in *Between Imitation and Innovation*, ed. Robert Boyer, Elsie Charron, Ulrich Jurgens, and Steven Tolliday (Oxford University Press, 1997), 216–30; Tetsuo Abo, "The Japanese Production System: The Process of Adaption to Natural Settings," in *States Against Markets: The Limits of Globalization*, ed. R. Boger and D. Drache (Routledge, 1996), 136–54.

[43] See, generally, Henry Yueng, *Transnational Corporations and Business Networks* (Routledge, 1998), 6; Richard Appelbaum, William Felstiner, and Volkmar Gessner, *Rules and Networks: The Legal Culture of Global Business Transactions* (Hart Publishing, 2001), 159–88.

[44] See, generally, Benjamin Cashmore, "Legitimacy and Privatization of Environmental Governance: How Non-state Market Driven Systems Gain Market Recognition," *Governance* 15, no. 502 (2002): 503–29.

[45] See Yuqing Xing and Neal Detert, *How the iPhone Widens the United States Trade Deficit with the People's Republic of China*, Asian Development Bank Institute, Working Paper Series, No. 257 (December 2010), available at http://www.adbi.org/working-paper/2010/12/14/4236.iphone.widens.us.trade.deficit.prc/.

[46] See Ram Mudambi, "Location, Control and Innovation in Knowledge-intensive Industries," Institute of Global Management Studies, Discussion Paper 08-0430 (April 2008), 21–4.

REGULATING FOR INNOVATION AND COMPETITIVE UPGRADING

A diverse range of studies shows that the communication of tacit knowledge is vital for collaborative innovation.[47] "Tacit knowledge is personal, context-specific, and therefore hard to formalize and communicate while explicit knowledge refers to knowledge that is transmittable in formal, systematic language."[48] Research by Fred Selnes and James Sallis, for example, demonstrates that "more than two-thirds of all technical development collaboration is done through informal interpersonal networks."[49]

Studies further reveal that tacit knowledge flows are difficult to control and assimilate using formalized learning patterns, such as structured meetings, hierarchical organizational systems, training courses, and organizational manuals. Conversely, the communication of tacit knowledge increases where collaboration, based on high-levels of personal trust, coordinates business activities – a process that is called relational learning.[50] It turns out that tightly knit relational groups, such as intra-Asian TPRs, generate the relational preconditions for the communication and absorption of tacit knowledge. Studies have identified a link between the collectivist long-term perspectives associated with intra-Asian TPRs and the creation of closely knit relational learning environments.[51] They also find a strong correlation between the collectivism promoted by intra-Asian TPRs and the communication of tacit knowledge.[52] Intra-Asian TPRs not only act like repositories of tacit knowledge, but also actively steer network members toward common innovative objectives.[53]

Other studies comparing innovation in East Asian MICs with Eastern European MICs shows how relational learning in intra-Asian TPRs provides a competitive advantage over more formally structured networks. The communication of tacit

[47] The literature is vast, but see Chung-Jen Chen, "The Effects of Knowledge Attribute, Alliance, Characteristics, and Absorptive Capacity on Knowledge Transfer Performance," *R&D Management* 34, no. 3 (2004): 311–21, at 314; Shahid Yusuf, "Intermediating Knowledge Exchange between Universities and Businesses," *Research Policy* 37, no. 8 (2008): 1167–74.

[48] See Chung-Jen Chen, "The Effects of Knowledge Attribute, Alliance Characteristics," 312.

[49] See F. Selnes and J. Sallis, "Promoting Relationship Learning," *Journal of Marketing* 67 (2003): 80–95, at 84.

[50] Relational learning is a joint activity in which two or more parties attempt to generate more value together than they would create individually. See M. S. Cheung, M. B. Myers, and J. T. Mentzer, "The Value of Relational Learning in Global Buyer-Supplier Exchanges," *Strategic Management Journal* 32, no. 10 (2011): 1061, 1064–5; C. Bartlett and S. Ghoshal, *Managing Across Borders: A Transnational Solution* (Harvard Business School Press, 1998).

[51] See D. Griffith and M. Myers, "The Performance Implications of Strategic Fit of Relational Norm Governance Strategies in Global Supply Chain Relationships," *Journal of International Business Studies* 36 (2005): 254–69; Yusheng Peng, "Kinship Networks and Entrepreneurs in China's Transitional Economy," *American Journal of Sociology* 109, no. 5 (2004): 1045–74.

[52] See F. Selnes and J. Sallis, "Promoting Relationship Learning," *Journal of Marketing* 67 (2003): 80–95, at 83.

[53] See M. Zellmer-Bruhn and C. Gibson, "Multinational Organization Context: Implications for Team Learning and Performance," *Academy of Management Journal* 49, no. 3 (2006): 501–18.

knowledge proved more important for innovation than the homegrown advantages of advanced research and development capacities and education systems in the Eastern European countries.[54] As an Asian Development Bank report recently concluded:[55]

> A high degree of trust among firms is increasingly regarded by [Multinational Corporations] MNCs as a critical ingredient for developing market-led production networks. Among other things, high levels of trust encourage positive collective behavior among firms – such as sharing of sensitive information, pooling of technical knowledge, and joint production and marketing activities – which is critical in technologically intense, efficient production networks.

A growing body of evidence suggests that East Asian firms linked to Euro-American TPRs are less innovative than comparable firms in intra-Asian TPRs. According to one study, most, but not all, Euro-American TPRs decouple innovative activities pursued in HICs from production in MICs.[56] Such TPRs use rule-based organizational processes to circumscribe innovation from routine production. Corporate governance rules, for example, limit the flow of tacit knowledge through personal interaction.[57] Protocols developed around intellectual property protection further decouple innovation from other processes. This type of "stickiness" in communicative linkages inhibits innovation in the supplier firms located in East Asian MICs.

Another factor limiting knowledge flows within Euro-American TPRs is the cultural distance separating firms based in Euro-American HICs and firms in East Asian MICs. Cross-border networks need to create shared knowledge so that member firms can conceptualize and devise common solutions to regulatory problems.[58] Studies demonstrate that, the greater the cultural distance between firms, the greater the need for the communication of tacit knowledge that explains the different assumptions underpinning regulation and innovation.[59] The formal organizational

[54] See Jochen Lorentzen, Peter Mollgaard, and Matija Rojec, "Host-country Absorption of Technology: Evidence from Automotive Supply Networks in Eastern Europe," *Industry and Innovation* 10, no. 4 (2003): 415–32, at 418–23. See also a comparison of African and Asian firms: Banji Oyelaran-Oyeyinka and Kaushalesh Lal, "Learning New Technologies by Small and Medium Enterprises in Developing Countries," *Technovation* 26 (2006): 220–31.

[55] Ganeshan Wignaraja, "Engaging Small and Medium Enterprises in Production Networks: Firm-level Analysis of Five ASEAN Economies," Asian Development Bank Institute, Working Paper Series, No. 361 (June 2012), available at http://www.adbi.org/working-paper/2012/06/01/5076.engaging.small.medium.enterprises/.

[56] See Ram Mudambi, "Location, Control and Innovation in Knowledge-Intensive Industries," Institute of Global Management Studies, Discussion Paper 08-0430 (April 2008), 14–16.

[57] See Henry Yueng, *Transnational Corporations and Business Networks* (Routledge, 1998), 5–6

[58] See A. K. Gupta and V. Govindarajan, "Knowledge Flows within Multinational Corporations," *Strategic Management Journal* 21, no. 4 (2000): 473–96.

[59] See Cheung, et al., "The Value of Relational Learning in Global Buyer-Supplier Exchanges," 1066; Clive Lawson and Edward Lorenz, "Collective Learning, Tacit Knowledge and Regional Innovative Capacity," *Regional Studies* 33, no. 4 (1999): 305–17, at 309.

structures in Euro-American TPRs constrain the flow of tacit knowledge required to bridge cultural divides.[60]

To summarize, the socioeconomic and relational learning literature shows how the communication of tacit knowledge is crucial to innovation and industrial upgrading in East Asia MICs. This kind of communicative interaction is facilitated more by intra-Asian than by Euro-American TPRs. The following case studies explore this proposition by comparing the communicative structures within intra-Asian and Euro-American TPRs.

CASE STUDY: INTEL

In 2006, Intel entered into a Code of Conduct (CoC) with Sai Gon Hi-tech Park (SHTP).[61] SHTP managed the industrial park where Intel had established its Vietnamese operations.[62] The CoC contained provisions that aimed to instill high ethical standards and transparent business practices in local component suppliers.[63] Intel was concerned about corruption in Vietnam and wanted SHTP to insulate them from local business suppliers.

Intel ran a series of training courses with SHTP staff to inculcate the anticorruption principles embedded in the CoC.[64] Some CoC provisions were already familiar to SHTP staff, as the Vietnamese government and media reports routinely criticized bribery and kickback commissions. Other aspects of the CoC generated confusion. SHTP staff did not understand the rationale for conflict of interest provisions designed to avoid the appearance of corruption. Business in Vietnam is conducted through relational networks, and without personal connections with regulators, firms struggle to enter new markets.[65] The absolute prohibitions against giving and

60 See Masahiko Aoki, *Information, Incentives and Bargaining in the Japanese Economy* (Cambridge University Press, 1988); Ronald Dore, "Inside Management and Board Reform: For Whose Benefits?," in *Corporate Governance in Japan Institutional Change and Organizational Diversity*, ed. Masahiko Aoki, Gregory Jackson, and Hideaki Miyajima (Oxford University Press, 2007), 370–98.

61 Author unknown, "Intel talks about investment environment in Vietnam" [Intel nói về môi trường đầu tư Việt Nam], *Vietnam Economic Times*, January 24, 2008.

62 VnExpress, "A state agency signs a commitment refusing bribes" [Một cơ quan nhà nước ký cam kết từ chối việc hối lộ], *Vietnamnet Bridge*, September 7, 2007, available at http://search.vnexpress.net/news?s=M%E1%BB%99t+c%C6%A1+quan+nh%C3%A0+n%C6%B0%E1%BB%9Bc+k%C3%BD+cam+k%E1%BA%BFt+t%E1%BB%AB+ch%E1%BB%91i+vi%E1%BB%87c+h%E1%BB%91i+l%E1%BB%99&g=0B439851-C644-4B23-904E-9D7B068D05F7&butS=yes.

63 The CoC contains five principles: Intel conducts business with honesty and integrity; Intel follows the letter and spirit of the law; Intel employees treat each other fairly; Intel employees act in the best interests of Intel and avoid conflicts of interest; and Intel employees protect the company's assets and reputation. See Intel Corporation, *Intel Code of Conduct*, May 2, 2007, available at http://www.intel.com/intel/finance/docs/code-of-conduct.pdf.

64 Interviews Lam Vu Thao, In-house counsel, Intel Vietnam, Ho Chi Minh City, October 14, 2008 and July 3, 2009 (conducted by Nguyen Hung Quang) and February 17 and 22, 2012 (conducted by John Gillespie).

65 See John McMillan and Christopher Woodruff, "Interfirm Relationships and Informal Credit in Vietnam," *Quarterly Journal of Economics* 114, no. 4 (1999): 1285; John Gillespie, "Testing the Limits to

receiving gifts also seemed inappropriate to SHTP staff, because Vietnamese traders made finely calibrated distinctions between gifts designed to show respect and develop goodwill and bribes disguised as gifts.

Training courses conducted by Intel were delivered in English and then translated into Vietnamese. Subsequent meetings were conducted in Vietnamese, unless senior American executives were present. Intel staff were encouraged to avoid conflicts of interest that might arise from socializing with SHTP staff. As a consequence, after five years, formal meetings had not ripened into the close personal relationships required for Intel staff to act like cultural intermediaries[66] and translate the CoC into the local idioms and practices familiar to SHTP staff.

Despite the limited personal interaction, Intel staff noticed changes in the regulatory outlook of SHTP staff. Initially, SHTP staff were reluctant to discuss corruption, which is considered a politically sensitive topic (*te nhi*) in Vietnam. Public discourse about corruption is usually conducted in ambiguous and figurative language, and reasoned discussion of the kind promoted by Intel is considered in bad taste as it shines too brightly on delicate matters. Over time, SHTP staff realized that the rules governing public discourse did not apply to their exchanges with Intel staff and began to openly engage with the CoC. SHTP is now marketing the industrial park as a model transactional environment and has encouraged other firms in the industrial park to enter into similar CoCs.

Interviews suggest that SHTP staff promoted the CoC, not from a deeply held conviction that it represented the optimal regulatory approach, but rather as a marketing strategy to attract more foreign investment to the industrial park. This reluctance to embrace the CoC is unsurprising given the large knowledge gap to overcome between Intel and SHTP. Intel developed the CoC to manage highly complex transnational production networks. Contrasting with this cosmopolitan world, SHTP staff spent their formative years working in government departments or state-owned enterprises. They considered themselves state officials and favored discretionary personalistic regulation – "state economic management" (*quan ly nha nuoc kinh te*) – to the immutable, universally applicable ethical standards in the CoC. Few SHTP staff had traveled outside Vietnam and gained familiarity with "rule of law" societies.

What this case study suggests is that Intel and SHTP staff lacked the close personal relationships that the institutional learning literature implies are necessary to absorb and integrate new regulatory practices. Intel did not effectively communicate the tacit knowledge that explained the CoC to SHTP staff. It made pragmatic sense for the SHTP staff to leverage the CoC to attract new investors, but they rejected aspects

the 'Rule of Law': Commercial Regulation in Vietnam," *Journal of Comparative Asian Development* 12, no. 2 (2008): 245–72.

66 The term *cultural intermediary* is used to describe a person who uses cross-cultural knowledge to adjust one regulatory system to the particularities of another system. See Lauren Benton, *Law and Colonial Cultures: Legal Regimes in World History* 1400–1900 (Cambridge University Press, 2002), 3–9.

of the CoC, such as avoiding conflicts of interest and gift giving, which contradicted deeply embedded regulatory practices. Intel presented the CoC as a fait accompli and used corporate governance rules to prevent interaction with SHTP staff that might have imaginatively reconfigured the CoC to accommodate domestic regulatory practices.

CASE STUDY: FOOTWEAR

In 1996, a foreign investor established a footwear manufacturing business in northern Vietnam.[67] The firm flourished and sold its products through production networks to transnational sporting goods firms based in the United States and Japan. Initially, the foreign investor ran the firm along conventional Vietnamese familial lines. He assumed the pivotal role in the firm, acting as the father and benefactor. Vietnamese managers acted as his lieutenants, and the employees were treated as members of a rather large family. Storylines attributed the firm's success to "good heart" (*tam*), compassion (*thong cam*), and sentiment between the managers and staff.

In 2001, Nike, one of the main buyers, insisted that the firm adopt a logistic management regime to track the manufacturing process. The corporate governance rules embedded in this regime required the firm to develop internal management rules that clearly identified positions and responsibilities. For example, the managers and staff were given detailed job descriptions, and internal review processes were grounded on output-oriented standards. These hierarchical organizational rules sharply contrasted with the preexisting loosely structured lines of control.

After many interviews, the senior managers conceded that without constant encouragement from the foreign investor, they would have treated the logistics regime as a mere formality (*hinh thuc*) and not fundamentally changed their organizational practices. They interacted daily with the foreign investor on professional and social levels. He acted like a cultural intermediary in explaining the logistics regime in a conceptual language that the managers understood. For example, he pointed out deficiencies in the existing organizational system that generated overlap and unnecessary competition and rivalry, and he showed how the imported logistics regime could create more precise lines of accountability that might resolve long-standing power struggles.

Reflecting upon ten years of reform, the senior managers could see profit arising from workplace specializations, clear hierarchical lines of authority, and more precise monitoring of manufacturing processes. Although they could not recall consciously deciding to change their management style, they agreed that the rules-

[67] Interviews with the senior managers of a sporting goods and footwear firm were conducted by the author with the assistance of NH Quang and Associates and research assistants between July 2004 and April 2010 in Hanoi, Vietnam. In total, six senior managers were interviewed three or more times over this period.

based regime had extensively, although not entirely, displaced relational management practices. More significantly, they linked this change to a shift in their identity. The logistics regime gave them a new set of values that reconceptualized their role within the firm. They incrementally changed from being leaders of an extended family to being professional managers.

In tandem with this cognitive shift, the senior managers increasingly acted out the role of modern, cosmopolitan professionals and began to socialize with other global business managers in tennis clubs and on golf ranges. They sent their children to international schools, vacationed overseas, and generally assumed the lifestyle of the expatriate business community. Their new identity not only shaped who they were, but also it influenced how they conceptualized business regulation.

This identity shift was not, however, complete. The senior managers blurred the organizational rules to favor family members. For example, performance standards were subtly adjusted to ensure that family members progressed rapidly through the firm, even though the rules were rigorously enforced for everyone else. Trust and solidarity among close family members subordinated objective rules and hierarchies.

A key difference between this case study and the Intel case study is the role played by the foreign investors. In this case the investor acted like a cultural intermediary and conveyed the tacit knowledge required by the senior managers to imaginatively reconstruct the logistic management regime in order to meet the requirements of Nike as well as the demands placed on them by family members.

CASE STUDY: COPPER-WIRE NETWORKS

During the mid-1980s, four household enterprises formed a transnational business network that now controls approximately 70 percent of the wholesale market for copper wire in northern Vietnam. Members of this distribution network spent the high-socialist period (1954–86) earning a precarious living in the underground economy. They were bound together by decades of business collaboration and intermarriage. Operating out of small shop fronts in Hang Bong Street in central Hanoi, the distribution network now controls warehouses on the city outskirts and employs approximately four hundred family members and staff. Currently, the network links South Korean copper-wire manufacturers with Vietnamese electrical transformer and appliance manufacturers in an intra-Asian TPR. What distinguishes this case from the Intel and footwear case studies is that the flow of regulatory knowledge takes place entirely among East Asian firms.

The Vietnamese distributors formed the TPR to gain a price advantage over competitors. In this industry, the value added in the manufacturing process is relatively low compared to the commodity cost of copper. By sharing market information, the purchase of copper by the wire manufacturers was closely matched to demand by the Vietnamese end users. This collaborative process enabled the members of the TPR not only to minimize inventory costs but also to take advantage of rapid fluctuations in the commodity value of cooper. Rival TPRs that purchased copper wire using contracts were insufficiently flexible to capitalize on short-term price variations.

What gave the copper-wire TPR flexibility was its capacity to coordinate the individual member firms. This regulatory architecture differed from the chains of contracts used by rivals firms, because it created a coordinating entity that existed outside of the member firms, linking them together for mutual benefit. Its chief advantage was to provide a form of multiparty coordination without the hierarchical rules that impeded knowledge flows within contract-based TPRs.

According to the Korean copper-wire manufacturers, who were familiar with intra-Asian and Euro-American TPRs, parties relying on contracts do not work as hard in maintaining close relationships. Faith is placed in the contract to regulate the transaction, a mental construct that distances the transacting parties and reduces knowledge flows. In low-margin production, rapid knowledge flows make the difference between profit and loss.

Members described the copper-wire TPR as following an "Asian business style." By this, they meant that decision making was anchored in sentimental bonds. To cultivate these bonds, members met frequently to discuss business and socialize over dinners, in karaoke bars, and at weddings and funerals. Despite the complexity and value of the transactions (some deals were worth millions of U.S. dollars), sales agreements were only formalized in writing to comply with customs declarations. The underlying transactions were recorded in handwritten notes that captured the basic transactional details without explicit or implicit reference to internal network rules, much less external legal or regulatory systems.

What this network lacked in abstract rules and guidelines, it made up for in a rich body of tacit knowledge. Over several decades, network members developed their own language to coordinate the distribution of copper wire. The members communicated in basic Vietnamese, but many of the terms concerning regulation and technical knowledge were borrowed from Korean, and to a lesser extent English. For example, members used the Vietnamese term *tuong tro lan nhau* to illustrate the mutual assistance that cemented their trading network, *mang luoi* to signify the relational network, and *tinh cam* to describe the sentiment that allowed them to focus on knowledge exchange rather than detecting opportunistic behavior. Korean terms were used to describe the technical specifications of the copper wire and English terms were used for international shipping documents and customs declaration forms.

Over many years, the network developed idiosyncratic routines that became embedded in business practices. For example, a ritual evolved that enabled members to share the risk of commodity price fluctuations. They held a special dinner at a particular Hanoi restaurant to average price fluctuations over the last quarter. Without this ritual, price movements might have destabilized the network. The routines created shared memories and habits that formed part of the tacit knowledge binding the network members. This shared knowledge facilitated the rapid exchange of market information and shaped common approaches to regulatory problems.

The Vietnamese distributors and Korean manufacturers identified closely with the network to define who they were and how they should behave. Unlike the footwear manufacturers, they did not self-consciously assume the identity of cosmopolitan business people and managed to negotiate cultural and regulatory differences using the collective identity provided by the network.

Network members used narratives and tacit routines to responsively regulate the distribution of copper wire. They responded innovatively to rapidly changing market conditions at every stage of the manufacturing and distribution cycle, rather than passively relying on formal organizational procedures or top-down instructions from the head office. By negotiating a plurality of regulatory ideas, the network rapidly absorbed and integrated knowledge flows, giving the members a competitive advantage over rivals.

TRANSNATIONAL NETWORKS AS REGULATORY AGENTS

The case studies advance the discussion by showing how the collaborative regulatory architectures associated with intra-Asian TPRs facilitate the exchange of tacit knowledge and innovative responses to market conditions. In the Intel case study, strict top-down, corporate governance rules discouraged personal connections with SHTP staff. Without close relationships, the Intel and SHTP staff lacked the shared tacit knowledge to come together to reconfigure the CoC to suit Vietnamese conditions. In the process, they missed the innovation that might have flowed from localizing these rules.

The foreign investor in the footwear case study acted like a cultural intermediary in conveying the tacit knowledge required by the senior managers to absorb and integrate the logistics management regime. Without his intercession, the senior managers would have formally complied with the regime without adapting it to enhance their firm's competitiveness. Their close personal connection with the intermediary also reduced the stress associated with switching identities[68] to deal with the cosmopolitan world of international trade and domestic familial relationships. These findings connect to other research showing the pivotal role played by cultural intermediaries in bridging knowledge gaps between firms in East Asian MICs and Euro-American HICs.[69]

68 See Andrew Molinsky, "Cross-Cultural Code-Switching: The Psychological Challenges of Adapting Behavior in Foreign Cultural Interactions," *Academy of Management Review* 32, no. 2 (2007): 622–40; Noriko Yagi and Jill Kleinberg, "Boundary Work: An Interpretive Ethnographic Perspective on Negotiating and Leveraging Cross-Cultural Identity," *Journal of International Business Studies* 42 (2011): 629–53.

69 See Frederic C. Deyo and Richard F. Doner, "Dynamic Flexibility and Sectoral Governance in the Thai Auto Industry: The Enclave Problem," in *Economic Governance and the Challenge of Flexibility in East Asia*, ed. Frederic C. Deyo, Richard F. Doner, and Eric Hershberg (Rowman and Littlefield, 2001), 107–36.

Cross-cultural complexities were largely absent from the copper-wire network. The Vietnamese copper-wire traders and Korean manufacturers came from similar regulatory traditions, were in psychological sync with each other, and drew tacit understandings about appropriate forms of regulation from a plurality of regulatory sources. They did not require a cultural intermediary to bridge their regulatory worlds.

In emphasizing nonhierarchical collaboration, the copper-wire network differed from conventional Euro-American TPRs. Network members were encouraged to look beyond their scripted responsibilities and create new pathways to achieve regulatory objectives. Although lacking a centralized command-and-control organizational structure, the network architecture seemed to unconsciously steer and coordinate the manufacture and distribution of copper wire. Most activities were governed by routines and rituals, but internal tensions and new business problems were resolved through dialogue. Sustained informal discussions made tacit practices explicit, enabling members to reflect on existing practices and propose innovative solutions to new commercial and organizational problems. Dialogue also enabled the communication of tacit assumptions and prevented unspoken, taken-for-granted assumptions (tacit knowledge) from blocking the development of new ideas. It also generated a complementarity of knowledge that promoted interdependence and regulatory stability within the network.

CONCLUSION

This chapter identifies a nexus between intra-Asian TPRs and wealth generation in East Asian MICs. Endogenous factors such as economic policies, education, and domestic institutions scale-up industrial capacities, but intra-Asian TPRs have driven firm innovation and industrial growth in East Asian MICs. This phenomenon raises important questions about the relationship between regulation and wealth creation in MICs. Why have intra-Asian TPRs, rather than Euro-American TPRs, promoted much of the recent growth in East Asian MICs? Is this phenomenon confined to East Asian MICs? How do intra-Asian TPRs influence the domestic regulatory regimes in East Asian MICs?

When comparing intra-Asian and Euro-American TPRs, it is important to recall the overlap and interconnections between these regimes. Nevertheless, despite this interplay, intra-Asian TPRs are generally less vertically and formally structured and more horizontally and relationally ordered than Euro-American networks. A high premium is placed on frequent personal interaction and the collaborative interpretation of knowledge. Governance within intra-Asian TPRs is based on routines that build tacit understandings about the nature of problems and the appropriate regulatory responses. It is this collaborative regulation that promotes innovation and flexible responses to the fragmented and protean East Asian markets. Moreover, the comparatively loose internal structures governing intra-Asian TPRs facilitate knowledge spillovers that build regional capacities in East Asian MICs.

In contrast, the top-down, command-and-control regulation promoted in Euro-American TPRs appears to inhibit innovation in supplier firms located in East Asian MICs. What little research exists in this area suggests that corporate governance rules, intellectual property, and contracts ordering Euro-American TPRs are presented to East Asian firms as immutable laws. Calls by East Asian firms to renegotiate and flexibly apply the rules are interpreted as breaches of good faith or legalized as contractual violations. Command-and-control rules create barriers that constrain the formation of the tightly knit relational connections that communicate tacit knowledge. This not only inhibits collaborative innovation, which requires complementary tacit knowledge, but also it limits the opportunities for East Asian firms to overcome cultural boundaries within the network. Research considered in this chapter suggests the need for cultural intermediaries to bridge the tacit knowledge gap separating Euro-American and East Asian firms.

These findings seem to contradict the law and development trope that business networks need formal rules and corporate governance to handle the complexity generated by increased size and industrial upgrading. This notion evolved in HICs when formal rules were required to standardize Fordist mass-production economies.[70] Research considered in this chapter suggests that formal regulation designed for Fordist production is insufficiency flexible for post-Fordist East Asian markets. The chief regulatory advantage of intra-Asian TPRs is their emphasis on rapid collaborative responses to changing market conditions.

Another question that warrants further research is whether East Asian TPRs can stimulate innovation in non-Asian MICs. For decades, East Asian firms have operated subsidiaries in both HICs and non-Asian MICs. Research shows that these networks take advantage of research and development skills in HICs, but little innovation occurs in non-Asian MICs.[71] Why this is so is less clear. For example, do TPRs function differently outside East Asia? Or do non-Asian MICs lack economic cooperation agreements with East Asian HICs? Or do non-Asian MICs fail to provide sufficient support to domestic firms?

It is also important to consider the interaction between intra-Asian TPRs and the domestic regulatory systems in East Asian MICs. As the case studies reveal, TPRs order the way network members perceive state-based laws.[72] But, more than this, as TPRs drive competiveness and wealth creation, the regulatory models in East Asian MICs seem to have evolved into a supporting role that focuses on the provision of infrastructure, while leaving business decisions increasingly to intra-Asian TPRs. In China, for example, the state adopted a bifurcated approach that retained tight control over industries considered strategic, while liberalizing other sectors to

70 See, generally, Charles Sabel, *Work and Politics* (Cambridge University Press, 1983), 33.

71 See Abo, "Hybridization of Japanese Production Systems in North America."

72 See, generally, John Gillespie, "Exploring the Role of Legitimacy and Identity in Framing Responses to Global Legal Reforms in Socialist Transforming Asia," *Wisconsin International Law Journal* 29, no. 2 (2011): 101–46.

encourage foreign investment and TPR linkages. The state mobilizes resources to enhance the competitiveness of industries in both sectors.[73] Smaller regional countries, such as Vietnam, Thailand, and Indonesia, have relied extensively on Japanese Official Development Assistance and bilateral development assistance programs to harmonize their domestic regulatory structures with intra-Asian TPRs.

Finally, it is pertinent to reflect on what these findings mean for law and development studies. They suggest the need to decenter law and development studies to take into account the regulatory function of intra-Asian TPRs. Global "best practice" regulation developed for Fordist markets may not provide the optimal regulatory environment for post-Fordist markets. Nevertheless, in the long term, reforms designed to increase state and firm accountability and minimize corruption are likely to play a critical role in promoting economic development in MICs. Rather than searching for economic development exclusively in one system, future research might usefully examine the dynamic interaction between these systems. It might investigate the market conditions in which rules-based hierarchies and responsive regulation pay the highest dividends.

[73] See B. Jessop and Ngai-Ling Sum, *Beyond the Regulatory Approach*, 201–6.

PART III

Good Governance and the Rule of Law in Middle-Income Countries

7

Law and Development in Central and Eastern Europe

The Neoliberal Developmental State and Its Problems

Bojan Bugaric

INTRODUCTION

The major part of the regulatory structures in contemporary Central and Eastern Europe (CEE)[1] was built during the age of the Washington Consensus. The term *Washington Consensus* usually refers to a set of policies advocating economic liberalization, privatization, and fiscal austerity, which were initially designed in the 1980s and 1990s by the International Monetary Fund (IMF), the World Bank, and the U.S. Treasury to respond to the economic crisis in Latin America.[2] Later, a similar set of policies was applied to former communist countries in CEE. As we know today, the Washington Consensus had a strong antistatist bias. More attention was paid to courts, judges, property law, and contracts, and less to administrative agencies, civil servants, and regulatory policies needed to implement various developmental policies of the state. The neoliberal ideology[3] underpinning the Washington Consensus was antistatist in the sense that it did not provide much room for the state as a regulator of economic activity. According to the mentality of the time, "the main thing that needed to be done was to get the state out of the way, and somehow everything else would take care of itself."[4] The only role left for the

[1] Among the CEE countries discussed here, the Czech Republic, Estonia, Hungary, Poland, Slovak Republic, and Slovenia belong to HICs, while Bulgaria, Romania, Latvia, and Lithuania belong to MICs.

[2] The term was coined by John Williamson in 1989. John Williamson, "What Washington Means by Policy Reform," in *Latin American Readjustment: How Much Has Happened*, ed. John Williamson (Institute for International Economics, 1989), 7. Subsequently, the term acquired a broader meaning and usually connotes a market fundamentalism or neoliberal agenda. Justin Yifu Lin, "Lessons from Great Recession," in *New Ideas on Development after the Financial Crisis*, ed. Nancy Birdsall and Francis Fukuyama (The John Hopkins University Press, 2011), 57.

[3] Neoliberalism represents the revival of economic liberalism that has been taking place since the late 1970s. Its main premise is that the market is seen as morally and practically superior to government and any form of political control. Andrew Heywood, *Political Ideologies: An Introduction* (Palgrave Macmillan, 2003), 54–5; David Harvey, *A Brief History of Neoliberalism* (Oxford University Press, 2005), 2.

[4] David M. Trubek, "The 'Rule of Law' in Development Assistance: Past, Present, and Future," in *The New Law and Development: A Critical Appraisal*, ed. David M. Trubek and Alvaro Santos (Cambridge University Press, 2006), 85.

state was to protect property rights, enforce contracts, and protect against arbitrary use of governmental power.[5] Apart from that, the market was considered the optimal mechanism for regulating the economic activity. As succinctly argued by David Kennedy, the aim of the legal program of neoliberalism "was not an improved exercise of state power but to disentangle the state from the market and establish more effective restrains on government rent-seeking and public choice bickering. All this was to be done by law."[6]

The neoliberal legal theory was highly formalistic. A great emphasis was placed on formal rules aimed at constraining public authority, on one hand, and at creating "the right rules" for market actors, on the other. The importance of formal rules was so great that the law and development paradigm from the early 1960s was replaced with "the rule of law" model.[7] As Sherman argues, "a central characteristic of this rule of law project was the idea that the formalization of Western-style law in the developing world was sufficient for promoting economic development."[8] Furthermore, according to the rule-of-law model, only one model of the rule of law was appropriate for all countries. This rule-of-law model was comprised of a set of institutions typically found in Anglo-American countries. Therefore, the rule-of-law model was accompanied by a strong belief in the possibility of legal transplantation.[9]

With a major emphasis on property, contracts, and the judiciary, the rule-of-law model almost completely disregarded the importance of public law, that is, the role of regulatory agencies, civil service, and public regulation of markets. It is hardly a surprise then that during the initial stage of the transition public administration reforms were not given the attention they deserved. As Ezra Suleiman argues, "one of the most striking aspects of the transition process in Central and Eastern Europe was the absence of recognition, at least in the essential phase of the transition, that a professional bureaucracy is crucial to both the consolidation of the democratic process and the imperatives of economic development."[10]

It was only during the accession period of European Union (EU) enlargement that reforms of public administration emerged high on the agenda both of the CEE governments and the EU commission. But given the prevalent mentality of the time, even the EU-initiated reforms of public administration could not escape from the dogmatic formalism of neoliberal development experts. Civil service reforms, anti-corruption campaigns, transparency initiatives, and, more recently, creation of new

5 Ibid.

6 David Kennedy, "Law and Development Economics: Toward a New Alliance," paper, Harvard Law School (2008), 29.

7 Trubek, "The 'Rule of Law' in Development Assistance," 86.

8 F. Charles Sherman, "Law and Development Today: The New Developmentalism," *German Law Journal* 10, no. 6 (2009): 1264.

9 Trubek, "The 'Rule of Law' in Development Assistance," 86.

10 Ezra Suleiman, *Dismantling Democratic States* (Princeton University Press, 2003), 287.

developmental agencies were mostly about creating more and more new rules. If the rules did not function, then they were replaced with a new set of rules.

After the crisis of 2008, a new Post Washington Consensus (PWC) is emerging and it is calling for a new role for the "visible hand." According to Francis Fukuyama and Nancy Birdsall, one of the consequences of the crisis is the rise of various new sorts of state intervention (industrial policy) that differ markedly from the old-style strategy of picking winners in East Asia and Japan.[11] Examples of such new forms of state intervention are found in countries like China, Brazil, India, and South Africa. The PWC also builds on ample historical evidence, showing that "today's most advanced economies heavily relied on government intervention to ignite and facilitate their take-off and catch-up process."[12] Alice Amsden, Ha-Joon Chang, Alexander Gershenkron, Robert Wade, and colleagues have shown how various forms of state intervention contributed to the rapid development of Britain before the eighteenth century; Germany, France, and the United States in the nineteenth century; and Nordic countries, Japan, Korea, Taiwan, Singapore, Malaysia, and other East Asian countries in the twentieth century.[13]

According to David Trubek, we are witnessing an emergence of a new type of developmental state, a New Developmental State (NDS).[14] One of the key features of NDS is its ability to foster the process of learning and discovery as the central ingredient for a successful developmental state. As a consequence, the proponents of NDS are critical of the "one-size-fits-all" approach:

> Scholars have pointed out that even if it is necessary to have institutions for certain functions, there are different ways to deal with such functional needs. And they have noted that given the social embeddedness of economic institutions, it is often impossible successfully to "transplant" institutions from one nation to another. They argue that development policy must allow each nation to shape its institutional structure according to its own needs and traditions.[15]

What distinguishes these NDS from the industrial policies of the 1960s and 1970s is their ability to coordinate between public and private actors in order to address coordination problems that discourage private investment in new industries and technologies. Some of the other key elements of NDS are a major role for the state in steering investment; coordinating projects and providing information especially in projects with multiple inputs and long-term payoff; extensive collaboration and

[11] Nancy Birdsall and Francis Fukuyama, "The Post-Washington Consensus," *Foreign Affairs* 49 (March/April 2012): 45–53.

[12] Justin Yifu Lin and Celestin Monga, "Growth Identification and Facilitation," The WB Policy Research Working Paper 5313 (May 2010), 8.

[13] Ibid., 7.

[14] David Trubek, "Developmental States and the Legal Order: Towards a New Political Economy of Development and Law." Paper presented at the Conference on Social Science in the Age of Globalization, National Institute for Advanced Study on Social Science, Fudan University, Shanghai (December 2008).

[15] Ibid., 9.

communication between public and private sectors; a strong interest in exports and relative openness to imports; and direct attention to entrepreneurships, innovation, and new product development.[16] As one of the key features of such new forms of developmental states is experimentation and learning, these new states need more flexibility and less formalism. As emphasized by Robert Wade, many NDSs "have low scores in terms of the formalization of their rules, yet have grown relatively fast over a sustained period."[17] Various authors emphasize that NDSs depend on capable and autonomous bureaucrats, such as those found at the upper levels in China, which are capable of managing and coordinating sophisticated policies. But unlike in the CEE countries, where a legalistic and formal approach to administrative reforms was dominant, the NDS emphasized the state's capacity "to coordinate agents, stabilize their confidence in the states' behavior and establish national development as an urgent overarching project."[18] As the key features of these NDSs, Wade lists evenly balanced power between the state and the business; an activist, public-service oriented mindset of public officials; creation of bifurcated political and economic administrative structures; and an absence of significant discretionary power of budget resources on the side of public officials who are doing the nudging of private firms.[19]

The situation in CEE countries could not be more different. CEE countries face the current economic crisis with regulatory structures and policies that are quite different from the ones of NDSs. Under the strong influence of the Washington Consensus, they developed a distinct type of developmental state, a neoliberal developmental state. Not an oxymoron, this type of developmental state is characterized by excessively formalized regulatory structures, a strong reliance on promarket (neoliberal) economic policies, and an almost complete neglect of autonomous developmental policies. As a consequence, CEE are ill prepared to tackle new challenges described by the PWC. While there is, as a result of the current economic crisis, an increased functional demand for all kinds of new regulatory policies and structures, there are only a few high-quality regulatory structures and policies in place in CEE. Civil service is prone to politicization and corruption; the public sector (e.g., education and health care) is in grave need of modernization and various regulatory bodies; and structures outside the core government (anticorruption commissions, developmental agencies, etc.) lack necessary independence and credibility. And paradoxically, there is still very little demand in these countries for autonomous developmental policies. But "development has never been something that the rich bestowed on the poor but rather something the poor achieved for

16 Ibid., 11.

17 Robert Wade, "After the Crisis: Industrial Policy and the Developmental State in Low-Income Countries," *Global Policy* 1 (May 2010): 157.

18 Ibid.

19 Ibid., 158–9.

themselves."[20] CEE countries are no exception. Without appropriate development structures and policies in place they may well remain geopolitically peripheral, the "unfinished part of Europe."[21]

During the last decade, many CEE countries have made improvements both in terms of economic growth and higher quality institutions. According to the latest World Bank data, Slovenia, the Czech Republic, Hungary, Poland, Slovakia, Croatia, and Estonia are now all high-income countries (HICs) by World Bank standards, and with the exception of Slovenia (23,610 gross national income [GNI]), all in the 12,480 to 18,500 GNI per capita range.[22] Similarly, these countries outperform CEE middle-income countries (MICs) on good governance indicators such as the rule of law, government effectiveness, and regulatory quality.[23] As far as rule of law is concerned, Estonia, Slovenia, Czech Republic, and Hungary are the top performers among CEE. However, if we compare the same indicators over the last twelve years for the same group of countries, we find only small improvements or no improvements at all. The latest Nations in Transit 2012 Freedom House Report "Fragile Frontier: Democracy's Growing Vulnerability in Central and Southeastern Europe"[24] shows a clear backsliding in key governance institutions across the region. Six out of ten EU member states in the region (Hungary, Bulgaria, the Czech Republic, Lithuania, Romania, and Slovakia) have experienced net declines over the past five years. As far as other MICs in the region are concerned, the Nations in Transit Report documents "an antidemocratic trend," a "democratic decline," "which raises real doubts about the prospects for widening the circle of democratic states in Europe."[25]

Despite much enthusiasm since they had joined the EU, which led serious thinkers to declare that while CEE may not look exactly like the old member states, they nonetheless belong to the same broad category of democratic and liberal states, the picture of CEE today is not so rosy. As a leading economic historian, Ivan Berend, observes: "Looking back to the last two centuries, the picture is rather depressing. In relative terms, comparing to Western Europe, Central and Eastern Europe is far behind its 1820 relative level, and could not reach the 1870 relative level either."[26]

20 Birdsall and Fukuyama, "The Post-Washington Consensus," 53.

21 Ivan Berend, "Central and Eastern Europe in the Word Economy: Past and Prospects," 1 *Development and Finance* (2011): 2.

22 See http://data.worldbank.org/about/country-classifications.

23 The World Bank, Worldwide Governance Indicators, available at http://info.worldbank.org/governance/wgi/index.asp.

24 Freedom House: Nations in Transit 2012: *Fragile Frontier: Democracy's Growing Vulnerability in Central and Southeastern Europe*, available at http://www.freedomhouse.org/report/nations-transit/nations-transit-2012.

25 Ibid.

26 Berend, "Central and Eastern Europe in the World Economy," 1.

Furthermore, if CEE countries continue to grow twice as fast as Western European countries, they would need at least half of the twenty-first century to catch up with the West.[27] If CEE economies are almost half a century behind the West, what conclusions can be drawn about the quality of their legal and political institutions?

According to the New Institutional Economics (NIE), an influential economic theory, institutions are a key variable that distinguishes between successful and failed development.[28] Under the influence of such thinking, the IMF and the World Bank substituted the market-oriented Washington Consensus with a good governance regime that sees the poor quality of institutions as the root cause of economic problems in developing countries.[29] Interestingly, although the good governance approach attributes high importance to institutions, its theory about "proper" institutions is not so different from its predecessor, the Washington Consensus.[30] According to the good governance approach, it is mostly institutions that maximize market freedom and most strongly protect private property rights, which are the best for economic development. One of the leading developmental economists, Ha-Joon Chang, criticizes this approach as assuming that the causality runs from institutions to economic development and neglecting the other direction, where economic development creates better institutions. As he argues, there is substantial historical evidence showing that the causality may be stronger in the latter direction: "Today's rich countries acquired most of the institutions that today's dominant view considers to be prerequisites of economic development after, not before, their economic development – democracy, modern bureaucracy, IPRs [Intellectual Property Rights], limited liability, bankruptcy law, banking, the central bank, securities regulation, and so on."[31]

Chang's arguments have two important implications for the development theory. First, if Chang is right about the causality, then developing countries would be better off to invest financial and human resources in policies that "more directly stimulate economic development – be they educational expenditure, infrastructural investments, or industrial subsidies – especially when they also indirectly promote institutional development, which can then further promote economic development."[32] Instead of trying to copy the institutions from developed countries, they should

[27] Ibid.

[28] Ha-Joon Chang, "Institutions and Economic Development: Theory, Policy and History," *Journal of Institutional Economics* 7, no. 4 (2011): 473.

[29] Ibid.

[30] Julio Faundez, "Rule of Law or Washington Consensus: The Evolution of the World Banks' Approach to Legal and Judicial Reform," in *Law in the Pursuit of Development*, ed. Amanda Perry-Kesaris (Routledge, 2010), 180–201; Tor Krever, "The Legal Turn in Late Development Theory: The Rule of Law and the World Bank's Development Model," *The Harvard Journal of International Law* 52, no. 1 (Winter 2011): 302, 305.

[31] Chang, "Institutions and Economic Development," 476.

[32] Ibid., 477.

develop their own development policy, which should be more directly oriented toward economic development and growth. Otherwise, as Chang argues, they may end up with institutions that are more developed than what their standards of material development would strictly demand, which further complicates their attempt to identify the exact relationship between institutions and development. Second, the good governance approach strongly advocates the so-called Global Standard Institutions, which are typically found in Anglo-American countries, and are said to maximize market freedom and protect private property most strongly. Chang criticizes this view as too simplistic and historically inaccurate. For example, during the Golden Age of Capitalism (1945–70), many rich countries adopted various forms of regulated capitalism and grew three to four times faster than during the period of classical liberalism (1820–1914) and twice as fast as than during the neoliberal period (1980–2009).[33] Moreover, the relationship between institutions and economic development changes over time. What might be good for one country in a certain period is not necessarily good for another country facing different circumstances. When developing countries fail to reach expected results, they are usually told to change the institutions instead of changing the policies that might not be appropriate for them. The latter course was usually not taken by developing countries because the straitjacket of neoliberal theory, undergirded by conditionality of financial support and loans offered to those countries, did not allow deviations from a seemingly universal applicability of various policy measures such as deregulation, privatization, or liberalization.

In the following section, I describe the origins of neoliberal developmental states in CEE. I start with the outline of administrative reforms during the age of the Washington Consensus and examine how the neoliberal legal policies and theories affected the administrative structures built in that period. I show that under the influence of the neoliberal "rule of law" model, CEE developed a distinctive neoliberal developmental state. During the early stage of administrative reforms, they followed a one-size-fits-all approach and hastened to transplant various Western-style administrative structures without paying sufficient attention to social context and disregarding the policy relevance of such rules. I use the example of civil service reforms because they were at the epicenter of the first stage of administrative reforms.

I then discuss the EU-inspired innovation development policies, which gradually emerged as a major albeit truncated version of developmental policy in CEE. Again, the inadequacy of the administrative structures built during the early stage of transition turned out to be one of the key inhibiting factors that prevented these new development policies from succeeding. However, as the Strategy for Poland, the only alternative development strategy to the Washington Consensus in the region shows, selection of adequate economic policies is as important as the creation of adequate legal and political institutions. Poland achieved remarkable economic

[33] Ibid., 484.

results with institutions considered to be inadequate by actors like the EU, the World Bank, and IMF. I conclude with general observations about the importance of CEE examples for development policies of other MICs in the region.

BUILDING NEOLIBERAL STATES IN CENTRAL AND EASTERN EUROPE

Reforms of national administration in CEE countries were not a key policy priority during the initial stage of the transition. Given the antistatist bias prevalent among the reformers of that time, this is not surprising. It is only during the accession negotiations with the EU that administrative reforms became an important item on the policy agenda of the CEE governments. More precisely, with very few exceptions, most of the governments started with various reforms of public administration only in the second half of the 1990s. Before that period, the neoliberal development experts were more interested in dismantling prior communist state structures than in building new ones.

As one early study on the transition reports, the neoliberal experts deliberately weakened potential agents of industrial restructuring in the region. For example, in Poland and Hungary, the World Bank explicitly required respective governments to disempower the ministries of industry, responsible for development and industrial policy, while providing both technical and financial assistance to ministries of privatization, which became the most effective government bureaucracies in the region. In Poland, the ministry of privatization had a special status within the government and was exempt from ceilings on civil service pay scales, which enabled it to attract the most capable staff members.[34] Next, the World Bank imposed a de facto ban on development banking. The Polish Development Bank's autonomy to lend directly to industry was limited by the World Bank's loan conditions. The theory behind such institutional destruction was the "do nothing policy," based on the idea that once proper institutions for the market economy had emerged, the markets would do the rest of the job. Instead of pursuing their own industrial or developmental policy, CEE countries invested heavily in various structural reforms, another term used by the Washington Consensus ideology, which amounted to deindustrialization rather than reindustrialization.

The EU-initiated accession negotiations with the candidate countries of CEE brought important modifications to the previous neoliberal antistatist policy. Because a vast part of the EU administration depends on indirect administration carried out by member states, it is unsurprising that the commission decided to scrutinize the administrative capacity of the CEE's national administrations to apply the "acquis." As A. J. G. Verheijen observes, "too wide a divergence in administrative capacities between member states to transpose and efficiently implement EU

[34] Alice H. Amsden, Jacek Kochanowicz, and Lance Taylor, *The Market Meets Its Match: Restructuring the Economies of Eastern Europe* (Harvard University Press, 1994), 119.

legislation could lead to serious distortions in the functioning of the Internal Market."[35]

Example: Civil Service Reforms

The EU Commission strongly insisted on the adoption of civil service legislation as a start for administrative reforms.[36] Adoption of civil service legislation, coupled with some additional measures such as the development of a training system, adequate policy development and policy-coordination capacities, became almost synonymous with administrative reform. While the adoption of civil service legislation was carefully scrutinized by the commission, other aspects played a less prominent role. Adoption of civil service laws was too often understood not as a first step in administrative reform but as an end in itself. The legalistic nature of civil service reforms can be explained by the insistence of the commission on adoption of civil service laws and by the prevailing legalistic tradition in CEE countries. As one of the principal Support for Improvement in Governance and Management in Accession Countries (SIGMA) advisors argued, their "approach to public administration reform has been basically and necessarily a legal approach because the change required from candidate countries by the EU is mainly about changing the rules of the game and building a new legal order for public administration that is compatible with EU membership aspirations."[37]

SIGMA[38] and the commission, sometimes implicitly, sometimes explicitly, promoted requirements for the adoption of the classical Weberian model of centralized hierarchy, with the emphasis on formalization of civil service management and the minimization of managerial discretion, which are needed to strengthen the principles of legality, professionalism, impartiality, and depoliticization.[39] The Weberian model comes close to the continental Rechtsstaat tradition of public administration with its roots in Max Weber's ideal type of rational/legal bureaucracy.[40]

35 A. J. G. Verheijen, "Administrative Capacity Development: A Race against Time?," WRR Working Documents, W 107, The Hague (2000), 15.

36 This section uses an updated version of parts of my earlier work. See Bojan Bugaric, "The Europeanization of National Administrations in Central and Eastern Europe: Creating Formal Structures without Substance?," in *Apres Enlargement: Legal and Political Responses in Central and Eastern Europe*, ed. Wojciech Sadurski, Jacques Ziller, and Karoline Zurek (European University Institute, Robert Schuman Centre for Advances Studies, 2006), 201–29.

37 Francisco Cardona, "Introducing the Rule of Law in Civil Service and Public Administration Reform: The Case of the EU Eastern Enlargement." Paper presented at conference on Reforming Public Administration through Functional Reviews, Sarajevo (May 5, 2004), 7.

38 SIGMA is an OECD unit principally sponsored by the EU.

39 Jan-Hinrik Meyer Sahling, "The Durability of EU Civil Service Policy in Central and Eastern Europe after Accession," *Governance* 24, no. 2 (2011): 240.

40 Christopher Pollitt and Geert Bouckaert, *Public Management Reform: A Comparative Analysis* (Oxford University Press, 2000), 59.

There was not much discussion of the New Public Management (NPM) model,[41] the most influential model for civil service reforms in Western Europe at that time, or of other models of development. Because the strong communist legacy of overt politicization of public administration was still alive in most of the CEE countries, one can understand why the commission and SIGMA sincerely believed that depoliticization and establishment of professional and neutral public administration should become a priority in administrative reforms in CEE. However, it is a little more difficult to understand why such a reform should preclude any borrowing from the NPM or other alternative models. As a consequence of the commission's insistence, most of the CEE countries hurried with the adoption of civil service laws. While before 1997 only Hungary, Poland, Latvia, Estonia, and Lithuania had passed civil service legislation, in the period from 1997 to 2002, all other CEE countries had done so. The Slovak law from 2001 "was a formality designed to satisfy the European Union."[42]

The strong insistence of the commission and SIGMA on the classical Weberian model limited the range of policy options available to CEE countries. One of the false dilemmas the CEE countries confronted was a choice between the classical Weberian model of bureaucracy and the more flexible model of civil service, favored by the NPM writers. The head of SIGMA argued that CEEs should first establish a classic Weberian model of public administration. He strongly urged the CEE not to experiment with NPM solutions, because too much NPM could lead to unpredictability and corruption. Such a preference for the classical, Weberian model of public administration, coupled with an overreliance on law and legislation, produced a distinctive "legalistic" approach to administrative reforms, where passing civil service laws became almost identical to administrative reform. As Verheijen critically argues, "the adoption of laws was considered the panacea for addressing problems such a politicisation, fragmentation and instability."[43]

The preaccession civil service systems in CEE suffered from some common problems and dysfunctions. These systems were plagued by a strong politicization of civil service; an absence of a culture of political neutrality; a lack of mobility in civil service personnel policy; decentralization and fragmentation of personnel and pay policy; the lack of a central agency responsible for the recruitment and dismissal of civil servants; poorly paid staff; and last but not least, a poor image of the civil service. Verheijen argues that adoption of civil service laws "has not resolved the problems of instability and politicisation and has rarely led to the development of a

41 The NPM usually refers to a broad set of programs that sought to introduce more managerial discretion, competition and flexibility into the "old" Weberian model of public administration.

42 Conor O'Dwyer, "Civilizing the State Bureaucracy: The Unfulfilled Promise of Public Administration Reform in Poland, Slovakia, and the Czech Republic (1990–2000)," Institute of Slavic, East European, and Eurasian Studies, Berkeley Program in Soviet and Post-Soviet Studies, University of Berkeley, California, paper (2002), 31.

43 A. J. G. Verheijen, "Public Administration in Post-Communist States," in *Handbook of Public Administration* ed. B. Guy Peters and Jon Pierre (Sage Publications, 2003), 491.

well-working system of long-term career development."[44] A World Bank study also reports about "a mixed picture of overall setbacks, especially since accession with some promising innovations, particularly in the Baltic States."[45] One of the setbacks has to do with the return of politicization. The study reports that "the very idea of an impartial and professional civil service, based on merit and continuity, appears to have lost its appeal to the political leadership of most of the new Member States."[46]

Quite paradoxically, few years after the accession, the politicization of civil service in Poland, Hungary, Slovenia, and Slovakia has reached a critical point, leading Adam Michnik to declare the Polish civil service corrupt.[47] Jan-Hinrik Meyer Sahling argues that Slovakia, the Czech Republic, Poland, and Slovenia are cases of postaccession reform reversal. Hungary is a case of reform reorientation. Only the three Baltic states continued with professionalization and depoliticization of civil service.[48]

The Polish, Hungarian, and Slovenian governments amended their civil service laws to allow more political appointments in the civil service. A major reform of civil service law in 2006 in Poland abolished civil service office and redefined senior civil service jobs such as directors general, directors of departments, and deputy directors of departments as political appointees. As a consequence, the entire civil service was under the direct control of the prime minister's office and special civil service examinations were abolished so that politically loyal but unqualified newcomers could replace existing civil servants.[49] The Polish government replaced hundreds of board members of state enterprises with their friends and cronies. Interestingly enough, new public management ideas did not influence Polish policy makers. The reforms were justified as part of the anticorruption crusade of the Kaczynski government of that time.

In Slovenia, politicization reaches downward toward nonmanagerial ranks in the civil service. Slovenia also passed a new Salary Act with the aim at centralizing and rationalizing the pay system in the public sector. The Salary Act is so rigid and formal that it leaves almost no discretion to heads of units and organizations for flexible pay policy. A recent Organisation for Economic Co-operation and Development study recommends a substantial reform of the act, criticizing the excessive rigidity and formalization of the entire pay system.[50]

44 Ibid.

45 The World Bank, "EU-8 Administrative Capacity in the New Member States: The Limits of Innovation?," Poverty Reduction and Economic Management Unit, Europe and Central Asia, Report Number: 36930-GLB (2006), 50.

46 Ibid., 10.

47 Adam Michnik, "The Polish Witch-hunt," *The New York Review of Books*, June 28, 2007.

48 Meyer Sahling, "The Durability of EU Civil Service Policy in Central and Eastern Europe after Accession," 231.

49 Ibid., 243.

50 OECD Public Governance Reviews, Slovenia, Review of the Public Sector Salary System (September 2011).

According to the first comparative study of politicization of senior civil service, Slovenia belongs to a group of countries with the highest score on politicization. The most politicized senior civil service is in Slovakia and Poland, followed by Hungary, the Czech Republic, and Slovenia. The lowest scores belong to the Baltic states, Estonia, Lithuania, and Latvia, which have the least politicized senior civil service.[51]

Hungary, in the 1990s the frontrunner in civil service reforms, continued with further politicization of senior civil service positions as well as human resource management responsibilities. Interestingly, the Gyurcsany government amended the civil service law in 2007 with a reformist program heavily influenced by new public management thinking.[52] A new government personnel center was established with the idea of improving the quality, competitiveness, and transparency of personnel policy. Moreover, the new competence-based evaluation system and modernized performance-related pay system were introduced. A new performance-related pay system allows an annual bonus of six monthly salaries as a reward for outstanding performance. The system has implementation problems also due to major resentment among civil servants. Given the unstable political situation in Hungary after March 2008 and with the new Orban government, it is unclear whether and how these reforms will be implemented.

Slovakia passed a major amendment to its civil service law in 2003 deregulating the salary system and introducing a highly discretionary bonus system. Furthermore, with another major amendment in 2006, Slovakia abolished the Civil Service Office and transferred civil service management authority to the Ministry of Labor and the Government Office. Slovakia politicized the rank of head of Service Office, the highest civil servant, and removed the job protection for directors general and other senior civil servants. Like in Hungary, a combination of more discretionary salary and performance systems with dismantling of job protection of senior civil servants in both countries led to increased politicization of civil service.[53]

On the other side of the spectrum we find the Baltic countries that have the least politicized senior civil service in the region. In Latvia, even the secretary of the state at the top of the civil service is subject to very limited political control. Latvia, known for introducing management contracts allowing ministers to negotiate salary deals with their officials, further modernized the salary system and introduced a performance-related pay system, thus strengthening the managerial discretion in the salary system. A similarly depoliticized, professionalized, and managerial performance pay system was introduced in Lithuania. Estonia's civil service, according to Meyer Sahling, "stands out with low levels of politicization and a well-entrenched

[51] Jan-Hinrik Meyer Sahling and Tim Veen, "Governing the Post-Communist State: Government Alteration and Senior Civil Service Politicization in Central and Eastern Europe," *East European Politics* 8, no. 2 (2012): 10–11.

[52] Meyer Sahling, "The Durability of EU Civil Service Policy in Central and Eastern Europe after Accession," 247.

[53] Ibid., 242.

ethos of professionalism."[54] The Baltic states, particularly Estonia, were heavily influenced by the Swedish and Finnish model of public administration. One of the key differences between the Scandinavian and other continental European models of public administration is a greater degree of flexibility and managerialism in the first group.

CEE countries, with the exception of Baltic states, adopted the wrong strategy of administrative reforms. With an overreliance on legislation, buttressed by a strong legalistic tradition already present there, CEE sought to adopt new civil service laws first, and reform people later. As Verheijen argued, first they should have designed appropriate strategic approaches, invested more in training and education, and devoted more time to tackle structural problems. For example, to tackle the problem of overt politicization with almost exclusive focus on legislative aspect of reforms is not a good strategy: "designing and adopting civil service legislation without attacking the root causes of the problems in the administration first has proved to be a highly inadequate reform strategy."[55]

Depoliticization of the civil service is an immensely difficult task. Most developed democracies in the West spent decades building a political culture of neutral and apolitical public administration. On the contrary, as Meyer Sahling shows, the political parties in the region were locked in the spiraling process of the continuous politicization of civil service, in which each newly elected government suspended or radically modified the administrative reforms of its predecessor.[56] In such a climate of heightened political distrust among the key political actors, it is nearly impossible to agree and even more difficult to implement any serious administrative reform. Administrative reforms in developed democracies are usually piecemeal and take several years to develop. They require the strong support of all major political forces. Without changing training and education systems first, it is very naive to believe that passing a new law would solve the problem by itself. Yet, in all CEE we can discern almost a fetishist focus on the production of new legislation that was often dissociated from its own implementation. Such processes often degenerated into "symbolic politics" resulting in adoption of laws that cannot be enforced.

Institution Building and/or Development Policies: The Polish Alternative?

As the example of civil service reforms shows, CEE, with the Baltic exception, still lack a competent and professional bureaucracy that is sufficiently capable and autonomous from political patronage. And yet, "promoting effective public sectors is one of the most daunting development challenges that the world faces."[57] Such a

[54] Ibid., 248.

[55] Verheijen, "Public Administration in Post-Communist States," 496.

[56] Jan-Hinrik Meyer-Sahling, "Civil Service Reform in Post-Communist Europe: The Bumpy Road to Depoliticisation," *West European Politics* 27, no. 1 (2004): 98.

[57] Birdsall and Fukuyama, "The Post-Washington Consensus," 51.

bureaucracy is a prerequisite urgently needed in a country contemplating any use of newer forms of industrial policy. Many Asian countries like Japan, Korea, or China relied on a long tradition of strong professional bureaucracy. Heavily influenced by the private rule-of-law formalism of neoliberal theory[58] and rigid Weberianism of EU policy makers,[59] CEE created institutions that, compared to the West, are "more formal, more constraining of public authority over the economy, less open to institutional variation and less well embedded in the local institutional, social and economic context."[60] As in private rule-of-law formalism, the focus shifted from public to private law, law then emerged primarily as a limit on the state – on the discretion of administrators and the mandate of legislation.[61] As Kennedy argues, "the goal was less to ensure that state functionaries understood the needs of national development, than that both public and private experts understand the needs of (largely foreign) capital and are able to formulate rules to 'open markets' and encourage its arrival."[62]

Quite paradoxically, as CEE focused on formalistic rules aimed at limiting discretion and undue political influence over bureaucracy, they ended up with civil service structures that are neither sufficiently competent nor autonomous from political pressure.

Civil service is not the only example showing such results. A very similar pattern can be found in other areas of institutional reforms in CEE such as anticorruption campaigns, transparency legislation, and creation of new developmental agencies.[63] The excessive focus on rules and legislation, disassociated from policy goals and social context, has largely contributed to the creation of such "formal structures without substance": that is, institutions that look similar to its Western-style counterparts, but fail to produce expected results.[64]

As Trubek[65] and Kennedy[66] argue, different theories about law and development are always embedded in different theories of political economy, which in turn means that law is embedded in different development policies. Hence, neoliberal developmental states and their legal institutions were embedded in various forms of

[58] Kennedy, "Law and Development Economics," 27.

[59] See example of civil service reforms.

[60] Kennedy, "Law and Development," 29.

[61] Ibid., 30.

[62] Ibid.

[63] Agnes Batory, "Why Do Anti-Corruption Laws Fail in Central Eastern Europe? A Target Compliance Perspective," *Regulation & Governance* 6 (2012): 66; Antoaneta Dimitrova, "Institutionalization of Imported Rules in the European Union's New Member States: Bringing Politics Back in the Research Agenda," EUI Working Papers, RSCAS 2007/37, EUI, Florence (2007), 11–12.

[64] Bojan Bugaric, "The Europeanization of National Administrations in Central and Eastern Europe: Creating Formal Structures without Substance?," in *Apres Enlargement: Legal and Political Responses in Central and Eastern Europe*, ed. Wojciech Sadurski, Jacques Ziller, and Karoline Zurek (European University Institute, Robert Schuman Centre for Advances Studies, 2006), 201–29.

[65] David Trubek, "The Political Economy of the Rule of Law: The Challenge of the New Developmental State," *Hague Journal on the Rule of Law* 1 (2009): 28–32.

[66] Kennedy, "Law and Development," 1–2.

neoliberal capitalism that emerged in CEE. During the first two decades of transition (1989–2009), CEE countries evolved into three distinct types of capitalism.[67] The first two types, present in the Baltic (Estonia, Latvia, and Lithuania) and Visegrad states (the Czech Republic, Poland, Hungary, and Slovakia), represent variations of neoliberal capitalism. Only the third type, found in Slovenia, represents a distinct type of neoliberalism embedded in corporativist institutions and a generous welfare state.[68] A common characteristic of these various neoliberal types of capitalism during the early transition period was almost a total absence of any indigenous developmental policies. A comparative study of industrial policy in the region finds that "[b]asically any government role in industrial development was challenged as a return to former policy practices, and a 'hands-off' pattern of industrial policy seemed to prevail in most CEECs [Central East European Countries]."[69]

Consequently, in the entire region there was very little demand for anything other than neoliberal developmental policies. Parts and pieces of industrial policy could be found in many different forms and variations but they never developed into a more comprehensive, systematic development policy. The only two major exceptions to this neoliberal preemption of alternative development strategies were the Polish "Strategy for Poland" plan in the 1990s and the innovation policies in some CEE countries initiated by the EU structural funds.

The Strategy for Poland was the only development strategy in the region to explicitly reject the doctrine of Washington Consensus. Its major architect was the Polish deputy premier and finance minister at the time, Professor Grzegorz W. Kolodko.[70] From 1994 to 1997, Poland achieved an outstanding economic performance topped by other measures that improved social welfare of Polish citizens. The left-center Polish government combined a pragmatic economic approach that included "heterodox" economic policies running against the neoliberal prescriptions, with gradual improvements in the market economy institutions. Instead of immediately privatizing the entire state sector, Kolodko's government implemented a commercialization of the public sector, which meant that state-owned enterprises were exposed to competitive pressure and subjected to tough budget constraints, similarly to the private sector. By contrast, privatization was "rationalized" in order to help improve the double goal of microeconomic efficiency and maximizing government revenue. In short, "neoliberal doctrinarism

67 Dorothee Bohle and Bela Greskovits, "Neoliberalism, Embedded Neoliberalism and Neocorporativism: Towards Transnational Capitalism in Central-Eastern Europe," *West European Politics* 30, no. 3 (2007): 443.

68 Dorothee Bohle and Bele Greskovits, "Capitalist Diversity in Eastern Europe," *Economic Sociology* 8, no. 2 (March 2007): 5.

69 Adam Torok, "Industrial Policy in the New Member Countries of the European Union: A Survey of Patterns and Initiatives since 1990," *Journal of Industry, Competition and Trade* 7, no. 3 (2007): 256.

70 G. W. Kolodko, "A Two-thirds Rate of Success: Polish Transformation and Economic Development," UNU/WIDER research paper no. 2009/14 (2009), 2.

was abandoned for a pragmatic approach based on economic rationalism."[71] Kolodko's government was also aware of the importance of institutional infrastructure required to make a market economy function.[72] Last but not least, Poland emphasized some things that were usually neglected by the IMF, such as the importance of democratic support for the reforms, which entailed its concern to keep unemployment low, to provide benefits for the unemployed and to adjust pensions for inflation, and also the importance of public dialogue and social partnership with trade unions and business organizations.[73]

According to Kolodko, the Strategy for Poland, together with the Programme of the Reform of Public Finance (2002–3), when he resumed the position of deputy prime minister and finance minister, essentially made Poland a success story among the postcommunist economies. Poland is the only country in the region to almost double its gross domestic product from 1989 to 2010. Nevertheless, as Kowalik shows, the story of Polish economic "success" is not without its own contradictions and problems.[74]

However, according to the new institutional economics, given the low quality of the Polish bureaucracy at the time, such poor-quality institutions could not have led to spectacular economic and social results as achieved in Poland. In order to explain the success of "East European Tiger," we have to return to the critique of NIE as developed by Chang and Fukuyama.

As Chang argues, the choice of appropriate policies, especially when they also indirectly promote institutional development, may be more important for development than the design of institutions as such. As he argues, the causality often runs from economic development and economic policies to institutions. Kolodko, being very much aware of the institutional aspects of development, has contributed a great deal to the theory of systemic change in transition economies[75] as well to unorthodox development economics.[76] Instead of focusing on the neoliberal formalized approach to institutions, Kolodko's government adopted more pragmatic and policy-oriented style of administrative reforms. Special attention was given to the recruitment of qualified people, special programs for teaching and training were established, and special code/regulation on civil service was introduced. Kolodko was doing his best to engage the nonpartisan technocrats and pay them as much as the budget could afford.[77]

[71] Ibid.

[72] Joseph E. Stiglitz, *Globalization and Its Discontent* (W. W. Norton and Company, 2004), 181.

[73] Ibid.

[74] Tadeusz Kowalik, *From Solidarity to Sellout: The Restoration of Capitalism in Poland* (Monthly Review Press, 2012).

[75] G. W. Kolodko, *From Shock to Therapy: Political Economy of Postsocialist Transition* (Oxford University Press, 2000).

[76] G. W. Kolodko, *Truth, Errors, and Lies: Politics and Economics in a Volatile World* (Columbia University Press, 2011).

[77] G. W. Kolodko, e-mail message (July 20, 2012).

This was quite different from other CEEs that were mostly preoccupied with building "ideal" institutions as propagated by the neoliberal "good governance" doctrine. With such "imperfect" institutions, the Polish government pursued pragmatic economic policies that in combination contributed to spectacular economic results. Therefore, the Polish alternative strategy does not show that institutions are not important. What it shows is that "effective institutions have to evolve indigenously, reflecting a country's own political, social, and cultural realities.... Institutions such as the rule of law will rarely work if they are simply copied from abroad; societies must buy into their content."[78] As Fukuyama argues, there are many countries, beginning with China, that have developed rapidly in the absence of "good governance" institutions. But there are also countries like the United States and Britain that made the industrial revolution with governments that were substantially more corrupt and less capable than they are today.[79] What matters most is, first, that institutions are relevant and appropriate for a country's development goals and policies, and second, that institution building is not treated as something prior or separate from formulation of development policies. And, as the Polish case reveals, it is equally important that country has a "right" development policy in the first place. By rejecting the neoliberal orthodoxy of "do-nothing" industrial policy and replacing it with more pragmatic "heterodox" economic policies, Poland achieved better economic results than countries that simply followed the neoliberal advice.

The second major exception to "do-nothing" industrial or development policy in CEE is the innovation policy that was heavily promoted and supported by the EU structural funds starting in 2004.

INNOVATION POLICY AS DEVELOPMENT POLICY

Since 2004, innovation policies in CEE represent the most important form of industrial policy with a much more active role of the state.[80] During the first stage of transition, innovation policy was basically substituted by the Washington Consensus policies of "structural adjustment." The innovation policy proper was not considered important to the neoliberal development experts. Almost all economic capacity building was directed toward macroeconomic issues: "Industrial policy thinking of the early transition governments was characterized by an outspoken liberal approach, leaving structural change entirely to the market."[81]

78 Birdsall and Fukuyama, "The Post-Washington Consensus," 51.

79 Francis Fukuyama, "Do Institutions Really Matter?," blog on *American Interest*, January 23, 2012, available at http://blogs.the-american-interest-com/fukuyama.

80 Rainer Kattel, Erik S. Reinert, and Margit Suurna, "Industrial Restructuring and Innovation Policy in Central and Eastern Europe since 1990," *Working Papers in Technology Governance and Economic Dynamics* 23 (May 2009): 2.

81 Torok, "Industrial Policy in the new Member Countries of the European Union," 255.

Already in the late 1990s, such an approach to industrial policy gradually began to shift to various forms of more horizontal innovation, technology, and regional policies, all representing an EU "implicit" version of industrial policy. All these various policies are part of the EU cohesion policy, which aims to reduce social and economic disparities and is conceptualized as "a partial counterbalance to the natural effects of the internal market by promoting a more balanced distribution of resources and economic development across the EU."[82] The main policy instruments of cohesion policy are the Structural and Cohesion Funds, which account for 40 percent of total EU budget (347 billion euros). During the 2007–13 financial perspective, the innovation policy as a part of a broader set of initiatives known as the "knowledge economy" became one of the key priorities financed through the structural funds.[83]

Most of CEE made extensive use of the EU structural funds to promote their "implicit" industrial policies. For that purpose, most of CEE created special purpose agencies: the Agency for Enterprise Development in Poland (2000), the Slovak Innovation and Energy Agency (2007), the Lithuanian Science Council (2008), the government's technology policy agency, the National Committee for Technological Development (OMFB) in Hungary and several ministerial executive agencies in Slovenia. Due to the requirements of EU law on structural funding requiring regional and local institutions to administer the EU funds, a multilevel, decentralized system of various implementation agencies and other bodies, on the national, regional, and local level was created subsequently. As a more complex, decentralized, and collaborative framework for industrial policy was created, it was clear from the outset that more traditional, top down, statist versions of industrial policy were ruled out in this policy area.

However, as it turned out later, it was precisely this decentralized and fragmented institutional network that caused some major problems in developing successful innovation policies in the region. As one comparative study of innovation policy in the region argues, one of the major problems was caused by "increasing usage of independent agencies in an already weak administrative capacity environment lacking policy skills for networking and long-term planning."[84] As a consequence, while Europeanization of innovation policy has had many positive effects, it has also contributed to "deepening and exasperating the existing problems of networking, clustering and coordination"[85] in CEE regulatory framework. Moreover, "the lack of tradition of partnership and inter-institutional coordination and cooperation between administrative levels on the other hand meant that most positive effects

[82] Neil Nugent, *The Government and Politics of the European Union*, 7th ed. (Palgrave MacMillan, 2010), 339.

[83] Ibid.

[84] Kattel, et al., "Industrial Restructuring and Innovation Policy in Central and Eastern Europe since 1990," 35.

[85] Ibid., 2–3.

of such agencies were not reaped and that they created in some cases more difficulties and problems than they solved."[86] What is particularly interesting is not that such problems existed during the accession period but that they were exacerbated during the current period. The same study reports that "almost all CEE innovation policy implementation problems go back to very weak and disorganized actors, coordination problems are rampant in policy design and innovation."[87] The fragmented policy-making system suffered from acute absence of cooperation and learning between different actors like governments, industry, and research organizations. Creation of multiple independent agencies was one of the key innovation policy problems in CEE.

As different comparative studies on independent agencies show, one of the most difficult tasks is to create agencies that are sufficiently independent but flexible enough (which usually means not too independent) to allow policy coordination.[88] Too much independence, coupled with fragmentation of the number of agencies, could lead to severe coordination problems between the principals (e.g., ministries and development bodies) and agents (e.g., independent agencies), as well as between the agencies. In such a context, it is not clear formal rules that usually help to ameliorate coordination problems, but other factors such as administrative culture, shared policy agenda among the actors, and informal channels of coordination. Most of these informal prerequisites are simply lacking in the CEE context. To make things worse, at the top of the system sits civil service, which also lacks most of the attributes important for policy coordination of the entire framework.

Innovation policies in CEE also suffer from wrong substantive policy choices that are not necessarily related to the previously described problems of policy structures. One of them has to do with a linear understanding of innovation ("from lab to market"), which assumes that there is a growing demand from industry for innovation products resulting from innovation policy: "Innovation is seen as something close to science and invention, and that there is a more or less linear correspondence between scientific discovery and high innovation performance, and that innovations behave like Nokia's mobile phones and thus search for the latter became the holy grail of CEE innovation policy."[89]

It is no surprise then that many of the innovation policies tend to solve the problems that are nonexistent in the industry. While the industry specializes in just few research-intensive and high-skill products, the innovation policies

[86] Ibid., 23.

[87] Ibid., 29.

[88] Christopher Pollitt and Colin Talbot, eds., *Unbundled Government: A Critical Analysis of the Global Trend to Agencies, Quangos and Contractualisation* (Routledge, 2004); Christopher Pollitt, Colin Talbot, Janice Caulfield, and Amanda Smullen, *Agencies: How Governments Do Things through Semi-Autonomous Organizations* (Palgrave Macmillan, 2004).

[89] Kattel, et al., "Industrial Restructuring and Innovation Policy in Central and Eastern Europe since 1990," 25.

concentrate on high-technology sectors, on commercializing university research, technology parks for start-ups, and so forth. Furthermore, the innovation policies are horizontal and less focused on specific sectors or industries, what in turn contributes to high fragmentation of policy measures. Coupled with already fragmented institutional framework, such misguided innovation policies cannot deliver expected results. As a recent EU annual scoreboard revealed, CEE lagged much behind West European countries in innovation policy results.[90]

While the example of innovation policy clearly shows the importance of an adequate institutional framework for a successful developmental policy, it also reveals that creating appropriate institutions is not a separate process from devising appropriate policies. The structure of a neoliberal developmental state, created to promote neoliberal agenda, turned out to be inadequate for "post neoliberal" innovation/development policies. The example is also important because it comes closest to examples of new forms of developmental policies as practiced by NDS. Trubek offers a list of key features of NDS. Among them we can find organized systems for public-private information sharing; cooperative public-private efforts to construct regulatory regimes that foster global competitiveness and domestic efficiency; extensive collaboration and communication between public and private sectors; an emphasis on innovation; and new product development.[91] As he further argues,

> It is impossible to know the right developmental paths in advance, finding these paths requires experimentation, experimentation must involve public-private collaboration, and a successful path must include the appropriate legal and regulatory framework... policy must be flexible enough to permit a variety of efforts and regulatory frameworks must be sufficiently revisable so that the fruits of learning can easily be incorporated.... If we wanted to sum up the NPED [New Political Economy of Development] in a few words, it might be in envisioning development as a process of discovery in which the state seeks to empower the private sector and state and market function best when they are linked in collaborative structures that foster experimentation and revision.[92]

While CEE innovation policies were clearly informed by some general ideas about the importance of education, research and development, and innovation, most of other elements of the new developmental state are missing. Again, like in the example of administrative reforms, CEE reformers subscribed to an unduly formalized approach to institution building, without paying enough attention to other informal features required for such collaborative and decentralized policy framework to deliver expected results.

[90] Jacy Meyer, "Central and Eastern Europe Lag in Innovation," *New York Times*, May 22, 2011.

[91] Trubek, "Developmental States and the Legal Order," 12.

[92] Ibid., 10.

More informal approaches to institution building of regulatory structures are not found only among East Asian countries.[93] They are also found in a diverse group of countries including Brazil, South Africa, and India. One cannot fail to notice a stark difference between an almost obsessive focus on formalization of administrative structures in CEE, and a more informal approach among the new developmental states. One lesson for CEE thus seems to be that these countries should abandon the overly formalistic approach to institution building and replace it with a new approach that understands the rule of law in a more informal, pragmatic, and revisable fashion. This is not to say that the rule of law does not require formalization to a certain degree. My point is that a proper mix of formal and informal rules can be found and designed only through an indigenous process of institution building that allows each nation to design its development policy and institutions according to its own needs and traditions.[94] The ideology of legal transplants, so typical for the age of the Washington Consensus, should be replaced by a new legal approach of experimentation and learning.

The innovation policies in CEE, with all their flaws, represent a truncated and less ambitious version of development policy if compared to a variety of policies practiced by the NDSs around the world. Unlike the NDS, CEE lacks both institutions and polices required for the more sophisticated approach to development. The examples from this article show that while, on the one hand, the new policies represent an important break with the neoliberal development thinking, on the other hand, they still continue to be influenced by a strong residuum of the neoliberal doctrines and policies. There is still very little demand for new autonomous developmental policies in CEE. As the case of innovation policy shows, even when they are in place, they are predominantly a result of the EU initiatives and less home driven. Nevertheless, these examples also show that devising a development strategy has to be done by the developing countries.

CONCLUSION: LESSONS FOR OTHER MIDDLE-INCOME COUNTRIES

The lessons of failures and successes of neoliberal developmental states in CEE are relevant not only for CEE countries but also for other developing countries in the region. In the conclusion, I briefly discuss some of the lessons that might be important for other MICs in the region. While all CEE that are EU member states belong to a category of consolidated democracies, most of the other MICs in the region fall into various categories of semiconsolidated democracies, transitional governments or hybrid regimes, semiconsolidated authoritarian regimes, and

[93] On the importance of "regulatory informalism" in East Asia for postcommunist countries, see Tom Ginsburg, "East Asian Regulatory Informalism: Implications for Post Communist Countries," in *Law and Informal Practices: The Post-Communist Experience*, ed. Denis Galligan and Marina Kurkchiyan (Oxford University Press, 2003).

[94] Trubek, "Developmental States and the Legal Order," 9.

consolidated authoritarian regimes.[95] As such, they will continue to attract intellectual and practical interest of international and domestic actors searching for solutions regarding how best to promote further development of these "nations in transit" toward democracy and the rule of law.

With the emergence of the PWC it has become clear that there is no development without an indigenously created developmental strategy by developing countries. This observation represents a clear shift in the development agenda. A history of law and development in the last four decades shows that such agenda was usually generated in the developed world to be implemented later in the developing world. As the examples of NDS show, successful development agendas have to primarily emerge and grow locally. With the growing importance of countries like China, India, Brazil, and South Africa, the developed world will have to accept the importance of their economic resources as well as their ideas. Ready-made models of legal texts, political institutions, or economic policies will have to be replaced by much more dialogical and contextual debate between the donors and the recipients of developmental aid. The developed world and international institutions will remain important providers and donors of international best practices and financial resources for developing countries, but actual configuration of appropriate development models will have to be done at home, in the periphery. Therefore, MICs in the region would be well advised not to follow the path of CEE countries that, with the exception of Poland, substituted their development strategies with neoliberal "do nothing" industrial policies. The absence of "appropriate" institutions in many MICs should not be an excuse for not trying to create different development strategies. Needless to say, they will vary according to political, social, and economic context of the country in question. As MICs in the region include some of the existing EU members (Lithuania and Latvia) with small and open economies and relatively well-developed institutions modeled upon their Scandinavian neighbors, but also countries with large continental economies, weak political institutions, and rich natural resources (Russia, Kazakhstan, and Azerbaijan), it is clear that development strategies of MICs will have to proceed along quite different developmental paths.

One of the most flawed views of the Washington Consensus was that there is a single set of most appropriate institutions, including the rule of law, which is required for successful development. Such a "one-size-fits-all" model prevailed in the development thinking of the last fourth decades. One of the first leading economists to criticize such approach was Joseph Stiglitz.[96] Roberto Unger developed a powerful legal critique arguing that such identification of institutional conceptions like representative democracy or a market economy with a single set of institutional arrangements represents a theoretically and historically flawed

95 "Freedom House Nations in Transit 2012: Democratization from Central Europe to Eurasia," available at http://www.freedomhouse.org/report/nations-transit/nations-transit-2012.

96 Stiglitz, *Globalization and Its Discontent*, 180–2.

version of "institutional fetishism." Defending his theory of democratic experimentalism, he further argues that "representative democracies, market economies, and free civil societies can assume legal-institutional forms very different from those that have come to prevail in the rich industrial democracies."[97] A more recent work on "varieties of capitalism" confirms that there are substantial differences among institutional forms of rich industrial economies.[98] Institutions like parliamentary democracy, corporate governance, civil service, or judicial review can assume many different forms. Only when we talk about them in highly abstract terms, it appears as if there are core institutional structures like an independent judiciary or accountable government, which any democracy based on the rule of law must assume. But with their further specification, we realize that there are many different forms that such institutional structures can assume. Civil service reforms in CEE offer a good example of such institutional fetishism. CEEs were ill-advised to follow specific models that turned out to be quite inappropriate from them.

As a consequence, the "one-size-fits-all" model of appropriate legal and political institutions has to be replaced with a plurality of different models, each suitable for a particular country or a group of countries. As Gunther Teubner argues, the logic of legal transplants has to be replaced with the idea of legal irritants. The theory of legal transplants wrongly suggests that "after a difficult surgical operation the transferred material will remain identical with itself, playing its old role in the new organism."[99] As he further argues, "[W]hen a foreign rule is imposed on a domestic culture, I submit, something else is happening. It is not transplanted into another organism, rather it works as a fundamental irritation which triggers a whole series of new and unexpected events."[100] Instead of being told to copy legal transplants from the rich industrial economies, MICs should be encouraged to experiment with various forms of institutional configurations most likely to advance and promote their development. CEE, for example, invested too many resources in formal transplantation of various transparency and anticorruption codes, without paying sufficient attention to incentive structures likely to render such codes workable. In countries like Albania, Romania, Bulgaria, or Belarus, it is even less likely that such formal transposition of transparency and anticorruption laws would work. As Agnes Batory suggests[101], policy makers should move from almost exclusive focus on sticks and consider the potential use of carrots. In many situations, rewards for reporting corruption may have a greater effect than penalties.[102]

[97] Roberto Mangabeira Unger, *What Should Legal Analysis Become?* (Verso, 1996), 7.
[98] Peter A. Hall and David Soskice, eds., *Varieties of Capitalism: The Institutional Foundations of Comparative Advantage* (Oxford University Press, 2001).
[99] Gunther Teubner, "Legal Irritants: Good Faith in British Law or How Unifying Law Ends Up in New Divergencies," *Modern Law Review* 61, no. 1 (1998): 12.
[100] Ibid.
[101] Batory, "Why Do Anti-Corruption Laws Fail in Central Eastern Europe?," 79.
[102] Ibid., 78.

More recent literature on industrial policy[103] reminds us that new development policies are by their nature experimentalist and process oriented. Because there is no single set of international best practices, new development policies require both learning and innovation. Such an approach requires a sufficiently capable and politically autonomous bureaucracy to exist. Needless to say, in most of the MICs, with the exception of Baltic states, such a bureaucracy does not yet exist. MICs in the region don't have a tradition of strong technocratic bureaucracy as it exists in the developed world or in China. As Birdsall and Fukuyama argue, countries without such a tradition should be more careful.[104] All these suggest that one of the top priorities for MICs should be promotion of effective public sectors. This will be especially difficult task in countries that have consolidated authoritarian or semiauthoritarian regimes. One of the prerequisites of effective public service is its autonomy and meritocracy. How to create such a bureaucracy in authoritarian regimes that also lack the legacy of a strong technocratic bureaucracy? As Birdsall and Fukuyama explain, "the development of impersonal bureaucracies in the West was the product of a long and painful process, with factors exogenous to the economy (such as the need to mobilize for war) playing a large part in creating state institutions (such as Prussia's famously efficient bureaucracy)."[105]

As Chang argues, today's rich countries acquired most of the institutions that are, according to the dominant view, prerequisite of economic development, after and not before their economic development. In many ways such institutions were rather a result than a cause of their economic development. Alina Mungiu-Pippidi came to almost the same conclusion: "The explanation for the performance of historical achievers is not to be found in their present organization (legislation, political institutions) which should not be viewed as a cause, since it acts for the maintenance, rather than the creation, of good governance."[106] This is particularly important for MICs that should avoid the institutional fetishism as promoted by the advocates of the Washington Consensus. They should invest more in economic policies likely to promote economic development and approach institution building more pragmatically than other HICs from the region did. This is not to argue that institutions are not important but only to reverse the priorities and follow certain elements of the East Asian Model for development as described by Randall Peerenboom.[107] They should initially focus on economic growth and adopt a

[103] Dani Rodrik, "Industrial Policy for the Twenty-First Century," available at www.ksg.harvard.edu/rodrik.

[104] Birdsall and Fukuyama, "The Post-Washington Consensus," 50.

[105] Ibid., 51.

[106] Alina Mungiu-Pippidi, *Becoming Denmark: Understanding Good Governance Historical Achievers*, available at http://www.againstcorruption.eu/uploads/norad/Becoming-Denmark-Historical-Lessons-Learned.pdf.

[107] Randall Peerenboom, "The Political Economy of Rule of Law in Middle-Income Countries: A Comparison of Eastern Europe and China," *UCLA Pacific Basin Law Journal* 28 (2010–11): 70–1.

pragmatic approach to economic reforms, but as the economy grows and wealth is generated, they should invest in human capital and institutions.

As a leading developmental economist argues, adopting such "second best" institutions in developing countries is a much better choice than trying to emulate the best practice institutions. The second-best institutions are those that take into account context-specific market and government failures that cannot be removed in short order. As such, they promise more effective institutional framework conducive for economic development than "best practice" institutions, which are "almost by definition, not contextual and do not take account these complications."[108] Almost the same conclusion is reached by Stephan Haggard and colleagues in their systematic review of the literature dealing with relationship between the rule of law and economic development: "Yet for countries at low levels of development, the types of informal institutions that generated trade in early modern Europe may be more relevant than the complex statute and demanding institutions of the American or current European legal systems."[109]

In trying to get the law right, legal reformers in CEE too often overlooked "that the life of the law, even in the well-appointed homes of the exporters of the rule of law, lies outside official institutions as much as, arguably more than, it does within them."[110] No surprise that "legal systems are among the most difficult and costly governmental systems to construct because they have huge infrastructure needs and require both human and physical capital."[111] The rule-of-law promotion in MICs should therefore follow a different strategy. New institutions in MICs may in the end resemble their Western models. But what is more important is that they actually work well for MICs, even if they look different than their Western counterparts.

[108] Dani Rodrik, "Second-Best Institutions," *American Economic Review: Papers & Proceedings* 98, no. 2 (2008): 100–4.

[109] Stephan Haggard, Andrew MacIntyre, and Lyidia Tiede, "The Rule of Law and Economic Development," *Annual Review of Political Science* 11 (2008): 233.

[110] Martin Krygier, "The Rule of Law and the 'The Three Integrations,'" *Hague Journal on the Rule of Law* 1 (2009): 24.

[111] Francis Fukuyama, "Transitions to the Rule of Law," *Journal of Democracy* 21, no. 1 (2010): 41.

8

Judicial Intervention in Civic-Military Relations

Evidence from Colombia and Mexico

Julio Ríos-Figueroa and Fernanda Gómez-Abán

INTRODUCTION

Middle-income countries (MICs) suffer from state weakness, limited institutional capacity, political and social instability, violence, and organized crime. While these problems are also present in high-income countries (HICs), in MICs they often take center stage and sometimes threaten the very existence and viability of the state. In the words of Douglas North and colleagues,[1] whereas HICs are "open access orders," MICs are "limited access orders" in which the state does not yet have a secure monopoly on violence, and society organizes itself to control violence among the elite factions. A common feature of limited access orders is that political elites divide up control of the economy, each getting some share of the rents. As a consequence, several hurdles arise in the way to developing the institutional capacity that scholarship on MICs has signaled out as crucial for escaping the "Middle Income Trap."[2]

To build the required institutional capacity necessary to leave the trap and take MICs to the next level is challenging. It is no longer sufficient, as in low-income countries (LICs), to just throw people and money into factories: innovation and a more productive use of labor and capital become essential. This is reflected in the advices offered to leave the trap, which come down to maxims such as: "invest more heavily in R&D [research and development]," "specialize on selected growth niches where global excellence can be achieved,"[3] or "create an active industrial policy."[4] In sharp contrast

We are grateful for comments and suggestions from participants in the conference on Law and Development in Middle-Income Countries, University of Chicago School of Law, April 20–1, 2012. In particular, thanks to Dan Brinks, Diane Desierto, Julio Faundez, Tom Ginsburg, Randy Peerenboom, and Jeff Staton. Research for this chapter was done with support from the project "Judges and Politics in Latin America" (CONACYT, México, Ciencia Básica # 8341).

1 Douglas North, John Joseph Wallis, and Barry Weingast, *Violence and Social Orders: A Conceptual Framework for Interpreting Recorded Human History* (Cambridge University Press, 2009).

2 Peter Fallon, Vivian Hon, Zia Qureshi, and Dilip Ratha, "Middle-Income Countries: Development Challenges and Growing Global Role," World Bank Policy Research Working Paper No. 2657 (2001): 3.

3 Yusuf Shahid and Kaouru Nabeshima, "Can Malaysia Escape the Middle Income Trap? A Strategy for Penang," World Bank Policy Research Working Paper, WPS4971 (2009), 3.

4 Eva Paus, "Can Latin America Escape the Middle-Income Trap? Lessons from a Trans-Regional Comparison." LASA Forum, vol. XLIII, no. 2 (2012): 20–1.

to the so-called Washington Consensus, which required a retreat of the state from the economy,[5] policy recommendations for leaving the middle-income trap emphasize direct involvement and participation from the government and state institutions.

However, not any kind of state intervention is desirable. Scholarship on MICs stresses that, for instance, intervention in industrial development requires "strategic, proactive, and coherent government policies for the advancement of social and firm-level capabilities."[6] To create growth niches, investment in R&D should also follow some plan developed between investors and well-formed and farsighted government officials. Similarly, as chapters in this volume show, in the handling of economic and social rights (ESR) cases that involve resource allocation issues and in which the courts cannot provide an effective remedy by themselves, neutral third parties that adopt a "consultative approach" that facilitates debate and negotiation among the interested parties are required. In sum, the question is no longer whether the government should intervene but rather how it should do so.

In this chapter, we go beyond the focus on economic issues in MICs' scholarship and show that for overcoming the middle-income trap, how governmental and state institutions intervene is important not only regarding industrial policy or commercial dispute resolution but also in jurisdictional and balance-of-power issues. In particular, this chapter argues that constitutional courts can contribute to improving the delicate matter of civic-military relations. Constitutional courts provide a forum in which military and civilian perspectives can be mixed under the values and principles of democratic constitutions. Constitutional judges may help strike a democratically accepted balance between the exercise of civilian authority and the legitimate needs of the military in its pursuit of order and national security. The chapter shows that constitutional courts can perform this function under conditions of security crises and emergencies, and that their role becomes even more relevant when the threats to the state come from within its borders.

The empirical focus of the chapter is Latin America, a region with a diverse collection of MICs that nonetheless share a long and troubled history of civic-military relations. Latin American countries also share a wave of institutional innovation since the end of the 1970s, in which recently created constitutional courts are paramount. In particular, the chapter analyzes in detail the changing constitutional jurisprudence on military jurisdiction in the contrasting cases of Colombia and Mexico. In Colombia, constitutional judges since the enactment of the new constitution in 1991 have crafted their decisions on military jurisdiction in such a way that the discussion on the role of the armed forces now revolves around basic constitutional principles and human rights. In contrast, Mexican Supreme Court judges have addressed the topic of military jurisdiction timidly and

5 Patricio Navia and Andrés Velasco, "The Politics of Second Generation Reforms," in *After the Washington Consensus: Restarting Growth and Reform in Latin America*, ed. Pedro Pablo Kuczynski and John Williamson (Institute for International Economics, 2003), 265–304.

6 Paus, "Can Latin America Escape the Middle-Income Trap?," 20.

inconsistently, even after the 1994 constitutional reform that delegated to them important powers of constitutional adjudication. While the constitutional jurisprudence on military jurisdiction is different in Colombia and Mexico, both countries suffer harsh internal security environments that have induced the government to rely on the armed forces to fight the organized crime and to provide security. Conditions have been harsher in Colombia where constitutional judges have taken a more active role.

A reaction from the armed forces is expected when military jurisdiction is limited by, for instance, excluding cases in which civilians or human rights abuses are involved. Like other interest groups – such as religious groups, corporations, trade unions, and the media – the military will attempt to safeguard its own power status by maintaining the political status quo. This is especially the case in Latin America, where military jurisdiction had become almost synonymous with impunity and lack of accountability. Current efforts to reform military justice in Colombia and Mexico allow us to discuss how constitutional jurisprudence can help or hinder bargaining between the civilian government and the military officers. As we discuss in the conclusion, intelligent and sensitive jurisprudence in Colombia has contributed to shaping the preferences of the main actors in this drama, opening new avenues and possibilities for reform. This jurisprudentially created framework for innovative bargaining under democratic principles is absent in Mexico.

The chapter is divided into three parts. The first part discusses the role of military interventions in democratic stability in Latin America. It also discusses how constitutional courts, a novel feature in Latin American constitutions since the transitions to democracy in the second half of the 1970s, can change civic-military relations not only during normal times but also during emergency situations. The second, and main part of the chapter, presents in detail a long-term perspective on the constitutional jurisprudence on military jurisdiction in Colombia (1945–2010) and Mexico (1920–2010). The last part concludes with a brief discussion about the possible causes of the jurisprudential patterns and with an assessment of how such jurisprudence has shaped current military reforms efforts in both countries.

Civic-Military Relations and Instability in Latin America

Latin America suffers from regime and, in general, institutional instability. It can be said that instability has been a hallmark of Latin American politics: although the region comprises fewer than 10 percent of the world's countries, 37 percent of transitions to and from democracy have occurred there. Juan Linz famously pointed to the presidential system of government as the main culprit for this instability. In his view, presidentialism's lack of incentives for coalition formation promote, in multiparty systems, minority governments and conflict between the executive and the legislature as well as legislative "deadlock." According to Linz, lacking a democratic principle or mechanism to solve this situation, such as parliamentarism's vote of no confidence or the call to early elections, deadlocked presidentialisms are prone to military interventions and democratic instability.[7]

Despite the appeal of the Linzian view, José Antonio Cheibub has convincingly argued that "the higher instability of presidential democracies can be entirely attributed to their authoritarian legacy; it has nothing to do with their constitutional structure."[8] According to Cheibub, the instability of presidential democracies is a consequence of their following military dictatorships that leave in place weakened regimes that are prone to military interventions, leading to a spiral of instability.

The spiral of instability results from the impact of authoritarian legacies, and the history of military interventions, on the relation between executives and armed forces during nonauthoritarian times. Latin American executives have long used military forces not only for external defense purposes but also against insurgency, internal conflicts, and organized crime within boundaries. Leaving internal security to the military to address crisis or emergencies during democratic times reinforces its capacity to intervene during other institutional crises, such as a perceived or real "legislative paralysis" or the potential electoral triumph of a political party considered extreme or dangerous by the governing elite.

The last round of authoritarianism and military interventions in the region took place during the Cold War. By 1970 all Latin American countries (with the exception of Colombia, Costa Rica, and Venezuela) were dictatorships, almost all of them led by the military. Things began to change in 1978 with the transition to presidential democracy in the Dominican Republic followed by Ecuador the next year, Peru in 1980, and since then practically all countries in the region. The spiral-of-instability logic suggests that most current presidential democracies should be inherently instable. However, Cheibub argues that this time democracy in the region should be more durable because of the higher income levels at which it is developing and because the military organizations are delegitimized due to the gross abuses perpetrated during the last round of authoritarian regimes.[9] The military is no longer a trustworthy intervening power (at least in some cases).

Figure 8.1 displays differences in armed forces' size, budget (absolute and relative), and legitimacy, in six Latin American countries. Interestingly, while the Brazilian, Colombian, and Mexican armed forces are by far the largest in the region, Chile and Columbia devote a higher share of gross domestic product to their armies. By 2007 less than 30 percent of people had confidence in the military in Argentina and Peru, although the percentage at least doubles for Brazil, Colombia, Chile, and Mexico (see Figure 8.1). The degree of civilian control of the military, the functions performed by the armed forces, and the transparency and accountability of the military's budget also

[7] Juan Linz and Arturo Valenzuela, *The Failure of Presidential Democracy: The Case of Latin America* (The Johns Hopkins University Press, 1994).

[8] José Antonio Cheibub, *Presidentialism, Parliamentarism and Democracy* (Cambridge University Press, 2007), 173.

[9] Ibid., 155.

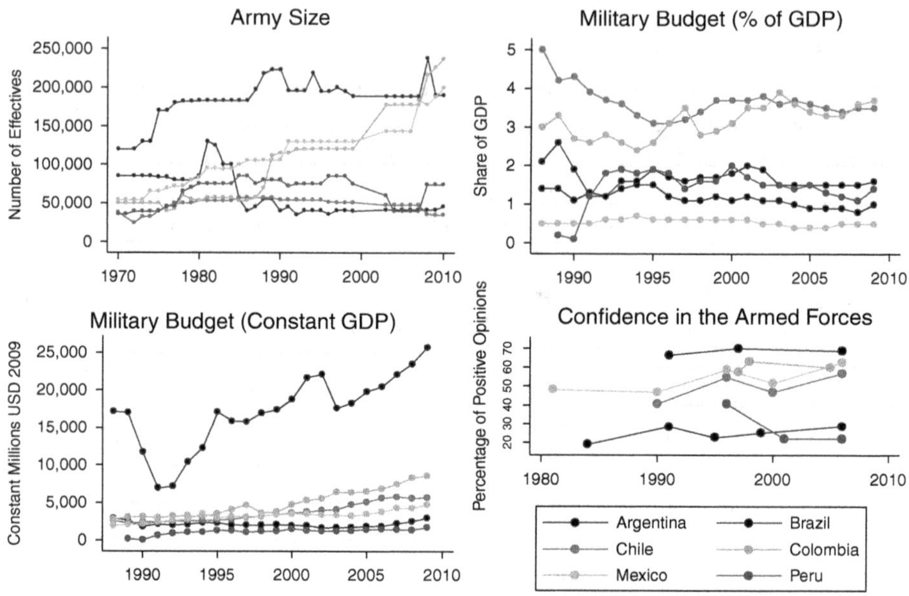

FIGURE 8.1. Armed forces in Latin America (selected countries).
Sources: Army size: The Military Balance, International Institute for Strategic Studies. Budget: SIPRI Military Expenditure Database 2011, available at http://milexdata.sipri.org. Confidence: The World Value Survey (WVS). Confidence in the armed forces reflects only the positive opinion about them, that is, we added the percent of people who approve the military "quite a lot" and "a great deal" (WVS include only four categories for response, the other two are negative).

vary across countries. For instance, while Argentina and Brazil have civilians exercise some ministerial and budgetary control over the military, this is practically absent in Mexico.[10] This diversity is partly explained by electoral competition[11] and by the strength and legitimacy of the military after the transition to democracy.[12]

Despite the differences across countries, the region is still haunted by the specter of a military intervention. In many countries, there is a current expansion of military influence that is hampering the efforts at building institutional capacity, and may actually derail again democratic politics. This fear is more pronounced in the

[10] Arturo Sotomayor, "Los civiles y militares en América Latina: Avances y retrocesos en material de control civil," Revista Mexicana de Política Exterior. No. 83, 2007.

[11] Wendy Hunter, "Continuity or Change: Civic Military Relations in Democratic Argentina, Chile, and Peru," *Political Science Quarterly* 12 (2007): 453–75.

[12] Anthony Pereira, "Virtual Legality: Authoritarian Legacies and the Reform of Military Justice in Brazil, the Southern Cone and Mexico," *Comparative Political Studies* 34 (2001): 555–74; Anthony W. Pereira, "Of Judges and Generals: Security Courts under Authoritarian Regimes in Argentina, Brazil, and Chile," in *Rule by Law: The Politics of Courts under Authoritarian Regimes*, ed. Tom Ginsburg and Tamir Moustafa (Cambridge University Press, 2008), 23–57.

countries that have increasingly turned to the armed forces in their fight against terrorism, drug trafficking, organized crime, and sometimes even regular street policing, such as Brazil, Colombia, Peru, Guatemala, Honduras, and Mexico.

Contemporary Latin American democracies are also different in another aspect that may contribute to build better civic-military relations: the delegation to judges of the power to interpret the constitution. Although judicial review has been present in some countries in the region since the second half of the nineteenth century, in the last three decades there has been a clear regional shift (though not in all countries at the same time) to delegate this authority to judges who were also made independent, at least on paper.[13] Autonomous constitutional courts have been created in some countries, such as Brazil or Colombia. Supreme Courts, or one of its chambers, have been invested with greater constitutional review powers, as in Costa Rica or Mexico. Access to constitutional justice has been broadened considerably in countries like Colombia or Costa Rica. The list of justiciable rights has been expanded in virtually all constitutions of the region. In general, the gist of this institutional change is the incorporation of a new actor, the constitutional judges, with power to breathe new life into new or reformed constitutions across the region.

But how exactly can constitutional judges contribute to generate better civic-military relations, more stable democracies, and greater institutional capacity? Constitutional judges can, and have in some cases, contribute to striking a democratically accepted balance between the exercise of civilian authority and the legitimate needs of the military in its pursuit of national security. Civilian control over the military is not a fact but a process that needs to recognize the specifics of the military organization. As Richard Kohn[14] puts it: "[The] military cannot perform its duty, nor can civilians exercise their authority, unless the machinery of government allows military and civilian perspectives to mix in the formulation of policy." Constitutional courts can be forums in which Kohn's concern is addressed, where military and civilian perspectives in the pursuit of order and security can be mixed, under the principles and values of the constitution. The role that constitutional courts can play in civic-military relationships is even more relevant during critical and emergency situations, especially when threats to the state come from within its borders.

The trade-off between security and liberty is as old as democracy,[15] but how to strike the balance between the two ideals varies considerably across space and time. In particular, there is an interesting debate on the role of the judicial power under emergency and critical situations.[16] Eric Posner and Adrian Vermeule argue that

[13] Julio Rios-Figueroa, "Institutions for Constitutional Justice in Latin America," in *Courts in Latin America*, ed. Gretchen Helmke and Julio Rios-Figueroa (Cambridge University Press, 2011), 27–54.

[14] Richard H. Kohn, "How Democracies Control the Military," *Journal of Democracy* 8 (1997): 140–53.

[15] Adam Przeworski, *Democracy and the Limits of Self Government* (Cambridge University Press, 2010).

[16] This discussion assumes that minimum conditions for exercising judicial power are in place (cfr. Lee Epstein, Jack Knight, and Olga Shvetsova, "The Role of Constitutional Courts in the Establishment of Democratic Systems of Government," *Law & Society Review* 35 [2001]): 362–77.

judicial review in times of emergency "cannot improve matters, because there is no reason to think that courts possessing limited information and limited expertise will choose better security policies than does the government."[17] Rather, the institutional structures that work to the advantage of courts during normal times hamper their effectiveness during emergencies: Courts are "slow, open and rigid," they "lack control over police and the military," and the ability "speak with one voice." The conclusion is clear: "In times of emergency, judges should get out of the government's way because government will choose good emergency policies and even when not, judicial intervention may only make things worse."[18]

Bruce Ackerman, among others, has warned about the dangers of unchecked delegation of power during emergencies: "unless careful precautions are taken, emergency measures have a habit of continuing well beyond their necessity. And governments should not be permitted to run wild even during the emergency – many extreme measures should remain off limits."[19] Posner and Vermeule are aware of the possibility that the government, or other political actors such as the military, can take advantage of emergency situations to advance its own agenda, which they call the "ratchet theory," but they reject it based on U.S. history. They argue that in the United States there are no important ratchet mechanisms that cause repeated wars or emergencies to push civil liberties in one direction in a sustained fashion. They argue that emergencies produce a cyclical pattern in which civil liberties are restricted during emergency and then reinstated, thanks to congressional and judicial independence, political culture, civil society, and federalism.[20]

Posner and Vermeule's assumptions are difficult to meet in Latin American and other MICs (and probably also in other HICs). First, in Latin American history there are many instances in which governments, and other political actors such as the military, act opportunistically to advance their own agenda during emergencies. Second, the history of military interventions and instability weaken the very factors that Posner and Vermeule posit as obstacles to the fulfillment of the ratchet theory, that is, congressional and judicial independence, civil society, and federalism. Third, and most important, in Latin American MICs emergencies and critical situations are frequent, threats to the state often come from within its borders often generated due to the government´s performance, and, for the same reasons, it is rarely the case that an enemy can be clearly identified. This contrasts with Posner and Vermeule's argument in which emergencies are rare, with a clearly identifiable enemy, and in which threats to the state are exogenous.[21] To make an analogy: in Posner and Vermeule's view threats to the state are like viruses that attack

17 Eric Posner and Adrian Vermeule, *Terror in the Balance: Security, Liberty and the Courts* (Oxford University Press, 2007), 12.

18 Ibid.

19 Bruce Ackerman, "Don't Panic: States of Emergency," *London Review of Books* 24 (2002): 15–16.

20 Posner and Vermeule, *Terror in the Balance*.

21 The exception is the U.S. Civil War from 1861 to 1865.

the body, while in Latin America they are more often like autoimmune diseases. The remedy for Latin America is not to leave the government alone and unchecked, but to make it function in a more responsive and inclusive way. Constitutional courts can be of help for this aim.

Even though Posner and Vermeule's arguments do not lead to the conclusion that courts in Latin American and other MICs should "get out of the government's way," it does not follow that any type of judicial intervention is desirable. The point is not whether judges should intervene but rather how they do it.[22] For instance, during emergencies it would not be advisable that every judge may limit the government but only those at the supreme or constitutional court. This would allow for faster and univocal judicial interventions. But the more important contribution that constitutional courts can make is based on what distinguishes these institutions from the other branches of government: to give reasons, weigh in and mix different points of view, and participate and promote public deliberation under the principles and limits of the constitution.[23]

In sum, constructive contributions by constitutional courts in delicate matters such as civil-military relations depend on how they intervene. Constitutional judges can help to recognize different views about the same issue, making congressmen, the executive, and the military better justify and potentially review their policy decisions.[24] In this way, constitutional judges do not merely provide a resolution to a case, they also promote participation and deliberation between all the actors involved in a constitutional problem and smooth relations between them making fine distinctions in complex situations. If a country has capable and prudent constitutional judges who are aware of their special role and value precedents, any departure from or exception to existing arguments is carefully justified,[25] thus clearly contributing to building institutional capacity. Colombia has made substantial progress in these directions while Mexico has not.

[22] cf. Thomas M. Franck, "Political Questions/Judicial Answers: Does the Rule of Law Apply to Foreign Affairs?," in *Comparative Constitutional Law*, ed. Vicki Jackson and Mark Tushnet (Foundation Press, 2006), 352–8.

[23] See, e.g., John Ferejohn and Pasquale Pasquino, "Constitutional Courts as Deliberative Institutions: Towards an Institutional Theory of Constitutional Justice," in *Constitutional Justice, East and West*, ed. Wojciech Saduurski (Kluwer Law International, 2003), 21–36; Martin Shapiro, "The Giving Reasons Requirement," in *On Law, Politics & Judicialization*, ed. Martin Shapiro and Alec Stone Sweet (Oxford University Press, 2002), 228–57; Barry Friedman, "Dialogue and Judicial Review," *Michigan Law Review* 91 (1993): 577–682; Roberto Gargarella, "Un papel renovado para la Corte Suprema. Democracia e interpretación judicial de la constitución," in *Tribunales Constitucionales y Democracia* (SCJN, 2008), 403–28. This is similar to the notion of "policy making," in contrast to "syllogistic," judges developed by Brinks and Forbath's chapter (Chapter 11) in this volume.

[24] cfr. Gargarella, "Un papel renovado para la Corte Suprema"; Friedman, "Dialogue and Judicial Review."

[25] cf. Diego Eduardo López Medina, *El derecho de los jueces* (Legis-Universidad de los Andes, 2009).

Constitutional Jurisprudence on Military Jurisdiction in Colombia and Mexico

Military jurisdiction, *fuero military* in Spanish, has traditionally been justified on the grounds that members of the armed forces require a separate body of law, prosecutors, and courts that take into account the specifics of their job in order to give stability to the institution and legal security to its members. Even though this justification has merit, in places with a history of military interventions, military participation in public security within national borders, and executive dominance, military jurisdiction gave way to impunity and arbitrariness. In particular, military jurisdiction became a blank check for members of the armed forces who committed crimes that had nothing to do with their specialized mission and a vehicle for repressing political opponents. In those places, members of the armed forces and executives got used to a very wide scope of military jurisdiction and usually resist attempts to reduce it, judicially or otherwise.

Military jurisdiction is the specification of who can be judged in military courts, and under what circumstances. Judges interpreting the constitution provide answers to these factual questions in which the interests of civilian governments and the armed forces clash.[26] The question "whom and when can be judged in military courts" can be answered, in general terms, in seven ways that can be ordered from the widest to the narrowest scope of military jurisdiction: (1) military personnel and civilians, under any circumstance; (2) military personnel and civilians, only during emergency situations; (3) only military personnel, under any circumstance; (4) only military personnel, only when crimes were committed during service; (5) only military personnel, only when strictly military crimes are involved; (6) not even military personnel when crimes against humanity and human rights violations are involved; and (7) nobody ever – the military jurisdiction is abolished.

While the extreme situations are theoretical possibilities that do not take place as such in reality, there are actual cases close to those extremes. For instance, Chile under the military regime expanded the scope of the military jurisdiction to include many ordinary crimes.[27] On the other end, Costa Rica abolished military jurisdiction, while France or Germany abolished military jurisdiction within their borders, accepting it only in cases of war abroad or aboard military ships.[28] Notice that among the intermediate categories where only military personnel can appear before military courts there are important differences. Whereas in (3) any type of crime, as long as it was committed by a member of the armed forces, is admitted in military courts, in (4) only service-related crimes are admitted thus limiting not the type of crimes

[26] These zones correspond to what ibid. (p. 154) calls "constitutional scenarios."

[27] Alberto Bovino, "El juzgamiento de civiles," in *Justicia Militar y Estado de Derecho*, ed. Jorge Mera Figueroa (Universidad Diego Portales, 1998), 47–71.

[28] Susana Pedroza de la Llave, "La reinterpretaciónconstitucional del fuero de guerra o militar en el marco del estadodemocrático," *Cuestiones Constitucionales* 25 (2011): 152–98.

WHO? WHEN?	Military Personnel and Civilians Always	Military Personnel and Civilians Emergencies	Military Personnel Always	Military Personnel Service-related crimes	Military Personnel Military crimes only	Nobody Crimes against humanity	Nobody Never
1920–5					35, 36, 43, 44		
1926–30					38, 39, 40, 41, 42		
1931–5			26, 34		33, 37		
1936–40		27	29, 30, 32	22, 24, 25, 28, 31	23		
1941–5		33					
1946–50				21			
1951–5							
1956–60				20			
1961–5			18, 19				
1966–70		30, 31, 32	29 16	17			
1971–5		23, 24, 25, 26, 27, 28		13, 14, 15			
1976–80		19, 21, 22	20	9, 10, 11, 12			
1981–5		18		7, 8			
1986–90		16	17	15 6			
1991–5		14		5			
1996–2000				11, 12 3	10, 13 4		
2001–05				8		2, 3, 4, 5, 6, 7, 9	
2006–10				2	1	1	

FIGURE 8.2. Scope of military jurisdiction in Colombia and Mexico: Who can be judged in military courts, and when?
Note: Numbers refer to court cases cited in the references section. Black numbers correspond to Colombian cases. The dotted arrows refer to jurisprudential tendencies in Colombia. White numbers correspond to Mexican cases. The solid arrows refer to jurisprudential tendencies in Mexico.

but the circumstance under which they take place; and in (5) only military crimes such as cowardice, insubordination, or treason are admitted in military courts.

Figure 8.2 shows a summary of the jurisprudential histories on military jurisdiction in Colombia and Mexico, according to the seven responses to "who can be judged in military courts, and when?" Each number in Figure 8.2 represents a case that is cited (with the same number) in the references section of this chapter. Black numbers refer to Colombian cases ordered from the most recent case on military jurisdiction decided by the constitutional court (number 1), to the oldest case on the same topic in our sample (number 33, decided by the Colombian Supreme Court in the 1940s).[29] White numbers refer to Mexican Supreme Court's so-called jurisprudential theses ordered from the most recent (number 1) to the oldest thesis (number 44 for Mexico, decided by the Mexican Supreme Court in the 1920s).

The arrows in Figure 8.2 show the patterns of constitutional jurisprudence on military jurisdiction in Mexico and Colombia. Consider first the solid arrows in Figure 8.2: they represent the patterns of constitutional jurisprudence on military jurisdiction in Mexico since the 1920s. There are basically two clear patterns. The first in the period from 1920 to 1934, during which the Mexican Supreme Court rather consistently held a quite narrow scope of military jurisdiction. The second in the period from 1940 to 2005 when, again quite consistently, the Mexican Supreme Court defended a wider scope of military jurisdiction. There are also two periods of interesting constitutional debates over the proper scope of military jurisdiction that are

[29] The sample of cases analyzed in this chapter does not include cases on military jurisdiction decided by the Colombian Supreme Court or by the *Consejo de Estado*, the highest administrative court, after 1991 (the year in which the Colombian Constitutional Court was created).

reflected in inconsistent jurisprudence: during the 1930s, which concluded favoring military justice over civilian courts, and the current period (since 2005), which appears to move in favor of civilian courts but a clear pattern has not yet emerged.

Consider now the dotted arrows in Figure 8.2: they represent the patterns of constitutional jurisprudence in Colombia since the 1940s. There are, again, basically two clear patterns. The first in the period from 1945 to 1987 during which the Colombian Supreme Court held a consistently wide constitutional interpretation of military jurisdiction. The second pattern, from 1987 to the present, is marked by an incremental and consistent jurisprudential move toward a narrower interpretation of military jurisprudence. The reminder of this section presents a detailed analysis of these patterns of constitutional jurisprudence on Mexico and Colombia.

Mexico

Article 13 of the Mexican Constitution of 1917 establishes and delimits military jurisdiction. It clearly states that:

> Article 13. . . . The military jurisdiction will deal with military crimes and offenses to the military discipline. The military tribunals never, and for no reason, will extend their jurisdiction to persons that do not belong to the armed forces. When a civilian is involved in a military crime or an offense to the military discipline the case will be decided in the correspondent ordinary court.

It is apparent that the scope of the military jurisdiction is defined very narrowly in the constitution. During the debates of the constituent assembly in 1916 some deputies even proposed to eliminate the military jurisdiction altogether.[30]

When the armed phase of the Mexican Revolution ended in 1920 and some kind of regular politics started to operate under a vigorous multiparty system, cases on military jurisdiction began to arrive at the Mexican Supreme Court. And the Court consistently upheld, in line with Article 13, a narrow scope of military jurisdiction. The Court also clearly stated that when a civilian is implicated in a crime committed with military officials, ". . . the same civil tribunal should decide the case, so that it is not split in two courts" (Mexico Case #42), presumably responding to the litigant's request that the military official should be judged in a military court and the civilian in a civil court.[31]

The Supreme Court's narrow interpretation of the military jurisdiction, in line with Article 13, was upheld until 1933–4 (see Mexico Case #33 and #35–44). That year, General Lázaro Cárdenas became president. Cárdenas and other generals considered that the multiplicity of political forces in place during the 1920s

[30] Manuel González Oropeza, "El fueromilitar en México. La injusticia en las Fuerzas Armadas," in *Estudios en homenaje a Marcia Muñoz de Alba Medrano. Estudios de derecho público y política* (UNAM, 2006), 177–95.

[31] cf. José Ramón Cossío, "El fueromilitar: alcances y limitaciones," *Cuestiones Constitucionales* 22 (2010): 321–62.

threatened the already precarious postrevolutionary regime. To channel this diversity of political forces, the revolutionary leader and former president General Plutarco Elías Calles had pushed for the creation of an umbrella political organization under the name of National Revolutionary Party (PNR, 1929). During the administration of General Lázaro Cárdenas (1934–40), the party successfully integrated the army, the organized workers, and the organized peasants into its structure and changed its name to *Partido de la Revolución Mexicana* (PRM, 1936).[32] Cárdenas also promoted a constitutional reform that changed the number of Supreme Court Judges from sixteen to twenty one, and changed their tenure from life to six years to make it coincide with the presidential administration. A transitory article allowed President Cárdenas to replace the full membership of the Supreme Court. Since then, and until the 1990s, the Supreme Court was successfully incorporated into the dynamics of a hegemonic party regime.

The Supreme Court's jurisprudence on military jurisdiction nicely reflects the loss of judicial independence from the government. The place to start is the code of military justice enacted in 1933 that in its Article 57 not only considerably expands the list of crimes that can be decided in military courts (including, e.g., fraud, robbery, and assault),[33] but also states that military courts have jurisdiction on service-related crimes committed by military personnel. The scope of military jurisdiction defined in Article 57 of the code of military justice is, therefore, manifestly wider than what Article 13 of the constitution stipulates. What did the Mexican Supreme Court do? After resisting a bit in erratic jurisprudence from 1934 to 1940, the Court interpreted the constitution in such a way that made the code constitutional. The Court adapted the constitution to the code, instead of the other way around.

From 1940 until 2009 – when an important dissenting opinion by a Supreme Court judge on military jurisdiction was published – the Mexican Supreme Court basically uphold a criteria based on the identity of the person involved in a crime: if the person belongs to the armed forces then the case belongs to military jurisdiction. The "personal-identity" criterion was somewhat attenuated by sensibly keeping out of military courts some conducts and situations that cannot be considered part of the military service, such as when the officer is on vacation (Mexico Case #11) or when a military officer killed the referee during a soccer game (Mexico Case #12).[34] But in some cases, the Mexican Supreme Court upheld the pure "personal-identity" criterion even in cases of rape of a woman (Mexico Case #13), robbery (Mexico Case #18), or murder of a civilian (Mexico Case #19). The Court explicitly invoked the "personal-identity" criterion as late as of 1991 (Mexico Case #5).

[32] A decade later, when the party took its current name *Partido Revolucionario Institucional* (1946), it had already been established its authority as the single most important political machine in the country.

[33] González Oropeza, "El fueromilitar en México."

[34] See, in general, Mexico Cases #8 to #15 for some restrictions to what is considered "service-related" crimes.

In 1994, the Mexican Supreme Court was empowered with new instruments of constitutional adjudication, and the formal guarantees of judicial independence were strengthened. In 1997, for the first time in decades, the Partido Revolucionario Institutional (PRI) lost a majority in the Chamber of Deputies, and a period of divided government began in Mexico. In 2000, the PRI lost for the first time in seventy-one years the executive power. These changes have had some effects on Mexican Supreme Court decisions.[35] However, regarding military jurisdiction the Court mostly kept a deferential silence, with the exception of some mild restrictions on what is considered military crimes for military jurisdiction (Mexico Cases #2 and #3). During more than a decade after the reform of 1994, the most important decisions of the Mexican Supreme Court regarding military justice were a handful of jurisprudential theses on the autonomy of the military jurisdiction on procedural matters, and a consequential 1996 decision in which the Court upheld the constitutionality of military participation in matters of internal public security.[36]

Things began to change in 2009 when Justice José Ramón Cossío published an important dissenting opinion in a case known as "Reynalda Morales." The case is named after the woman who filed an *amparo* suit against a lower court that granted jurisdiction to a military tribunal over a case related to her husband's death by military officers. The Mexican Supreme Court dismissed the *amparo* arguing that Ms. Morales lacked the "juridical interest" in this case required to file an *amparo* suit. Justice Cossío published a dissenting opinion in which he basically argues for the unconstitutionality of Article 57 of the code of military justice and proposes a radical jurisprudential change on military jurisdiction. The importance of the dissenting opinion lies in the fact of its close resemblance with a recent opinion by the Mexican Supreme Court (Mexico Case #1), where the scope of military jurisdiction is interpreted in very narrow terms (the so-called Radilla Case). Interestingly, on the Radilla Case the Mexican Supreme Court merely issued an opinion agreeing with the holding by the Interamerican Court of Human Rights that pointed to, among other things, the unconstitutionality of Article 57 of the code of military justice.

Whether the opinion by the Mexican Court in the Radilla case will set the tone of future judicial decisions on military jurisdiction, and their impact on civic-military relations, remains to be seen. Apparently, the Supreme Court has decided to continue its construction of a more limited interpretation of military jurisdiction. During the summer of 2012 the Mexican Supreme Court issued a series of decisions

[35] See, e.g., Julio Ríos Figueroa, "Fragmentation of Power and the Emergence of an Effective Judiciary in Mexico, 1994–2002," *Latin American Politics and Society* 49, no. 1 (2007): 31–57.

[36] Miguel Carbonell, "El rol de lasfuerzas armadas en la constitución mexicana," *Iuset Praxis* 8 (2002): 35–51; Pedroza, "La reinterpretaciónconstitucional del fuero de guerra o militar en el marco del estadodemocrático."

upholding and even extending its holding in the Radilla case, arguing that cases of human rights violations do not belong to military courts, and started to delimit the type of crimes that can properly be heard in military courts, as well as the definition a crime committed "during a military service." While human rights groups immediately applauded these decisions, the reaction of both the armed forces and the current government is still unclear.

Colombia

Military jurisdiction in the Colombian Constitution of 1886 was specified in Article 170 that literally says: "Article 170. – Crimes committed by military personnel in active service and related to such service, will be heard in military tribunals according to the prescriptions of the criminal military code." If we compare the text of Article 170 with that of Article 13 of the Mexican constitution it is clear that in Colombia the scope of military jurisdiction was wider from the outset. Figure 8.2 reflects this difference in the opposite starting points of the constitutional jurisprudence in Colombia and Mexico. In Figure 8.2, however, the Colombian jurisprudential line starts in the 1960s not in 1886. Some context is necessary to explain that starting point before we proceed to analyze the Colombian Supreme Court decisions.

The Colombian Constitution of 1886 was in force for more than a hundred years, until 1991, when it was replaced by the current constitution. During this long period the country enjoyed a limited but stable democracy that mostly revolved, in political terms, around two parties: the Conservatives and the Liberals. Since the enactment of the 1886 constitution and until about 1930, Colombia was dominated by successive Conservative governments. From 1930 and until about 1946, the country was ruled by successive Liberal governments. The tensions between these two main political groups led to an undeclared civil war in the second half of the 1940s and the 1950s (called *La Violencia*). This violent period was ended by a brief military government (1953–7) led by General Rojas Pinilla, which facilitated a pact between the two groups that crystalized in a series of constitutional reforms in 1958.

In political terms, the reforms of 1958 sealed the so-called National Front (*Frente Nacional*) of 1958–74: a pact for Conservatives and Liberals to share all positions of power equally for the following sixteen years. Regarding the justice system, the reforms transformed the appointment of Supreme Court judges from a method in which a congressional majority selected one of three candidates proposed by the executive, to a self-appointment, or *co-optation*, method. Interestingly, it was the government of General Rojas Pinilla that appointed the first set of judges to the Supreme Court after the reform of 1958. While the co-optation method of appointment made Supreme Court judges quite independent from the political parties represented in the elected branches, it also made them deferential toward the military. Some critics suggest that the military decided to remove the elected branches from the appointment process because they wanted to prevent a possible trial against them.[37]

The Colombian Supreme Court cases analyzed in this chapter that come from the 1960s actually upheld a quite expansive interpretation of military jurisdiction, previously set by a 1945 decision (Colombia Case #1). The 1945 decision upheld the constitutionality of a presidential decree that allowed for the expedite creation of war tribunals to process military and civilians suspected of having participated in attempted coup d'état against then president López Pumarejo.[38] The Colombian Supreme Court from the second half of the 1960s until 1987 basically upheld that both civilians and military personnel could be judged in military tribunals under emergency situations. In some decisions, the justification for this expansive interpretation is the celerity with which military courts can proceed in times of emergency (Colombia Case #22 and #30). The main problem with this criterion problem is that Colombia during those years practically lived under state of emergency.

During the National Front years three elements emerged that are still part of the Colombian political landscape: guerrillas (such as the Revolutionary Armed Forces of Colombia (*Fuerzas Armadas Revolucionarias de Colombia*) and the National Liberation Army (*Ejército de Liberación Nacional*); illegal drug processing and trafficking; and the paramilitary phenomenon.[39] From the end of the National Front and throughout the 1980s, the country's situation became extremely difficult with the government's declaration of a "war against drugs," the closeness of the Colombian political system, and the power of the drug cartels to produce a spiral of violence and narco-terrorism. To deal with this situation, Colombian presidents constantly declared a "state of exception" (they could do that unilaterally), which not only implied the delegation of legislative powers to the executive but also limited the scope of civil rights and, as we said, expanded the military jurisdiction. Of the forty-two years between 1949 to 1991 Colombia spend thirty five (83 percent of that time) under "state of exception."[40]

The Supreme Court automatically reviewed the constitutionality of the declaration of states of exception, and the decrees issued under them, but very rarely restricted the government. The Supreme Court limited itself to check whether such declarations were procedurally correct. Regarding military jurisdiction, the Supreme Court consistently upheld that both military personnel and civilians could

[37] Rodrigo Uprimny Yepes, "Entre el protagonismo, la precariedad y las amenazas: las paradojas de la judicatura," in *En la encrucijada. Colombia en el Siglo XXI*, ed. Francisco Leal Buitrago (Norma, 2006), 81–111.

[38] Antonio Barreto Rozo, *La generación del estado de sitio. El juicio a la anormalidad institucional en la Asamblea Nacional Constituyente de* 1991 (Universidad de los Andes, 2011), 36–8.

[39] Francisco Gutiérrez Sanin. *¿Lo que el viento se llevó? Los partidos políticos y la democracia en Colombia*, 1958–2002 (Norma, 2007).

[40] Uprimny Yepes, "Entre el protagonismo, la precariedad y las amenazas."

be judged by military tribunals under emergencies[41] (Colombia Case #30-18) Things began to change in 1987 when the Supreme Court issued a historical decision (Colombia Case #17, and also #15) stating that "the judging of civilians by military personnel is more than a simple transfer of competencies, it actually amounts to a substantial alteration of the equilibrium of powers and a radical change of the idea of administration of justice."

One of the motivations of the historical jurisprudential change in 1987 was the death of several members of the Supreme Court and the Council of State in November of 1985 during the assault to the *Palacio de Justicia* perpetrated by the M-19 guerrilla group.[42] The military handled very poorly the response to the assault and many members of the judiciary, and part of the public opinion, considered that the military did not keep in high regard the life of the judges. The attack on the Justice Palace was only one of several tragedies that took place in Colombia during the 1980s, that included the assassination of two ministers of justice, of the owner of a national leading newspaper, of four presidential candidates, and several terrorist attacks to public buildings.

In the difficult political context of the second half of the 1980s, Colombian presidents Virgilio Barco (1986–90) and his successor César Gaviria (1990–4) managed to convene the constituent assembly that produced the Constitution of 1991: a transformative document that opened the political arena to previously marginalized actors, created a complex machinery of checks and balances, and in general brought the government and the state closer to citizens. The Constitution of 1991 also transformed the justice system by creating the constitutional court, granting its judges with guarantees of independence and broad powers of judicial review. Interestingly, one thing that practically did not change in 1991 was the constitutional article that defines the military jurisdiction. The new Article 221 is literally the same as Article 170 of the 1886 Constitution. An important difference, however, is that the new Article 213 states that "in no case civilians can be investigated or judged in the military jurisdiction." The jurisprudential change of 1987, therefore, was constitutionalized in 1991.

It did not take the new Constitutional Court long to begin to interpret the new constitution creatively and expansively. As early as 1992 the Court decided that it was its duty to check the constitutionality not only of the procedural requirements but also of the content of the executive´s declarations of "states of exception." In open contrast with previous jurisprudence on this issue, the constitutional judges adopted a series of decisions establishing that they could evaluate whether the events invoked by the executive actually required the temporary suspension of certain constitutional

[41] See Librado Ariza, "Fuerzas Armadas, justicia penal militar y discurso judicial: entre el garantismo y el eficientismo," in *Derecho Constitucional: Perspectivas Críticas* (Universidad de los Andes/Siglo del Hombre, 1999), 3–38; Gina Cabarcas Maciá, *Militares, política y derecho. Sobre los silencios de la constituyente de* 1991 (Universidad de los Andes, 2011); Barreto Rozo, *La generación del estado de sitio.*

[42] Barreto Rozo, *La generación del estado de sitio*, 63.

features; the measures adopted by the executive should be proportionate to the dangers specified in the declaration; and the executive decrees issued during the emergency but not directly connected to it should be unconstitutional.[43]

The jurisprudence of the new Constitutional Court on military jurisdiction also started to change sooner rather than later. Right in 1993, the court announced its new ideas about military jurisdiction. That year, the Court reviewed an executive decree that allowed civilians to be judged in military tribunals (Colombia Case #14). The court upheld the constitutionality of the decree, despite the letter of Article 213, but included in the sentence clear argumentation of the very exceptional nature of this case, in a way prudently announcing what the government could expect in this regard for future cases. That future arrived in 1997, when the Constitutional Court narrowed the scope of military jurisdiction beyond prohibiting that civilians be judged in military courts: the court also clearly argued that not even military personnel can be judges in military courts when human rights are violated (Colombia Case #13).

After the leading case of 1997, the Court issued another important decision in 2000 (Colombia Case #10). In this decision, the Constitutional Court not only reiterates the criterion established in 1997, it also starts distinguishing carefully what does it mean for a crime to be "service-related." In particular, the Court discusses the requirements that need to be fulfilled for a crime to be considered as part of the military service. These careful distinctions continued in a series of cases (Colombia Case #3-12), building step by step a simple but powerful argument: the ultimate mission of the armed forces is to defend the country and its constitution; the constitution of the country is grounded upon universal principles and human rights; therefore, human rights violations of human rights by military officers, even if they take place under a specific service, sever the link between the armed forces and their ultimate mission (Colombia Cases #13 and #8). The conclusion is clear: human rights violations do not belong, under any circumstance, to the military jurisdiction.

The jurisprudence of the Constitutional Court on military jurisdiction has made a huge impact, although it has not been easy for the Court to handle the reactions of other actors to its decisions.[44] For a number of years, the decisions by the Constitutional Court were mostly ignored by the military tribunals and by the Judicial Council, the organ in charge of deciding conflicts of competence between the civil and military jurisdictions. However, for different reasons, among which is the persuasiveness of the Court's argumentation, in recent years the criteria established by the Court has been adopted not only by the Judicial Council, but also on

[43] The effect of this change in interpretation was quite dramatic: from 1992 to 2002, from a total of twelve declarations of state of exception, three were declared unconstitutional, and four partially unconstitutional. Because of this Colombia was in a state of exception less than 20 percent (rather than 80 percent) of the time. Uprimny Yepes, "Entre el protagonismo, la precariedad y las amenazas."

[44] Revenga Sánchez and Girón Reguera, "La Corte Constitucional colombiana ante las medidas de seguridad y defense nacional del gobierno de Uribe."

the Highest Military Court that has already sent voluntarily some cases to the civil jurisdiction.[45]

CONCLUSION

Scholarship on how to overcome the middle-income trap has emphasized that government intervention is crucial to build the institutional capacity required for a strategic optimization of resources and improvements in productivity. The literature, however, has focused on economic issues, such as industrial policy, international trade, or resolution of ESR cases. In this chapter, we showed that careful and prudent constitutional argumentation, based on values and principles but also taking into account political realities, can be a fundamental resource for the improvement of conflictive political relations such as that between civilians and military officers. We argued that this is something that judges can do better than executives or legislators, even during emergencies and critical situations. This judicial intervention, which is possible in Latin American countries because of the judicial empowerment produced during the third-wave transitions to democracy, can be consequential for the future and quality of democracy in a region marked by instability and conflictive civic-military relations. Stability is a *sine qua non* condition for building the much-needed institutional capacity to leave the middle-income trap.

Colombia, in particular after 1991, has made considerable progress in building such careful and prudent jurisprudence, but Mexico has not. To answer why the judicial empowerment is sometimes effective but not others is beyond the limits of this chapter. However, some clear lessons stem from the comparison of the contrasting cases of Colombia and Mexico. First, when judges lack independence their jurisprudence is likely to reflect the interests of those who directly or indirectly control the judges. In both Mexico and Colombia there was a moment when the armed forces managed to exert undue influence on the judges (in Mexico after the reforms in 1934 and in Colombia after the reforms of 1958), and this was almost automatically reflected in a jurisprudential shift toward an expansion of the military jurisdiction.

Second, legal reforms that make judges independent do not automatically produce independent and creative jurisprudence, which makes these legal changes a necessary but not a sufficient condition to produce a change in behavior. Interestingly, the legal reforms to the justice system in Colombia carried out in 1991 effected a faster change in jurisprudence than similar reforms implemented in Mexico in 1994. One of the reasons of the belated change in interpretation in Mexico vis-á-vis the quick change in Colombia is that Mexican constitutional judges

45 Ariza, "Fuerzas Armadas, justicia penal militar y discurso judicial"; Cabarcas Maciá, *Militares, política y derecho*.

enjoyed less judicial review powers. Another reason may be related to the nature of the institutional change: a wholesome constitutional transformation in Colombia versus an amendment of only some articles related to constitutional justice in Mexico. It is thus important to investigate more deeply what exactly fills the gap between institutional and behavioral change.

How have the armed forces reacted to restrictions in the military jurisdiction in Colombia and Mexico? Current (summer of 2012) efforts at creating a new legislative framework for military justice in both countries show that negotiating in the shadow of creative and serious constitutional jurisprudence is an advantage in the tense relations between military officers and civilian authorities. In Mexico, where such jurisprudence is lacking, the efforts at reforming military jurisdiction have been slow and erratic. Mexican president, Felipe Calderón, engaged the army in a cruel fight against drug cartels since the very beginning of this administration in 2006. The costs in terms of human rights violations are undeniable: just in 2011, the National Commission for Human Rights received 1,695 complaints for military abuses.[46] However, after a long six-year administration, Calderón has failed to deliver even an acceptable legal framework for the armed forces. One of his legislative initiatives proposed that "ordinary courts presided by military judges [*sic*]" decide cases in which military officers have presumably violated human rights. Needless to say, such initiative undermines the principle of having separate jurisdictions and a neutral third party deciding such cases. The issue will continue to be in the interest of multiple actors not only because the initiative is pending, but also because the military will likely continue to play a key role in internal security and the fight against drug cartels and because of the recent decisions by the Mexican Supreme Court that are beginning to draw the boundaries of military jurisdiction.

In contrast, in Colombia civil-military negotiations have taken place under the shadow of constitutional jurisprudence. Colombian president, Juan Manuel Santos, has pushed for a reform to military jurisdiction in order to both deal with scandals such as the "false positives"[47] and to provide legal security to the military men that participate in internal security affairs. To deal with the situation, and to find an agreement with the main parties and institutions, the government created a High Commission formed by experts, civilian and military. Interestingly for the argument of this chapter, some of the civilian members of the commission are the very former constitutional judges who drafted some of the most important decisions limiting the military jurisdiction. The process of reform is not yet finished and has been criticized on a number of grounds by NGOs and Colombian analysts. However,

[46] *La Jornada*, May 25, 2012. Available at http://www.jornada.unam.mx/2012/05/25/politica/002n1pol.

[47] "False positives" are innocent victims in military operations against guerrilla and drug-trafficking groups that are deliberately misreported as members of such groups. Around 3,500 military officers are reported to be involved in this practice. See Colombia Reports, February 18, 2012, available at http://colombiareports.com/colombia-news/news/22286-colombia-withdraws-controversial-military-justice-proposal.html.

the innovative proposals generated by the High Commission and the negotiation between the armed forces and the civilian government are noteworthy, especially if we compare this deliberative process of reform with the Mexican one. For instance, all parties have agreed upon a list of crimes that do not belong under any circumstance to military jurisdiction (informed by constitutional jurisprudence) and they have agreed that difficult cases be heard in a committee with ordinary and military judges that would decide to which jurisdiction the case belongs.[48] There are other problems with the reform but, as Manuel José Cepeda put it, the process reflects a bargain between the armed forces and the civilian authorities that balances the clashing aims of protecting human rights by limiting military jurisdiction and providing legal security and procedural rights to the members of the armed forces taking into account their participation in risky and dangerous missions.[49]

REFERENCES

Sample of cases used in the chapter (starting with most recent)

Colombia

1. C-533 de 2008
2. C-228 de 2003
3. T-932 de 2002
4. C-802 de 2002
5. C-1024 de 2002
6. C-251 de 2002
7. C-1214 de 2001
8. SU-184 de 2001
9. C-361 de 2001
10. C-878 de 2000
11. C-368-00 de 2000
12. T-298-00 de 2000
13. C-358 de 1997
14. C-034 de 1993
15. Corte Suprema de Justicia. Sentencia del 15 de diciembre de 1988
16. Corte Suprema de Justicia. Sentencia del 26 de mayo de 1988
17. Sala Plena. Corte Suprema de Justicia. Sentencia 20 del 5 de marzo de 1987
18. Corte Suprema de Justicia. Sentencia 57 del 3 de julio de 1984
19. Sala Plena. Corte Suprema de Justicia. Sentencia del 30 de octubre de 1978

[48] See *Revista Semana*, May 22, 2012, available at http://www.semana.com/politica/senado-no-amplia-fuero-militar-para-combatir-bacrim/177573-3.aspx.

[49] *El Espectador*, February 25, 2012, available at http://www.eltiempo.com/justicia/ARTICULO-WEB-NEW_NOTA_INTERIOR-11221141.html.

20. Corte Suprema de Justicia. Sentencia del 3 de marzo 1978
21. Sala Plena. Corte Suprema de Justicia. Sentencia del 27 de enero 1977
22. Corte Suprema de Justicia. Sentencia del 2 de diciembre de 1976
23. Corte Suprema de Justicia. Sentencia del 31 de julio de 1975
24. Corte Suprema de Justicia. Sentencia del 10 de julio de 1975
25. Corte Suprema de Justicia. Sentencia del 23 de septiembre de 1973
26. Corte Suprema de Justicia. Sentencia del 5 de abril de 1973
27. Corte Suprema de Justicia. Sentencia del 19 de octubre de 1971
28. Corte Suprema de Justicia. Sentencia del 31 de marzo de 1971
29. Corte Suprema de Justicia. Sentencia del 19 de agosto de 1970
30. Corte Suprema de Justicia. Sentencia del 13 de agosto de 1970
31. Corte Suprema de Justicia. Sentencia del 6 de noviembre de 1969
32. Corte Suprema de Justicia. Sentencia del 30 de octubre de 1969
33. Sala Plena. Corte Suprema de Justicia. Sentencia del 12 de junio de 1945

Mexico

1. Expediente Varios 912/210 ("Radilla Case"), June 2011
2. CONTRADICCIÓN DE TESIS 105/2005-PS. 9a. Época; 1a.Sala; S.J.F. y su Gaceta; XXIII, Febrero de 2006; Pág. 248
3. CONTRADICCIÓN DE TESIS 67/95. 9a. Época; 1a.Sala; S.J.F. y su Gaceta; VIII, Julio de 1998; Pág. 71.
4. AMPARO DIRECTO EN REVISIÓN 698/96. 9a. Época; Pleno; S.J.F. y su Gaceta; VI, Septiembre de 1997; Pág. 122.
5. COMPETENCIA 224/90. Suscitada entre el Juez Cuarto de Distrito con residencia en Matamoros, Tamaulipas y el Juez Octavo de Distrito en Materia Penal en el Distrito Federal. 4 de marzo de 1991. Unanimidad de cinco votos.
6. AMPARO DIRECTO 501/86. 21 de octubre de 1986. 7ª. Época; Sala Auxiliar Informe 1986, Segunda Parte, Sala Auxiliar, tesis 7, página 9.
7. COMPETENCIA 146/81. 7ª. Época; Primera Sala. Abril 1984.
8. AMPARO DIRECTO 1256/82. 7ª Época; Primera Sala; Apéndice al S.J.F. 1917–1975, Segunda Parte, Primera Sala, tesis 144; 23 de julio de 1982; página 299.
9. AMPARO DIRECTO 1260/79. 7ª Época; Primera Sala; 13 de marzo de 1980.
10. AMPARO DIRECTO 3349/77. 7ª Época; Primera Sala; 17 de agosto de 1978. Informe 1978, Segunda Parte, Primera Sala, tesis 27, página 17.
11. AMPARO DIRECTO 751/76. 7ª Época; Primera Sala; 6 de septiembre de 1976. Informe 1976, Segunda Parte, Primera Sala, tesis 25, página 24.
12. AMPARO DIRECTO 4638/75. 7ª Época; Primera Sala; 8 de marzo de 1976.
13. AMPARO DIRECTO 94/74. 7ª Época; Primera Sala; 6 de marzo de 1975.
14. COMPETENCIA 6/73. 7ª Época; Primera Sala; 21 de septiembre de 1973.

15. COMPETENCIA 36/72. 7ª Época; Primera Sala; 13 de noviembre de 1972.
16. COMPETENCIA 46/68. 7ª Época; Primera Sala; 17 de julio de 1969. (Citada en Pedroza 2011).
17. COMPETENCIA. 6ª Época; Pleno; S.J.F. Primera Parte L, p. 22, registro 258142. (Citada en Pedroza 2011).
18. COMPETENCIA.6ª Época; Pleno; S.J.F. Primera Parte, XLI, p. 210, registro 804058. (Citada en Pedroza 2011).
19. COMPETENCIA. 6ª Época; Pleno; S.J.F. Primera Parte, LXIV, p. 37, registro 257974. (Citada en Pedroza 2011).
20. COMPETENCIA 83/57. 6ª Época; Pleno; 21 de octubre de 1958.
21. AMPARO PENAL EN REVISIÓN 7638/45. 5ª Época; Pleno; 23 de enero de 1946.
22. COMPETENCIA 136/39. 5ª Época; Primera Sala; 10. de abril de 1940. Apéndice 1917–1985, Segunda Parte, Primera Sala, últimatesisrelacionada con la jurisprudencia 34, página 95.
23. AMPARO PENAL DIRECTO 830/39. 5ª Época; Primera Sala; 30 de agosto de 1939.
24. COMPETENCIA 119/38. 5ª Época; Pleno; 3 de abril de 1939.
25. TESIS AISLADA. 5ª Época; Pleno; Informe 1938, página 72.
26. COMPETENCIA. 5ª Época; Pleno.
27. AMPARO PENAL DIRECTO 4074/38. 5ª Época; Primera Sala; 14 de noviembre de 1938.
28. AMPARO PENAL EN REVISIÓN 5216/38. 5ª Época; Primera Sala; 8 de noviembre de 1938.
29. COMPETENCIA 122/37. 5ª Época; Pleno; 13 de junio de 1938.
30. AMPARO PENAL DIRECTO 453/36. 5ª Época; Primera Sala; 8 de abril de 1937.
31. COMPETENCIA 44/36. 5ª Época; Pleno; 2 de noviembre de 1936.
32. COMPETENCIA 179/36 5ª Época; Pleno; 26 de octubre de 1936.
33. COMPETENCIA PENAL 208/33. 5ª Época; Pleno; 12 de febrero de 1934.
34. COMPETENCIA 337/33 (11 de diciembre de 1933), COMPETENCIA 70/33 (11 de diciembre de 1933), COMPETENCIA 310/33 (11 de septiembre de 1933). 5ª Época; Pleno.
35. AMPARO PENAL DIRECTO. 5ª Época; Pleno; 18 de diciembre de 1924.
36. COMPETENCIA. 5ª Época; Pleno; 23 de junio de 1924.
37. TESIS AISLADA. 5ª Época; Pleno; S.J.F., tomo V, página 900. (Citada en Cossío 2009).
38. TESIS AISLADA. 5ª Época; Pleno; S.J.F., tomo VI, página 853. (Citada en Cossío 2009).
39. TESIS AISLADA. 5ª Época; Pleno; S.J.F., tomo VII, página 1140. (Citada en Cossío 2009).

40. TESIS AISLADA. 5ª Época; Pleno; S.J.F., tomo X, página 788. (Citada en Cossío 2009).
41. TESIS AISLADA. 5ª Época; Pleno; S.J.F., tomo XII, página 70. (Citada en Cossío 2009).
42. TESIS AISLADA. 5ª Época; Pleno; S.J.F., tomo XII, página 913. (Citada en Cossío 2009).
43. TESIS AISLADA. 5ª Época; Primera Sala; S.J.F., tomo XXV, página 873. (Citada en Cossío 2009).
44. TESIS AISLADA. 5ª Época; Primera Sala; S.J.F., tomo XXX, página 1643. (Citada en Cossío 2009).

9

The Prospects for Anticorruption Law in Middle-Income Countries

Kevin E. Davis

INTRODUCTION

All countries struggle to prevent public power from being used for private gain. Middle-income countries (MICs) are certainly no exceptions. Corruption is widely viewed as a substantial impediment to development in these countries, and ever-increasing amounts of attention are being paid to methods of controlling corruption.

Contemporary anticorruption programs have a strong legal flavor. Tremendous amounts of effort have been invested in creating international legal instruments that bind states and international organizations to take various steps to combat corruption. In many cases those steps require further legal action, such as the creation of new organizations; changes in the structure of existing organizations; enactment and enforcement of prohibitions and disclosure requirements; or changes in the terms of contracts.

These initiatives reflect remarkable optimism about the potential of law to effect positive social change. They presume that legal institutions can be used instrumentally to combat corrupt practices. Some of these initiatives also embody faith in the power of legal institutions that operate across national boundaries. The most innovative new approaches go beyond treaties and international organizations and try to recruit foreign courts, prosecutors, regulators, and plaintiffs into the project of combating local corruption, hopefully in a way that complements local efforts. It might be unreasonable to place this kind of faith in the legal institutions of low-income countries (LICs), where state capacity is sharply limited by resource constraints. But in MICs the state is not bound by these kinds of constraints and so should, in principle, be capable of creating effective anticorruption institutions.

Experiences in other contexts, however, suggest grounds for skepticism about whether anticorruption law can live up to these hopes. In the general literature on

I am grateful to participants in the Conference on Law and Development of Middle-Income Countries, especially Randy Peerenboom and Alberto Simpser, for helpful comments, as well as to Zachary Rynar for research assistance.

law and development, skeptics about the efficacy of legal reforms raise several recurring concerns:[1]

- Law is epiphenomenal; legal norms and outcomes are ultimately shaped by more fundamental economic, political, or cultural forces.
- Law does not have a significant impact on behavior in comparison to other forms of social control.
- Foreign actors lack the knowledge, capacity, and legitimacy to craft legal interventions that promote development.

Each of these arguments provides grounds for skepticism about the efficacy of anticorruption law. Taken together they imply that domestic rather than foreign actors will play the most direct and critical roles in reducing or mitigating the effects of corruption; domestic actors will not necessarily rely on legal mechanisms to achieve their goals; and they will not be able to rely on law without also effecting fundamental economic, political, or cultural changes in their societies. The skeptical view also implies that progress in combating corruption cannot be measured simply by examining legal instruments or even the activities of legal officials, especially at the international level.

This chapter will examine and contrast optimistic and skeptical views of the prospects of anticorruption law. The focus is on MICs that, on the one hand, appear to experience distinct forms of corruption from high-income countries (HICs) and, on the other hand, have greater ability to mount legal responses to corruption than LICs. The chapter begins by describing the problem: What is corruption and why do people believe it is such an impediment to development? The next section outlines the consensus view on the appropriate form of anticorruption law. The following sections set out, in turn, optimistic and skeptical views of the role that anticorruption law can play in combating corruption.

THE PROBLEM OF CORRUPTION

Corruption is conventionally defined as the abuse of public power for private benefit. Those abuses can take several forms. Perhaps the most notorious form is bribery, use of public office in exchange for a benefit from another party. Another important form of corruption is embezzlement, that is, misappropriation of public assets. Nepotism and conflicts of interest are the other main forms of corruption.

Sometimes corruption is transnational in scope. For instance, bribes might be paid by foreign actors, as in cases in which a foreign enterprise pays a bribe to a public official to obtain a benefit such as a contract, concession, or an exemption

[1] David Trubek and Mark Galanter, "Scholars in Self-Estrangement: Some Reflections on the Crisis of Law and Development Studies in the United States," *Wisconsin Law Review* (1974): 1062; Kevin E. Davis and Michael Trebilcock, "The Relationship between Law and Development: Optimists versus Skeptics," *American Journal of Comparative Law* 56 (2008): 895.

from customs duties. Alternatively, corruptly procured assets might be transferred overseas or a corrupt local actor might physically move to a foreign jurisdiction.

There is now a consensus that corruption, broadly defined, is an impediment to development. Cross-country evidence suggests that societies in which levels of corruption are perceived to be high tend to have lower rates of economic growth. There are several plausible reasons why corruption might retard development. First and foremost, corruption, by definition, involves deviations from official public policy. In many cases the deviations will be detrimental to public welfare. The public suffers when unqualified drivers obtain drivers' licenses, when mobile telephone contracts are awarded to firms that offer inferior technology, when unqualified nephews become public officials, or when firms pay bribes in order to be permitted to continue polluting. Second, some forms of corruption lead to unpredictable official behavior and consequently discourage investment. Third, large-scale corruption transfers wealth from the state to public officials, often at the expense of much poorer people who would otherwise have benefitted from public expenditures. These transfers are objectionable in terms of distributive justice. Over time they may also have undesirable economic effects. The prospect of enrichment through public office creates incentives to fight for public appointments. The resources invested in those fights usually could be put to better use. There is also no guarantee that the people who win such battles will be the ones who are most committed to and capable of serving the public. Fourth, corruption undermines the legitimacy of public institutions. This might in turn diminish the population's willingness to cooperate with the state, in a variety of contexts.

Nonetheless, describing in a summary fashion the consensus that corruption poses a significant problem masks the fact that different countries experience the problem quite differently. This variation has been a major theme of Michael Johnston's writing about corruption. His research identifies four different "syndromes" of corruption,[2] three of which are prevalent in LICs and MICs. These syndromes can be distinguished by both the types of actors involved in corruption and their relative power.

The first syndrome, "Elite Cartel" corruption, is "centralized, organized and relatively predictable."[3] It involves relatively stable elites comprising top politicians, business figures, bureaucrats, and military and ethnic leaders. The state is reasonably effective, in the sense that courts and other state agencies are capable of enforcing their decisions, but does not necessarily serve broad public interests. Johnston[4] associates this type of corruption with MICs such as Argentina, Botswana, Brazil, Chile, Paraguay, South Africa, and Zambia, as well as HICs such as Italy and Korea.

² Michael Johnston, *Syndromes of Corruption: Wealth, Power and Democracy* (Cambridge University Press, 2005).

³ Ibid., 90.

⁴ Ibid., 222.

Johnston labels his second syndrome "Oligarchs and Clans." In these settings, the participants in corrupt activities are not members of stable elites. Instead they include a variety of public officials and private actors, including some who obtain wealth and power through violence or participation in illicit activities. Public officials do not necessarily wield significant power, meaning that their decisions can be ignored by powerful private actors, and disputes are sometimes resolved through violence. Johnston associates countries such as Bangladesh, Colombia, India, Jamaica, Mexico, Pakistan, the Philippines, and Russia with this syndrome.

Johnston's third syndrome is that of "Official Moguls." This dynamic involves powerful public officials who face little competition from other actors and so can engage in corruption with impunity. This often involves large-scale misappropriation of resources using the power of the state. Sometimes there is only one Official Mogul in the country. In other cases there are several Official Moguls, all operating independently and without constraint. Johnston cites China, as well as Indonesia during and following the Suharto years, as paradigmatic examples of Official Mogul corruption. Other examples include Algeria, Cameroon, Egypt, Gabon, Jordan, Morocco, Nigeria, Syria, and Tunisia.

Johnson's fourth syndrome is labeled "Influence Markets." In this syndrome moneyed private interests purchase access to a wide range of powerful public officials predominantly through legal means such as campaign contributions. This syndrome can coexist with varying degrees of political competition. Influence Markets are characteristic of HICs such as Germany, Japan, and the United States, which tend to experience relatively low levels of other forms of corruption.

Johnston groups countries as victims of the same syndrome even when it seems clear that some members of the group exhibit more severe symptoms than others. Botswana, for instance, is characterized as being governed by an elite cartel because although it is formally a multiparty democracy it has been dominated by a single party since independence. To be sure, allegations of corruption have been leveled at government ministers from time to time and members of the government often have significant interests in commercial enterprises. Yet at the same time, Botswana is perceived as the least corrupt country in sub-Saharan Africa and among the least corrupt countries in the world.[5]

As Johnston points out, each of these syndromes presents different kinds of obstacles to economic and political development. For instance, the experience of countries such as Botswana and Korea suggests that Elite Cartel corruption is not a fatal impediment to economic growth. Both those countries have state governments that have proven capable of pursuing public policies that have generated sustained development. The Oligarchs and Clans form of corruption, by contrast, seems likely

[5] Norad (the Norwegian Agency for Development Cooperation), *Contextual Choices in Fighting Corruption: Lessons Learned*, Report 4/2011-Study, available at http://www.norad.no/en/tools-and-publications/publications/publication?key=383808, at 64; Johnston, *Syndromes of Corruption*, 115–17.

to induce frequent and unpredictable deviations from official public policy. Meanwhile, Official Moguls corruption, at least in its centralized form, may lead to very predictable public policy but also to large-scale redistribution of wealth to high-level officials.

These syndromes also seem likely to vary in terms of their susceptibility to legal interventions. In Elite Cartels cases there are public officials capable of effectively enforcing anticorruption norms, whereas this is less likely in countries afflicted by Oligarchs and Clans or Official Moguls corruption. Influence Markets pose still different problems because they often involve legal behavior. Consequently, effective legal responses to Influence Markets involve formulation of new anticorruption norms rather than enforcement of existing norms. Because Influence Markets are not characteristic of MICs, the discussion that follows will focus on the other three syndromes.

THE GLOBAL MODEL FOR ANTICORRUPTION LAW

The beginning of the twenty-first century marked global convergence on a single model for states' anticorruption laws. That model is embodied in the UN Convention against Corruption (UNCAC)[6], which was adopted in 2003 and came into force in December 2005. Although there are other international treaties dealing with corruption, none are as comprehensive as UNCAC.

UNCAC requires states to take various steps to prevent and sanction corruption on the part of their own public officials. The recommended forms of prevention include transparency in public administration, codes of conduct for civil servants, and requirements that public procurement processes be open, competitive, and accountable. UNCAC also contains somewhat more specific requirements to criminalize bribery, embezzlement, abuse of power, and laundering of the proceeds of corruption (Articles 15, 17–23) and to treat corruption as a factor in civil proceedings such as proceedings to annul or rescind contracts. At the institutional level, a notable feature of UNCAC is that it encourages states to adopt independent anticorruption bodies (Articles 6, 36).

UNCAC also encourages states to assist in efforts to control bribery of foreign public officials and officials of international organizations. The key provision here is Article 16, which encourages states to make bribery of foreign public officials a criminal offence. An entire chapter (IV) is devoted to encouraging states to cooperate in proceedings involving other states, through extradition, prisoner transfers, mutual legal assistance, joint investigations, and so forth. Another chapter (V) contains innovative provisions requiring parties to cooperate in both the recovery of assets that qualify as either proceeds or instruments of corruption and in the collection of compensatory damages for harm caused by such corruption. In these respects UNCAC builds on a foundation laid by the U.S. Foreign Corrupt Practices

[6] UN Convention against Corruption, 2349 U.N.T.S. 41, in force December 14, 2005.

Act (FCPA)[7] and, later, the Organisation for Economic Co-operation and Development (OECD) Convention on Combating Bribery of Foreign Public Officials in International Business Transactions. The FCPA, enacted in 1977, prohibits bribery of foreign public officials and requires all sorts of payments to be accounted for properly. The OECD Convention, concluded in 1997, requires its signatories to enact prohibitions comparable to those found in the FCPA and to cooperate in international proceedings.

International financial institutions' anticorruption policies also represent an important component of the global anticorruption regime. Those policies focus on ensuring that the proceeds of grants or loans are not used for corrupt purposes. The policies include detailed procurement codes and procedures for canceling agreements with firms or governments found to have engaged in improper activity and disqualifying guilty firms from receiving further funds. International financial institutions, in concert with other actors, have pressed developing countries to adopt international norms concerning government procurement, including those set out in instruments such as the UN Commission on International Trade Law's Model Law on Procurement of Goods, Construction and Services and the World Trade Organization's Agreement on Government Procurement.[8] Many of those norms are clearly designed to prevent corruption. For instance, the Agreement on Government Procurement generally requires open competitive bidding, acceptance of the lowest qualified tender, the establishment of procedures for bringing challenges to the procurement process before an independent tribunal, and abandonment of discrimination in favor of local suppliers.

OPTIMISTIC CLAIMS

Optimistic assessments of anticorruption law share the view that concerted legal action, by both domestic and foreign actors, can make a meaningful contribution to reducing the problem of corruption. There is little concrete evidence to support this belief, but it is sustained by a combination of anecdotes and theoretical analysis.

As far as anecdotes are concerned, the story of Hong Kong's anticorruption reforms serves as something of a founding myth for the optimistic view of anticorruption law. In 1973 corruption was, by all accounts, rampant in Hong Kong. The police force was especially notorious, with syndicates of police officers banding

7 Foreign Corrupt Practices Act of 1977, Pub. L. No. 95-213, § 102, 91 Stat. 1494, codified as amended at 15 U.S.C. §§78m(b), (d)(1), (g)–(h), 78dd-1, 78dd-2, 78dd-3, 78ff; amended by Foreign Corrupt Practices Act Amendment of 1988 (part of Omnibus Trade and Competitiveness Act of 1988), Pub. L. 100-418, 102 Stat. 1107, 1415 (1988), and International Anti-Bribery and Fair Competition Act of 1998, Pub. L. 105-366, 112 Stat. 3302 (1998).

8 Christopher McCrudden and Stuart G. Gross, "WTO Government Procurement Rules and the Local Dynamics of Procurement Policies: A Malaysian Case Study," *European Journal of International Law* 17 (2006): 151–85; Agreement on Government Procurement, April 15, 1994, WTO Agreement, in force January 1, 1996.

together to extort payments from both legal and illegal enterprises. In the middle of that year, however, a senior police officer named Peter Godber fled to Britain while under investigation for having amassed large amounts of unexplained wealth. The ensuing outcry led to the creation of a new anticorruption agency, the Independent Commission Against Corruption (ICAC). The ICAC was independent of the police force and reported directly to the governor. The ICAC adopted a three-pronged approach to anticorruption efforts, but the initial priority was enforcement of criminal prohibitions, beginning with a concerted effort to prosecute members of the police syndicates. The other two prongs were public education and the prevention of corruption through consultation with legislative drafters and government departments. The impact of the ICAC was dramatic. Immediately after its establishment, the number of corruption incidents reported more than doubled.[9] As for the police syndicates, by mid-1977 the head of the ICAC reported to the governor that "no major syndicates were known to exist."[10] According to Manion, "by the mid-1980s (or late 1980s, at worst) corruption in government was no longer a routine practice."[11]

The Hong Kong ICAC story has two noteworthy transnational aspects. First, in 1974 Hong Kong was a British colony and its governor, Murray MacLehose, was a Scottish career diplomat appointed by the queen. MacLehose was the prime mover behind the creation of the ICAC, and, although he was the chief executive of the colony, he also undoubtedly qualified as a foreign actor. Second, the most high-profile anticorruption case handled by the ICAC in its early years was the prosecution of Peter Godber, who was extradited from England in 1975. This prosecution clearly would not have been possible without the assistance of the UK police and courts.

The ICAC case is exemplary because it shows the multifaceted role that law might play in response to corruption. The case teaches that law has the potential not only to influence the incidence of corrupt activity but also to shape beliefs about corruption – that is, beliefs about what counts as corrupt activity, about the prevalence of such activity, and about the extent to which it ought to be condemned.

When it comes to influencing the incidence of corruption, law, first, defines *opportunities* for corruption by assigning power among public officials and defining the appropriate ways of exercising that power. Second, legal sanctions create *incentives*. Imprisonment, fines, awards of damages, asset forfeiture, avoidance of contracts, and debarment – laws that impose these sanctions for engaging in corrupt activity create incentives to avoid it. Third, law provides a source of *moral instruction*. Many people are influenced in part by a desire to do the right thing. Laws,

9 Melanie Manion, *Corruption by Design: Building Clean Government in Mainland China and Hong Kong* (Harvard University Press, 2004), 35–72, at 35–6.

10 Ibid., 40.

11 Ibid., 72.

including legislation and rulings issued in the course of adjudicating individual cases, delineate the boundaries between acceptable and unacceptable behavior. Fourth, legal norms can require disclosure, and thus legal processes can be sources of *information*. Fifth and finally, the ICAC case demonstrates the potential benefits of foreign involvement in lawmaking and law enforcement.

The ICAC's preventive efforts exemplify the ways in which institutional design, including through legal reform, can limit opportunities for officials to engage in corruption. For example, when Hong Kong legalized off-track betting it instantly eliminated the need for payoffs to the police and thereby reduced opportunities for police corruption. On a larger scale, Chile's success in controlling corruption has been attributed in part to constitutional reforms that expanded the budgetary authority of the executive branch and limited Congress' ability to enact legislation designed to benefit specific constituencies.[12] Finally, Brazil's *ficha limpa* ("clean record") legislation illustrates yet another way in which law can define opportunities for corruption. That legislation, passed in May 2010, bars people who are convicted of violations of electoral statutes or crimes involving the use of public funds from running for public office.

The most familiar effect of law, however, is the creation of incentives. Hong Kong's crackdown on police corruption was presumed to be effective in large part because it led to a dramatic increase in the probability of punishment and a corresponding decline in incentives to engage in corruption. Singapore's legal system is similarly known for creating high-powered incentives to refrain from corruption.

Hong Kong's experience is also consistent with the idea that law serves as a source of moral instruction. The ICAC's investments in educational programs were premised on the idea that simply explaining the concept of corruption to the public would discourage misconduct and encourage reporting. When the ICAC was created there was an unusually strong need for this kind of instruction. Many residents of Hong Kong in 1973 were migrants from mainland China who actually did not know what the law demanded of police officers and other public officials. The combination of the education program and efforts to publicize prosecutions served to change popular perceptions of what is appropriate conduct.

The Hong Kong experience also illustrates law's informational role. Legal proceedings can disseminate information about who-took-what, who-paid-how-much-to-whom, or who-was-friends-with-whom. Most legal proceedings require such information to meet a fairly high standard of proof, meaning that it tends to be fairly reliable. These kinds of information not only shape beliefs about the prevalence of corruption, but can also trigger various sorts of nonlegal sanctions against the people whose misbehavior has been disclosed. More recently, lawmakers have begun to

[12] Norad, *Contextual Choices in Fighting Corruption*.

adopt substantive norms that require transparency in government and disclosure of public officials' income and assets.

Finally, the story of the ICAC provides historical support for the idea that foreign actors might play key roles in both motivating reforms to domestic anticorruption laws and combating transnational corruption. The plausibility of this claim rests on the idea that local law enforcement institutions confront two significant obstacles in cases of transnational corruption. First, much of the evidence of wrongdoing will be located overseas. Obtaining that evidence will require navigating a foreign legal system, and will typically demand a great deal of time and expensive legal expertise. Second, it is difficult for local institutions to impose meaningful sanctions on actors who engage in transnational corruption – including foreign bribe-payers, foreign institutions that help launder proceeds of corruption, and the corrupt officials – if the relevant individuals and assets are located in foreign jurisdictions. Foreign institutions can help to overcome both of these obstacles by criminalizing the bribery of foreign public officials and the laundering of the proceedings of corruption; providing mutual legal assistance; helping to recover stolen assets; extraditing fugitives; and refusing to enforce corruptly procured contracts. At the margins, fear of punishment by foreign actors diminishes the incentives for public officials and their potential accomplices to engage in corruption. Condemnation by foreign institutions might also play a role in shifting attitudes toward corruption, forcing officials and the general public to reexamine beliefs about what should and should not be tolerated. Finally, information generated by foreign legal institutions can be used by local law enforcement agencies and the media, thus serving as a catalyst for domestic law enforcement.

It is often implicitly assumed that foreign institutions will be less vulnerable to political capture than local institutions. This assumption seems reasonable to the extent that the institutions in question have proven to be relatively immune to corruption in dealing with purely local cases. This assumption is less obviously valid, however, when the relevant foreign institutions are located in a country that is struggling with corruption. For instance, given the amount of foreign investment undertaken by Chinese companies, vigorous enforcement of China's prohibitions on bribery of foreign public officials might have a significant impact on overall levels of transnational bribery. But it is an open question whether China's anticorruption institutions can be relied on for effective enforcement. Even in these situations, however, it may be sensible to have faith in foreign institutions. Physical and social distance may limit opportunities for corrupt officials and foreign law enforcement officials to form the kinds of personal relationships that help to sustain corrupt relationships.

As an aside, the arguments in favor of relying on foreign actors to hold public officials accountable for corruption parallel the arguments in favor of using foreign or international tribunals to hold officials accountable for human rights abuses.[13] In

[13] See, generally, Kathryn Sikkink, *The Justice Cascade: How Human Rights Prosecutions Are Changing World Politics* (W. W. Norton, 2011).

each situation, the argument is that foreign intervention is required to overcome impunity. Increasing acceptance of these kinds of foreign intervention in the human rights context might very well smooth acceptance of foreign anticorruption interventions.

SKEPTICISM ABOUT ANTICORRUPTION LAW: AN OVERVIEW

Anyone versed in the literature on law and development is intimately familiar with objections to the optimistic assertion that law plays a significant causal role in achieving social change. In their landmark critique, David Trubek and Marc Galanter associated this kind of optimism with a model they called "liberal legalism." In a now-famous passage, they summed up the limitations of the liberal legalism model in the following terms:

> Empirically, the model assumes social and political pluralism, while in most of the Third World we find social stratification and class cleavage juxtaposed with authoritarian or totalitarian political systems. The model assumes that state institutions are the primary locus of social control, while in much of the Third World the grip of tribe, clan, and local community is far stronger than that of the nation-state. The model assumes that rules both reflect the interests of the vast majority of citizens and are normally internalized by them, while in many developing countries rules are imposed on the many by the few and are frequently honored more in the breach than in the observance. The model assumes that courts are central actors in social control, and that they are relatively autonomous from political, tribal, religious, or class interests. Yet in many nations courts are neither very independent nor very important.[14]

This set of ideas is consistent with a well-established tradition in the political science literature of treating corruption as a symptom of overall economic and political underdevelopment rather than of defective institutional design. Daniel Treisman[15] defends this viewpoint on empirical grounds. His statistical analysis finds that levels of perceived corruption for the period of 1996 through 1998 were explained mainly by the following factors: national income, whether the country was a former British colony, the percentage of Protestants in the population, whether the country had been a democracy continuously since 1960, openness to trade (although the effect was small), and whether the country was a unitary (as opposed to federal) state. Most of these factors are immune to the influence to short-term policies. Thus he concludes that, "Controlling for predetermined factors that themselves influence the choice of policies, policy decisions themselves either have little significant impact on corruption or else work painfully slowly."[16]

[14] Trubek and Galanter, "Scholars in Self-Estrangement," 1075–6.

[15] Daniel Treisman, "The Causes of Corruption: A Cross-national Study," *Journal of Public Economics* 76 (2000): 399–457.

[16] Ibid., 441.

THE RISK OF CAPTURE

One of Trubek and Galanter's central complaints was that "in many developing countries rules are imposed on the many by the few. . . ." The concern here is that legal institutions will be captured by actors who represent narrow interests and will be used in ways that are incompatible with the common good.[17]

Johnston's typology suggests three different ways in which powerful actors might be able to capture anticorruption institutions and influence their orientation. In Official Moguls countries, officials at the top of the hierarchy are so thoroughly dominant that they and their cronies can engage in corruption with impunity. If the institutions are used at all, they are used only against enemies of the moguls. In Oligarch and Clans countries, anticorruption institutions are not independently effective but can be used by powerful interests as effective weapons against members of other weaker factions. Thus vulnerability to anticorruption institutions depends upon a constantly shifting balance of power. By contrast, in Elite Cartel countries, anticorruption institutions can be used effectively against most members of society other than members in good standing with the elite group.

There are two main ways in which these kinds of external influences over anticorruption institutions might impair their performance. First, they might be aimed at people who are not corrupt. In cases in which the targets are truly innocent this kind of mistargeting leads to obvious injustice. It also diminishes incentives to behave honestly; if people expect to be sanctioned whether they are honest or corrupt, then the incentive to be honest is diminished. Going beyond purely incentive-based arguments, this kind of injustice seems likely to undermine the moral authority and credibility of the legal system as a whole. A system that permits the innocent to be persecuted is unlikely to be regarded as a source of either moral instruction or reliable information. Finally, targeting people who are honest is a waste of public resources.

A second possibility is that capture of anticorruption institutions will allow people who actually are corrupt to escape sanctions. People who enjoy impunity obviously have no incentive to avoid corruption. A system captured in this fashion may also struggle to retain its moral authority.

Suspicions have periodically been raised about anticorruption institutions being used to pursue political vendettas. For instance, Peter Larmour[18] describes how, in December 2006, the leader of a military coup in Fiji tried to use an anticorruption campaign to disable political opponents and shore up his legitimacy without presenting clear evidence of corruption on the part of many of the targeted

[17] Trubek and Galanter, "Scholars in Self-Estrangement," 1080.

[18] Peter Larmour, "Populist Anti-corruption and Military Coups: The Clean-Up Campaign in Fiji 2006–07," in *Governments, NGOs and Anti-Corruption: The New Integrity Warriors*, ed. Luís de Sousa, Peter Larmour, and Barry Hindess (Routledge, 2009), 120–32.

individuals. Similarly, Ivan Krastev[19] reports that in postcommunist Eastern Europe, allegations of corruption slung at one another by political opponents have led politicians and the public to obsess about corruption to the exclusion of other important policy considerations.[20] Mark De Weaver[21] argues that a Chinese anticorruption campaign launched in or around 2003 was motivated in part by a desire "to remove people loyal to former party chairman Jiang Zemin." Going further back in time, in a study focused on the Middle East and North Africa, Kate Gillespie and Gwenn Okruhlik[22] identified many examples of ineffective anticorruption campaigns that were either empty public relations exercises or designed primarily to target political opponents.

There are also many examples of MICs in which corrupt officials appear to enjoy impunity. For example, according to U.S. State Department reports, in Brazil and India, "officials frequently engaged in corrupt practices with impunity." In these kinds of MICs, the problem typically is not that legal institutions are completely impotent. The State Department also reports examples of officials in these countries being accused of corruption and subjected to real legal sanctions, such as seizure of assets and dismissal from public office. Rather, the problem is that sanctions are not imposed consistently. This often stems from the judiciary being susceptible to bribery or political influence.

ALTERNATIVES TO LAW AS A FORM OF SOCIAL CONTROL

Optimists assume that a society's laws have meaningful effects on the behavior of its members. Trubek and Galanter's critique challenged this assumption as well. One of their central complaints was that "The [liberal legal] model assumes that state institutions are the primary locus of social control, while in much of the Third World the grip of tribe, clan, and local community is far stronger than that of the nation-state."[23] Over thirty years after this critique was published, there remain many countries in which it still makes sense to ask whether legal institutions really are the primary locus of control over political corruption.

The answer to this question varies from country to country. In some countries, the legal system is an important means of social control. Whether they are independent or not, legal institutions impose sanctions for corrupt behavior that can reasonably

[19] Ivan Krastev, *Shifting Obsessions: Three Essays on the Politics of Anti-corruption* (Central European University Press, 2004).

[20] See also Daniel Smilov, "Anti-corruption Bodies as Discourse-controlling Instruments: Experiences from South-East Europe," in de Sousa, et al., *Governments, NGOs and Anti-Corruption*, 85–101.

[21] Mark A. De Weaver, "Hidden Motives in Anti-corruption Campaign," Asia Times Online, October 29, 2005, available at http://www.atimes.com/atimes/China_Business/GJ29Cb05.html.

[22] Kate Gillespie and Gwenn Okruhlik, "The Political Dimensions of Corruption Cleanups: A Framework for Analysis," *Comparative Politics* 24 (1991): 77–95.

[23] Trubek and Galanter, "Scholars in Self-Estrangement," 1075–6.

be expected to limit authority, deter misconduct, provide moral guidance and generate reliable information.

The People's Republic of China, however, presents a very different situation. There, control over public officials is vested almost entirely in the Chinese Communist Party (CCP) as opposed to the formal legal system. According to Fu Hualing:

> While the legal reform in China since the late 1970s may have witnessed the reemergence of a legal system which is functioning and effective in civil and commercial matters, the CCP is in direct control over matters of political significance, especially those concerning the direct interest of the Party, including corruption perpetrated by its members.[24]

The CCP has its own mechanisms for investigating and disciplining party officials. There are also specialized legal anticorruption investigative teams in the procuracy. Although the CCP's investigators sometimes conduct joint investigations with their legal counterparts, the CCP has superior jurisdiction. This means that party officials can halt proceedings by the legal authorities.

At the same time, the mere fact that the CCP's anticorruption mechanisms are political rather than legal does not necessarily mean they are ineffective. The CCP has repeatedly emphasized its commitment to fighting corruption and does from time to time authorize the prosecution of party members of the highest rank. Nonetheless, although severe sanctions have been imposed in a few cases, punishments are generally lenient.

Countries that are more democratic than China sometimes rely on elections – another kind of political mechanism – as alternatives to legal controls over corruption. Take, for example, Argentina. Argentina's legal system is widely viewed as ineffectual at combating corruption. One of the most high-profile failures involved a contract to produce national identity cards. The contract was awarded in 1998. In December 2008 Siemens, a German multinational company, admitted to U.S. and German authorities that its Argentine subsidiary had paid bribes of approximately U.S.$100 million to obtain and retain the contract. Allegations of the bribes began circulating in Argentina almost as soon as the contract was awarded and were substantiated by Siemens' admissions to the U.S. and German authorities. Nevertheless, fourteen years later not one person had been indicted by the Argentine authorities. Yet at least in this case, focusing exclusively on the absence of, or at least delay in, legal accountability would be misleading. Argentine voters were swift to punish the government that awarded the contract at the ballot box. In December 1999 voters threw the incumbent government out of power, and the successor government promptly canceled the Siemens contract.

[24] Fu Hualing, "The Upward and Downward Spiral of China's Anti-Corruption Enforcement," University of Hong Kong Faculty of Law Research Paper, 2011, available at http://papers.ssrn.com/sol3/papers.cfm?abstract_id=1883348.

Internalized moral norms are important methods of social control that serve as alternatives to legal norms. Some people are simply more inclined to be honest than others. This may explain why purges of corrupt agencies are sometimes effective. For example, in 2004 the newly elected government of Georgia implemented its anticorruption platform by firing and replacing all of the members of the notoriously corrupt traffic police. Corruption declined dramatically.

Moral norms do not necessarily evolve independently of legal institutions. To the extent that legal norms serve as forms of moral instruction they influence prevailing moral norms. Typically this kind of instruction is a by-product of the more conventional activities of legal institutions, but sometimes it is quite deliberate. For example, as noted in the preceding text, since early in its history Hong Kong's ICAC has offered public education programs – including an extensive program aimed at school-aged children – designed to inculcate values that inhibit participation in corrupt activities and to encourage reporting.

THE LIMITS OF FOREIGN INTERVENTION

A third commonly cited lesson of the law and development movement is that legal reforms driven primarily by foreign actors have limited chances of success, at least not without significant input from, consultation with, and participation from local actors. One reason for this is that foreign actors may lack the inclination to follow through on initial commitments and make sustained investments in solving another country's problems. This is a particular concern when the other country is a MIC and thus not a strong candidate for international redistribution. A second concern is that foreign actors acting alone often lack the power to have meaningful influence over the behavior of local actors. A third concern is lack of knowledge. Foreign actors may be inclined to prescribe reforms drawn from global templates, even though when it comes to legal institutions one size does not necessarily fit all. The current wisdom is that context matters and legal institutions have to be tailored to fit the needs of the societies in which they operate. But this kind of tailoring requires local knowledge that foreign actors may not possess. A fourth concern is that foreign actors may lack legitimacy. Sometimes local solutions are preferred and are viewed as more legitimate simply because they are local.

In the anticorruption context, foreign actors are involved in both the design and enforcement of legal norms. First, as we have already seen, MICs are under pressure to adopt anticorruption laws based on the global template set out in UNCAC. Quantitative assessments of their impact support the skeptical view of externally driven interventions. Ratification of UNCAC is not correlated with declines in perceived levels of corruption, nor is the creation of a specialized anticorruption commission.[25] Meanwhile, the jury is still out on the effects of transnational law

[25] Norad, *Contextual Choices in Fighting Corruption.*

enforcement. The coming into force of UNCAC coincided with a very visible increase in the level of enforcement of laws against foreign bribery, particularly on the part of the United States. There have also been some successful efforts to recover stolen assets shipped overseas by officials in developing countries and even a few successful prosecutions of officials who have moved overseas. There is some evidence that laws against foreign bribery deter investment in relatively corrupt countries – which is a mixed blessing – and the actions against corrupt officials have no doubt had salutary effects. There is, however, no hard evidence linking any of these initiatives to amelioration of corruption in MICs or LICs.[26]

There are several possible explanations for these findings. Lack of inclination may be one. This kind of law enforcement activity is expensive; even for the wealthiest countries economic self-interest weighs against devoting scarce resources to solving other countries' problems. Current data suggest that many countries exert very little real effort on enforcement. The 2010 Annual of Report of the OECD Working Group on Bribery shows that of thirty-eight parties to the OECD Convention, only thirteen imposed any sanctions for foreign bribery between the date the convention came into force in 1999 and the end of 2010. According to Transparency International, only a handful of even those countries could be described as having actively enforced their legislation.[27]

There are also clear limits on the power of foreign actors to influence the course of events in any given MIC. Unlike in the case of colonial Hong Kong, sovereignty generally prevents foreign actors from directly changing domestic law. Foreign actors have more power to effect change through enforcement actions aimed at transnational corruption, although even in those cases cooperation from local institutions is often helpful. Yet there are limits to how much any given country's corruption problem is inherently transnational. Transnational corruption is likely to be a serious problem in countries whose wealth is derived primarily from exports of extractive resources and whose economies and financial systems are too small to hold large amounts of corruptly procured assets locally. In those countries, it makes sense to consider foreign law a potent and important means of controlling corruption. But that is simply not the case in countries with more diversified economies and where it is practicable to hold corruptly procured wealth in domestic assets. It may be conceivable for foreign institutions to play a substantial role in combating corruption in Angola, but not in, say, Brazil. Yet even in the Angolas of this world, the costs of initiating transnational proceedings might be prohibitive for all but the biggest cases.

Another concern is lack of knowledge. The UNCAC approach to corruption control may be optimal, or may not be. Perhaps independent anticorruption

[26] Kevin E. Davis, "Does the Globalization of Anti-Corruption Law Help Developing Countries?," in *International Economic Law, Globalization and Developing Countries*, ed. Julio Faundez and Celine Tan (Edward Elgar, 2010), 283–306.

[27] OECD Working Group on Bribery, 2010 *Annual Report* (OECD, 2010).

agencies are good for Hong Kong but elsewhere competition among less "independent" law enforcement agencies is preferable. Perhaps prosecuting firms that pay bribes causes more harm than good by deterring investment in precisely those countries that are already struggling to control corruption. Or perhaps in an age in which communication technology provides broad swathes of the population with access to almost limitless information, transparency in government will be sufficient to check corruption without the need to resort to criminal prosecutions. Either way, without good information about local circumstance, it is quite possible that deploying global best practices in anticorruption law will do some countries more harm than good.

Finally, there is the question of legitimacy. This is likely to become a particular concern if it becomes more common for foreign states to bring legal actions against individual public officials. At some point questions will be asked about whether such proceedings are legitimate, in much the same way that these questions are being asked about the idea of using foreign or international tribunals to prosecute individual public officials for human rights violations.

CONCLUSION

Despite recent trends there are sound theoretical reasons to be uncertain – neither optimistic nor skeptical – about the extent to which anticorruption law can be used instrumentally to mitigate the effects of corruption in MICs. In this sense anticorruption law is no different from other forms of law and their relation to development. Law is generally a powerful means of social control, but its significance and amenability to manipulation vary from place to place and from time to time. It is particularly difficult to generalize about the extent to which foreign actors can use legal tools for instrumental purposes. Under these circumstances, the trend toward convergence on a single global model of anticorruption law seems misguided. A more fruitful approach might be to build a global regime that encourages ongoing search for anticorruption laws that represent the best responses to the problems facing particular societies at particular points in time.

10

The Delivery of Justice in Middle-Income Countries

Juan Carlos Botero

INTRODUCTION

In a recent survey conducted among female victims of violence in Pakistan, formal courts were described by the users as "frightening." Respondents were also asked to list what they would change about the formal court process for women. Their response was an "overwhelming demand for less delays and quicker disposal of cases."[1] Formal courts in developing countries – civil law and common-law countries alike – are perceived to be not only bureaucratic and ineffective, but also inaccessible and threatening. There seems to be a global crisis of justice delivery, and it is particularly serious in low- and middle-income countries (MICs). The poor and other marginalized segments of society face significant limitations to access formal judicial institutions in developing countries.[2] Cultural and language barriers, overly complex procedures and cumbersome legal requirements, financial limitations, mistrust for institutions derived from a colonial past, and radically different views on the nature and role of justice in society,[3] among other factors, hamper the ability of low-income citizens to effectively resolve their disputes in official courts.[4]

1 Hannah Irfan, "'Honor' and Violence Against Women in Pakistan," in *Marginalized Communities and Access to Justice*, ed. Yash Ghai and Jill Cottrell (Routledge, 2010), 162.

2 United Nations Development Program (hereafter referred to as UNDP), Report of the Commission on Legal Empowerment of the Poor, *Making the Law Work for Everyone*. V.1, UNDP, 2008; Paul Collier, *The Bottom Billion: Why the Poorest Countries Are Failing and What Can Be Done About It* (Oxford University Press, 2007); Botero, et al., "Judicial Reform," *World Bank Research Observer* (2003): 61–88, at 18, 1; Michael R. Anderson, "Access to Justice and Legal Process: Making Legal Institutions Responsive to Poor People in LDC," *Institute of Development Studies* (2003).

3 See, e.g., Barry Bearak, "Women Are Defaced by Acid and Bengali Society Is Torn," *New York Times*, June 24, 2000; Gunter Bierbrauer, "Toward an Understanding of Legal Culture: Variations in Individualism and Collectivism between Kurds, Lebanese, and Germans," *Law & Society Review* (2004): 243–64, at 28.

4 See, e.g., Fidelis Kanyongolo, *Malawi, Justice Sector and the Rule of Law* (Open Society Initiative for Southern Africa, 2006); Benjamín Boumakani, "L'Etat de Droit en Afrique," *RJP* [Revue juridique et politique des états francophones] (2003): 445–69.

In old ages, people used customary justice systems to resolve their disputes, ranging from the Cheyenne "conference of tribal chiefs,"[5] to the Afghan *Jirgas*, to the Liberian chiefdoms, to the Amazonian shamans. While many of these systems continue to operate today, the European colonization process of the past few centuries brought with it a new dispute-resolution system to all corners of the planet. In some places the old forms were completely abandoned while in others a dual arrangement emerged. Parallel systems of dispute resolution coexisted and interacted in most countries. In some places customary justice was formally and hierarchically integrated into the formal (European) judicial machinery, while in others they remained in operation de facto, mostly ignored or tolerated by the formal courts. For decades (in Africa and parts of Asia) or centuries (in Latin America and other parts of Asia), the formal courts were perceived mostly as instruments for resolving disputes among the descendants of European colonizers, the global and local business community, and the local elites. By design, in most colonies and pseudocolonies around the world formal courts were not intended to be widely accessible to ordinary folk. However, this was not seen as a problem per se, because people still had access to their customary justice systems.

Several new factors have emerged in the last few decades, starting with the end of the Cold War, which pose a serious challenge to the existing arrangements. These factors include, among others, increasing globalization and integration of markets; growing migration and urbanization; exponential expansion of access to communication technologies; unprecedented universal access to information for all segments of the population; growing cultural self-assertiveness;[6] and growing awareness among marginalized populations about their own rights (and decreasing tolerance to abuses and exclusion). The Arab Spring is the most graphic example of the powerful impact of the combination of these factors. The impact of these changes for the machinery of justice is clear: the "Wig and Gown" justice of the colonizers and their heirs is no longer acceptable to an increasingly cultural assertive and well-informed population, at the same time that the "Sassy-wood" justice[7] of the local chiefs is no longer effective in a globalized world. The system is broken.

In many low-income countries (LICs), coexisting informal (customary, traditional, aboriginal) dispute-settlement mechanisms, such as the village elders,[8]

[5] Karl N. Llewellyn and E. Adamson Hoebel, *The Cheyenne Way: Conflict and Case Law in Primitive Jurisprudence* (William D. Hein and Company, 2002).

[6] Samuel P. Huntington, *The Clash of Civilizations and the Remaking of World Order* (Touchstone Books, 1998).

[7] Trial by ordeal by poisoning in contemporary Liberia, Gambia, and other Sub-Saharan African countries.

[8] See, e.g., Yash Ghai and Jill Cottrell, eds., *Marginalized Communities and Access to Justice* (Routledge, 2010); Erica Harper, *Customary Justice: From Program Design to Impact Evaluation* (IDLO, 2011); Keebet von Benda-Beckmann, "Globalisation and Legal Pluralism," *International Law Forum Du Droit International* (2002): 19–25 at 4, 1; O. Oko Elechi, "Human Rights and the African Indigenous Justice System." Paper presented at the International Conference of the International Society for the Reform of Criminal Law, Montreal, Canada, August 2004, 1–30; O. Oko Elechi, *Doing Justice without the State: The Afikpo (Ehugbo) Nigeria Model* (Routledge, 2006), 1–256.

continue to fill the justice gap. Yet increasing internal migration and urbanization in developing countries over the last few decades (particularly in MICs) have eroded the ability of large segments of society to have their disputes resolved by customary justice institutions. Newly arrived migrant peasants and members of indigenous groups are often unable to keep their traditions and ancestral dispute-settlement mechanisms alive in big cities, while they are also unable to understand and incorporate the abstruse legal procedures of the formal courts, which are often perceived as a foreign "transplant."[9] While there is ample evidence of structural deficiencies in the delivery of justice for vast segments of society in both MICs and LICs, the situation in MICs is peculiar, as most people in these countries no longer have access to a "backup system" (customary justice) to resolve their disputes.

This chapter proposes a simple framework to compare justice outcomes across legal families and across countries of different levels of development. It also provides new metrics of effectiveness of civil and criminal justice and private arbitration for a large sample of high-income countries (HICs) and MICs.

THE "JUDICIAL EQUILIBRIUM" – ACCESSIBLE, IMPARTIAL, AND EFFICIENT JUSTICE

Rule 1 of the U.S. Federal Rules of Civil Procedure states that the rules of procedure "should be construed and administered to secure the *just, speedy, and inexpensive* determination of every action and proceeding."[10] These characteristics relate to the broader concepts of impartiality, efficiency and accessibility of dispute-resolution systems.[11] From the point of view of the ordinary user, the overall effectiveness of a judicial system encompasses three dimensions:[12]

Access (absence of procedural, financial, and other hurdles)[13]
Impartiality (independent and unbiased adjudication)
Efficiency (enforceable results within reasonable time)

9 See, e.g., Alan Watson, *Legal Transplants: An Approach to Comparative Law* (University of Georgia Press, 1993); O. Kahn-Freund, "On Uses and Misuses of Comparative Law," *Modern Law Review* (2011): 1–27, at 37, 1; Lauren Benton, *Law and Colonial Cultures: Legal Regimes in World History, 1400–1900* (Cambridge University Press, 2002); Oko Elechi, "African Indigenous Justice System," 1–30; Boumakani, "L'Etat de Droit en Afrique," 445–69; Erica Harper, "Customary Justice: From Program Design to Impact Evaluation," *International Development Law Organization* (2011): 26–30; Stephen Breyer, "For Their Own Good: The Cherokees, the Supreme Court, and the Early History of American Conscience," *New Republic* (2010): 7; Botero, et al., "Judicial Reform."

10 "U.S. Federal Rules of Civil Procedure, Rule 1," last modified December 1, 2010, available at http://www.law.cornell.edu/rules/frcp/Rule1.htm (emphasis added).

11 While "just" is a synonym of "impartial," "speedy" refers to only one of the critical dimensions of efficiency, and "inexpensive" speaks only about one of the key component of access. Botero, et al., "Judicial Reform," 61–88.

12 Ibid., 80.

13 For a comprehensive description of the concept, see, Debora Rhode, *Access to Justice* (Oxford University Press, 2004).

Procedures in all countries aim at balancing these dimensions of judicial effectiveness. There is no magic formula to achieve the right balance among them. Just as with any other service – such as telephone communication or the financial services – there is an inescapable compromise among speed, cost, access, and quality of the service. Judicial procedures everywhere face the challenge of guaranteeing the widest possible access to justice; maintaining speed and cost of litigation within reasonable limits; and ensuring a fair and enforceable outcome of the procedures, while simultaneously preserving effective alternatives to litigation.[14] Evidently there are multiple definitions of these concepts, and especially the concept of "impartiality." Different types of process deliver different types of justice. But regardless of these variations, justice is – or at least it is supposed to be – the outcome of the judicial process.[15]

Rules of procedure are the safeguard of fairness.[16] Procedures are established to guarantee the litigant's right to have her case decided in accordance with the law. Without due process of law, litigants would be subject to the unfettered discretion of the judge. Therefore, rules of procedure may rightfully impose some restrictions on the efficiency of proceedings and citizens' access to courts, in order to guarantee the impartiality (accuracy) of judicial decisions. In the words of Professor Purwoto Gandasubrata, "in connection with the nature of the judicial process itself and considering the formal, punctual and rather complicated manners and usages upheld by the courts according to the Law on Procedure, it could be said that *correct judgment cannot be performed in a short time*."[17] This is the basic compromise of the adjudicative process. While there is no magic formula to achieve a perfect balance among these elements (efficiency, access, and impartiality), and societies may reach different equilibriums at various points in time, there are some boundaries within which these equilibriums may be considered "reasonable."[18]

Legal families and countries around the world have reached different equilibriums regarding the interaction of the various dimensions of judicial effectiveness (efficiency, access, and accuracy). The most salient differences are those between the civil law and the common-law traditions that are discussed in the next section. In civil law countries procedural and substantive safeguards tend to restrict judicial efficiency to protect the defendant and enhance procedural and substantive fairness.

[14] The public service provided by the judicial system may be subject to the same efficiency-quality-access analysis as any other service, such as the telephone or water supply. Perfect telephone communication, 100 percent pure water, and immaculate judicial decisions, which are available only at prohibitive costs or after unbearable delay, are all examples of poor quality services.

[15] More precisely, the outcome of the process of adjudication through formal or informal (customary) justice institutions.

[16] See, e.g., J. A. Jolowicz, *On Civil Procedure* (Cambridge University Press, 2000).

[17] Purwoto Gandasubrata, "Indonesia," *Administration of Justice: Procedural Reforms on Court Congestion* (1980): 7, at 2, 1 (emphasis added).

[18] E.g., Common-law countries use the "reasonable prudent person" standard in torts and contracts. Civil law countries have a similar standard, inherited from Rome: the good *pater familias* (head of household).

In common-law countries, conversely, the guarantee of procedural fairness heavily relies on judicial discretion.[19] A number of practical consequences flow from this basic conceptual difference.

TWO MODELS OF ADJUDICATION: LEGISLATIVE CONTROL (CIVIL LAW) VERSUS JUDICIAL DISCRETION (COMMON LAW)

Comparativists have long proposed the idea that the laws of all countries may be aggregated into a handful of legal families. Similar institutional designs within these families have been said to stem from shared legal traditions. As the late professor John Henry Merryman defined it:

> A legal tradition, as the term implies, is not a set of rules of law about contracts, corporations, and crimes, although such rules will almost always be in some sense a reflection of that tradition. Rather it is a set of deeply rooted, historically conditioned attitudes about the nature of the law, about the role of law in the society and the polity, about the proper organization and operation of a legal system, and about the way law is or should be made, applied, studied, perfected, and taught. The legal tradition relates the legal system to the culture of which it is a partial expression. It puts the legal system into cultural perspective.[20]

The evolution of procedure in civil law and common-law countries allows us to delineate two models of adjudication. In civil law countries procedural and substantive safeguards tend to restrict judicial efficiency to protect the defendant and enhance procedural and substantive fairness. In common-law countries, conversely, the guarantee of procedural and substantive fairness heavily relies on judicial discretion.[21] Renowned comparativists – R. C. van Caenegem, Mirjan Damaška, Rene David, John P. Dawson, Mary Ann Glendon, Merryman, Rudolf Schlesinger, Konrad Zweigert, and Hein Kotz – differ on a number of issues related to the divide between civil law and common law, but they all tend to agree on the fact that specific historical developments led to a rather distinct view of the role of the judge in society. Evidently there are variations among individual countries – each one has its own history – but the trends seem clear and they help to understand the particular situation of each country in a broader perspective.

However, the increased procedural rigidity of the civil law tradition, which has been found to be associated with increased burden and cost of litigation,[22] arguably

[19] John Henry Merryman, *The Civil Law Tradition: Introduction to the Legal Systems of Western Europe and Latin America* (Stanford University Press, 1970), 123.

[20] Ibid., 2.

[21] Ibid., 123.

[22] Djankov, et al., "Courts: The Lex Mundi Project," *The Quarterly Journal of Economics* (2003): 118, 2; Aron Balas, et al., "The Divergence of Legal Procedures," Working Paper No. w13809, National Bureau of Economic Research (2008); "Doing Business Report 2004 to 2009 (Enforcing Contracts)," *World Bank* (2008).

reflects a comparatively higher and perhaps fully justified desire to ensure substantive justice. It may simply reflect a different, and possibly better, compromise between judicial efficiency, access to justice, and procedural guarantees. Professor John Langbein convincingly argues that the governing role of the judge and the inquest procedures of the civil law system, adequately address the fundamental inequality problem of the adversarial common law, that is the "inequality of weapons." In his words:

> The German system gives us a good perspective on another great defect of adversary theory, the problem that the Germans call "Waffenungleichheit" – literally, inequality of weapons, or in this instance, inequality of counsel. In a fair fight the pugilists must be well matched. You cannot send me into a ring with Muhammed Ali if you expect a fair fight. The simple truth is that very little in our adversary system is designed to match combatants of comparable prowess, even though adversarial prowess is a main factor affecting the outcome of litigation. Adversary theory thus presupposes a condition that adversary practice achieves only indifferently.... Disparity in the inequality of legal representation can make a difference in Germany, too, but the active role of the judge places major limits on the extent of the injury that bad lawyering can work on a litigant. In German procedure both parties get the same fact-gatherer – the judge.[23]

When the outcome of litigation depends so much on the parties, as it does in adversarial systems, the most affluent party – who can afford the best lawyer – is more likely to win. Thus the German judge intervenes to protect the weak. In sharp contrast, let us consider the role of the judge according to the U.S. Supreme Court:[24]

> In our adversary system, in both civil and criminal cases, in the first instance and on appeal, we follow the principle of party presentation. That is, we rely on the parties to frame the issues for decision and assign to courts the role of neutral arbiter of matters the parties present ... as a general rule, "[o]ur adversary system is designed around the premise that the parties know what is best for them, and are responsible for advancing the facts and arguments entitling them to relief." [*Castro v. United States*, 540 U.S. 375, 386 (203)] (SCALIA, J., concurring in part and concurring in judgment). As cogently explained: "[Courts] do not, or should not, sally forth each day looking for wrongs to right. We wait for cases to come to us, and when they do we normally decide only questions presented by the parties." *United States v. Samuels*, 808 F. 2d 1298, 1301 (CA8 1987) (R. Arnold, J., concurring in denial of reh'g en banc).

In sum, while the U.S. judge is an impartial umpire, the blindfolded *Lady Justice* with the scales, the civil law judge emerges as the protector of the weak

[23] John H. Langbein, "The German Advantage in Civil Procedure," *University of Chicago Law Review* (1985): 843, at 52, 4.

[24] *Greenlaw v. United States*, 554 U.S. 237, 243 (2008) (footnote omitted).

(or the *Buddha of Compassion* in the Japanese variant), and this fact alone may fully justify allowing for comparatively more lengthy and cumbersome procedures.[25]

Civil law and common-law traditions seem to have achieved different equilibriums. In civil law countries procedural and substantive safeguards tend to restrict judicial efficiency to protect the defendant and enhance procedural and substantive fairness. In common-law countries, conversely, the guarantee of procedural fairness heavily relies on judicial discretion (and substantive fairness partly relies on efficient markets[26]). This may explain why common-law countries have been found empirically to have more efficient proceedings than civil law countries, at least for simple litigation. Civil law tends to be more protective of the weaker party in the dispute, which is commonly the defendant.

The next question is whether these variations among civil law and common-law countries are by design – that is, they reflect slightly different cultural notions of what is "fair" or "just" in England, France, and Germany over the centuries – or simply a product of historical chance or political compromise. In the case of "mother" countries it may be both. The different judicial equilibrium among civil law and common-law countries reflects a slightly different understanding of what is fair, which in turn is deeply rooted in history and long-forgotten political compromises.[27] In the United States, justice means fair play, the judicial process is a contest, and the judge is an umpire. The function of the American judge is to guarantee an efficient and fair process. In contrast, in civil law countries the judge is the good old Roman *pater familias*, who has a say and becomes involved in every dispute within the family. The function of the civil law judge is to ensure a fair outcome. Moreover, in other civil law countries that have millenary autochthonous traditions, justice is represented by the Buddha of Compassion; "the Japanese criminal law system has harmony as its goal."[28] In this civil law variant, the function of the judge is to restore social harmony.

[25] In his seminal paper Professor Langbein goes one step further; he argues that German civil procedure is not only better than its American counterpart in terms of substantive fairness, but it is also more efficient: "Our lawyer-dominated system of civil procedure has often been criticized both for its incentives to distort evidence and for the expense and complexity of its modes of discovery and trial. ... My theme is that, by assigning judges rather than lawyers to investigate the facts, the Germans avoid the most troublesome aspects of our practice. ... The primary reason that German courts do less fact-gathering than American lawyers is that the Germans eliminate the waste" (Langbein, "The German Advantage," at 823 and 846).

[26] See, e.g., landlord-tenant disputes in New Zealand.

[27] E.g., a different power balance between the Crown and the feudal lords. See Mirjan Damaska, *The Faces of Justice and State Authority* (Yale University Press, 1986).

[28] Carl F. Goodman, *The Rule of Law in Japan: A Comparative Analysis*. 2nd rev. ed. (Kluwer Law International, 2003), 504.

MIDDLE-INCOME COUNTRIES AND LEGAL "TRANSPLANTS"

Professor Merryman instructs us that, "the legal tradition relates the legal system [of a particular country] to the culture of which it is a partial expression. It puts the legal system into cultural perspective."[29] Or does it?

Most European legal institutions have been transplanted from the "mother" countries into their colonies and other territories. Procedures have not been adopted by recipient countries upon a reasoned finding – after careful examination – that these procedures would fit the culture and needs of these particular societies. Quite to the contrary, laws and procedures have been largely copied and adopted in transplant countries because the adoption was either forcefully imposed by the colonizers, or voluntarily adopted by local elites as instruments to perpetrate existing power allocation arrangements. As Hannah Irfan tells us, in Pakistan "one of the major reasons that women victims are reluctant to take action against violence through the courts is that they fear the system of which they have no knowledge. The inadequacy of knowledge and information about the legal processes made the thought of even going to court frightening."[30]

As we saw previously, Langbein convincingly argues that the governing role of the judge and the inquest procedures of the civil law system adequately address the fundamental inequality problem of the adversarial common law, that is the "inequality of weapons." However, this may be true for Germany, Austria, France, and Holland. When the day-to-day reality of access to justice for everyday folks in Mexico and Colombia is put into the magnifying glass, the role of the judge as the protector of the weak is seriously called into question. Moreover, because almost all litigation is written and in most cases the judge never meets the parties, the opposite seems to be true – extensive empirical research in Mexico and other Latin American countries seem to confirm this view. This is even clearer when, as in many countries, the various stages of the procedure are handled by different officers.[31]

Judicial stagnation in MICs is not a recent phenomenon; the gap between developed and developing countries on judicial efficiency has been documented

[29] Merryman, *Civil Law Tradition*, 2.

[30] Irfan, *"Honor" and Violence Against Women in Pakistan*, 162.

[31] "Those under the influence of the French tradition have what the French call 'la phase de l'instruction.' This is an investigatory phase conducted only by one of the subsequent decision-makers and not accessible to the public, should it include oral elements." "L'instruction or, as it is called of late, 'la mise en état' and 'la trattazione' are much more than just the taking of evidence. . . . In France [the investigatory judges] even belong to a special category of judges appointed as 'judges de la mise en état.' They are expected to handle 200 to 250 cases every year. They have to do everything needed for a full clarification of the factual issues in dispute including, so to speak, if it is unavoidable, the taking of evidence. The judge has to set deadlines for procedural acts to be committed, particularly for completing factual allegations, submitting evidentiary materials and requesting that evidence be taken. Only after his conclusion that everything is clarified or that no further clarification is obtainable, may he return the case to the deciding body." Charles Platto, ed., *Economic Consequences of Litigation Worldwide* (Kluwer Law International, 1999), 78–80.

for decades. For instance, the average duration of a civil dispute in first instance in Germany in 1993 was of 4.2 months (County Court), of 4.9 months in second instance (District Court), and of 8.7 months before the Higher Regional Court.[32] For the same year, the average duration of a case in France was of 4.8 months in the *Tribunal d'Instance*, of 9.3 months in the *Tribunal de Grande Instance*, and of 13.3 months in the Court of Appeals.[33] In contrast, in India "in 1993 it was taking between 12 and 15 years for a case to be tried before the Bombay High Court, with an additional period of 10 to 12 years before all appeals would be exhausted."[34] The elements of the judicial equilibrium introduced previously (efficiency, access, and impartiality) do not seem to be in balance.

CUSTOMARY JUSTICE IN LOW-INCOME COUNTRIES AND MIDDLE-INCOME COUNTRIES

The access to justice gap is filled in many countries – particularly in LICs – by coexisting informal (customary, traditional, aboriginal) dispute-settlement mechanisms, such as the village elders. Traditional justice is widely used because:

> The formal legal system proves less efficient and less accessible in terms of infrastructure, language and facilities as well as actual delivery of justice to the citizens, and hence there has been an increased reliance on this alternative and traditional form of dispute resolution in Pakistan. It is argued that local tribunals because of their proximity substantially reduce the cost of dispute settlement for the poor, and are decided on the basis of customary law, which the villagers can comprehend. Most importantly, however, the contrast drawn between the formal system and the informal tribal system is that the decisions of the tribal system enjoy the "sanction of tradition and are more readily and willingly acceptable" by the parties. State laws are rarely understood by the uneducated masses and "court decisions do not inspire confidence either in merit or impartiality."[35]

Yet, as previously mentioned, these mechanisms no longer deliver accessible and efficient justice in MICs. Increasing internal migration and urbanization in MICs have eroded the ability of large segments of society to resort to customary justice. Newly arrived migrant peasants and members of indigenous groups are often unable to keep their traditions and ancestral dispute-settlement mechanisms alive in big cities, while they are also unable to understand and incorporate the abstruse legal procedures of the formal courts. While this problem is also present in some LICs, it is particularly acute among MICs.

[32] Ibid., 173.
[33] Ibid., 159.
[34] Ross Cranston, "Access to Justice in South and South-East Asia," in *Good Government and Law*, ed. Julio Faundez (The British Council, St. Martin's Press, 1997), 241.
[35] Irfan, *"Honor" and Violence Against Women in Pakistan*, 162.

QUANTITATIVE ANALYSIS OF THE DELIVERY OF JUSTICE IN HIGH-INCOME COUNTRIES AND MIDDLE-INCOME COUNTRIES

This section presents a statistical analysis of cross-sectional data on the delivery of justice in a large sample of countries. This analysis compares the overall effectiveness of the judicial system in delivering impartial, efficient, and accessible justice (the judicial equilibrium) across legal families for a large sample of HICs and MICs. The analysis includes civil and criminal justice, and private arbitration.

The purpose of this analysis is to determine whether (1) the overall effectiveness of the judicial system in delivering impartial, efficient, and accessible justice, is determined by policy choices inherent to the legal architecture of the main legal traditions of the world – the civil law and the common law; (2) these policy choices have effectively migrated from mother to transplant countries within legal families; and/or (3) other factors beyond the legal architecture or the level of resources – such as the prevalence of corruption – explain the overall effectiveness of civil and criminal justice across countries.

Methods

Eight new indicators (civil access, civil efficient, civil impartial, criminal efficient, criminal impartial, ADR [Alternative Dispute Resolution] access, ADR efficient, and ADR impartial) are produced based on the components of the *WJP Rule of Law Index* 2011 that measure justice.[36] These new indicators measure the judicial equilibrium presented in the first section of this paper, for a large sample of countries.

The *WJP Rule of Law Index* rankings and scores are built from more than four hundred variables drawn from two new data sources: a general population poll, designed by the World Justice Project (WJP) and conducted by leading local polling companies using a probability sample of one thousand respondents in the three largest cities of each country; and a qualified respondents' questionnaire completed by in-country experts in civil and commercial law, criminal law, labor law, and public health. To date, more than sixty-six thousand people and two thousand experts have been interviewed in sixty-six countries and jurisdictions.[37]

[36] Factor 7, civil justice, and Factor 8, criminal justice. The *WJP Rule of Law Index* provides new data on nine dimensions of the rule of law: limited government powers, absence of corruption, order and security, fundamental rights, open government, effective regulatory enforcement, access to civil justice, effective criminal justice, and informal justice. These factors are further disaggregated into fifty-two subfactors. Together, they provide a comprehensive picture of rule-of-law compliance. Agrast, et al., "The WJP Rule of Law Index 2011," *The World Justice Project* (2011), available at www.worldjusticeproject.org.

[37] A full description of the methods employed to collect, weight, aggregate, and normalize the data, as well as the precise definition of the more than 150 variables employed to construct the relevant judicial components of the *WJP Rule of Law Index* 2011, are provided in J. Botero and A. Ponce, *Measuring the Rule of Law*, The World Justice Project Working Paper No. 1. 2011, available at www.worldjusticeproject.org. A statistical assessment of the reliability of the *WJP Rule of Law Index* data is also

The dependent variables included in this analysis are constructed through the aggregation of relevant subfactors of the *WJP Rule of Law Index* 2011. These variables are:

Civil Access: This variable measures the accessibility of the civil justice system. It is coded as the average of subfactors 7.2 and 7.3. Subfactor 7.2 measures whether people can access and afford legal advice and representation, and subfactor 7.3 measures whether people can access and afford civil courts.

Civil Impartial: This variable measures the impartiality of the civil justice system. It is coded as the average of subfactors 7.4, 7.5, and 7.6. Subfactor 7.4 measures whether civil justice is free of discrimination, subfactor 7.5 measures whether civil justice is free of corruption, and subfactor 7.6 measures whether civil justice is free of improper government influence.

Civil Efficient: This variable measures the efficiency of the civil justice system. It is coded as the average of subfactors 7.7 and 7.8. Subfactor 7.7 measures whether civil justice is not subject to unreasonable delays, and subfactor 7.8 measures whether civil justice is effectively enforced.

Criminal Impartial: This variable measures the impartiality of the criminal justice system. It is coded as the average of subfactors 8.4, 8.5, 8.6, and 8.7. Subfactor 8.4 measures whether the criminal justice system is impartial, subfactor 8.5 measures whether the criminal justice system is free of corruption, subfactor 8.6 measures whether the criminal justice system is free of improper government influence, and subfactor 8.7 measures whether the criminal justice system accords the accused due process of law.

Criminal Efficient: This variable measures the efficiency of the criminal justice system. It is coded as the average of subfactors 8.1, 8.2, and 8.3. Subfactor 8.1 measures whether crimes are effectively investigated, subfactor 8.2 measures whether crimes are effectively and timely adjudicated, and subfactor 8.3 measures whether the correctional system is effective in reducing criminal behavior.

ADR Access: This variable measures the accessibility of the private arbitration mechanisms available in the country. It is coded as subfactor 7.9.1, which measures whether commercial arbitration mechanisms are accessible.

ADR Impartial: This variable measures the impartiality of the private arbitration mechanisms available in the country. It is coded as subfactor 7.9.3, which measures whether commercial arbitration is free of improper influence (corruption).

ADR Efficient: This variable measures the efficiency of the private arbitration mechanisms available in the country. It is coded as the average of subfactors 7.9.4 and 7.9.5, which measure whether commercial arbitration is not subject to unreasonable delays, and if it is effectively enforced.

available at Michaela Saisana and Andrea Saltelli, "Rankings and Ratings: Instructions for Use," *Hague Journal on the Rule of Law* (2011): 247–68, at 3, 2; and M. Agrast, J. Botero, and A. Ponce, "Statistical Test of the WJP Rule of Law Index," in *WJP Rule of Law Index* 2011 (The World Justice Project, 2011), at 123.

Independent variables employed are legal origin, gross domestic product (GDP) per capita, and absence of corruption. Legal origin is taken from Djankov, et al. Income groups follow the World Bank standard classification – upper and lower MICs are grouped together. Absence of corruption is taken from the overall score of Factor 2 of the *WJP Rule of Law Index* 2011, which measures absence of corruption.[38]

First, bivariate analyses are conducted by legal origin and income-level group. Secondly, multivariate analyses are conducted for civil and criminal justice indicators by legal origin, controlling by per capita income and prevalence of corruption. For each variable of civil or criminal justice effectiveness, three models are analyzed for a subsample of all HICs and MICs. In the first model only legal origin is included; common law is used as comparison category against French and German legal origin. In the second model GDP per capita is introduced in the analysis, under the rationale that the overall level of resources available in society may determine the effectiveness of justice delivery across countries, regardless of legal architectures derived from policy choices of the civil and common-law traditions. In the third model absence of corruption is included. Corruption is included as a proxy for other variables. The rationale is that other characteristics of the judicial system, which are independent of the design of the system per se, such as the prevalence of corruption, may determine the effectiveness of the delivery of justice beyond the policy choices of the legal families and the level of resources available in society.

The analysis was conducted with SPSS 20. Inclusion criterion was to be listed in the *WJP Rule of Law Index* 2011. No country was excluded. Results of these analyses are presented in Table 10.1.

Legal Traditions

Table 10.1 shows the country scores obtained by the twenty-three HICs[39] included in the sample, grouped by legal tradition.

Table 10.2 presents the results of independent sample T-tests comparing high-income countries HICs by legal family.

These analyses support the notion that the civil law and common-law traditions have developed different judicial equilibriums. Among HICs in both traditions justice appears to be equally impartial. However, there are statistically significant differences between common-law and civil law countries in terms of the trade-off

[38] There is a partial overlap between one of the dimensions of Factor 2 (absence of corruption) and one of the dimensions of impartiality of civil and criminal justice (subfactors 7.5 and 8.5). In the *WJP Rule of Law Index* 2011, Factor 2 includes data for three subfactors: 2.1. Government officials in the executive branch do not use public office for private gain; 2.2. Government officials in the judicial branch do not use public office for private gain; and 2.3. Government officials in the police and the military do not use public office for private gain.

[39] The table includes twenty-two countries and one jurisdiction, Hong Kong SAR China.

TABLE 10.1. *Country Scores of HICs by Legal Tradition*

Country	Civil Access	Civil Impartial	Civil Efficient	Criminal Impartial	Criminal Efficient	ADR Access	ADR Impartial	ADR Efficient
Australia	0.57	0.73	0.60	0.82	0.62	0.83	0.89	0.84
Canada	0.57	0.77	0.53	0.83	0.67	0.73	0.80	0.77
Hong Kong SAR	0.66	0.64	0.74	0.81	0.89	0.42	0.89	0.76
New Zealand	0.77	0.85	0.66	0.90	0.77	0.87	0.93	0.80
Singapore	0.46	0.76	0.71	0.83	0.82	0.39	1.00	0.74
United Arab Emirates	0.58	0.75	0.67	0.81	0.89	0.75	0.93	0.58
United Kingdom	0.66	0.75	0.65	0.80	0.70	0.67	0.87	0.78
United States	0.52	0.67	0.61	0.71	0.67	0.82	0.90	0.70
Common law	0.60	0.74	0.65	0.81	0.75	0.68	0.90	0.75
Belgium	0.77	0.77	0.59	0.77	0.63	0.33	0.75	0.74
France	0.71	0.71	0.50	0.77	0.55	0.67	1.00	0.77
Italy	0.66	0.66	0.30	0.80	0.64	0.63	0.55	0.70
Netherlands	0.79	0.81	0.74	0.89	0.71	0.67	0.86	0.85
Spain	0.72	0.70	0.48	0.76	0.63	0.67	0.77	0.64
French origin	0.73	0.73	0.52	0.80	0.63	0.59	0.78	0.74
Austria	0.73	0.76	0.62	0.84	0.73	0.58	1.00	0.75
Croatia	0.77	0.55	0.33	0.58	0.39	0.53	0.94	0.64
Czech Republic	0.74	0.71	0.36	0.84	0.66	0.67	0.89	0.78
Estonia	0.72	0.86	0.52	0.81	0.67	0.78	0.88	0.83
Germany	0.83	0.88	0.61	0.82	0.73	0.83	1.00	0.72
Japan	0.62	0.79	0.68	0.81	0.69	0.83	0.70	0.89
Poland	0.68	0.65	0.34	0.84	0.56	0.67	0.80	0.62
South Korea	0.65	0.67	0.58	0.70	0.66	0.62	0.90	0.79
German origin	0.72	0.73	0.51	0.78	0.64	0.69	0.89	0.75
Norway	0.71	0.94	0.65	0.88	0.83	1.00	1.00	0.92
Sweden	0.73	0.83	0.69	0.89	0.69	0.22	1.00	0.88
Scandinavian	0.72	0.88	0.67	0.89	0.76	0.61	1.00	0.90
HICs (avg.)	0.68	0.75	0.57	0.80	0.69	0.66	0.88	0.76

between access and efficiency of justice. The delivery of civil justice in common-law countries appears to be more efficient <T-stat–2.62*> and less accessible < T-stat –3.98**> than in civil law countries. Scandinavian countries, by contrast, outperform both civil law and common-law countries in terms of judicial efficiency, while also providing as much access to civil justice as the French and German origin

TABLE 10.2. *Independent Sample T-tests of HICs by Legal Tradition*

	Civil Access	Civil Impartial	Civil Efficient	Criminal Impartial	Criminal Efficient	ADR Access	ADR Impartial	ADR Efficient
Independent sample T-tests								
Common law vs. civil law	-3.98^{c}	-0.32	2.62^{b}	0.45	2.33^{b}	0.45	0.81	-0.59
Common vs. French	-2.80^{b}	0.28	2.06^{a}	0.50	2.82^{b}	0.94	1.86^{a}	0.11
Common vs. German	-2.92^{b}	0.15	2.56^{b}	0.93	2.17^{b}	-0.08	0.31	-0.19
Common vs. Scandinavian	-1.69	-2.79^{b}	-0.53	-1.80	-0.09	0.18	-2.33^{b}	-2.60^{b}

[a] $p < 0.1$.
[b] $p < 0.05$.
[c] $p < 0.01$.

countries. They also obtain significantly higher scores in terms of the impartiality of the civil justice system.

In terms of criminal justice, the numbers suggest that both civil law and common-law countries deliver equally impartial justice. However, criminal justice is statistically significantly more efficient in common-law countries <t-stat 2.33*>. Unfortunately, no measure of access to criminal justice is available. Finally, there appears to be no significant difference in the efficiency, accessibility, and impartiality of alternative dispute-resolution mechanisms available in civil law and common-law countries.

Legal Traditions among Transplant Countries

When the same comparison is applied to MICs, results are very different. Table 10.3 shows the country scores obtained by thirty-five MICs included in the sample, grouped by legal tradition.

Table 10.4 presents the results of independent sample T-tests comparing MICs by legal family.

Results are very interesting. When only MICs are taken into account, the differences across legal families observed among HICs disappear. There are no statistically significant differences between civil law and common-law countries in terms of the efficiency and impartiality of civil and criminal justice, or in the accessibility, efficiency, and impartiality of private arbitration. Only a statistical trend is noted in the case of accessibility of civil justice, where civil law countries appear to be more accessible than their common-law counterparts <t-stat −2.00†>. This stands in

TABLE 10.3. *Country Scores of MICs by Legal Tradition*

Country	Civil Access	Civil Impartial	Civil Efficient	Criminal Impartial	Criminal Efficient	ADR Access	ADR Impartial	ADR Efficient
India	0.56	0.58	0.28	0.56	0.45	0.65	0.62	0.60
Jamaica	0.61	0.64	0.37	0.63	0.36	0.50	0.50	0.65
Malaysia	0.52	0.50	0.44	0.50	0.55	0.72	0.86	0.63
Nigeria	0.58	0.60	0.48	0.48	0.32	0.59	0.73	0.57
Pakistan	0.48	0.30	0.15	0.40	0.30	0.60	0.30	0.32
South Africa	0.51	0.66	0.51	0.66	0.42	0.70	0.85	0.74
Thailand	0.49	0.52	0.37	0.66	0.60	0.62	0.67	0.40
Common law	0.54	0.54	0.37	0.56	0.43	0.63	0.65	0.56
Albania	0.70	0.45	0.36	0.43	0.33	1.00	0.63	0.57
Argentina	0.69	0.57	0.46	0.47	0.28	0.67	0.91	0.50
Bolivia	0.55	0.37	0.50	0.35	0.28	0.62	0.65	0.52
Brazil	0.68	0.67	0.37	0.56	0.37	0.33	0.94	0.61
Cameroon	0.55	0.43	0.23	0.44	0.28	1.00	0.13	0.47
Chile	0.78	0.66	0.50	0.66	0.50	0.54	0.73	0.72
Colombia	0.74	0.60	0.37	0.51	0.32	0.50	0.80	0.61
Dominican Republic	0.52	0.55	0.50	0.56	0.37	0.54	0.85	0.62
El Salvador	0.73	0.56	0.35	0.51	0.25	0.53	0.50	0.68
Guatemala	0.47	0.48	0.40	0.49	0.33	0.73	0.83	0.54
Indonesia	0.67	0.58	0.35	0.66	0.52		0.25	0.63
Iran	0.65	0.51	0.59	0.46	0.54	0.67		0.70
Jordan	0.64	0.60	0.46	0.56	0.55	0.87	1.00	0.76
Kazakhstan	0.67	0.52	0.58	0.48	0.51			0.66
Lebanon	0.58	0.44	0.41	0.51	0.44	0.58	0.50	0.50
Mexico	0.51	0.43	0.38	0.38	0.20	0.59	0.56	0.59
Morocco	0.55	0.46	0.50	0.35	0.40	0.89	0.33	0.71
Peru	0.47	0.51	0.40	0.62	0.35	0.30	0.83	0.79
Philippines	0.50	0.49	0.30	0.50	0.38	0.54	0.67	0.58
Romania	0.63	0.59	0.37	0.62	0.51	0.62	0.71	0.75
Russia	0.57	0.57	0.41	0.62	0.66	0.67	0.86	0.56
Senegal	0.61	0.50	0.32	0.46	0.47	1.00	1.00	0.56
Turkey	0.64	0.61	0.48	0.47	0.38	0.48	0.50	0.81
Ukraine	0.52	0.34	0.38	0.39	0.46	0.00	0.40	0.51
Venezuela	0.61	0.39	0.24	0.30	0.29	0.59	0.85	0.46
Vietnam	0.46	0.45	0.51	0.52	0.58	0.78	0.50	0.54
French origin	0.60	0.51	0.41	0.49	0.41	0.63	0.66	0.61
Bulgaria	0.62	0.55	0.41	0.37	0.20	0.80	0.75	0.65
China	0.65	0.37	0.57	0.52	0.73	0.67	0.44	0.63
German origin	0.64	0.46	0.49	0.45	0.47	0.73	0.60	0.64
MICs (avg.)	0.59	0.52	0.41	0.50	0.41	0.63	0.66	0.60

TABLE 10.4. *Independent Sample T-tests of MICs by Legal Tradition*

	Civil Access	Civil Impartial	Civil Efficient	Criminal Impartial	Criminal Efficient	ADR Access	ADR Impartial	ADR Efficient
Common law vs. civil law	−2.00^{a}	0.84	−1.14	1.56	0.33	−0.01	−0.13	−1.26
Common vs. French	−2.66^{b}	0.74	−1.01	1.47	0.46	−0.00	−0.18	−1.17
Common vs. German	−2.88^{b}	0.88	−1.18	1.37	−014	−1.73	0.30	−0.78

TABLE 10.5. *Independent Sample T-tests by Income Level*

	Civil Access	Civil Impartial	Civil Efficient	Criminal Impartial	Criminal Efficient	ADR Access	ADR Impartial	ADR Efficient
High income vs. middle income	3.72^{d}	9.30^{d}	5.38^{d}	13.45^{d}	8.34^{d}	0.50	4.92^{d}	5.77^{c}
High income vs. low income	5.00^{d}	8.47^{d}	2.96^{c}	10.48^{d}	6.35^{d}	−0.51	4.65^{c}	4.23^{c}
Middle income vs. low income	3.15^{c}	2.95^{c}	−041	1.92	0.08	−083	2.83^{c}	0.54

Note: The following key is to be used for Tables 10.4 and 10.5.
^{a} $p < 0.1$.
^{b} $p < 0.05$.
^{c} $p < 0.01$.
^{d} $p < 0.001$.

sharp contrast to the strongly significant variations across legal families found among HICs.

Income Groups – Sixty-six Countries

Table 10.5 presents the results of independent sample T-tests comparing sixty-six countries (twenty-three HICs, thirty-five MICs, and eight LICs) by income levels.

When countries are grouped by income level, income appears to be a defining factor for all justice effectiveness variables, except one. The delivery of justice in HICs significantly outperforms MICs and LICs in all dimensions, with the only exception of the accessibility of private arbitration.

MICs significantly outperform LICs in the delivery of accessible and impartial civil justice, and impartial private arbitration. Interestingly, the justice gap between HICs and MICs appears to be wider than that between MICs and LICs,[40]

[40] Upper and lower MICs are grouped together in this analysis. While there are some variations among these two subgroups of countries, they are comparatively smaller than those between HICs, MICs, and LICs.

TABLE 10.6. *Civil Access*

	High Income			Middle Income		
	β	β	β	B	β	β
Legal origen common law	Comparison category					
Legal origen French	.602[c]	.632[c]	.645[c]	.347[a]	.347	.472[b]
Legal origen German	.625[c]	.697[c]	.718[c]	.282	.282	.322[a]
GDP per capita		.178	.169		.000	.153
Absence of corruption			.053			.434[b]
(constant)	[d]	[d]	[b]	[d]	[d]	[d]
R^2	.423	.450	.452	.118	.118	.285

[a] $p < 0.1$.
[b] $p < 0.05$.
[c] $p < 0.01$.
[d] $p < 0.001$.

particularly with regard to criminal justice outcomes. The efficiency of civil justice, as well as the efficiency and impartiality of criminal justice in MICs, are not higher than in LICs.

Legal Origin, Income Level, and Corruption

Tables 10.6–10.10 present the results of a series of linear regression analyses of the five variables of civil and criminal justice effectiveness, among twenty-three HICs and thirty-five MICs.

Among HICs both French and German civil law countries deliver more accessible justice than their common-law peers. These results hold after introducing GDP per capita and absence of corruption in models 2 and 3. Among MICs, however, results are different. When GDP per capita is taken into account, civil law countries do not deliver more accessible justice than their common-law peers. Interestingly, legal origin turns significant when absence of corruption is introduced.

Among HICs, common-law countries deliver more efficient justice than their civil law (French and German) peers. These results hold after introducing GDP per capita. However, when absence of corruption is taken into account, differences across legal families disappear. Among MICs there are no statistically significant differences across legal families in the efficiency of the civil justice.

Legal origin and GDP per capita are not significant predictors of impartiality of civil justice among HICs or MICs. As expected, absence of corruption is a strong predictor of impartiality of civil justice among both income groups.

TABLE 10.7. *Civil Efficiency*

	High Income			Middle Income		
	β	β	β	B	β	β
Legal origin common law	Comparison category					
Legal origin French	−.413^{b}	−.403^{a}	−.221	.189	.056	.137
Legal origin German	−.521^{b}	−.498^{a}	−.201	.277	.203	.230
GDP per capita		.058	−.065		−.260	−.160
Absence of corruption			.735^{d}			.282
(constant)	^{d}	^{d}		^{d}	^{d}	^{c}
R^2	.253	.256	.684	.069	.121	.192

^{a} $p < 0.1$.
^{b} $p < 0.05$.
^{c} $p < 0.01$.
^{d} $p < 0.001$.

TABLE 10.8. *Civil Impartial*

	High Income			Middle Income		
	β	β	β	B	β	β
Legal origin	Comparison category					
Legal origin French	−.056	−.010	.197	−.140	−.270	−.077
Legal origin German	−.041	.067	.406	−.214	−.286	−.223
GDP per capita		.265	−.124		−.255	−.017
Absence of corruption			.840			.672
(constant)						
R^2	.003	.064	.623	.040	.091	.493

Among HICs, legal origin, and GDP per capita are not significant predictors of impartiality of criminal justice. Among MICs, legal origin is not significant when taken alone (model 1), but it becomes significant when GDP per capita is introduced (model 2). As expected, absence of corruption is a strong predictor of impartiality of criminal justice among both income groups.

Legal origin is a significant predictor of criminal efficiency among HICs when taken alone and when GDP per capita is considered (models 1 and 2), but it loses significance

TABLE 10.9. *Criminal Impartial*

	High Income			Middle Income		
	β	β	β	B	β	β
Legal origin common law	Comparison category					
Legal origin French	−.096	−.094	.107	−.273	−.408[b]	−.217
Legal origin German	−.252	−.247	.082	−.261	−.336[a]	−.273[a]
GDP per capita		.011	−.125		−.264	−.028
Absence of corruption			.816[d]			.665[d]
(constant)	[d]	[d]	[b]	[d]	[d]	[d]
R^2	.051	.051	.579	.083	.137	.531

Note: The following key is to be used for Tables 10.8 and 10.9.
[a] $p < 0.1$.
[b] $p < 0.05$.
[c] $p < 0.01$.
[d] $p < 0.001$.

TABLE 10.10. *Criminal Efficiency*

	High Income			Middle Income		
	B	β	β	B	B	β
Legal origin common law	Comparison category					
Legal origin French	−.490[b]	−.489[b]	−.338[a]	−.078	−.217	−.102
Legal origin German	−.525[b]	−.525[b]	−.278	.069	−.008	.030
GDP per capita		.000	−.102		−.271	−.129
Absence of corruption			.612[c]			.399[b]
(constant)	[d]	[d]		[d]	[d]	[b]
R^2	.290	.290	.586	.015	.073	.214

[a] $p < 0.1$.
[b] $p < 0.05$.
[c] $p < 0.01$.
[d] $p < 0.001$.

when absence of corruption is introduced in model 3; it only remains as a trend for French origin countries. Among MICs legal origin and income per capita are not significant predictors of criminal efficiency. Absence of corruption is significantly associated with criminal efficiency in both income groups.

DISCUSSION AND CONCLUSION

This last section discusses the findings of the quantitative analysis of judicial outcomes presented in the previous section, in light of the comparative law and development law perspectives introduced in Chapter 1.

The Influence of Legal Families in High-Income Countries and Middle-Income Countries

The data supports the notion that among HICs, the civil law and common-law traditions have developed significantly different judicial equilibriums. These results confirm empirically our expectations from the comparative law literature and other qualitative and anecdotal evidence presented in the preceding text. The civil law and common-law traditions have achieved significantly different balances among accessibility, efficiency, and impartiality of justice. Consistent with the comparative law literature, procedural, and substantive safeguards in civil law countries tend to restrict judicial efficiency to protect the weak party and to enhance procedural and substantive fairness. Similarly, access to justice in civil law countries is enhanced by a comparatively larger cadre of young professional judges tasked with the duty to implement the law (rather than creating it or adapting it to the particular circumstances of the case).[41] In common-law countries, conversely, the guarantee of procedural fairness heavily relies on a body of comparatively more selective, less numerous, less accessible, more senior, and more autonomous judges. Comparative deficiencies in judicial outcomes across legal traditions appear to be the result of different policy choices made by the legal families with regard to the inescapable trade-off among efficiency, impartiality, and accessibility of justice. Common law chose comparatively more efficient and independent justice, while civil law opted for more accessible and protective or "equalizing" justice. The tenant-friendly procedure of France, Germany, and Japan largely reflects a different (not necessarily better or worse) notion of fairness than the plaintiff-friendly procedure of the United States, Australia, and New Zealand.[42] In sum, among HICs, the overall effectiveness of the judicial system in delivering impartial, efficient, and accessible justice (the judicial equilibrium) is determined by policy choices inherent to the legal architecture of the main legal traditions of the world – the civil law and the common law.

[41] While Jean-Ethienne-Marie Portalis expressly refers to judges as those who adapt the inflexible words of the law to the fluid circumstances of the particular case (*Discours Preliminaire do Premier Project de Code Civil*), the revolutionary movement largely limited the role of the judge to specific instances of legal interpretation, which were governed by statue. This represents a significant departure from the Germanic role of the judge in the *pais de droit coutumiere*. The Napoleonic Civil Code and the Code of Civil Procedure had a long-lasting legacy in civil law countries around the world, including a more limited role of the judge. German civil law countries arrived to an intermediate position between the common law and the French family; by adopting through *The Reception* the Roman law of the late (Justinian) period, they inherited a somewhat limited role of the judge, as the final period of Roman procedure was characterized by the "bureaucratization" of justice. See, e.g., R. C. van Caenegem, "History of European Civil Procedure," *International Encyclopedia of Comparative Law* 16, no. 2 (1973): 54–61; Mirjan Damaska, *The Faces of Justice and State Authority* (Yale University Press, 1986); Carl F. Goodman, *The Rule of Law in Japan: A Comparative Analysis*, 2nd rev. ed. (Kluwer Law International, 2003).

[42] See detailed description of landlord-tenant disputes in civil law and common-law countries in the author's unpublished SJD dissertation at Georgetown Law School entitled "The Three Faces of Justice: Legal Traditions, Legal Transplants, and Customary Justice in a Multicultural World," 2013.

Yet, this analysis also suggests that the judicial equilibrium developed by mother countries does not appear to have effectively migrated to transplant countries; there seems to be a fundamental disconnect between the architectural design of judicial institutions and the practical delivery of justice in developing countries. Justice outcomes among MICs do not appear to reflect policy choices of the legal families. Comparative deficiencies in judicial outcomes are not the result of implicit policy choices documented in the comparative law literature. Overall, the characteristics of the delivery of justice in MICs do not mirror those of high-income members of their respective legal families, despite the fact that a number of the actual codes, statutes, and procedures applicable in MICs are identical or remarkably similar to those of their legal "mothers." The judicial equilibrium appears to be broken.

Legal origin fails to explain judicial outcomes in MICs in all dimensions of judicial effectiveness analyzed in this chapter, with the possible exceptions of access to civil justice and impartiality of criminal justice. Overall, the data shows a significant decline in influence of the legal traditions in the delivery of justice outcomes. Legal origin partially explains differences among MICs in accessibility of civil justice, that is the comparatively less accessible justice delivered by MICs that belong to the common-law family, as compared to their civil law income-level peers, may be an expression of a deliberate compromise for a relatively more independent and senior judiciary. Thus less accessible civil justice in common-law MICs does not necessarily mean worse justice; it probably reflects more independent justice. Yet, more independence does not necessarily translate into more impartiality. According to the evidence presented in the third section of this chapter, there are no statistically significant differences between legal families in terms of impartiality of civil justice. Nonetheless, when GDP per capita is taken into account, MICs of the common-law tradition seem to deliver more impartial criminal justice than their civil law (French and German) income-level peers. These appear to be remnants of an old compromise between accessibility of justice and judicial independence, which was probably driven by legal tradition.

The Justice/Income Gap

Another finding of this study is to provide empirical confirmation to the justice gap between HICs and MICs. People and companies in MICs face statistically significantly bigger restrictions to access courts than people and companies in HICs. Moreover, the quality of justice in MICs is also statistically significantly lower. Both civil and criminal courts and ADRs are less efficient and less impartial in MICs than among HICs. There is a significant justice gap in all dimensions of judicial effectiveness between HICs and MICs. These findings confirm empirically the expectations from very extensive qualitative and anecdotal evidence from the development and legal empowerment literature.[43]

Among MICs we find a complex amalgam of "mixed systems," systems that do not entirely follow either the civil law or the common-law traditions. The distinction between French and German legal origin countries is blurred among MICs. More importantly, all these mixed systems deliver suboptimal outcomes: civil and criminal justice in MICs is significantly less accessible, impartial, and efficient than in HICs. ADRs are also less impartial and efficient. None of these findings appear to reflect deliberate policy choices of the legal families. This suggests that the determinants of justice effectiveness in HICs may not be the same as those in MICs.

Finally, our basic bivariate analyses of LICs suggest another big gap in the delivery of justice between MICs and LICs. Just as the determinants of justice effectiveness among HICs and MICs are not uniform, those determinants among MICs and LICs appear to vary. This fact has interesting policy implications for those working on judicial reform in developing countries. Nonetheless, results must be taken with a grain of salt, given the small size of our sample of LICs.

Corruption and Beyond

Consistent with extensive economic development literature, the overall level of corruption emerges as an important determinant of justice outcomes among MICs in all dimensions of judicial effectiveness analyzed in this study.

Professor Merryman was wrong; the legal tradition does not "relate the legal system [of a particular country] to the culture of which it is a partial expression." Outside of the "metropolis" (HICs), the legal tradition only relates the legal system to the culture and needs of the colonizers. For the vast majority of the population of developing countries, the legal system often remains a distant and even frightening transplant, not an integral part of their culture. Even if we could argue that the tenant-friendly procedure of France, Germany, and Japan reflects a different notion of fairness than the plaintiff-friendly procedure of the United States, Australia, or New Zealand,[44] it is hard to believe that these different cultural choices are equally representative of the cultural values of lay people in, say, El Salvador or Ghana. Samuel Huntington argues that "the sources of conflict are in fundamental differences in society and culture."[45] This seems to be true for many legal and procedural transplants. In many developing countries the "transplantation" process may have contributed to create a fundamental disconnect between the intended outcomes of the formal judicial institutions and the practical delivery of justice for vast segments

[43] See, e.g., Collier, "Commission on Legal Empowerment"; Collier, *The Bottom Billion*; Anderson, "Access to Justice," among many others.

[44] See detailed description of landlord-tenant disputes in civil law and common-law countries in Botero, "The Three Faces of Justice," 13.

[45] Huntington, *The Clash of Civilizations*, 225.

of the population. Factors such as the prevalence of corruption, which are not dependent upon the legal architecture of the civil law and common-law traditions, largely explain the overall effectiveness of civil and criminal justice across MICs.

Sophisticated legal elites in LICs and MICs around the world, from Mexico to Sierra Leone, continue to hold fast to the historical principles and institutions of the legal families (civil law and common law), and they rely on these theoretical underpinnings to justify structural inefficiencies of the legal process, and perpetrate insurmountable barriers to access the legal system for large segments of the population. These barriers help the elites to maintain control over the formal dispute-resolution system, which delivers suboptimal results for the society as a whole, and especially for the urban poor. The system is broken, particularly in MICs where the two faces of justice (bureaucratic formal courts and customary justice) are increasingly misaligned with the changing reality of an urban and multicultural population. A third face of justice appears to be needed.[46]

APPENDIX 1. LEGAL ORIGIN – SIXTY-SIX COUNTRIES

Table 10.11 presents the results of independent sample T-tests comparing sixty-six countries of all income levels by legal family.

TABLE 10.11. *Independent Sample T-tests, Full Sample by Legal Family*

	Civil Access	Civil Impartial	Civil Efficient	Criminal Impartial	Criminal Efficient	ADR Access	ADR Impartial	ADR Efficient
Common law vs. civil law	−3.84[d]	0.45	0.80	1.32	1.37	0.02	−013	−0.03
Common vs. French	−2.80[c]	1.68[a]	1.35	2.70[c]	2.29[b]	0.24	0.66	1.01
Common vs. German	−4.55[d]	−1.33	−025	−1.04	−067	−086	−1.45	−1.56
Common vs. Scandinavian	−2.42[b]	−2.50[b]	−1.61	−6.44[d]	−1.44	0.10	−1.59	−2.42[b]

[a] $p < 0.1$.
[b] $p < 0.05$.
[c] $p < 0.01$.
[d] $p < 0.001$.

[46] This new face of justice may assume different shapes. There are a number of examples around the world of more accessible approaches to deliver timely and efficient justice for the urban poor, for instance, paralegals in Sierra Leone, the *tutela* proceeding in Colombia, or small claims courts in the United States. While the problem described in this chapter appears to be present in most MICs, the search for a solution requires a case-by-case approximation. A detailed analysis of a number of relevant considerations in the search for this third face of justice, is included in the author's unpublished SJD dissertation at Georgetown Law School, "The Three Faces of Justice."

When countries of all income levels are taken into account, common-law countries appear to deliver less accessible justice than civil law countries, and more impartial and efficient criminal justice than the French variant of the civil law family. However, these findings have little practical significance, as they must be considered in light of the relatively higher income of German origin and common-law countries. Scandinavian countries outperform civil and common-law countries, but these results have no practical relevance, as this legal family does not include any MICs or LICs.

APPENDIX 2. LOW-INCOME COUNTRIES

Table 10.12 shows the country scores obtained by the eight LICs included in the sample.

TABLE 10.12. *Country Scores of LICs*

	Civil Access	Civil Impartial	Civil Efficient	Criminal Impartial	Criminal Efficient	ADR Access	ADR Impartial	ADR Efficient
Bangladesh	0.50	0.37	0.30	0.48	0.50	0.75	0.30	0.55
Cambodia	0.51	0.23	0.37	0.37	0.42	1.00	0.00	0.36
Ethiopia	0.49	0.48	0.58	0.41	0.44	0.75	0.58	0.47
Ghana	0.54	0.65	0.47	0.67	0.39	0.83	0.75	0.78
Kenya	0.47	0.33	0.44	0.52	0.44	0.53	0.71	0.71
Kyrgyzstan	0.63	0.27	0.45	0.34	0.38	0.67	0.33	0.57
Liberia	0.25	0.42	0.37	0.37	0.21	0.33	0.00	0.48
Uganda	0.45	0.44	0.41	0.47	0.50	0.73	0.45	0.71
LICs (avg.)	0.48	0.40	0.42	0.45	0.41	0.70	0.39	0.58

PART IV

Socioeconomic Challenges in Middle-Income Countries

11

The Role of Courts and Constitutions in the New Politics of Welfare in Latin America

Daniel M. Brinks and William Forbath

Like many middle-income countries (MICs), Latin American welfare states are squeezed between demands for basic social goods and neoliberal policy prescriptions backed by the pressures of a globalized economy. They are pressed to limit taxes, services, and the public sector in order to grow their economies by neoliberal lights; but they have sufficient resources to make the prospect of providing basic goods for their vulnerable populations more than a pipe dream. In MICs across the world, but perhaps especially in Latin America, social movements and reformers seeking ways to resist pressures to limit the welfare state have turned to economic and social rights (ESR) as a tool of mobilization. In alliance with courts, these advocates for ESR have sometimes been successful in tempering the harsher impulses of neoliberalism, and even in expanding and broadening the reach of public provision of goods like health care, housing, or water.

It is our suggestion that the politics of the welfare state in MICs are often shaped by the nature of this alliance between courts and ESR advocates. When courts take a more active role, they can become the central axis of debate, conflict, and cooperation among legislators, members of the executive, and social movements; when courts take a back seat, the debate remains more traditional, and social movements and their allies are generally weakened. Moreover, the forms that judicial "activism" may take also make a critical difference. Courts' interventions can be more policy oriented, or less so; they can address individual grievances or systemic problems, and this too shapes how their intervention will affect politics. In many countries, courts have come to supply crucial deficits in the state, prodding inert central ministries into action; spotlighting large and small gaps in public policy; and lending political leverage and moral authority to ESR movements and advocates. In this way courts can compensate, in some measure, for deficits in responsiveness and accountability toward the mass of poor and vulnerable citizens on the part of bureaucrats, elected officials, and party elites, even under conditions of democratization.

At the same time, however, it is clear that courts are not a panacea, either for activist groups seeking to preserve or broaden social programs, for central governments seeking to monitor compliance with centrally developed policies, or for MICs seeking to negotiate the perilous terrain of development with equity. Often in tension with technocrats who do not wish to cede authority to the courts and with economists fearful of immodest demands on the national fisc, ESR movements and courts find they must engage with many other actors in many-sided strategies and dialogues to succeed.

Recently, though, economic and social rights-based reform has gotten a surprising boost from the demise of the neoliberal Washington Consensus among state elites. State economists, planners, and policy makers, the technocracy, have begun turning away from free market orthodoxy over the past decade. The region has seen a shift toward models of the "new developmental state," or what some have called "Latin American neostructuralism."[1] This new account of development and economic growth has many facets, some of them hotly debated, as we will note, but one precept has gained real traction: ending extreme poverty and assuring a decent minimum of goods like food and water, health, housing, and education are no longer the hoped-for results of good economic policy, but instead are essential ingredients of it. What the ESR-minded lawyers call the progressive realization of social and economic rights, the new developmentalist-minded economists call "investment" in "human capital" through health care, education, broad access to social assistance, and other improvements in the material welfare of the population.

To be sure, efficiency-minded state technocrats can be expected to be leery of the seeming absolutism of rights talk. But whereas free market fundamentalism insists on holding social policy austerely apart from economic policy, the new developmentalism enjoins state economists to wed the two. And while some of the region's important Constitutional Courts remain wedded to a formalist style of jurisprudence, others have adopted a more pragmatic, contextualized, policy-minded style of legal reasoning. Thus, as we will see, the ESR-bearing provisions of the new Latin American constitutions seem to have new salience in the corridors of state power, and a new space has opened for commerce between constitutional courts and ESR advocates, on the one hand, and technocrats in the administrative state, on the other. When and where this happens, the ESR movements seem likely to be more successful in mobilizing all the different aspects of their repertoire toward advancing what several new constitutions call the progressive realization of ESR.

What has emerged in Latin America and other MIC regions, then, as a consequence of the peculiar position in which MICs find themselves in the global economy today, is a set of social and institutional practices around ESR. Their goal is to refound a welfare state in the context of a global economy and the dominance and discontents of neoliberal economic policy. Over the last twenty-five years, in MICs around the world, social democratic-minded attorneys and

[1] Fernando Ignacio Leiva, *Latin American Neostructuralism: The Contradictions of Post-neoliberal Development* (University of Minnesota Press, 2008). See also David Trubek, "Developmental States and the Legal Order: Towards a New Political Economy of Development and Law," unpublished paper, University of Wisconsin (2010), on file with the authors.

health care and other professionals along with social movements and nongovernmental organizations (NGOs) have mobilized a discourse of ESR from constitutions and international human rights documents toward this end. Confronting the lack of both adequate social provision and the political will or administrative state capacity to deliver it to broad swathes of the citizenry, these actors have sought to leverage the new prestige and authority of liberal democratic constitutions and constitutional courts. Through the courts, they have made new ESR-based claims on the state, polity, and expanding economic pie of MICs. The peculiar subject matter of these rights, however, and the difficulties inherent in realizing them, have forced sophisticated advocates into a new blend of legal, social movement, and more traditional alliance-building and policy-making strategies. Sometimes they have pushed the courts – and sometimes, conversely, sophisticated courts have pushed them – into a new style of adjudication that is more cooperative and open ended than traditional judicial styles.

In this chapter we first describe the constitutional developments that laid the foundation for ESR-based politics. Then in very brief and stylized fashion we outline the history of the welfare state in Latin America, as an example of the policy context facing ESR-oriented groups in MICs around the world. Next we detail the groups' strategies and the courts' response to these demands. We end with a brief account of what some groups have achieved, in some countries. The goal is neither to offer a comprehensive account, nor a representative sample of experiences. Rather, we outline general patterns and possibilities, as a way to open a window on the pressures MICs face to balance development and social justice, and the ways organized civil society and courts have interacted, using the language and tools of ESR to promote these ends.

THE BURGEONING OF ECONOMIC AND SOCIAL RIGHTS IN 1980S–1990S LATIN AMERICAN CONSTITUTIONS – SOCIAL DEMOCRATIC PROMISSORY NOTES IN NEOLIBERAL POLITICAL ECONOMIES

Most countries in Latin America, as most MICs globally, have incorporated a broad range of ESR into new constitutions, or through significant amendments to old constitutions. Even countries that have long had such rights at the formal level have strengthened the institutional framework for claiming these rights, by reforming their constitutional courts, crafting new forms of action, and easing access to justice. The global history of the constitutionalization of ESR begins in Latin America, with the Mexican constitution of 1917. To cite only one example, this constitution promises remarkable labor rights under Article 123, including humane and healthy working conditions, limits on child labor, and a minimum wage.[2] During the first

[2] Constitución Política de los Estados Unidos Mexicanos [Political Constitution of the United Mexican States], art. 123.

half of the twentieth century, the social rights in this constitution found an echo in other constitutions. President Getulio Vargas's short-lived 1934 Constitution for Brazil was the first constitutional guarantee of ESR in that country. President Juan Perón wrote a social constitution for Argentina in 1949, which was derogated after the 1955 coup that sent him into exile. But Mexico's constitutional promises were poorly realized, if at all, and an alliance between the military and elite economic interests soon scotched the early expressions of populist ESR-oriented constitutionalism in Argentina and Brazil. Though many of the provisions remained in constitutional texts, social constitutionalism, as a source of democratic energy, protest, and claim making, was fully derailed when the region plunged into dictatorship and repression in the 1970s and 1980s.

ESR and social constitutionalism truly became the dominant pattern in Latin America as the region began to return to democracy in the 1980s. If the first generation of economic and social rights-bearing provisions in Latin American constitutions were the fruits of authoritarian populism, aimed at heading off radical leftist demands, the new social constitutionalism arose in a different conjuncture. This time the revolutionary left frequently had a seat at the drafting table – sometimes having forsaken the armed struggle in direct exchange for a role in the constitution-making process – and this time their more conservative negotiating partners were representatives of political and economic elites with genuine commitments to a liberal democratic constitutional order. The gulf between them lay in the elites' sometimes equally deep commitments to safeguarding a neoliberal political economy. The upshot was often a Janus-faced constitutional text that looked toward institutionalizing the Washington Consensus of strong property rights, independent central banking, and the like, even as the text also brimmed with social democratic aspirations and promises.

A signature example was the drafting of Colombia's 1991 constitution. This constitution is an amalgam of neoliberal and social democratic impulses. César Gaviria, an economist who had been instrumental in bringing the neoliberal project to Colombia, was president at the time of Colombia's constitutional convention.[3] Pushed into the convention by popular demands, Gaviria aimed to crystallize that project in the new constitution. The president's constitutional draft protected property rights, removed barriers to foreign investment, allowed for private ownership of former state enterprises, and created an autonomous central bank. But the M-19, a leftist guerrilla movement with its origins in the urban middle class, was returning to politics and won the largest block of votes of any organized group at the constitutional convention.

Whether out of partiality for strong judicial enforcement of rights and other rule-of-law values, a need to keep the ex-guerrillas on board, or a general impatience with

[3] Rodrigo Nunes, "Ideational Origins of Progressive Judicial Activism: The Colombian Constitutional Court and the Right to Health," *Latin American Politics & Society* 52 (2010): 67–97.

civil law–trained members of the Colombian legal elite – or, most likely, a combination of all these – Gaviria charged a group of young U.S.-trained lawyers to work as drafters alongside his U.S.-trained economists.[4] Led by a future justice of that court, Manuel José Cepeda, these lawyers negotiated for an extensive battery of ESR in the constitution. The package of social-democratically inflected ESR was sufficiently comprehensive that the M-19 merely adopted the government's proposal, rather than putting forth their own set of demands.[5] The result, as we shall see, is that Colombia now has a constitution with a neoliberal spine and a social democratic heart, enforced by one of the most ambitious and canny constitutional courts in the world.[6]

The Brazilian constitution was crafted a few years earlier, in 1988. Widely known as "the citizenship constitution,"[7] it has less of the neoliberal impulse in it, but is equally founded on the hopes of various progressive groups that a robust constitution, including social and economic rights, might serve to bring Brazil's marginalized classes into full citizenship. Just as in Colombia, the 1988 Brazilian constitutional assembly included a number of former leftist guerrilla fighters who had put down their arms to enter politics in a world dominated by neoliberal economic thought. Just as in Colombia, these revolutionaries understood that they could perhaps gain, in this constitution-making moment of flux and uncertain transformation, important economic concessions that they could not win in the legislature.[8] And finally, just as in Colombia, enthusiasm for ESR served as a bridge between the revolutionary left and the establishment liberals and moderates; for the latter saw the promise of a decent welfare state as an authentic aspiration of civilized, liberal modernity, a source of long-term social stability, and a way to bring the revolutionaries on to the civilizing plane of parliamentary politics and lawmaking. The Brazilian judiciary went on to forge a jurisprudence of constitutional social rights on the basis of the 1988 Constitution; the nation's courts, as we will see, would become central actors in decision making around basic goods like health care.[9]

Other examples of social constitutionalism abound. Even in Argentina, where the basic constitutional text dates back to an earlier era, amendments in 1994

4 Ibid. The president's disillusionment with Colombian civil law–minded attorneys trained in Spain was highlighted as an explanation for this recruitment of young U.S.-trained lawyers in the authors' personal conversation with Manuel José Cepeda on February 13, 2012.

5 Ibid.

6 M. J. Cepeda, "The Judicialization of Politics in Colombia: The Old and the New," in *The Judicialization of Politics in Latin America*, ed. R. Sieder, et al. (Palgrave Macmillan, 2005): 67–103. See also Nunes, "Ideational Origins of Progressive Judicial Activism."

7 In Portuguese it is known as "a constituição cidadã," which loosely translates as the citizen constitution or citizenship constitution.

8 Personal conversation, William Forbath with Nelson Jobim, August 2011.

9 F. Hoffman and F. Bentes, "Accountability for Social and Economic Rights in Brazil," in *Courting Social Justice: Judicial Enforcement of Social and Economic Rights in the Developing World*, ed. V. Gauri and D. M. Brinks (Cambridge University Press, 2008), 100–45; Flavia Piovesan, "Brazil," in *Social Rights Jurisprudence: Emerging Trends in International and Comparative Law*, ed. Malcolm Langford (Cambridge University Press, 2009), 182–91.

incorporated many ESR explicitly and then, for good measure, incorporated by reference all the rights included in all human rights treaties to which Argentina is party, including the International Covenant on Economic, Social and Cultural Rights (Article 22). Costa Rica's constitution has long included labor rights, but in the 1990s also included international human rights (including ESR) and environmental rights, among others, in the repertoire of rights enforceable through the *amparo* mechanism. The successful Nicaraguan revolutionaries, the Sandinistas, drafted Nicaragua's 1987 constitution to include a full set of social rights, from health, to housing, to working conditions. Mexico's constitution continues to fall in this camp. In general, one is currently hard-pressed to find a constitution in Latin America that does not contain a robust set of economic and social rights.

THE ACTUALLY EXISTING WELFARE STATES

And yet, at the same time as constitutional texts were expanding and entrenching formal welfare rights, the welfare states in the region were coming under increasing pressure from neoliberal reforms. As we have glimpsed, the pioneers of welfare-state-building in early twentieth-century Latin America had been more or less authoritarian populist regimes with a narrow, urban, unionized base of support. As a result, these welfare states tended to reinforce as much as ameliorate socioeconomic inequalities, targeting the urban formal sector of the labor market and largely ignoring the vast rural and urban informal sectors. The results were social welfare states that were "deep but not wide."[10] Even the more democratic countries focused largely on workers in those industries essential to the mid-century economic development strategy that went under the banner of import substitution industrialization (ISI). In both cases, then, state provision was often tied to labor unions and therefore, by definition, limited to the formal sector.[11] To make matters worse, labor market rigidities led to the dramatic growth of the unprotected informal sectors of nations' labor markets,[12] leaving large numbers of people utterly outside whatever kinds of labor standards, social goods, and social insurance were on offer from the welfare state. Brazil is a case in point. As late as the mid-1980s, when the dictatorships were beginning to collapse, as many as 80 percent of Brazil's rural workers, and up to

[10] Stephan Haggard and Robert R. Kaufman, *Development, Democracy, and Welfare States: Latin America, East Asia, and Eastern Europe* (Princeton University Press, 2008), 5, 12, 79. See also Eric Hershberg, et al., *Latin America after Neoliberalism: Turning the Tide in the 21st Century?* (New Press, 2006), 4–5.

[11] Ibid., 64.

[12] Ibid., 63. See also Marilyn Carr and Martha Alter Chen, "Globalization and the Informal Economy: How Global Trade and Investment Impact on the Working Poor," paper commissioned by the International Labor Organization (2002), 1, available at http://www.ilo.org/global/publications/lang–en/index.htm (noting that, by the 1990s, the nonagricultural informal sector accounted for about 55 percent of the workforce in Latin America).

one-third of its urban informal workforce, were not even registered in the social security and pension systems, let alone receiving any benefits.[13]

At this constitutional crossroads, however, between the final decade of the old authoritarian regimes and the dawn of the new democratic orders, even the narrow and unequal Latin American welfare state came under fierce attack. Reigning economists on the national and international scenes, international financial organizations, and financial elites, public and private, all blamed ISI and the welfare state for much of the 1980s debt crises and hyperinflation. The Washington Consensus famously enjoyed greater sway in 1980s Latin America than it did among domestic policy makers in 1980s Washington. So, in Latin America, ISI was dismantled and welfare states dramatically rolled back. And yet, the trickle down prosperity that the Washington Consensus promised did not come. Instead, as social provision declined, inequality increased, and poverty became an increasingly acute problem.

Moreover, with democratization, poverty had acquired a great deal more political bite. The new liberal democratic orders rested on a far broader social base than had the dictatorships. The informal sector, the urban poor, indigenous groups, and hard-hit rural populations all became electorally relevant in the aftermath of democracy. From all these quarters, demands for public social provision mounted. And for progressive activists throughout the region, the ESR of the new democratic constitutions beckoned like official promissory notes. Much as the more left-leaning constitutional drafters had hoped and promised, the ESR-bearing constitutions, the "citizenship constitution," might be the platform for demanding that the state and polity actually take up the long-deferred project of distributive justice.

In the end, the neoliberal project failed, in Latin America as in many of the MICs, to produce prosperity for all, and the constitutional aspiration for social citizenship has proved to demand a far more conscious and arduous ESR politics. The perceived failure of the Washington Consensus, however, and its rejection by many Latin American state elites, has given ESR politics an unexpected boost. State economists, planners, and policy makers have turned away from rigid free market orthodoxy (or, as in Brazil, found their opposition to much of that orthodoxy confirmed) over the past decade. The region has seen a marked shift toward models of the "new developmental state," or what some have called "Latin American neostructuralism."[14] The new developmentalism, according to David Trubek and his collaborators,[15] represents an emerging, but still uncertain and unsettled, marriage of key features and insights of neoliberalism, on one hand, and some of the

[13] Kurt Gerhard Weyland, *Democracy without Equity: Failures of Reform in Brazil* (University of Pittsburgh Press, 1996), 134–5.

[14] Leiva, *Latin American Neostructuralism*. See also David M. Trubek, "Developmental States and the Legal Order: Towards a New Political Economy of Development and Law," Discussion Paper No. 1075 (Wisconsin Law School, 2009).

[15] Ibid. See also David M. Trubek, et al., "Toward a New Law and Development: New State Activism in Brazil and the Challenge for Legal Institutions," *The World Bank Legal Review* (2012), 281–314.

premises and arrangements of the older tradition and institutions of state-led developmentalism, on the other. It also borrows from the "new governance" models afoot in the North.[16] Thus, like neoliberalism, the new developmentalism abjures direct state ownership of industry and is relatively open to imports; it emphasizes making national firms competitive rather than shielding them from competition. Likewise, new developmentalism aims to cultivate local entrepreneurship and innovation, rather than relying on imported technology and know-how. At the same time, however it envisions a robust role for the state in steering and coordinating industrial development, promoting globally competitive "national champions" and underwriting education, research and development, and technological innovation. It makes heavy use of public-private partnerships in everything from information sharing and regulatory regimes to infrastructure investments. In sharp contrast to neoliberal orthodoxy, new developmentalist-minded state actors believe that government can "pick winners," at least in regard to industrial sectors. There remains much debate about how much of the new developmentalism represents a genuinely important array of innovative new policies and institutional arrangements, and how much it is merely a new rhetoric that may mask an older set of state practices, subsidizing already well-established industries with strong political influence. One thing, however, is certain: both at the level of rhetoric and in their real-world policies and practices, new developmentalism-minded state elites in Brazil, Colombia, and elsewhere have embraced the idea that social solidarity matters, inequality must be reduced, and ending mass poverty and including the rural and urban dispossessed in the social enterprise are not only moral or political issues but matters of long-term growth and economic health. Brazil's expanding and expansive Bolsa Familia is a famous case in point.

To be sure, the Washington Consensus in many of its iterations used the language of "investing in human capital"; but in this case, it is the new developmentalists who are practicing what was often just preaching by supporters of the Washington Consensus.[17] On their account, assuring a decent minimum of goods like food and water, health, housing, and education are no longer the hoped-for results of good economic policy, but instead are essential ingredients of it. What the ESR-minded lawyers call the "progressive realization of social and economic rights," the "new developmentalist" economists call "investing in human capital" and "human development" as "a critical input into expanding economic growth."[18]

16 Trubek, "Developmental States and the Legal Order," 24–5.

17 See Peter Evans and Patrick Heller, "Human Development, State Transformation and the Politics of the Developmental State," in *The Oxford Handbook of Transformations of the State*, ed. Stephan Leibfried, et al. (Oxford Press, forthcoming).

18 Peter Evans, "The Capability Enhancing Developmental State: Concepts and National Trajectories." Paper presented at the UNRISD-KOICA conference (2011), on file with authors, available at http://www.proac.uff.br/cede/sites/default/files/TD63.pdf. See also Michael Boozer, et al., "Paths to Success: The Relationship between Human Development and Economic Growth" Discussion Paper No. 874 (Economic Growth Center, Yale University, December 2003), cited in Evans, "The Capability Enhancing Developmental State."

As a result of these developments, the ESR provisions of the new constitutions have acquired a new salience in the corridors of state power. What is more, there is a surprising measure of antiformalist, contextualized, pragmatic, and policy-oriented thinking in the ESR jurisprudence of some Latin American constitutional courts. And so, as we will see, for example, in the case of Colombia's health care litigation, a new space seems to have opened up for commerce between such courts and reform-minded technocrats in the administrative state elites.

ECONOMIC AND SOCIAL RIGHTS ADVOCACY AND ADJUDICATION – EXPERIENCE IN THE COURTS, STATES, AND POLITIES OF MIDDLE-INCOME COUNTRIES OF LATIN AMERICA

When long lists of ESR began appearing in the new constitutions of MICs in Latin America and elsewhere, the idea of taking such rights to court generally found a skeptical, even hostile, reception, as much among scholars and activists on the left as among traditionalist judges. Skeptics posed many practical objections – that ESR advocacy was an antipolitics, a diversion of resources and energy from the necessary tasks of movement building and political engagement, and required an unwarranted faith in the policy-making capacity and coercive power of courts. In addition, the notion of "judicializing" ESR has met with principled objections. Under democracy, the meaning and content of new ESR commitments – what does it mean to ensure a right to education, or decent housing, health care, or employment; and how should resources be allocated and priorities set? – are questions whose technical dimensions require the expertise of policy professionals and whose normative dimensions should be addressed in the polity, through the active engagement of the citizens for whom ESR were enacted.[19]

Unifying many of these critiques was an image of what ESR advocacy and adjudication was destined to look like. "ESR-based demands" would become the subject of purely legal battles, waged solely in courtrooms, and entrusted to legal and social elites. Judicial victories, when and if they arrived, would mean government by judicial decree: courts would issue nonnegotiable, absolute demands that must be satisfied to their fullest extent, without consideration of their broader institutional or allocative impact. More often than not, however, events have given the lie to such conventional images of "judicialization."

The real work of reforming and building welfare policies on the basis of ESR demands is robustly political; it engages the dispossessed, would-be ESR-bearing

[19] Jeremy Waldron, "A Rights-Based Critique of Constitutional Rights," *Oxford Journal of Legal Studies* 13 (1993): 18–51; Frank B. Cross, "The Error of Positive Rights," *UCLA Law Review* 48 (2001): 857; Ran Hirschl, *Towards Juristocracy – The Origins and Consequences of the New Constitutionalism* (Harvard University Press, 2004); Gerald N. Rosenberg, *The Hollow Hope: Can Courts Bring about Social Change?*, 2nd ed. (University of Chicago Press, 2008).

citizenry; and the courts' response has been, in many cases, more nuanced than many expected. Contrary to the stylized "juristocratic" vision sometimes presented, ESR movements across the world pursue a comprehensive rights-based mobilization strategy in which social movements work in tandem with courts and other legal actors, at the same time that they continue to work the streets and legislative hallways. Courts are often central actors, but rather than issuing imperious, detailed decrees, they often choose to engage all the relevant parties in extensive and productive dialogue around concrete problems until new policy solutions are worked out.[20] We will develop these two points in their turn.

The first point is that the typical domestic ESR movement looks very different from the "juristocratic"[21] model on which many critiques are based. The vocabulary of ESR enshrined in constitutions and conventions imbues the language of these social movements, and the strategies certainly include litigation. But the latter is often not the primary focus of the various actors, even in countries like Brazil, where certain rights, like the right to health, have been thoroughly judicialized.[22] In many rights-based campaigns judicial action is subordinate to and at the service of political action. Lawsuits support mobilization; fill in gaps; generate greater oversight of bureaucrats and policy makers; provide leverage to ESR movements' allies and collaborators in the legislature, the technocracy, and the party and administrative state elites; and encourage the wedding of the technocratic, efficiency-based rationality wielded by state elites to constitutional ESR commitments and normative reasoning. There is nothing apolitical or demobilized about these movements.

Take, for example, the right to health movement in Colombia, which secured one of the more ambitious judicial orders in this area. The Colombian legal system was being flooded with hundreds of thousands of individual claims for violations of the right to health.[23] The Court processed these hundreds of thousands of individual claims in a fashion that generated a right to health movement, new NGOs, and massive grassroots support for the Court's activism. The Court's generous responses to individual *tutela* actions led – predictably enough – to enormous hostility on the

20 Gauri and Brinks, *Courting Social Justice*; Daniel M. Brinks and William E. Forbath, "Social and Economic Rights in Latin America: Constitutional Courts and the Prospects for Pro-poor Interventions," *Texas Law Review* 89 (2011): 1943; Lucie White and Jeremy Perelman, *Stones of Hope: How African Activists Reclaim Human Rights to Challenge Global Poverty* (Stanford University Press, 2011); William Forbath and Geoff Budlender (with assistance from Zackie Achmat and Mark Heywood), "Cultural Transformation, Deep Institutional Reform, and ESR Practice: South Africa's Treatment Action Campaign," in White and Perelman, *Stones of Hope*; Varun Gauri and Daniel M. Brinks, "Human Rights as Demands for Communicative Action," *Journal of Political Philosophy* (2012): 407–31.

21 See Ran Hirschl, *Towards Juristocracy – The Origins and Consequences of the New Constitutionalism* (Harvard University Press, 2001).

22 Hoffmann and Bentes, "Accountability for Social and Economic Rights in Brazil."

23 Alicia Ely Yamin, et al., "Colombia – Judicial Protection of the Right to Health: An Elusive Promise?," in *Litigating Health Rights: Can Courts Bring More Justice to Health?*, ed. Alicia Ely Yamin and Siri Gloppen (Harvard University Press, 2011), 103–31.

part of key figures in the executive branch, which responded with a number of emergency decrees. The president's decrees set out to quell the Court's solicitude for the right to health by imposing spending constraints and shutting down access to the Court in the name of safeguarding the solvency of the public health system. Broadly unpopular as well as legally dubious, the president's intervention triggered mass protests and even more public mobilization around the right to health. Protesters carried placards declaring "A Tutela Saved My Life."[24] ESR attorneys brought a challenge to the president's intervention to the Constitutional Court, garnering no less than 1,200 amicus briefs by many grassroots organizations and unions.[25]

Buoyed by popular support, the Court overturned the president's actions. Revealingly, however, the Court also stepped away from its previous path of simply liberally granting individual *tutela* claims. Instead, the Court married its overturning of the presidential decrees to a structural reform decree of its own. Rather than spurning the executive branch's worries about budgetary chaos, the Court took the fiscal problems seriously. It refused to simply decree a reformation of the public health care system that met the demands of right to health advocates, but it insisted that the new social movement's activists, attorneys, and reform-minded public health experts have a seat at the table, where structural reforms would be hammered out under the Court's prodding and supervision.

In the process, the Court summoned the nation's financial ministry and social budget officials along with the heads of the various key elements of Colombia's disjointed health care system to appear before it. And with a canny sense of where the state's most reform-minded technocrats were to be found, it put them to work, demanding what the state's isolated and arthritic bureaucracies had never produced: a systematic cost accounting of the public health system's budget and performance. With this accounting in place, both the court and the bureaucrats were finally in a position to truly gauge how much the system's notorious disjointedness and inefficiencies were to blame for its shortcomings, and how far the shortfall really was between current budgetary allotments and the right to health care advocates' account of a minimally adequate system of health care provision. More startlingly, the Court also directed the ESR advocates and their experts and the state officials and technocrats to collaborate and bring back to the Court a plan for the merger and cross-subsidization of the hitherto separate schemes of free public health care available to the poor and the contributory health care system available to those who can pay.[26]

Here, the Constitutional Court was taking a leaf from the new developmentalist economists' playbook. Old-fashioned social democratic health care thinking leaned

[24] Julieta Lemaitre and Katharine Young, "The Comparative Fortunes of the Right to Health: Notes from Colombia and South Africa," unpublished manuscript, p. 13, on file with author.

[25] Ibid.

[26] See Corte Constitucional [Constitutional Court of Colombia], July 31, 2008, Sentencia T-760/08 (Colom.).

toward free and universal coverage; that was the ideal of a social right to health. In a post–welfare state world, the human development-minded strains of neoliberal social policy have evolved more sophisticated, hybrid ideas. Among these are "responsibilizing" poor people by making them "coproducers" of and "active participants" in their own health care (i.e., maintaining certain kinds of copayments and disciplinary conditions on public health care provision), while also merging the old bifurcated systems of free and contributory health care. This way, one can bring the resources as well as the cost controls of the former to bear on the latter, and use cross-subsidization to provide a fuller measure of health care for the poor, in the process assuring one of the key ingredients of long-term economic growth. To put it in the Colombian Constitutional Court's rubric, "[e]fficiency and financial sufficiency are not necessarily incompatible with solidarity."[27] The economists' and technocrats' tools and touchstones could be put in the service of the constitutional mandate of progressive realization of the social right to health.

In general, the Court's intervention was a far cry from a judicial decree commanding the state to fully fund a public health care system that measured up to a human rights advocate's standards; it called for blending such standards with economists' measures, and left open how the two would be combined, and whether the Court would demand or the state cooperate with cashing out a decent minimum of health care coverage for poor citizens. All this remained up for grabs, in the internal dynamics of the peak-level policy negotiations over which the Court presided, and in the polity, where the judicially buoyed right to health movement continued to mobilize and exert pressure. The proof of the pudding, thus far, has been an announcement by the president that his administration is going forward with a plan to merge the public and contributory branches of health care provision for the nation's children in the name of economy and solidarity, but without mention of the judicial prodding.[28]

As with the right to health, the Court has played an outsized role in empowering the "internally displaced persons" (IDP) movement and the activists and advocates representing the millions of citizens uprooted by the conflict. The IDP movement has pushed for adequate housing, education, health care, and basic support, and like the right to health movement, it has done so with a blend of litigation and political mobilization. As one participant describes it, the final hearing in the landmark IDP case before the Colombian Constitutional Court included three hundred "lawyers, activists, grassroots leaders, journalists, government officials, and academics," while the square outside was filled with protesters drawn from among the displaced persons.[29] At issue in that case was not a single identifiable human rights violation,

[27] Corte Constitucional [Constitutional Court of Colombia], February 2, 2003, Sentencia C-150/03, para. 4.5, quoted in René Urueña, "The Rise of the Constitutional Regulatory State in Colombia: The Case of Water Governance," *Regulation and Governance* 6 (2012): 282.

[28] Personal conversation, Manuel Jose Cepeda, February 13, 2012.

[29] César Rodríguez Garavito, "Beyond the Courtroom: The Impact of Judicial Activism on Socioeconomic Rights in Latin America," *Texas Law Review* 89 (2011): 1669.

but what the Colombian Constitutional Court called "an unconstitutional state of affairs," the product of systematic failures on the part of the government to deal with the situation of the people rendered homeless and displaced by Colombia's violent internal conflict.

Once again, the Court did not attempt to decree a substantive solution. Instead, it called for hearings, reports, fact finding, and the design of new solutions by government officials and agencies. Using the individual *tutelas* or constitutional complaints of 1,150 displaced families as "diagnostics" of the systemic failures of government, the Court set about orchestrating and demanding a coordinated response on the part of all the social and governmental actors with an interest in the matter. Again, as with the right to health movement, the Court assured the IDP advocates a seat at the table and a significant portion of bargaining power.[30]

It is instructive to compare the interplay of social movements and Constitutional Court in the Colombian context with that in South Africa, another middle-income nation with great resources, vast inequality, a renowned Constitutional Court, and a progressive new constitution forged in the early 1990s and brimming with economic and social rights. As in Colombia, social movements of post-apartheid South Africa seized on the ESR language of the nation's new democratic constitution to frame their demands that government make good on the social transformation the new constitution promised for the nation's poor. As in Colombia and much of Latin America, in the late 1990s and early 2000s, South Africa's ESR movements confronted an administration committed to a neoliberal political economy. Like their Latin American counterparts, Mandela's and then Thabo Mbeki's African National Congress (ANC) party policy-making elite envisioned a market-friendly path to social democracy. As the ANC's path failed to bring redistribution and new social goods for the mass of poor South Africans, poor South Africans did not abandon the party that had led the anti-apartheid struggle; instead, ESR movements became vehicles for popular rage and disappointment. And again, as in Colombia, ESR advocates found in the Constitutional Court a crucial ally in their efforts to push government for the realization of these rights, in the areas of social provision, health, housing, water, and other social goods.

What sets the two countries' social movement/Court collaborations apart from one another is the much less sweeping, more narrowly crafted, and gingerly role that South Africa's ESR movements have carved out for litigation – a far less central and commanding, less managerial role, matching the more circumscribed role that South Africa's Constitutional Court has insisted that the judiciary play in the service of realizing ESR. Court victories have not been the primary objects of ESR movement campaigns, but instead one important source of political leverage and moral authority to promote pro-poor policy changes and institutional reforms.

30 Ibid.

Take the Treatment Action Campaign (TAC), which arose in the late 1990s in response to the nation's tragic HIV/AIDS pandemic and the Mandela and then the Mbeki administrations' death-dealing refusal to implement any substantial HIV/AIDS treatment or prevention programs in South Africa's public health sector. Many of the most seasoned and sophisticated organizers, activists, and advocates of the anti-apartheid era joined the movement for the right to health care for HIV/AIDS sufferers, and they made the polity and local, national, and international public spheres the key arenas for TAC's right to health care claims. Movement and coalition building, policy proposals and political initiatives, publicity and lobbying as well as civil disobedience campaigns: all these were forged ahead of litigation strategy, and the latter was subordinate to them.

First, TAC took to the international stage, demanding affordable antiretroviral drugs (ARVs) for the nation's public health system using intensive, media-savvy campaigns (including gripping demonstrations at international financial institutions, and open defiance of laws against bringing generics to South Africa) against the pharmaceutical industry and the Clinton administration. Then, with concessions from both of these, the TAC sought out reform-minded provincial officials to undertake local rollouts and experiments, demonstrating that the drugs could be effectively administered in the rickety public health clinics; and it waited – staging public protests to dramatize HIV/AIDS's relentless toll – while the state's medical board assessed the medicine's alleged dangers, costs, and benefits.

When TAC finally brought its landmark case, it demanded only that the public health system roll out the single dosages of ARVs needed for prevention of mother-to-child transmission of HIV. The lower court granted and the Constitutional Court upheld the decree TAC sought. In keeping with the Court's emerging ESR jurisprudence, the justices framed the issue as one concerning the "reasonableness" of government's refusal to roll out the simple medical regimen notwithstanding its *de minimis* cost and proven safety and effectiveness – both premises substantially attributable to the TAC's earlier groundwork. This refusal, the Court declared, violated the affected mothers' and babies' constitutional social right to health care.

Combining caution and boldness, the Constitutional Court's decision offered a distinctive vision of judicial collaboration with civil society organizations like TAC in the realm of ESR. The opinion offers a subtle account of the interplay of ESR claims and arguments in the polity and legal-constitutional interventions on the part of courts: the first a matter of organizations like TAC backing up claims of right with the exchange of views, information, and expert opinion between state and civil society using petitions, proposals, reports, conferences, joint commissions, hearings, and negotiations; the second a matter of the courts keeping the civil society/state exchanges and negotiations open and vital, and prodding and compelling the state when it falls short of its procedural or substantive constitutional duties and commitments.

The Court was also at pains to stress the limits of its role. It refused, as it already had in *Grootboom*, an earlier landmark right to housing decision, to hammer out the content of a "minimum core" definition of the right to basic health care, in the HIV/AIDS context, or any other. The UN Committee on Economic, Social and Cultural Rights had endorsed and adopted the "minimum core" idea, as a way of giving substance and direction to national ESR efforts and adjudications. But the Court rejected the notion: demanding, charting, and hammering out the evolving, substantive content of the constitution's ESR were tasks that belonged to civil society and the legislature and executive branches. The judiciary's main contribution would be a more traditionally legal, process-based one: to "guarantee that these democratic processes" through which deliberation, debate, and contestation over the achievement of ESR "must unfold ... are protected to ensure accountability, responsiveness and openness."

As far as the substantive content of policies was concerned, the judiciary's role was simply to demand, as it did in the *TAC* case, that government explain and justify its actions when these are challenged. The South African Constitutional Court made plain in *TAC* and subsequent cases that it has no stomach for the kind of magisterial judicial oversight of ongoing processes of policy formation or state building that the Colombian Court has embraced. As South African Constitutional Court Justice Yvonne Mokgoro observed recently, even – or perhaps especially – a committed social democratic judge must recognize that litigation "tends to be the privilege of the economically empowered"; therefore, a "vigilant civil society" must "agitate for change and monitor implementation" using "more accessible and direct strategies."[31]

This was how TAC finally pushed the South African state and the obdurate ANC leadership to roll out a full-blown HIV/AIDS program in the public health system: agitation and disobedience, politicking, policy making in collaboration with sympathetic high state and party officials, and monitoring – invoking the Court's ringing affirmation of the right to health care for HIV/AIDS sufferers, but keeping litigation in a backup role.

WHY COURTS?

In light of the indispensable role of social mobilization, agitation, politicking, policy making, and monitoring to ESR movements, then, why are the courts occupying as much space as they do in the ESR movements' repertory? Why not simply go into the streets, or lobby for more generous policies? The first answer is that courts sometimes break open stalemated politics and provide wedges into authoritarian power structures. One of the foremost practitioners of ESR litigation in Argentina

[31] Yvonne Mokgoro, "Constitutional Claims for Gender Equality in South Africa: A Judicial Response," *Albany Law Review* 67 (2003): 565–6.

argues that the need for litigation grows as the space for political participation shrinks.[32] Unfortunately, democratization has sometimes not been followed by a truly pluralistic and open politics. In some cases, due in part to constitutional and electoral system design, we observe a drift toward a quasi-one-party state. South Africa is a case in point, where the constitutional vision of open, responsive, deliberative, and participatory democratic state and party institutions are not to be found within the executive and legislative branches or in the party political apparatus. Rather, it has fallen to the social movements, civil society organizations, the press, and the judiciary to challenge these failures. For the "new South Africa," the courts and the public sphere of social rights advocacy have become the spaces for accountability through opposition politics and participatory and deliberative policy making. In other cases, representative politics are hampered by corruption and incompetence. When political roadblocks exist that are preventing the expression of widely felt demands, courts can sometimes become the spaces for contestation and deliberation that cannot be found in the other branches of government.

Moreover, courts are often called in because of some shortcoming or weakness in the administrative state. In Brazil, patient groups use litigation to sue for more up-to-date treatments, arguing that the agency in charge of updating the public health offering is failing to keep up with advances in medical technology.[33] Other times, they act to ensure that frontline bureaucrats are carrying out the legislative mandate and national policy – 65 percent of the drugs being demanded through litigation in Brazil are on the approved list, but patients are unable to secure them.[34] In Colombia, until the major decision in 2008 that sought to completely restructure the public health system,[35] the vast majority of the tens of thousands of cases seeking medical treatment and medications were demands for goods and services that were already included in legislated mandates, and that should have been supplied by the private providers who were being sued.[36]

Other times, the demands focus on extending universal promises to neglected and stigmatized groups that cannot at first get a hearing. In country after country, AIDS activists spearheaded the movement for legal enforcement of health rights.[37] The

32 Centro de Estudios Legales y Sociales, *La Lucha por el Derecho* (Siglo Veintiuno, 2008), 13. See also ibid., 25.

33 Hoffman and Bentes, "Accountability for Social and Economic Rights in Brazil."

34 João Biehl, et al., "Between the Court and the Clinic: Lawsuits for Medicines and the Right to Health in Brazil," *Health & Human Rights* 14 (2012): 1.

35 Corte Constitucional [Constitutional Court of Colombia], July 31, 2008, Sentencia T-760/08 (Colom.).

36 Yamin, et al., "Colombia – Judicial Protection of the Right to Health"; Yamin and Gloppen, *Litigating Health Rights*; Alicia Ely Yamin and Oscar Parra-Vera, "Judicial Protection of the Right to Health in Colombia: From Social Demands to Individual Claims to Public Debates," *Hastings International & Comparative Law Review* 33 (2010): 431.

37 Gauri and Brinks, eds., *Courting Social Justice*; Hoffmann and Bentes, "Accountability for Social and Economic Rights in Brazil"; Magdalena Sepúlveda, "Colombia," in *Social Rights Jurisprudence: Emerging Trends in International and Comparative Law*, ed. Malcolm Langford (Cambridge University Press 2009), ch. 7.

groups carrying the ESR banner are often the most marginalized: rural-indigenous, landless, roofless, the informal working sector. This is perhaps clearest in the many rights-based movements for land and dignified housing. In Latin America the pro-poor right to land movement is strongly radicalized. In Brazil we find the right to land mobilized by the *Movimento Sem Terra*, the Movement of the Landless, and the right to housing deployed by the *Movimento dos Sem Teto*, the Movement of the Roofless.[38] In Argentina, we see similar rights-based language mobilized by the squatter movement – a loosely organized network of groups that occupy residential buildings and factories, collectively known as *Okupas*, or Occupiers, claiming legitimacy under the right to work and the right to housing. These groups have only rarely turned to the courts, but over the past two decades, since the creation of the new constitutions, they have turned from older discourses of religious and revolutionary protest to framing their demands in the language of ESR. Even those who have not gone to court have gained a new sense of legitimate entitlement and claims on the state, in virtue of the new constitutions' inclusive promises to the poor and dispossessed and the efforts of advocates, jurists, and ESR-minded state elites to realize them.

This last discussion highlights one important change from the politics of the traditional welfare state in Latin America: the politics of ESR includes groups far removed from the world of traditional beneficiaries, of formal sector, unionized workers. To be sure, many of the movements are rooted in urban, middle-class groups with a common interest – say a particular illness, or a desire to see urban green spaces protected. But many more are explicitly anchored in marginalized and excluded groups: the poor, the hungry, the homeless. In both cases, claims on the state tend to be channeled, in whatever broad and collective or narrow, individual shape, through attorney advocates.

Thus claimants engage the state's legal apparatus in a variety of ways. They rely on litigation and extensive informal contacts with key judges to shape jurisprudence; and they provide crucial agendas and constituencies for courts interested in bringing constitutional ESR to earth using a broad reach into social policy. They engage with public prosecutors in places like Brazil, where the Public Ministry has a broad portfolio that includes the realization of constitutional rights, and with ombudsmen's offices and national human rights commissions elsewhere. They also develop ad hoc partnerships with political entrepreneurs and parties in order to advance common goals. They are not tied to any particular party, but they often do work with politicians to propose bills and advance policy objectives, turning to the courts often only as a last resort.[39]

[38] The full name of these two movements often includes a reference to "the workers" – Movimento dos Trabalhadores Rurais Sem Terra, and Movimento dos Trabalhadores Sem Teto – but they are most often referred to simply in terms of what they lack – land, a roof.

[39] Daniel M. Brinks and Varun Gauri, "A New Policy Landscape: Legalizing Social and Economic Rights in the Developing World," in Gauri and Brinks, *Courting Social Justice*, 303–52.

What has been the overall shape of the courts' response to these growing demands? If, as we have suggested, courts are often at the center of clashes over the contours of an ESR-based welfare state, still, different courts have responded to the challenge in very different ways. These differences in turn have had much to do with the subsequent texture of welfare state politics, sometimes more juriscentric, as in Colombia; sometimes more multifaceted, as in South Africa; and sometimes joining individual vindications through the courts with more concerted action in the legislature, as in Brazil. Different legal traditions, judicial attitudes, and modes of decision making both determine and take shape from these disparate ESR movement strategies and approaches.

We can map the various courts' decision-making styles along two dimensions. The first dimension concerns judicial deference versus assertiveness toward the legislature and the executive branch; it involves what constitutional lawyers call "separation of powers"; and it runs along the path between what is often called "judicial restraint" versus "judicial activism." The second dimension looks at styles of judicial reasoning. It concerns the contrast between what jurisprudes and legal theorists call "formalism" versus "pragmatism" or "policy" and "purposive" reasoning. "Formalist" judges present their judgments as logical, even syllogistic deductions from the legal or constitutional provisions at hand applied in a more or less mechanical fashion to the facts of the case. "Pragmatist" judges, by contrast, tend to acknowledge that logical deductions from the often highly general, open-ended phrases in the constitutional text (like the "right to health" or the guarantee of "freedom of speech") cannot decide concrete cases; instead, pragmatist judges reason in a more or less openly policy-minded and value-laden fashion, having regard to the "underlying purposes" and "principles" animating the legal or constitutional text, and also taking account of the broader, systemic consequences of their rulings. The "pragmatist" judge is more comfortable, for example, discussing the allocational trade-offs that inevitably attend decisions about ESR; and she is more at home crafting collective remedies to address collective problems. But notice: there is no necessary connection between a court's outlook regarding judicial deference versus activism, on one hand, and its style of reasoning, on the other. The courts and cases we have used as examples herein can be arrayed along these two dimensions (see Table 11.1).

Thus, for example, both South Africa's and Colombia's Constitutional Courts employ a style of judicial reasoning that falls on the pragmatic side of the spectrum. The South African Court is somewhat more candid than its Colombian counterpart about the inescapably value- and policy-laden nature of constitutional adjudication and the extent to which decisions about ESR cannot be derived through formal reasoning from the text or the factual record. Yet, on our other dimension, as we have seen, South Africa's Constitutional Court is substantially more restrained and deferential toward the legislative and executive branches than Colombia's Court.

TABLE 11.1. *Judicial Decision-Making Models in ESR Cases*

	Deferential	Assertive
Pragmatic	Many Brazilian decisions can be located here,[a] but perhaps better known are the South Africa Constitutional Court cases, most clearly *Soobramoney* (kidney dialysis) and *Mazibuko* (water rights/ privatization) – slightly less deferential are *Grootboom* (right to housing) and *TAC* (Nevirapine/right to health).	Colombia Constitutional Court in *T-760* (public health system case) and *T-025* (IDP case); Argentine Supreme Court in *Viceconte* (Hemorrhagic fever vaccine) and in *Mendoza* (Riachuelo clean up) case.
Syllogistic	Traditionally, Chilean constitutional court, but also thought to be the dominant model in Latin America, if not the entire civil law world.	Lower courts in health rights cases in Brazil; lower courts in individual *tutela* cases in Colombia.

[a] *Source:* Diana Kapiszewski, *High Courts and Economic Governance in Argentina and Brazil* (Cambridge University Press, 2012).

Traditionally, Latin American courts were seen as the very model of syllogistic reasoning and deference toward the executive branch.[40] As Javier Couso and Elisabeth Hilbink describe the traditional approach of the Chilean Constitutional Court, "[f]rom early in the country's republican history, Chilean judges were trained to be slaves of the law, but in a context in which law, particularly public law, was understood as the will of the executive."[41] Such a combination is unlikely to produce a court that will function as an effective ally in battles to reform and expand welfare provision. More recently, however, across Latin America, the courts of Mexico, Costa Rica, Peru, Colombia, Brazil, Argentina, and even Chile, to some degree, have become more assertive. Some, like the Colombian Court, have also adopted a broader policy-oriented mode of reasoning, while others have limited themselves to a more syllogistic style of decision making.[42] The combination of assertiveness and pragmatic, policy-style reasoning signals a more wholehearted adoption by judges of their central role in the construction of a new welfare state. One can see this most

[40] Keith S. Rosenn, "The Protection of Judicial Independence in Latin America," *Inter–American Law Review* 19 (1987): 1–35.

[41] Javier Couso and Elisabeth C. Hilbink, "From Quietism to Incipient Activism: The Institutional and Ideational Roots of Rights Adjudication in Chile," in *Courts in Latin America*, ed. Julio Rios-Figueroa and Gretchen Helmke (Cambridge University Press, 2011): 99–127.

[42] See the discussion by Miguel Schor of the move from a syllogistic approach to one that engages in the balancing of competing considerations, which is conceptually related to the one we describe here, though restricted to the form of legal reasoning deployed by the judges in their decisions. Miguel Schor, "An Essay on the Emergence of Constitutional Courts: The Cases of Mexico and Colombia," *Indiana Journal of Global Legal Studies* 16 (2008): 173–94.

clearly exemplified, in its robustly assertive variant, by the Colombian Constitutional Court.

This Court, regarded by many other courts in Latin America as a leader in ESR jurisprudence, has developed a series of key concepts that give it the latitude to play a central role in developing the new welfare state. The first is reliance on the figure of a "*mínimo vital*" – or minimum requirements for a dignified existence[43] – a notion loosely related to the "minimum core" idea fashioned by the UN Committee on Economic, Social and Cultural Rights and spurned, as we saw, by the South African Constitutional Court. This concept allows the Colombian Court to unmoor its rulings from specific language and provisions in the constitution, tying them instead to a broad view of what is necessary to give all human beings, including the poor and the politically marginalized, full human agency and social membership.[44] While it would be impossible to catalogue here all the disparate claims that have emerged under the sign of ESR, this is the idea that ties them all together – states are required to, and can be compelled to, create the conditions that enable all individuals to gain access to full social and political membership and a dignified existence.

In its pursuit of that goal, the Columbian Constitutional Court has developed another crucial doctrine, that of the "unconstitutional state of affairs." Under this rubric, the court can identify a general condition that fails to live up to the robust promises of the constitution, even if it is not clear that anyone in particular, much less any individual state actor, is directly responsible for a constitutional violation. We encountered the doctrine in the IDP litigation described previously. The Columbian Constitutional Court has applied the doctrine in a variety of cases, not all of them of transcendental significance: "Since 1997, the court has handed down seven decisions of this kind, in greatly varying circumstances including non-compliance with the state's obligation to affiliate numerous public officials to the social security system, massive prison overcrowding, lack of protection for human rights defenders, and failure to announce an open call for public notary nominations."[45] The Columbian Constitutional Court, then, has crafted a powerful doctrinal grounding for embarking on broad policy-making and state-building projects: a broad normative basis – "human dignity"; an abstract and malleable substantive standard – "mínimo vital"; an expansive notion of constitutional harms – an

[43] Sepúlveda, "Colombia." See also Rodolfo Arango and Julieta Lemaitre, eds., *Jurisprudencia Constitucional sobre el derecho al mínimo vital* [Constitutional Jurisprudence about the right to minimum subsistence] (Ediciones Uniandes, 2002).

[44] Other courts also anchor their jurisprudence in this idea of human dignity: "'Thus, from human dignity all other rights stem, insofar as they are necessary for man to integrally develop his personality.' Dignity means that individuals have 'the right to choose, in a free and autonomous manner, their life project. … Hence, the recognition of the right to the free development of one's personality.'" Alejandro Madrazo and Estefanía Vela, "The Mexican Supreme Court's (Sexual) Revolution?," *Texas Law Review* 89 (2012): 1863, quoting a 2006 Mexican Supreme Court *amparo* decision on rights of transgendered people.

[45] Garavito, "Beyond the Courtroom," 1670, citations omitted.

"unconstitutional state of affairs"; and relaxed standing requirements – thanks to the *tutela*, anyone can file a constitutional claim, and the court can then aggregate claims in any way it pleases in order to craft a case, not to mention its powers of abstract review.

Meanwhile, in South Africa, we have seen how the normative and strategic outlook on the part of social movements and ESR advocates has shaped and been shaped by the South African Constitutional Court's own somewhat more deferential conception of its role in respect of social rights.[46] For various reasons, the South African Constitutional Court approach is one of gingerly prodding and monitoring government along both procedural and substantive lines. Thus the South African Constitutional Court and the High Courts have condemned and forced changes in the government's social-policy-making processes in service of greater transparency and participation and greater attention to the needs and demands of the nation's poorest citizens; and they also have condemned and forced changes in the substantive content of those policies, in service of the constitution's command that government take reasonable steps to realize citizens' social rights. Some of the High Courts have been more forthcoming than the South African Constitutional Court with ESR-based structural decrees ordering the development of new plans, programs, and policies, as well as orders forbidding evictions of squatters and cutoffs of water.

In what seems like a less promising approach, the Brazilian courts have prompted what detractors have labeled an "epidemic" of health rights litigation, without ever stopping to consider why so many individual cases are being filed, how the accumulation of individual decisions might affect the public health system, or how it might address the issue in a more systemic way. This has prompted critiques that its decisions shift the provision of public health toward the better off.[47] The courts have largely disregarded the government's protestations that they should take into consideration fiscal constraints, the individual (let alone the cumulative) impact of these decisions on the broader public health system, or even the established process for determining the safety and appropriateness of particular medications and treatments. In case after case, they defer entirely to the decision of the treating physician, so that all that is required to succeed is a prescription.[48] Some of this may be changing in the wake of a decision by the Supremo Tribunal Federal (Brazil's highest constitutional court) that purports to introduce public policy considerations, and set a sliding scale standard for deciding these cases,[49] but it is fair to say that the dominant model is still as described previously.

[46] The South African Constitutional Court has recently become more deferential and has come under fire for abdicating its role in ways in which it had not been criticized before.

[47] Octavio Luiz Motta Ferraz, "Harming the Poor through Social Rights Litigation: Lessons from Brazil," *Texas Law Review* 89 (2011): 1643.

[48] Ibid.; Hoffman and Bentes, "Accountability for Social and Economic Rights in Brazil."

[49] See Brinks and Forbath, "Social and Economic Rights in Latin America," for a discussion of this decision and its implications for the dominant decision-making model in Brazil's health rights litigation.

In summary, the courts need not be, and often are not, the central arena for the new welfare state politics. At the same time, given that the demands are anchored in constitutional and human rights, the attractiveness of taking a more judicial route hinges in part on the relative likelihood of securing ESR policy goals in the political arena versus the courts. When the former seems more closed and little prone to good governance, the courts are presented with more demands for both policy making and accountability. Conversely, when the courts show themselves to be more inclined to vigorous enforcement of ESR, they are more apt to be called in earlier in the policy process. At times, the judicial intervention remains at the level of improving the process and ensuring that everyone has a voice. At others, it becomes more substantive and directive. The texture of welfare state politics is the result of this complex interplay between courts, social movements, and public officials.

Regardless of the ways in which demands are processed, the social bases of ESR movements include vast numbers of the truly poor. No wonder, then, that the agenda comprises the basic requirements identified in ESR, and a demand for a "basic income." To be sure, job creation, expanding the formal economy, and the base of good waged work – these remain integral to the broader economic demands from the organized left, and unions around the world continue to pursue them. But after two decades of the Washington Consensus, and after its failure to provide the promised employment and prosperity, fewer and fewer progressive forces expect the market to do more than pick up a small portion of the poor. The politics of welfare, in MICs around the world, goes far beyond demands for better industrial policy, to include explicit guarantees of basic goods. Given the prominence of ESR in constitutions and the political imagination, many of these demands are being processed with significant involvement by constitutional courts.

Importantly, many of these demands have been successful. South Africa may have been the pioneer in ESR enforcement, ushered in by the well-known *Grootboom* case, which recognized a judicially enforceable constitutional right to housing, followed recently by *Occupants of Olivia Road, Residents of Joe Slovo Community* and *Abahlali Basemjondolo Movement*. Social assistance rights were the subject of a string of important decisions, including *Ngxusa, Khosa/Malaule, Mashava*, and *Kate*. Health rights are also central to the ESR jurisprudence of the South African Constitutional Court, with the already discussed *TAC* decision, but also in decisions concerning the health rights of inmates (*Van Biljion, DuPlooy*, and *Westville*), decisions regarding drug pricing (*PMA, Hazel Tau*, and *Affordable Medicines*), and decisions easing restrictions on state purchasing of medications (*Interim Procurement*).[50]

50 See, generally, the discussions in Jonathan Berger, "Litigating for Social Justice in Post-Apartheid South Africa: A Focus on Health and Education," in Gauri and Brinks, *Courting Social Justice*, 38–99; and S. Liebenberg, *Socio-Economic Rights: Adjudication under a Transformative Constitution* (Juta Academic, 2010).

While South Africa is one of the best-known cases, Latin America has a very substantial experience with ESR demands. Health rights have appeared as central to the more judicialized demands of the new welfare state politics. This issue marks the jurisprudence of Costa Rica's constitutional chamber,[51] Argentina's Supreme Court,[52] the Brazilian constitutional court,[53] and Colombia's Constitutional Court and lower courts.[54] But the agenda encompasses many other rights as well. The right to water and other environmental rights have been litigated in different contexts, with varying degrees of success. The right has been litigated in contexts marked by deprivation – the antidisconnection movement is all about providing water for those who cannot afford it. It has been deployed by marginalized populations affected by industrial pollutants (as in the *Mendoza/Riachuelo* case, in Argentina) and by indigenous groups seeking to protect a cultural heritage and a way of life (unsuccessfully in Chile,[55] more successfully in Nicaragua[56]). ESR have firmly entered the political realm and transformed the actors involved, the discourse, and the locus of political conflict around distributive issues in Latin America. There have been some successes, although there is much still to do to establish robust and comprehensive welfare states.

There has been criticism of this approach as tending to benefit the better off, at the expense of the poor. Octavio Ferraz, for example, argues forcefully that bringing the courts into the center of the debate is simply a recipe for solidifying the advantages of the already advantaged urban middle class.[57] Our sense is that these concerns are overdrawn. We have argued elsewhere that these critiques focus on a misleadingly narrow slice of health rights litigation, and that, if one were to broaden the view, the conclusion might be quite different.[58] Moreover, there is empirical evidence emerging that the poor do not fare too badly, even when we limit the focus to judicial outcomes as opposed to broader policy and political strategies and results.[59] And in

51 Bruce M. Wilson, et al., "Legal Opportunity Structures and Social Movements: The Effects of Institutional Change on Costa Rican Politics," *Comparative Political Studies* 39 (2006): 325; Bruce M. Wilson, "Rights Revolutions in Unlikely Places: Colombia and Costa Rica," *Journal of Politics in Latin America* 1 (2009): 59.

52 Paola Bergallo, "Courts and Social Change: Lessons from the Struggle to Universalize Access to HIV/AIDS Treatment in Argentina," *Texas Law Review* 89 (2011): 1611.

53 Hoffman and Bentes, "Accountability for Social and Economic Rights in Brazil."

54 Yamin, et al., "Colombia – Judicial Protection of the Right to Health," in Yamin and Gloppen, *Litigating Health Rights*; Wilson, "Rights Revolutions," supra n. 52.

55 Anne Skjaevestad, "The Mapuche People's Battle for Indigenous Land: Litigation as a Strategy to Defend Indigenous Land Rights," in *Cultures of Legality: Judicialization and Political Activism in Latin America*, ed. Javier Couso, et al. (Cambridge University Press, 2010).

56 For a discussion of this, see *Awas Tingni Community v. Nicaragua*, Rep. Inter-Am. Ct. H.R. (ser. C) No. 79 (2001), a decision by the Interamerican Court of Human Rights.

57 Ferraz, "Harming the Poor through Social Rights Litigation." See also, V.A. Da Silva and F.V. Terrazas, "Claiming the Right to Health in Brazilian Courts: The Exclusion of the Already Excluded?," *Law & Social Inquiry* 36 (2011): 825–53.

58 Brinks and Forbath, "Social and Economic Rights in Latin America."

59 Daniel M. Brinks and Varun Gauri, "The Law's Majestic Equality? The Distributive Impact of Litigating Social and Economic Rights," World Bank Policy Research Working Paper No. 5999 (2012), available at http://ssrn.com/abstract=2024823.

all these cases, it is clear that the demands arise because the state has, at least so far, not addressed the perceived need.

Whether the broad legal and constitutional turn in welfare politics and movement strategies is wise policy or economic brinksmanship; whether it embodies nothing more than a palliative and a veil for the harsher side of neoliberal political economy; or whether instead it is a new and promising kind of social democracy that marries the market- and efficiency-minded insights of technocrats and policy makers to the egalitarian commitments of ESR advocates – these questions remain open. But we, at least, are encouraged. Many of the approaches to a new developmental state emphasize exactly the kind of issues that are at the core of ESR movements across the world, in particular, health care and education. Investments in these issues, they argue, will strengthen the economic position of states struggling to compete in a globalized economy at the same time that they offer a floor of economic and social inclusion that supports human dignity and broad political participation.

CONCLUSION

In short, the language of ESR has been deployed in many MICs to prompt a new politics of the welfare state in a postneoliberal moment. The phenomenon seems to have its global center of gravity in the MICs, perhaps because they are caught between the imperative of development in a globalized economy and the tantalizing promise of prosperity in countries that already command a certain amount of resources. This language has channeled demands for many of the basic goods that are central to the old welfare states of high-income countries (HICs) in Western Europe, and has pushed some of the MICs to broaden and deepen their own welfare states. The strategies of social groups seeking to expand the range of, and access to, state services include both traditional lobbying and mobilization, and newer litigation-based efforts. These strategies are usually deployed sequentially or together, in a multipronged effort to change both legislation and practice. The strategies are not always successful, nor are the judicial responses always enlightened. But in many MICs, the politics of the welfare state are marked by signature victories achieved by these groups. The *TAC* case in South Africa is a global standard bearer for access to modern, state-of-the-art medication, in the face of obstinate refusals by elected officials and appointed bureaucrats. The T-760 health care reform case in Colombia is a dramatic example of how a judicial strategy can eventually engage the entire policy-making community in a joint effort to recraft the national health care system in a country.

These efforts are characteristic of MICs, to a much greater extent than either the HICs or the low-income countries (LICs) in the world. The LICs simply do not have the infrastructure to support robust ESR demands. The HICs, for their part, have neither whole-heartedly embraced the constitutional language of ESR nor encouraged judicial interventions to the same degree. We can speculate that this is because courts in MICs are standing in for other policy-making and -monitoring structures that are stronger in the HICs, but this observation deserves additional research. None of this has eradicated poverty and need. But there is considerable evidence emerging that it can make a difference, and that, done well, it can benefit those who have been left behind by existing MIC welfare states.

12

The Judicialization of Health Care

Symptoms, Diagnosis, and Prescriptions

César Rodríguez-Garavito

INTRODUCTION

Middle-income countries (MICs) are, by definition, in a gray zone. As with middle classes within domestic societies, they find themselves in an intermediate ground between precariousness and opulence. Their essence is one of contrasts, as shown by the disparate geography of their large cities, from São Paulo and Delhi to Jakarta and Johannesburg.

Economic contrasts go hand in hand with institutional contrasts. The institutions of MICs are hybrids: in them coexist elements of weakness and strength, incapacity and capacity. On some occasions, there is disparity between different institutions – for example, between an authoritarian government captured by private interests, on the one hand, and an independent judiciary that protects citizens' rights, on the other. In others, the asymmetry is found within a single institution – for example, a tax-collecting agency or police force that is efficient in the cities, but absent or incapable of fulfilling its mission in the rest of the country.

This double economic and institutional contrast makes MICs particularly fertile ground for the judicialization of conflicts regarding socioeconomic rights (SERs). Among the economic variables that favor judicialization, income level and distribution stand out. By definition, MICs have more resources than low-income countries (LICs), but tend to have a distribution of wealth just as or more unequal than the latter.[1]

The aforementioned institutional asymmetry increases the probability that these demands turn into litigation. This is because governmental agencies are not sufficiently strong to adequately and regularly resolve citizen petitions, but (in contrast to what happens in LICs) do tend to be sufficiently strong and accountable to fulfill

I gratefully acknowledge the critical support of Camila Soto, José Rafael Espinosa, Laura Lozano, María Rojas, and Celeste Kauffman in the research that led to this chapter. Funding from the Office of the President of the University of los Andes made possible the study that led to the Spanish-language version of the paper, which was published in *La salud en Colombia* (Óscar Bernal and Catalina Gutiérrez, eds. [Ediciones Uniandes, 2012]).

[1] A prominent exception is India, which has a relatively low (albeit rising) Gini coefficient. I am grateful to the editors for bringing this fact to my attention.

TABLE 12.1. *Number of Cases of Right to Health Per Capita (approximate data)*

Country	Actions	Population (millions)	Cases of Health per Capita (Actions per 1,000,000)
Colombia	150,000[a]	45.6	3,289
Brazil	40,000[a]	193.7	206
Costa Rica	500[a]	4.6	109
Argentina	1,159[a]	40.2	29
South Africa	17[b]	49.3	0.3
India	218[b]	1,150	0.2

[a] Annual data.
[b] Accumulated data.
Source: Ottar Mœstad, Lise Rakner, and Octavio Ferraz, "Assessing the Impact of Health Rights Litigation," in *Litigating Health Rights: Can Courts Bring More Justice to Health?*, ed. Alicia Yamin and Siri Gloppen (Harvard University Press, 2011), 282.

judicial orders. When courts are independent and have adequate institutional capacity, litigation offers a particularly promising route to demand the fulfillment of SERs.

This combination of factors is particularly notable in the more well-off MICs, that is, those referred to as upper-MICs. To avoid the risk of overgeneralization associated with the use of the extremely broad MIC category, my arguments in this chapter are confined specifically to those countries with higher incomes within that category and a democratic political system committed to the rule of law. I have in mind, above all, those democratic upper middle-income countries (DUMICs) in which courts have been particularly active in the protection of SERs, such as South Africa, India, Brazil, Colombia, Argentina, and Costa Rica.

To empirically support my analysis, I focus on the right to health, which is the most litigated in these countries. Table 12.1 gives a general idea of the level of litigation regarding health in these countries.

As shown in the table, Colombia is, by far, the most prolific country in health litigation. Therefore, it represents an extreme case that allows us to see more clearly, as though under a magnifying glass, the causes and effects of the intervention of courts in the distribution of resources in DUMICs. With this methodological logic, in this chapter I focus on the analysis of the evidence regarding Colombia.

The chapter has two main goals. First, from an analytic point of view, I seek to examine how and why conflicts over the right to health have arrived en masse to Colombian courts and tribunals. Put in terms of research questions, I explore the following puzzles: What has been the magnitude of these constitutional claims regarding health? Who goes to court and what do they request? Why is Colombia the country with the largest amount of legal cases on the topic? What has been the response of judges? What impact have their decisions had? And, crucially, what does the Colombian story tell us about the factors underlying the judicialization of health in DUMICs at large?

Second, from a prescriptive point of view, I aim to use the findings on Colombia to tackle questions of institutional design and practice that have sparked much public debate and numerous regulatory reform proposals in DUMICs. Who should resolve the disputes on the right to health (and SERs in general), so that the solutions are at the same time efficient and comply with constitutional norms and international treaties on SERs? What administrative and legislative reforms can reduce the volume of health litigation? In what cases should courts intervene? How should they intervene? What mechanisms of institutional dialogue between the judiciary, on one hand, and the other branches of state power and relevant sectors of civil society, on the other, can maximize transparency, citizen participation, and the protection of the right to health and SERs at large?

To tackle these questions, I divide the article into three sections. I begin by exploring, in a medical manner, the symptoms of the phenomenon of judicialization of health. I combine original and secondary data to delineate the evolution of constitutional litigation on health in Colombia. Continuing with the medical analogy, I then offer a diagnostic of the situation, that is, an analysis of the causes and effects of the massive use of the courts in health disputes. I conclude the chapter and the medical parallel with a prescription section, in which I delineate administrative and judicial approaches that, while preserving a key role for courts, avoid the inequities and inefficiencies of the indiscriminate judicialization of health, and promote citizen participation in complex decisions about the health care system.

My argument is twofold. First, with respect to the diagnosis, I maintain that the judicialization process stems from a combination of factors that, albeit particularly marked in Colombia, are common to other DUMICs, that is, deep and persistent failures of the health system; a particularly accessible and proactive judiciary in the protection of SERs; and civil society actors that have gone to the courts en masse to resolve conflicts regarding the right to health. With respect to the impact of this type of case, I maintain that although it has offered an indispensable escape valve for the claims stemming from the profound failures of the health system, and has been the most efficient mechanism for protection of the right to health, it has also had counterproductive effects. In order to theorize and empirically document the positive and the negative consequences of judicialization of health in Colombia and DUMICs at large, I present a typology of effects of rulings on SERs.

Second, in relation to institutional and jurisprudential reforms, I maintain that the most promising approach is one that promotes public deliberation and dialogue among the courts, the executive, and the legislature about the complex decisions related with the health care system. This approach combines insights from the fields of public health and public policy,[2] and developments in constitutional theory and

[2] Norman Daniels, *Just Health: Meeting Health Needs Fairly* (Cambridge University Press, 2008); Norman Daniels and J. Sabin, *Setting Limits Fairly: Can We Learn to Share Medical Resources?* (Oxford University Press, 2002).

adjudication that support a move to "dialogic judicial activism"[3] on SERs, which focuses on structural remedies as opposed to case-by-case litigation.

THE SYMPTOMS OF JUDICIALIZATION

Since the entering into force of the 1991 Constitution, Colombian courts have solved more than one million constitutional cases brought before them by individuals alleging the violation of their right to health and asking, through *tutela* writs,[4] that the courts order that a public or a private health care provider supply a given good or services (e.g., medicines, treatments, medical appointments, or clinical tests). The evolution of *tutelas* regarding health can be divided into three periods: an opening phase that cleared the path to individual actions of this type, a phase of explosion of *tutelas*, and a more recent phase marked by an attempt to rationalize the use of the latter and address its structural determinants. Let us look briefly at each of them.

The Opening Phase (1992–1997)

Since its first rulings, the Colombian Constitutional Court (CCC) ordered the provision of medicines, surgeries, appointments, and other goods and services. The Court established that although the right to health was not directly justiciable because it is not a fundamental constitutional right, it could be claimed before courts when the lack of a good or service endangered the life of the claimant or his or her possibility to lead a dignified life.

This jurisprudential position would lead to the second trait of the initial period, which would have a profound impact in later years. After a 1993 statute (Law 100) established the existing health care system, the emerging jurisprudence of the Court was confronted with difficult cases in which a patient resorted to a court to request a treatment or medicine that had been prescribed by his or her doctor, but that was not included in the list of benefits that, according to a regulatory committee created by Law 100, would be covered by the health care system. The CCC's decision was to apply the criteria of connectedness to these cases as well, and order the provision of what was prescribed by the attending physician, even if it was not included in the official benefits list. This would be the beginning of a long line of cases that, faced

3 César Rodríguez-Garavito, "Beyond the Courtroom: The Impact of Judicial Activism on Socioeconomic Rights in Latin America," *Texas Law Review* 89 (2011): 1669–98; Roberto Gargarella, "Dialogic Justice in the Enforcement of Social Rights: Some Initial Arguments," in *Litigating Health Rights: Can Courts Bring More Justice to Health?*, ed. Alicia Yamin and Siri Gloppen (Harvard University Press, 2011), 232–45.

4 *Tutela* actions are judicial mechanisms established by the 1991 Constitution to process complaints regarding the violation of constitutional rights. Unlike most other legal actions, *tutelas* are remarkably accessible; they can be initiated by plaintiffs (without the intermediation of a lawyer) through an informal procedure. *Tutelas* are also notable (and popular) because of their exceptionally swift processing: courts must adjudicate this type of cases within a period of ten working days.

TABLE 12.2. Tutela *Actions Regarding the Right to Health* (1999–2011)

Year	*Tutela* Actions on the Right to Health
1999	21,301
2000	24,843
2001	34,319
2002	42,734
2003	51,944
2004	72,033
2005	81,017
2006	96,226
2007	107,238
2008	142,957
2009	100,490
2010	94,502
2011	105,947

Source: National Ombudsman's Office.

with the noncompliance of successive administrations' duty to update the list, would create a series of "jurisprudential benefits," that is to say, the broadening in the practice, case by case, of the medicines and treatments that should be provided to patients.[5]

The Explosion of Tutelas (1998–2008)

The marked increase in cases regarding health was already evident in 1999, the first year for which there exist data comparable to current data, compiled by the National Ombudsman's Office. According to these figures, in this year the participation of the right to health in *tutelas* had reached 24 percent. This percentage would keep growing throughout this period, closing with an impressive 41 percent in 2008. The right to health thus became one of three most litigated rights (together with the right to petition and the right to life) and surpassed these two in 2007.

The explosion of this type of litigation is evident not only in terms of percentages, but also in absolute terms. The number of *tutelas* grew rapidly and constantly in each year of this period, as shown in Table 12.2. In effect, between 1999 and 2008, the volume of cases multiplied by a factor of almost seven, going from 21,301 to 142,957. *Tutela* writs on health filed in this period amounted to a remarkable 674,612 cases.

How did the courts rule on these cases? The large majority of the disputes ended with a ruling favorable to the patient, and the success rate of *tutela* actions continued

[5] See, e.g., Judgments SU-043/95, T-271/95, T-502/95, T-088/95, T-312/96, T-546/96, and T-648/96.

to rise, increasing from 72 percent in 1999 to 86 percent in 2008. The favorability of *tutelas* for plaintiffs becomes even more patent through a more fine-grained analysis than the official data of the Ombudsman's Office permit. The analysis of an original random sample of one hundred cases processed by the Colombian courts between April and June 2010[6] showed that the majority of rulings unfavorable to the claimants do not correspond to cases in which the judge denies the medication or treatment, but rather cases in which, while the *tutela* action was being processed, the patient received what he or she was requesting. Once these cases are added, the percentage of writs that leads to a favorable outcome for the plaintiff reaches 95 percent.[7]

The routinization and unidirectional trend of rulings are largely explained by the fact that close to two-thirds of the cases have to do with lack of provision of medicines, surgeries, and treatments that are included in the legally mandated benefit plan, but that public or private providers fail to provide. Thus, as we will see, most of the litigation stems from routine failures and strategic behavior on the part of providers, which have exploited the regulatory loopholes and the lack of oversight in the health system.

Paradoxically, the explosion of cases was partly caused by the CCC's first attempts to systematize its case law and rationalize the use of *tutelas*. In Judgment SU-111 of 1997, the Court attempted to counteract the vagueness and broadness of the connectedness standard by replacing it with another: that of the "vital minimum," which defined the set of basic conditions of material well-being that give content to the standard of "dignified life." In SU-480 of 1997, the CCC established that, when courts ordered the provision of a good or service that was not included in the legally mandated benefit plan, health care providers could recover the cost from a public fund (Fosyga).[8]

Nonetheless, the effect of these decisions was the opposite. On one hand, the "vital minimum" criterion continued to be interpreted in a manner as broad as that of connectedness. Therefore, it led to the provision of a large number and variety of treatments and medicines by judicial order that were considered necessary to guarantee the vital minimum. On the other hand, the recovery mechanisms created by the second decision would come to be a powerful incentive for judicialization, encouraging different actors of the system (patients, private health care providers,

[6] The sample was collected by students of the Program on Global Justice and Human Rights of the University of los Andes, under the coordination of this chapter's author.

[7] This success rate is not unusual when compared with that of other DUMICs whose courts frequently adjudicate health cases, such as Argentina and Brazil, where the rate is close to 90 percent. See Paola Bergallo, "Argentina, Courts and the Right to Health: Achieving Fairness Despite 'Routinization' in Individual Coverage Cases?," in Yamin and Gloppen, *Litigating Health Rights* 43–75; Octavio Ferraz, "Brazil, Health Inequalities, Rights and Courts: The Social Impact of the Judicialization of Health," in Yamin and Gloppen, *Litigating Health Rights*, 76–102.

[8] The Fosyga (Solidarity and Guarantee Fund) is an account under the Ministry of Social Protection. It does not have legal personality or its own staff. It is managed by trusteeship and its resources are devoted to investment and health.

doctors, pharmaceutical companies, and so forth) to resort to or promote the use of *tutela* actions even more intensely. For instance, because the cost of medicines that were not covered by the benefit plan was passed on to a public fund, private providers and pharmaceutical companies have encouraged patients to demand them through *tutela* actions, and then charged the medicines to the public fund at exorbitant prices. This strategic behavior, with its associated corruption, has resulted in the financial bleeding of the system, as charges ("recoveries") from the providers to the public fund grew exponentially during this period, from 2,816 million pesos in 2001 to a figure 370 percent higher (1,039,520 million pesos) in 2008.[9]

The Structural Approach and Attempts at Dejudicialization (2009–2012)

The most recent phase is marked by various efforts from the judiciary as well as the executive and legislature to reduce the flow of *tutelas* and address their structural causes. The first measure of this type was Law 1122 of 2007, which sought to reduce recoveries by creating incentives so that committees of physicians within private health care providers would rigorously assess and filter the claims for high-cost medicines not included in the benefit plan. In cases in which such committees did not carry out the assessment and the patient later won a *tutela*, the law determined that the provider could recover only 50 percent of the costs from the public fund, and had to cover the other half with its own funds. Additionally, it broadened the judicial and conciliation jurisdiction of the National Health Superintendent to resolve claims that were arriving en masse to the courts.[10]

Shortly thereafter, the CCC issued a key ruling that shifted its jurisprudence in a similar direction. In Judgment T-760 of 2008 (heretofore *Health Care Crisis*), the CCC moved from a casuistic approach to the *tutela* conflicts, to a structural approach that focuses on resolving the systemic failures underlying the avalanche of individual disputes. For this, the Court turned to the jurisprudential mechanism of structural injunctions, used by tribunals in other countries (such as the United States and India), which involves multiple public and private actors and whose compliance is periodically monitored by the Court. For this, the CCC collected twenty-two cases that constituted a sample of the most common disputes included in separate *tutelas*. In addition to declaring the right to health a fundamental right (and, therefore, capable of being protected by writ independently), the Court issued

9 Figures submitted to the CCC by the national government during the constitutional review process of the social emergency decrees issued by the government in 2009 and 2010 to reform the health system (Judgment C-252 of 2010).

10 The CCC endorsed the constitutionality of this law and broadened its scope in Judgment C-463 of 2008, which extended the rule of copayment of the writs between private providers and the public fund to all cases of medicines and services in which the providers' physicians' committee had failed to assess the patient's claim.

orders directed to all the relevant actors of the health system to attend to, within strict time limits, the structural failings of the policies underlying the judicialization of health.

In part to comply with the orders of this decision, the government has joined the efforts to streamline the *tutelas*. As we will see, the most notable advance in this direction has been the promulgation of the Law 1438 of 2011, submitted by the government to Congress for this purpose.

As a result, the upward trend of this type of dispute was reversed in 2009 and 2010. Between 2008 and 2009, *tutelas* on health fell around 30 percent; between 2009 and 2010, they fell an additional 6 percent. Although still substantial (94,502 in 2010), they retreated from their peak in 2008. However, they unexpectedly went back up in 2011 (105,947).

In sum, over the last twenty years, Colombia has witnessed what is probably the highest level of litigation on health rights in the world, as claims that were not satisfactorily resolved by the health system were turned into more than a million *tutelas*. The upward trajectory of litigation has been partially countered by legislative, administrative, and judicial measures in recent years.

What explains such remarkable levels of litigation? What impact has it had on the fulfillment of the right to health, and the efficiency and equity of the health care system? More generally, what does the analysis of the Colombian story tell us about the judicialization of SERs in DUMICs? To these diagnostic questions I now turn.

THE DIAGNOSIS: CAUSES AND CONSEQUENCES OF JUDICIALIZATION

The Causes

An Explanatory Model

A nascent, dynamic literature has empirically examined the causes and consequences of judicial activism on distributive issues in DUMICs. For the purposes of this article, the work of Varun Gauri and Daniel Brinks is particularly useful, as it distills, based on evidence from various countries, the factors behind the legalization of disputes regarding SERs.[11]

Their explanatory model includes three types of causes, which involve different actors. The first is the action of citizens, nongovernmental organizations (NGO), state entities (such as the Ombudsman), and private companies (such as the health care providers) that initiate or promote litigation. In economic terms, the legal strategies of these actors constitute the demand for legal solutions to controversies regarding the right to health.

[11] Varun Gauri and Daniel Brinks, "Introduction: The Elements of Legalization and the Triangular Shape of Social and Economic Rights," in *Courting Social Justice: Judicial Enforcement of Social and Economic Rights in the Developing World*, ed. Varun Gauri and Daniel Brinks (Cambridge University Press, 2008), 1–37.

The second type of relevant factors has to do with features of the system of administration of justice that encourage or discourage the judicialization of complaints. It is about factors that determine the supply of legal resolutions. Among such factors are accessibility of courts, which in turn depends on the formal requirements and the costs that the legal system places on citizens who want to file a judicial action. The supply also depends on the attitude of judges to this type of complaint. While a judiciary that is permeable and favorable to the enforcement of SERs tends to produce decisions solving these disputes, an impermeable and passive judiciary tends to close this path of processing complaints.

The last set of causes relates the institutional arrangements and policies regarding the service involved. These factors concern the public and private actors in charge of the regulation, administration, or provision of the service, which are potential defendants in legal actions. The response of this set of actors influences the number of complaints that end up as court cases.

Gauri and Brinks's typology cogently captures the central causes of the judicialization of SERs in DUMICs. Nonetheless, it sheds limited light on the interaction between them, and over the sequence between them. Therefore, in order to exploit the potential of the model to explain phenomena such as the proliferation of constitutional writs on health in Colombia and other DUMICs, it is necessary to develop these aspects of the typology.

To elucidate the sequence between the factors, we must distinguish two moments of the response of the actors that are potential targets of litigation (i.e., the third category of the model). This distinction can be seen at play in right-to-health litigation. On one hand, there is prejudicial moment, in which the potential litigants (e.g., users of the health system and patients' organizations) make their petitions directly to the actors of the system (e.g., the health care providers). If the response is satisfactory for the petitioner, the process ends at this phase; if not, the complaint can become a lawsuit, depending on two other types of factors (demand and supply of legal solutions). For the petition to receive an adequate response depends, in turn, on structural factors (such as institutional arrangements of the health system and the procedures for dispute resolution) and attitudinal factors (such as the receptiveness of actors of the system toward citizen requests).

On the other hand, the volume of writs also depends on the responses given by the same actors in a postjudicial phase. Once the complaint has arrived before tribunals and the judges have ruled, the health system actors should comply with the orders of the decision, subject to penalties for contempt. But compliance can be of various types and have different effects. For instance, the execution of the majority of *tutelas* consists simply in that a health care provider supplies the required medicine, treatment, or service. Therefore, with the exception of structural decisions, such as *Health Care Crisis* in Colombia, the postjudicial reaction leaves intact the structural and attitudinal factors behind the unsatisfactory response that led to litigation. For example, despite thousands of court rulings granting medicines not

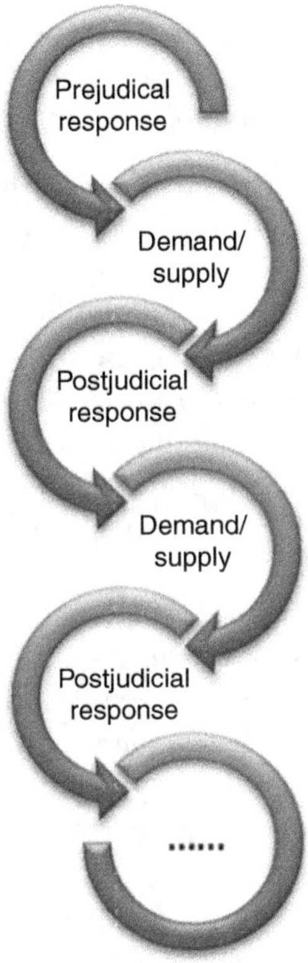

FIGURE 12.1. The judicialization spiral.

included in the benefit plan, the regulators of the health care system did not respond by systematically updating the benefits plan; this omission, in turn, perpetuated the structural faults that led to the massive judicialization of similar new petitions.

In sum, there is a feedback loop between prejudicial and postjudicial responses of system's actors. This suggests that the cycle of judicialization describes a spiral trajectory: absent institutional reforms, the procedural and policy flaws that motivate the *tutelas* remain in place, which in turn encourages new writs. Figure 12.1 portrays the logic of what I refer to as the judicialization spiral and the interaction of the factors that influence it.

In addition to specifying the causal sequence, this variation of the model allows a more precise diagnosis of the structural gaps and the bottlenecks of the institutions and policies that lead to litigation, as well as their interaction with supply and demand factors. The model also has a prescriptive utility, to the extent that the diagnosis sheds light on the precise points of the process of judicialization where interventions (legislative, administrative, and judicial) can be made that interrupt the spiral. The analysis of the Colombian spiral of *tutelas* illustrates these points.

THE TUTELA SPIRAL

The Prejudicial Responses of System Actors

At the start of the spiral are the factors that underlie the unsatisfactory responses of the system to petitions and complaints of patients. The principle failings of this kind are:

The absence of efficient mechanisms of dispute resolution: the institutional architecture of Law 100 of 1993 did not contemplate an agency or mechanism to quickly and opportunely resolve patients' complaints.[12] The agencies whose functions are closest to this type of authority, such as the Superintendent of Health, in practice have not carried out this role.[13] Unsurprisingly, until 2010, the majority of conflicts went directly to judges, without passing through an effective administrative filter to resolve them.

Noncompliance with contractual or legal obligations by the health care providers: as explained, close to two-thirds of the *tutelas* arise from claims for services that, despite being included in the benefits plan, are not supplied by providers.

Existence of "gray zones" in the benefit plan: a good number of *tutelas* originate not from the noncompliance of providers, but rather the fact that the benefit plan does not determine with precision if a specific treatment, medicine, or procedure is included.[14]

Absence of regulation regarding the updating of the benefit plan: Colombian law does not fix precise criteria on this matter, and the governmental regulation that was designed to fill this gap gave a closed character to the benefit plan, excluding any possibility that insurers or providers provide services not included in it.[15] Added to the inexistence of mechanisms to resolve petitions about these services and the lack of periodic updating of the benefit plan, this inflexibility has sent thousands of these petitions to courts, which offer the only venue to process them.

The weakness of the inspection, oversight, and control system: the transparent, equitable, and efficient functioning of the institutional design of Law 100, which gave a central role to the private sector of the health system, requires an equally robust role for public entities charged with overseeing insurers and private providers. Nonetheless, the agencies entrusted with this function have been very far from fulfilling it.[16] The inspection, oversight, and control system has suffered from a

[12] Procuraduría General de la Nación and Dejusticia, *El derecho a la salud: en perspectiva de Derechos Humanos y el Sistema de Inspección, Vigilancia y Control del Estado Colombiano en Materia de Quejas de Salud* (PGN & Dejusticia, 2008).

[13] Everaldo Lamprea, *La constitución de 1991 y la crisis de la salud* (Ediciones Uniandes, 2011).

[14] Alicia Yamin, Oscar Parra-Vera, and Camila Gianella, "Colombia, Judicial Protection of the Right to Health: An Elusive Promise?," in Yamin and Gloppen, *Litigating Health Rights* 103–31.

[15] Lamprea, *La constitución de 1991 y la crisis de la salud*, 123.

[16] Procuraduría General de la Nación and Dejusticia, *El derecho a la salud*.

high dispersion of functions between its main agencies (Ministry of Health, National Regulatory Commission on Health, and the National Health Superintendent), whose infrastructure, budget, and technical capacity has been far below that required to fulfill their duties.

The Supply Side

Institutional flaws, even if they are as deep and recurrent as the ones just described, do not explain in and of themselves the existence of massive litigation. In order for this to be possible, it is also necessary that the legal system be accessible and receptive to plaintiffs. In the case of the *tutelas*, the key factors that contribute to explaining the high number of court rulings (i.e., the "supply" of legal solutions) are the following:

Informality and efficiency of tutelas: the social impact and popularity of the writ lie largely in that the action can be filed by any citizen and before any judge, without the need for an attorney. This contrasts with the majority of DUMICs' legal systems with activist courts (e.g., South Africa and Brazil), in which the need to be represented by an attorney and overcome complicated procedures are powerful reasons that dissuade citizens from going to court. The fact that the writ must be resolved in a period of ten days is an equally important incentive for its use.

Generous legal protection of the right to health: in addition to containing an explicit clause on the right to health, the Colombian constitution includes a provision that automatically incorporates, at the same level as the constitution, the rights established in international treaties ratified by Colombia (e.g., the International Covenant on Economic, Social and Cultural Rights). This has given courts a legal basis for interpreting expansively the content of the right to health, as well as for further broadening it by incorporating soft-law guidelines such as those emanating from the UN Rapporteurship on the Right to Health.

The breadth of jurisprudential criteria: consequently, the CCC's standards on the procedural and substantive issues of the *tutelas* on health have been broad. Both the criteria of "connectedness" with the right to life that it used in the first phase of its jurisprudence, as well as the "vital minimum" that it adopted since 1997, left a large margin of interpretation, which the courts have tended to use in favor of the patients.

The nonbinding nature of CCC's rulings vis-à-vis lower courts: as heir of the continental European civil law model, the Colombian legal system gives each court autonomy in deciding the *tutelas* it receives. Unlike what happens in other countries where courts have been protagonists in the health system (such as India and South Africa), the judge deciding the writ does not have a strict obligation to follow the jurisprudence fixed by the CCC, and thus abide by the latter's efforts to rationalize the use of this judicial mechanism (e.g., the structural approach of *Health Care Crisis*). This key institutional trait further promotes the proliferation of court rulings on the matter.

The Demand Side

The combination of structural failings of the health system, on one hand, and the accessibility and receptivity of the judiciary, on the other, has created a propitious context for the judicialization of health. In sociological terms, they offer a favorable "opportunity structure."[17] A conducive structure, nonetheless, does not in itself lead to judicialization. An additional necessary condition is the existence of a set of social actors that mobilize to take advantage of the conditions of this context. In the Colombian setting, the main mechanisms of this demand for legal solutions have been the following:

The social diffusion of the tutelas *as a strategy of individual litigants:* as explained, cases are initiated by hundreds of thousands of patients who, in individual actions, request a concrete service that was denied by their health care provider. Thus, the very volume of actions and its constant growth until 2008 acted as efficient mechanisms of diffusion of this strategy, to the point that it became widely known to patients that heard of it through the experiences of relatives or acquaintances, or through the media and other channels. To put it in the epidemiological terms of social network theory, the *tutela* spiral has acted in part through a phenomenon of informal "contagion," in which awareness of this legal strategy has circulated with greater intensity as cases and petitioners have increased throughout the years.

The promotion of the tutelas *by public interest law and human rights organizations:* in an indeterminate number of cases, the diffusion of the *tutelas* has taken place through more institutional channels, through public and private organizations that promote the protection of human rights. Facing requests from thousands of patients that have not received a satisfactory response to their petitions, entities such as the Ombudsman's Office, university legal clinics, and NGOs that offer legal services advise the use of this legal mechanism.

The promotion of the tutelas *by actors of the health system:* a paradoxical twist in the spiral of the *tutelas* is that the very actors of the system induced part of the demand. As we shall see, the response of some defendants (e.g., many private health care providers) and other actors (such as physicians) has been to actively encourage, for various reasons, the use of the courts.

The Response of Health System Actors

The last element of the explanatory model that I propose, and that which gives it its spiral form, is the response to litigation by regulators, insurers, providers, and health system overseers. In the Colombian context, the key responses have been the following:

[17] Siri Gloppen, "Litigating Health Rights: Framing the Analysis," in Yamin and Gloppen, *Litigating Health Rights*, 17–42.

The (lack of) response from the executive branch: until recently, the executive branch remained relatively inactive in the face of the institutional failings and the policies that motivate the *tutelas*. Such inaction perpetuated the failures that motivated the *tutelas* and led to new cases. For example, in spite of the evidence of high cost to the national budget associated with health care providers' charges to the state for the medicines that had not been included in the benefits list but were routinely granted by courts (e.g., antiretrovirals to treat patients with HIV/AIDS), successive administrations did not make comprehensive updates of the benefits list. A particularly consequential omission was the failure to establish an expedient and accessible administrative mechanism for processing petitions on treatments and medicines not included in the benefits list.

In the worst case, the response of some public officials was to take advantage of the institutional gaps and exploit the *tutelas* as mechanisms for the embezzlement of public funds. The attorney general and the comptroller general have revealed alliances between ex-officials of the Ministry of Social Protection and private companies (e.g., health care providers and pharmaceutical companies) to get the public health fund (Fosyga) to pay medicines to the latter at exorbitant prices.[18]

The (lack of) legislative response: until the expedition of the Law 1122 of 2007, Congress remained equally passive to the causes of litigation. And when it did intervene through this law, it did so through a local surgery to specifically moderate the impact of the recoveries for high-cost medicines, instead of carrying out a general surgery to attend to the structural gaps of the institutions and policies of the health system. This type of intervention would have to wait until the Law 1438 of 2011, which marked the first significant step of Congress and the government (who proposed it) in this direction.

The response of the private and public health care providers: contrary to what could be expected, the main defendants of the *tutelas* have had an ambiguous reaction to judicialization.[19] On one hand, throughout the years, they have maintained a public stance against the intervention of the courts. On the other hand, as the costs of court orders' were passed on to the national budget, health care providers began to encourage, even advising, their affiliates to demand medicines and treatments that were not part of the benefits list. This response has been highly lucrative strategy to providers. For instance, providers have been able to inflate of the costs of medicines when recovering them from the public budget.[20]

[18] "Contralora pide un replanteo del actual sistema y arremete contra las EPS," *El Tiempo*, November 12, 2011.

[19] José Rafael Espinosa, "'Perder es ganar un poco': percepción y beneficios por parte de las EPS de la acción de tutela en Salud," JD thesis, Universidad de los Andes (2010).

[20] "FMC vuelve a encontrar demasiadas inconsistencias en la información de recobros suministrada por el Consorcio Fidufosyga," Federación Médica Colombiana, October 17, 2010, available at http://www.med-informatica.net/BIS/BisBcm42de2010_11a17oct10.htm.

The response of the judiciary: until the ruling in *Health Care Crisis*, the Constitutional Court would intervene case by case, without adopting a structural approach that addressed the systematic failures in the responses of the other actors. Thus it tended to perpetuate the wave of *tutelas*, and even encourage it through the unintended side effects of some of its systematizing decisions.

In sum, the judicialization of health in Colombia stemmed from institutional failures that gave rise to complaints that were not resolved by the health system, and, due to the accessibility of the justice system, have generated a high demand for judicial solutions. The cycle repeats itself when the responses of the system's actors leave intact the original failures or explicitly encourage judicialization.

Although magnified by the scale of health litigation in Colombia, these supply, demand, and response factors (as well as the spiral that ties them together) are not unique to this country. Similar developments have been documented in other DUMICs, such as India, Brazil, Nigeria, Indonesia, South Africa, and Argentina.[21] In line with the argument I laid out in the introduction, these common factors are largely rooted in the institutional and economic asymmetries that characterize DUMICs. As the Colombian story lays bare, the institutional weakness of key actors in the health care system (e.g., the National Superintendent's Agency responsible for processing patients' complaints and overseeing private health care providers) gives rise to unsatisfactory prejudicial and postjudicial responses that perpetuate the litigation spiral. At the same time, the relative institutional strength and efficiency of the *tutela* courts open up a channel for the massive judicialization of unmet claims. Economic asymmetries have a similar effect. On the one hand, poverty and wealth inequality translate themselves into a dual health care system, in which citizens unable to pay private health coverage resort to litigation to seek redress for the failures of publicly subsidized health care. On the other hand, the Colombian state does have the wherewithal to reimburse health care providers for the cost of the treatments, medicines, and other provisions mandated by the courts that are not part of the benefits plan. Although, as we will see, this has heavily strained the finances of the system and created some counterproductive effects, it also signals the availability of funds to be redistributed through litigation. Together with more idiosyncratic features (e.g., the existence of strong NGOs litigating the right to health), these defining factors of DUMICs go a long way toward explaining the process of judicialization in Colombia and other DUMICs.[22]

Against this background, in order to systematically assess the judicialization of health in these countries, an additional diagnostic question must be explored: What

[21] See Gauri and Brinks, *Courting Social Justice*.

[22] For an empirical analysis and theoretical exploration of the asymmetries of Colombian institutions at large, see César Rodríguez-Garavito, "The Colombian Paradox: A Deep Institutionalist Analysis," in *Institutions Count: Their Role and Significance in Latin American Development*, ed. Alejandro Portes and Lori Smith (University of California Press, 2012), 85–112.

are the consequences of this process? To this question I now turn, on the basis of the case study on Colombia.

EFFECTS OF THE JUDICIALIZATION OF HEALTH

Frequently, the evaluations regarding the appropriateness of court interventions in complex matters such as health adopt a narrow view of the effects of such interventions. Both advocates and critics of judicialization tend to take into account only a few effects, and occasionally their disagreement is owed to their focus on different effects. To appreciate the entire set of impacts of judicialization and decide which should be preserved and which should be avoided, a broader and more systematic view of the consequences of the court interventions is needed.

Based on the typology developed for another study,[23] I propose to capture the multiple effects of the *tutelas* on health through a classification that is reflected in Table 12.3.

First, the decisions can have direct or indirect effects. The direct effects consist of actions ordered by the judge that affect the participants of the case, be they litigants, beneficiaries, or state agencies that are recipients of the orders. In the cases studied, the direct effect of typical individual writs is the provision of a treatment, a medicine, or another service to the patient requesting it.

The indirect effects are all the consequences that, without being stipulated in the court's orders, are derived from the decision. They affect not only the parties to the case, but also other social actors. For example, it is probable that, by generating millions in recovery from the national budged (on occasions with considerable overhead), the massive *tutelas* have prevented the allocation of this budget to other public health needs.

Second, as the vertical axis of the table shows, legal decisions can produce material or symbolic effects. The first category refers to tangible changes in the conduct of groups or individuals. The examples just mentioned fall into this

TABLE 12.3. *Classification and Examples of the Effects of* Tutelas

	Direct	Indirect
Material	Provision of treatment, medicine, etc.	Updating of the benefits list through repetitive writs; redistribution of public funds toward the fulfillment of writs
Symbolic	Definition of the health crisis as a rights problem	Transformation of public opinion about the urgency and gravity of the health crisis

Source: Adapted from Rodríguez-Garavito, "Beyond the Courtroom," 1679.

[23] Rodríguez-Garavito, "Beyond the Courtroom."

category, as they affect the behavior of the health care providers and other actors in the health system. Symbolic effects are changes in the ideas, perceptions, and collective social conceptions relative to the issue that is the object of litigation. In terms of social theory,[24] they imply cultural or ideological modifications with respect to the problem raised by the case.

For example, when the decisions receive wide coverage by media, they can shape the way the media and public opinion understand the problem. This is what occurred with the *Health Care Crisis* ruling, which led to the reframing of the public health debate in Colombia. The empirical investigation underlying this chapter included an analysis of the content of the news and opinion articles about health published by the two principal printed media (*El Tiempo* and *Semana*). The analysis indicates that before the Court's decision, the most probable context in which the topic was discussed was that of "institutional crisis," which dominated 60 percent of the pieces published between 2004 and mid-2008 (when the ruling was handed down). The reframing process can be clearly seen in action in the press coverage that followed the decision: between mid-2008 and the end of 2010, the dominant frame in the large majority (72 percent) of the pieces was the "right to health."

Beyond its analytic utility, the typology allows us to detect the effects that the courts and advocates of judicialization favor, on one hand, and those that the critics emphasize, on the other. The classification also permits the comparison of the criteria of justice that both use, and to make a value judgment over the positive and negative effects of *tutelas* and of the judicialization of SERs in DUMICs at large.

The debates about court rulings on health tend to focus on material effects, as they are more tangible and require controversial economic, political, and legal choices. Judges and advocates of judicial activism focus on the direct material effects, that is, in the attention of concrete and immediate (and occasionally imperative) needs of patients whose health is at risk. In terms of the criteria of justice used to assign scarce resources of the health system,[25] it involves a nonconsequentialist reasoning that attends to the immediate case in order to guarantee a dignified life for the petitioner. Thus it usually fails to consider the indirect and collective impact that this type of decision could have (e.g., the reallocation of scarce public funds to treat high-cost illnesses or cover medicines covered by patent protection sought at the expense of other public health needs).

Critics of judicialization (especially economists among them) tend to focus precisely on these indirect material effects. In accordance with the criterion of justice prevailing in economics, critics tend to follow a utilitarian reasoning,

[24] Ann Swidler, "Culture in Action: Symbols and Strategies," *American Sociological Review* (1986): 273.

[25] Ottar Moestad, Octavio Luiz Ferraz, and Lise Rakner, "Assessing the Impact of Health Rights Litigation: A Comparative Analysis of Argentina, Brazil, Colombia, Costa Rica, India and South Africa," in Yamin and Gloppen, *Litigating Health Rights*, 273–303.

which focuses on the opportunity costs of judicial activism and the impact of court decisions on economic and social policy, rather than on the resolution of specific cases.[26]

The direct effects are relatively easy to measure, as demonstrated by the figures regarding the trajectory of the *tutelas* presented earlier. What is the evidence regarding indirect effects? In particular, in spite of the benefits that it provides in concrete cases, does the *tutelas* have inequitable collective effects? Contrary to the vision of critics (who respond positively to the question) and of the judges and advocates of the *tutelas* (who tend to ignore it), the data show that the indirect effects are mixed: some make the system more equitable, others deepen its inequality, and others do not seem to have an impact either way.

A first approach to these effects is the data regarding the geographic concentration of litigation by region. Critical studies of legal interventions in health, such as the carried out by Ferraz in Brazil,[27] maintain that the inhabitants of wealthier regions and members of the middle class are the most frequent beneficiaries of judgments because they enjoy greater access to the legal system. This, in turn, increases the inequalities of the health system.

Contrary to this conclusion regarding Brazil, and the one extracted by Yamin and colleagues regarding Colombia,[28] the combination of the most recent data (2010) on the number of *tutelas* per inhabitant and the human development index (HDI), shows that there is not a significant relationship between them. Although Figure 12.2 shows that some of the departments (states) with fewer *tutelas* per inhabitant (such as Chocó and Guajira) are among those that have the lowest HDI, and that some of the departments that enjoy a higher HDI have a higher concentration of writs per capita (e.g., Antioquia), there are equally conspicuous exceptions, and the correlation between both variables is not statistically significant at 90 percent.

Regarding the social equality of the use of the *tutelas*, the most relevant data is the distribution of petitions among affiliates of the private regime and affiliates of the public, subsidized regime (which, as in other dual health care systems, cater to the haves and the have-nots, respectively). The 2010 figures show that both sides make requests to judges at similar rates: while in the subsidized regime the rate was 3.4 requests per one thousand affiliates, in the contributive it was 3.2 petitions per one thousand affiliates. There is no proof, therefore, of bias in access to the *tutelas* that has as an indirect effect the deepening of inequality in the health system. On the contrary, the bias is slightly favorable to users of the subsidized regime.

The evidence is also inconclusive in relation to the cost-effectiveness of court orders regarding medicines and their impact on the public budget. The most detailed international study about the topic, done by Ole Norheim and Siri

[26] D. Pinto and M. Castellanos, "Caracterización de los recobros por tutela y medicamentos no incluidos en los planes obligatorios de salud," *Revista Gerencia y Politicas de Salud* 56 (2004): 40–61.

[27] Ferraz, "Brazil, Health Inequalities, Rights and Courts."

[28] Yamin, et al., "Colombia, Judicial Protection of the Right to Health?"

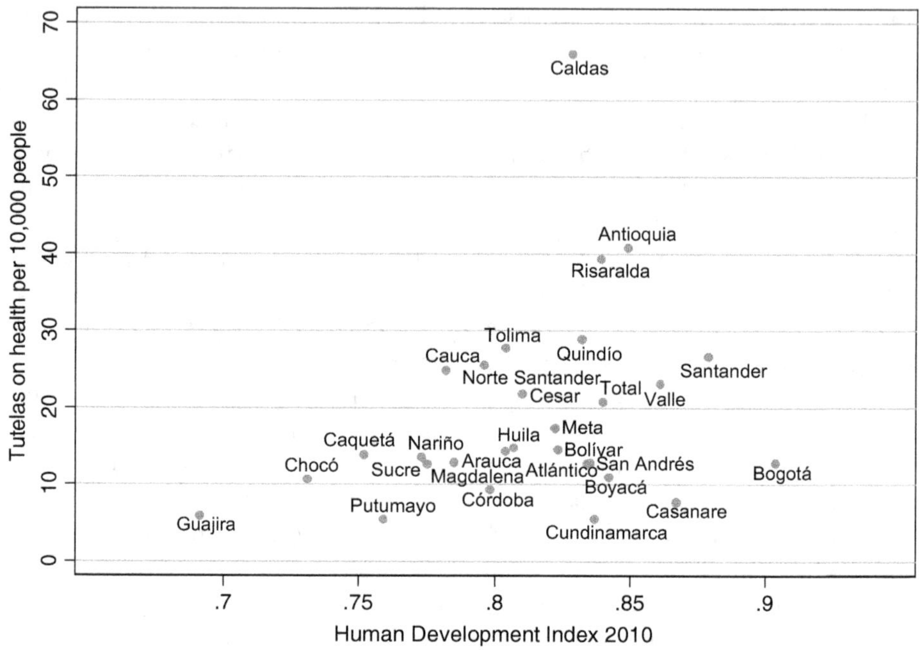

FIGURE 12.2. Colombia: Correlation between Human Rights Index and *tutelas* per 100,000 inhabitants, per Department (state).

Gloppen,[29] shows that the Colombian case is "mixed." Some of the medications most often granted through *tutelas*, such as tamoxifen (for breast cancer) and prednisolone (for rheumatoid arthritis) are cost-effective, relatively inexpensive, and routinely used in other countries with similar levels of economic development. By contrast, the cost-effectiveness of other medicines recurring in *tutelas*, such as donepezil (for Alzheimer's) and etanercept (for psoriatic arthritis), is low. This analysis does not take into account the practices of collusion and corruption that have sprung up around the system of cost recovery by private providers, which stem from the failures of state supervision and monitoring rather than the *tutelas*.

An indirect effect that seems to have been positive is the pressure that the judicial cases have placed for the inclusion of some medicines and treatments in the benefits list that, although cost-effective and necessary in light of the evolution of the epidemiological profile of Colombians, continued to be excluded from coverage due to the periodic updating of the list. Some examples are the viral load test and the medicine lopinavir/ritonavir for patients with HIV/AIDS.

Nonetheless, the adjudication of the *tutela* cases has also had clearly negative indirect impacts, as much in terms of efficiency as in terms of equality. With respect to the inefficiencies created by massive litigation, it is evident that legal processes are

[29] Ole Norheim and Siri Gloppen, "Litigating for Medicines: How Can We Assess Impact on Health Outcomes?," in Yamin and Gloppen, *Litigating Health Rights*, 304–32.

an imperfect substitute for decisions that should be made by interdisciplinary committees of specialists through expedited procedures. To the cost of court backlogs due to *tutelas*, are added the very considerable costs of orders that generate, case by case, cost recoveries from the public purse, without an overall assessment of prioritization among various medicines and treatments.

With respect to inequality, two indirect effects are especially important. First, from an economic point of view, there is evidence of the high opportunity costs of *tutelas*. For example, the funds paid out by the public fund (Fosyga) to cover excluded services would have had a more equitable alternative use in the broadening of the coverage of the subsidized system, or in emergency public health interventions.[30] Second, from a constitutional point of view, the casuistic concession of what patients request can generate inequalities in treatment contrary to the constitution. Because in Colombia (and in other DUMICs with civil law legal systems) lower courts are not bound by the CCC's decisions, two similarly situated patients claiming the same medicine or medical treatment may end up getting widely different responses from different courts.

Given this set of consequences of judicialization as exemplified by *tutela* litigation, the central institutional design challenge in Colombia and other DUMICs is how to strengthen the positive effects and avoid the negative ones. In the following section, I close my analysis by tackling this question.

PRESCRIPTIONS: A DIALOGIC AND STRUCTURAL APPROACH TO JUDICIALIZATION

The case study on Colombia lays bare the two sets of parameters that DUMICs need to balance in designing or reforming institutional mechanisms to fulfill SERs. First, institutional arrangements must be congruent with constitutional and international legal obligations on SERs. This requires, among other things, accessible judicial mechanisms for individuals and civil society organizations to bring complaints before independent courts. Second, institutional arrangements need to promote administrative efficiency and overall equity of the health system. Coupled with respect for the separation of powers, this entails the need for strengthening administrative mechanisms of dispute settlement, to make them more expedited, efficient, and just.

Reconciling these two types of parameters calls for an intermediate route between the two opposing positions that were described in the previous section: the non-consequentialist position that tends to inform court decisions (which focus on the first parameter and on the resolution of specific cases) and the utilitarian position

30 Pinto and Castellanos, "Caracterización de los recobros por tutela y medicamentos no incluidos en los planes obligatorios de salud," 40–61.

that predominates among critics (which privileges the second type of parameter and the overall impact of court rulings).

Based on a broader work on SERs adjudication,[31] I suggest an intermediate, dialogic approach whereby courts focus on addressing structural policy and institutional flaws (instead of solely on individual cases) and setting procedural standards for a public conversation and collaboration with the executive, the legislature, and civil society. In the realm of health, this approach requires two types of institutional adjustments. First, it entails reforms to fill institutional gaps underlying the unsatisfactory responses of the health system. Second, it requires changes in the responses of judges in such litigation, through jurisprudential adjustments that avoid the disadvantages of the casuistic judicial approach that is common in civil law countries like those of Latin America. The aim is to introduce adjustments in different links of the spiral, so that they may reinforce one another and alter the trajectory of the spiral.

To harmonize the two parameters and types of reform, an appropriate criterion for prioritization of health needs is required. Norman Daniels's "accountability for reasonableness" model is particularly promising for the dialogic approach to judicialization that I have in mind.[32] From a substantive point of view, this model is equidistant from both the utilitarian and nonconsequentialist points of view, and, therefore, offers an intermediate point between opposing positions regarding litigation. From a procedural point of view, the emphasis of this model in conditions of transparency, participation, accountability, reasonableness, and due process fit well with the dialogic conception of SERs adjudication that I posit.

This affinity becomes evident when we examine the conditions postulated by this approach as necessary to arrive at just decisions in matters of health. Although these conditions apply generally to decisions of prioritization in the system (e.g., to the updating of the benefits list), for our purposes they are relevant inasmuch as they set standards for dispute-resolution mechanisms, be they administrative or judicial. The conditions are the following:[33]

Publicity: the decisions of the agencies in charge of conflict resolution should be open to the public.

Relevance: conflict resolution authorities should explain the reasons of their decision, which should be based on relevant evidence, reasons, and principles within the given social, legal, and economic context. These reasons should be open to the scrutiny of all persons and organizations potentially interested or affected by the decisions.

[31] Rodríguez-Garavito, "Beyond the Courtroom."

[32] Daniels, *Just Health*; Norman Daniels and J. Sabin, *Setting Limits Fairly: Can We Learn to Share Medical Resources?* (Oxford University Press, 2002).

[33] Daniels and Sabin, *Setting Limits Fairly*, 118–19.

Review and appeal: there should be mechanisms to appeal decisions, and, in general, to review the criteria upon which these are based, in light of new evidence and arguments.

Execution: there should be institutional mechanisms to demand that the system's actors fulfill the previous requirements.

This is the direction in which Colombian legislation, administrative procedures, and jurisprudence have moved recently, which helps explain the gradual reduction of health litigation in the country. In 2011, Law 1438 revamped administrative dispute resolution by establishing a two-tier system that goes a long way to addressing some of the procedural flaws that have led to massive litigation. In the first tier, physicians' petitions for medicines and treatments that are not included in the benefits plan are reviewed by an independent medical committee set up within the health care provider's administrative structure. The committee makes a decision within a period of ten days, and provides a justification for it in writing. The patient or the provider can appeal this decision to the National Health Superintendent's Office, which constitutes the second tier of the procedure. Together with other administrative measures that tackle structural failures of the health care system (e.g., the systematic updating of the benefits plan in late 2011), this more agile and transparent procedure made progress toward fulfilling the criteria of accountability for reasonableness, as well as toward stemming the flow of disputes to courts. However, the fact that the volume of *tutelas* went back up in 2011 indicates that they have been insufficient.

Given that in Colombia and other DUMICs (e.g., Argentina, Brazil, and Costa Rica), the right to bring *tutelas* and other writs is enshrined in the constitution, regulatory reforms cannot (and should not) shut down the possibility of citizens' turning to the courts to demand the right to health and other SERs. Thus changes in administrative mechanisms of conflict resolution may turn out to be inconsequential unless they are accompanied by a change in the courts' approach to the right to heath. If judges in civil law systems with activist courts continue to decide case by case without taking into account the overall effects of their jurisprudence over equity and the sustainability of the system, the negative effects of the judicialization of health are likely to continue (while undermining the positive effects of the judicial enforcement of SERs).

This observation was the CCC's starting point in *Health Care Crisis* (T-760 of 2008), which marked the turning point toward a structural approach to adjudication on the right to health. The CCC had issued similar judgments to treat other structural problems of public policy that violated basic human rights in a serious and repeated manner. The Court has called these situations "unconstitutional state of affairs."[34] Since 1997, it has issued several decisions of this kind in various circumstances, among them was the situation of prison crowding (Judgment T-153

[34] César Rodríguez-Garavito, "Más allá del desplazamiento, o cómo superar un estado de cosas inconstitucional," in *Más allá del desplazamiento*, ed. César Rodríguez-Garavito (Uniandes, 2009), 435–92.

of 1998) and the humanitarian emergency of forcefully displaced persons (Judgment T-025 of 2004).[35] In these decisions, the Court accumulated numerous *tutelas* on the same topic, and issued long-term orders aimed not only at resolving these specific cases, but also the regulatory and political gaps that led to them.

Although *Health Care Crisis* did not formally declare an unconstitutional state of affairs, in practice it has had the same features and effects as decisions of this type. The Court accumulated twenty-two individual *tutelas* that were representative of the fault lines in the institutional framework of health care. To address these flaws, it issued orders aimed at multiple actors in the system (e.g., the Ministry of Protection, the private providers, and the Superintendent on Health), the execution of which requires long-term efforts. The orders sought five main objectives: (1) promote the precision, updating, unification, and access to benefits plans; (2) improve the sustainability and flow of financial resources; (3) enhance the transparency of the health system through the creation and dissemination of patients' bills of rights and duties; (4) move toward universal health coverage; and (5) develop indicators for periodic monitoring of compliance with the Court's orders.

As in other structural decisions, the Court has followed up on this ruling with a monitoring process that includes new decisions and public hearings, and that promotes a dialogue with actors of the health system (backed by the pressure of coercive orders) to address the causes of litigation. It is thus a jurisprudential approach and a judicial role very different to those of previous Court decisions, and to the approach that continues to dominate the jurisprudence of activist courts in civil law DUMICs such as Argentina and Brazil.

In closing, I argue that this structural and dialogical approach is the necessary counterpart to regulatory reforms aimed to improve the transparency, efficiency, accessibility, and fairness of health care systems in these countries. It is the jurisprudential face of the accountability for reasonableness approach, insomuch as it promotes the transparent, public, and reasoned deliberation about difficult decisions of prioritization in the health system. As K. Syrett comments, decisions of this type encourage reasoned deliberation because they require "open articulation of rationales for limit-setting decisions within the court room and, in consequence, [provide] stimulus for further debate upon such matters within the political branches of government and in broader civil society."[36] And, instead of unilaterally imposing judges' criteria, these decisions promote efficiency, transparency, and accountability in decision making within the health system.

Legal interventions of this type have three additional advantages over the casuistic approach that has dominated health litigation. First, they respond to the objection regarding judges' lack of technical knowledge. By following up on the compliance with their rulings through a monitoring process that involves not only public

[35] César Rodríguez-Garavito and Diana Rodríguez-Franco, *Cortes y cambio social* (Dejusticia, 2010).

[36] Keith Syrett, *Law, Legitimacy, and the Rationing of Health Care: A Contextual and Comparative Perspective* (Cambridge University Press, 2007), 233.

officials, but also a wide variety of actors with relevant knowledge (e.g., physicians' associations, academic experts, patients' associations, and human rights organizations), dialogic courts can promote the collaborative search for solutions, or at least a public discussion about the alternatives for action.[37] The direct and indirect effects that can emerge from this dialogue include the unfreezing of public policy processes, the improvement of coordination among public agencies that were previously disconnected, and the creation of public policy framed in the language of rights. These changes, in turn, can prevent the indiscriminate judicialization of disputes.

Second, this type of decision offers a solution to the criticism that, when a judge grants a medical service, she encroaches upon the government's and the legislature's competence. In judgments such as *Health Care Crisis*, the judge promotes the reform process, but does not decide its contents, because most of its orders are means oriented rather than outcome oriented. For example, the *Health Care Crisis* court – instead of demanding specific outcomes from the government – ordered the latter to put in place procedures and a plan of action to address public policy failures, that is, to formulate a contingency plan to avoid the bankruptcy of the public health system, create administrative procedures to resolve patient complaints, and establish mechanisms to efficiently supervise insurers and providers. But, unlike other courts that use the procedural, structural approach (such as the South African Constitutional Court), the CCC set strict time limits for compliance and the government's obligation to inform the Court on its progress, which the Court has enforced through a monitoring process that continues to this day.

Finally, structural, dialogic decisions can deepen the positive effects of legal interventions and, at the same time, mitigate the risk of negative effects. With respect to positive effects, they cannot only induce institutional and policy changes, but also enhance symbolic effects, for example, by making the flaws of the health system visible to public opinion, which generates citizen pressure to address the causes of litigation. With regards to the negative effects, by definition, judicial interventions avoid casuistic and unequal treatment of disperse litigation, and counteract, in this way, the risk of inequitable outcomes.

37 Charles Sabel and William Simon, "Destabilization Rights: How Public Law Litigation Succeeds," *Harvard Law Review* 117 (2004): 1015–1101.

13

Nascent Protections in Emerging Giants

Struggles to Judicialize Labor Rights in China and Indonesia

William Hurst

INTRODUCTION

Roughly 930 million people go to work each day across Indonesia and China. Like many middle-income counterparts, both countries share a history of repression of independent labor organizations and a general lack of respect of labor rights as generally defined in North America or Western Europe. Over the past decade, as China has sought to restore greater equity to its version of "market socialism" and Indonesia has felt its way toward democratization after half a century of military authoritarianism, both have enacted significant measures with an aim of judicializing labor rights and protections. Broadly speaking, Indonesia has created new institutions to facilitate the adjudication of labor rights, while China has laid down new rules to specify labor protections more clearly and forcefully.

Indonesia and China have dramatically different political systems and different levels of per capita gross domestic product (China's was nearly $1,500 higher than Indonesia's in 2010, according to the World Bank). They are nevertheless comparable in that they are both large, middle-income countries (MICs) in Asia with developmentalist authoritarian legacies. Tracing the processes by which these two states have moved toward judicialization of labor rights over the past decade thus sheds light on a number of aspects of legal development and change in large MICs.

Though the distinction between new rules in China and new institutions in Indonesia is useful analytically and heuristically, it does risk oversimplifying a complex reality. China has certainly added new institutions, both since the 1970s and even within courts more recently – including adding special divisions to courts, for example, some intermediate-level courts in coastal provinces like Guangdong and Jiangsu,[1] specifically for handling labor-related disputes. Indonesia has also added many new rules – not least Law 13.2003 (discussed later in detail), which provided the statutory basis for a large percentage of suits brought to the new labor relations courts. With this in mind, I maintain a primary focus on rules in China and institutions in Indonesia for purposes of clarity in this chapter.

[1] I am grateful to Jonathan Kinkel for bringing this to my attention.

CONCEPTUALIZING JUDICIALIZATION

Judicialization, generally speaking, is the extension of judicial authority into previously legislative or executive spheres or previously unregulated aspects of social interaction.[2] Alec Stone Sweet provides perhaps the best specific definition of the concept as the, "process by which a tryadic dispute resolution mechanism appears, stabilizes, and develops authority over the normative structure governing exchange in a given community."[3] The tryadic dispute-resolution mechanism to which he refers is the basic archetype of legal adjudication – that is, some system for deciding or settling disagreements involving the two parties to a case plus an impartial judge or arbiter.[4] This view of judicialization can thus apply to both extensions of judicial power into previously unregulated spheres of social interaction or the shift toward a judicial-style mechanism of dispute resolution in areas previously regulated by some other principle.

A slightly different definition of judicialization is the specific extension of judicial authority into previously demarcated executive or legislative areas. This can be observed whenever courts attempt to make rules that might otherwise be expected to have originated from legislatures (as many critics have said of the U.S. Supreme Court under Chief Justice Earl Warren, e.g.) or whenever courts step into regulatory or enforcement roles otherwise discharged by executive agencies (as, e.g., sometimes occurs in cases of American environmental or health-related litigation).

Some have recently applied and refined this idea in discussions of courts in authoritarian and developing contexts.[5] In this context, the thrust of arguments has usually been about either the extension of state power into previously unregulated realms of social interaction or attempts by a heavy-handed state to reduce the degree of direct executive coercion needed to smooth the resolution of disputes. Such processes have double advantages of strengthening and streamlining the state's apparatus of social control, while simultaneously bolstering the regime's popular and international legitimacy.

[2] Alec Stone Sweet, *Governing with Judges: Constitutional Politics in Europe* (Oxford University Press, 2002); Martin M. Shapiro and Alec Stone Sweet, *Law, Politics, and Judicialization* (Oxford University Press, 2002); Ran Hirschl, *Towards Juristocracy: The Origins and Consequences of the New Constitutionalism* (Harvard University Press, 2004).

[3] Alec Stone Sweet, "Judicialization and the Construction of Governance," *Comparative Political Studies* 32 (1999): 147–84, at 164.

[4] Martin M. Shapiro, *Courts: A Comparative and Political Analysis* (University of Chicago Press, 1981).

[5] See, e.g., Tom Ginsburg and Tamir Moustafa, eds., *Rule by Law: The Politics of Courts in Authoritarian Regimes* (Cambridge University Press, 2008); Tom Ginsburg and Albert Chen, eds., *Administrative Law in Asia* (Routledge, 2009); Hualing Fu, "Access to Justice in China: Potentials, Limits, and Alternatives," in *Legal Reforms in China and Vietnam: A Comparison of Asian Communist Regimes*, ed. John Gillespie and Albert Chen (Routledge, 2010), 163–87; John Gillespie, "Exploring the Limits of the Judicialization of Land Disputes in Vietnam," *Law & Society Review* 45 (2011): 241–76; Jonathan Kinkel and William Hurst, "Access to Justice in Post-Mao China: Assessing the Politics of Criminal and Administrative Law," *Journal of East Asian Studies* 11 (2011): 467–99.

Seldom, however, have scholars tried to assess just when and how specific developing states might take steps toward judicialization of key areas of social or economic life. China and Indonesia, as developmentalist authoritarian states, both had deliberately excluded labor from the polity and sought to downplay or directly repress labor rights.[6] Since 2000, however, both countries have significantly enhanced labor protections enshrined in law and facilitated the adjudication of labor disputes or rights claims through formal legal processes. The following sections trace how Indonesia's new institution of labor relations courts and the new rules China has enacted over the past five years have helped push each country toward judicialization of labor rights.

That said, both China and Indonesia offer a spectrum of relatively more or less judicialized mechanisms and venues for adjudicating labor disputes. In China, street protests can often obtain formal government accommodation.[7] Petitions, letters, and visits (*xinfang*) offer an only slightly more institutionalized, though also often successful, path to official redress.[8] Arbitration and mediation, either within the firm or facilitated by the local government, offer institutionalized but extrajudicial venues for adjudicating labor disputes. The relatively new and increasingly popular mode of "grand mediation"[9] and more direct intervention into cases by the state or Party Committee provide political mechanisms for settling large or high-profile disputes. Finally, courts and judges face powerful incentives to induce parties to settle through court mediation (*fayuan tiaojie*), rather than allowing cases to come to trial and adjudicating them formally.

Indonesia offers fewer alternative venues and labor-related street protests there are relatively much rarer (and still less frequently efficacious). Still, manpower bureaus in most cities accept cases for mediation, and this appears to be an at least informally expected step before workers can viably bring certain cases to the courts. These bureaus, however, seem frequently to find for workers without substantial investigation or deliberation and their decisions do not appear final or enforceable – Indonesian manpower office mediation is a step in a sequence that ends with a court decision, not a true alternative dispute-resolution venue operating in parallel to the courts.

[6] Vedi R. Hadiz, *Workers and the State in New Order Indonesia* (Routledge, 2008); William Hurst, "A "China Model" or Just a Broken Mould?," in *Development Models in Muslim Contexts: Chinese, "Islamic" and Neo-Liberal Alternatives*, ed. Robert Springborg (Edinburgh University Press, 2009), 13–25.

[7] Yang Su and Xin He, "Street as Courtroom: State Accommodation of Labor Protests in South China," *Law and Society Review* 44 (2010): 157–85.

[8] Isabelle Thireau and Hua Linshan, "The Moral Universe of Aggrieved Chinese Workers: Workers' Appeals to Arbitration Committees and Letters and Visits Offices," *The China Journal* 50 (2003): 83–103.

[9] Jieren Hu, "Grand Mediation in China: Mechanism and Application," *Asian Survey* 51 (2011): 1065–89.

While workers and firms frequently operate at many points along the continuum from street protests to formal lawsuits that come to trial, new rules and institutions explicitly aim to drive more disputes in the direction of judicialization. The rest of this chapter explores the ways in which these reforms were implemented and in which social and political actors – workers, firms, courts, and government agencies – made use of them to advance their interests and agendas.

NEW INSTITUTIONS IN INDONESIA

Background

In 2003, Indonesia's parliament, the *Dewan Perwakilan Rakyat* (DPR), made a sharp legislative break with its New Order era politics of exclusion toward the working class by passing Law 13.2003, guaranteeing a variety of labor protections. Among the most important rights eventually promised workers under Law 2.2004, which followed in 2004, was the ability to press several types of claims in special labor relations courts, to be called *Pengadilan Hubungan Industrial* (PHI). These special courts were to be established throughout the country and were to function as stand-alone entities in parallel to the regular operations of courts of the first instance (*Pengadilan Negeri*). Not only was this a marked departure from Indonesia's recent past, but it was also the first time any developing Asian country had taken so bold a measure to create purpose-designed judicial institutions for the protection or workers' rights.[10]

Special courts, however, were discussed in various areas of Indonesian law as early as the 1970s and were established for administrative and Islamic law by New Order during the 1980s.[11] Administrative courts have the longest history (and are perhaps more comparable to the new labor relations courts than the also well-established Islamic courts), but have been plagued with problems, for example in their overuse by people upset over the allocation or enforcement of land rights and the uneven regional distribution of case loads and access (i.e., courts in Jakarta, Surabaya, Bandung, Semarang, Makassar, and Medan are busy, while those in places like Denpasar, Kupang, and Jayapura are hardly utilized).[12] Still, three of the busiest courts processed only 182 cases between them over a five-year period in the 1990s, rejecting thirty (17 percent) and upholding twenty-six (14 percent) of plaintiffs' claims – a remarkable 126 cases (69 percent) were withdrawn, declared inadmissible, or settled out of court.[13] While the precedent of administrative courts' work is

10 Teri L. Caraway, "Protective Repression, International Pressure, and Institutional Design: Explaining Labor Reform in Indonesia," *Studies in Comparative International Development* 39 (2004): 28–49.

11 Adriaan Bedner, "'Shopping Forums': Indonesia's Administrative Courts," in *New Courts in Asia*, ed. Andrew Harding and Penelope Nicholson (Routledge, 2009), 209–30, at 209.

12 Ibid., 214.

13 Ibid., 221.

important for understanding Indonesia's labor relations courts, issues surrounding case loads, access, and jurisdiction have played out quite differently in the latter.

Although implementation of Law 2.2004 was delayed by executive order,[14] by 2006, PHI had been established across the archipelago in Jakarta, Surabaya, Makasar, Medan, Palembang, Bandung, Pekanbaru, Yogyakarta, and – at least in theory – every *Pengadilan Negeri* located in the capital city of a province or in a locality deemed by the president to be an essential center of industry (Law 2.2004: Bab III, Pasal 59). Perhaps not surprisingly, workers began filing suits as soon as these venues became available. Observers and advocates also began drawing conclusions about the efficacy of PHI almost as soon as they came into being, often noting how slow and cumbersome the process was.[15] We have little sense so far, however, of just how these new institutions have come to actually function, with only one nongovernmental organization report[16] and one conference paper[17] addressing the subject to date.

Creating Special Courts of Industrial Relations

Quickly after Suharto's fall and New Order's demise in May 1998, a scramble began to reorganize Indonesian labor governance.[18] Despite an initially moribund response by labor to this opportunity,[19] the debate quickly shifted in workers' favor.[20] The key turning point was the promulgation of Order Number 150 (*Keputusan Menteri Tenaga Kerja R.I. No. Kep-150/Men/2000*, often referred to simply as Kep-150) in June of 2000 by the then-Minister of Manpower, Bomer Pasaribu.[21] Crucially, this edict established very strict criteria for when and how workers could be dismissed with cause from their employment (Kep-150: Bab II). It also laid out procedures employers must follow to obtain clearance for laying off workers (Kep-150: Bab III), as well as formulae for calculating the severance pay and other benefits due workers upon their dismissal (Kep-150: Bab IV). These new regulations shifted the terms of debate, helping ensure that future revisions to Indonesian labor governance would take a rather prolabor set of standards as a starting point.

14 Erman Rajagukguk, "The New Indonesian Labor Court," paper presented at the Conference on New Courts in the Asia-Pacific Region, Melbourne, Australia, July 2007, 1–2.

15 See, e.g., Marsen Sinaga, *Pengadilan Perburuhan di Indonesia* [Labor Courts in Indonesia] (Perhimpunan Solidaritas Buruh, 2006), 74–5.

16 Surya Tjandra and Marina Pangaribuan, *Kompilasi Putusan Pengadilan Hubungan Industrial Terseleksi, 2006–2007* [Compilation of Selected Decisions of Courts of Industrial Relations, 2006–2007] (Trade Union Rights Centre, 2007).

17 Rajagukguk, "The New Indonesian Labor Court."

18 Caraway, "Protective Repression, International Pressure, and Institutional Design."

19 Jeffrey A. Winters, "The Political Economy of Labor in Indonesia," *Indonesia* 70 (2000): 139–49, at 148–9.

20 Caraway, "Protective Repression, International Pressure, and Institutional Design," 32.

21 Ibid., 37–9.

Law 13.2003 did just this in 2003, regulating everything from required job training (Law 13.2003: Bab V), to the use of foreign workers (Law 13.2003: Bab VIII), to the welfare provisions different categories of workers are entitled to (Law 13.2003: Bab X), and the meaning of labor relations (Law 13.2003: Bab IX). It also spelled out very clearly the right of workers to form unions, the rights for these unions to function minimally by, for example, accumulating strike funds, and rules for handling strikes and lockouts (Law 13.2003: Bab XI, Pasal 102, Pasal 104, Pasal 136–149). Crucially, Chapter 12 of the law expands upon and codifies the regulations laid out in Kep-150, regarding the terms under which workers can be dismissed and the severance and other payments due to workers upon dismissal (Law 13.2003: Bab XII). Law 13.2003 created many new rights and categories of worker protections, but left vague many aspects of how these should be enforced or adjudicated.

Law 2.2004 sought to address this gap by setting out procedures for handling a variety of workplace disputes. It describes procedures and rules for mediation and arbitration and specifies when each type of adjudication is appropriate. It establishes PHIs, sets out their mandate and organizational structure, defines where they should be established, and specifies processes for adjudication of labor disputes from simple bargaining and mediation through to trial[22] (Law 2.2004: Bab II–Bab IV). Importantly, the PHI system seems genuinely intended to protect workers' rights and expedite the adjudication of labor-related cases, not simply to remove jurisdiction from corrupt or incompetent ordinary courts (as some have claimed was the case for earlier special courts).[23]

Law 2.2004 begins (Law 2.2004: Bab I, Pasal 2; Bab III, Pasal 56) by specifying the types of suits that can be brought: contract, or "rights," disputes (*Hak*), disputes over the terms or conditions or employment (*Kepentingan*), disputes over dismissals (*Putusan Hubungan Kerja*, or PHK), and disputes between trade unions seeking bargaining or representational rights for workers in a given factory (*Perselisihan antara Serikat Buruh hanya dalam satu Perusahan*). These categories are meant to bring conceptual clarity to the court's mission and help litigants and experts decide which disputes are actionable.[24] Other parts of Chapter 3 set out the qualifications for judges, as well as the provision (Law 2.2004: Bab III, Pasal 70) that at least five ad hoc, lay judges be appointed to each PHI from labor unions, along with another five from employers' federations. Chapter 4 of Law 2.2004 then establishes the procedure for adjudicating cases in PHIs (Law 2.2004: Bab IV).

PHIs are meant to function in a manner basically similar to the ordinary *Pengadilan Negeri*, to which they are attached (Law 2.2004: Bab III, Paragraf 2 "Pemeriksaan dengan Acara Biasa," Paragraf 3 "Pemeriksaan dengan Acara

[22] Rajagukguk, "The New Indonesian Labor Court," 6–11.

[23] See, e.g., Bedner, "Shopping Forums."

[24] Sri Subiandini Gultom, Aspek Hukum Hubungan Industrial [Aspects of Industrial Relations Law] (Inti Prima Promosindo, 2008), 61–3.

Cepat"),[25] but with a few important departures. Their cases are adjudicated by panels of three judges, *Majelis Hakim*, as is the norm in Indonesian criminal and civil courts, but the PHIs' panels are to be composed of one professional judge (acting as chair) and two ad hoc lay judges (one from a labor union, the other from an employers' group) (Law 2.2004: Bab IV, Pasal 88). Also, the PHI are bound by an important substantive provision (Law 2.2004: Bab IV, Pasal 96) that if an employer is found during the course of hearings to have violated a worker's rights under Law 13.2003 (Law 13.2003: Pasal 155) to be paid wages and benefits while the PHI's decision on his or her termination is still pending, the chair of the three-judge panel (Ketua Majelis Hakim) must issue an interim judgment (*Putusan Sela*, sometimes translated as "Interval Verdict") forcing the employer to pay. Also, procedurally, when considering cases involving both dismissals and either contracts or working conditions issues, the PHI are bound to adjudicate those parts of the case first, before dealing with the dismissal (Law 2.2004: Bab IV, Pasal 86). Finally, parties to contract or dismissal cases heard in PHIs have the right to petition the Supreme Court for appeal directly, without having to first approach a higher-level court at the provincial level (Law 2.2004: Bab IV, Pasal 110).

How Workers, Firms, and Government Agencies Interact with the New Courts

In March 2010, I was able to compile basic data on all cases brought before Surabaya's PHI. All Indonesian courts keep "registers," usually handwritten ledger books roughly 80 cm × 40 cm in size, in which the type of case, first outcome, and subsequent appellate action are meant to be recorded. These vary greatly in quality and comprehensiveness. Many court's registers are also destroyed (euphemistically termed "sent to the warehouse") after about five years. Surabaya's PHI is small and staffed by professional and committed judges and clerks (at least some of whom specifically asked to be transferred from the prestigious and centrally located *Pengadilan Negeri* to the newly created PHI, established in a substandard building in a working-class area close to the major industrial areas at the southern edge of the city – close to the border with Sidoarjo Regency). It began accepting cases in 2006, and has had a relatively light total caseload (never more than three hundred in any given year, compared with more than four thousand – roughly 3,500 criminal and more than 600 civil – at Surabaya's *Pengadilan Negeri*). These factors made basic data collection, by sitting in the court clerks' office and copying down information from the registers into a notebook, relatively easy.

A few broad trends clearly stand out. First is that the case load steadily increased, from 192 in 2006 to 274 in 2009, but not at such a high rate as might have been anticipated. Second, more than 80 percent of all cases filed since the court's

[25] Rajagukguk, "The New Indonesian Labor Court," 13.

inception have revolved around the issue of dismissals (PHK), while very few were related to workplace conditions (*Kepentingan*) or union representation (only four dealt with unions). Third, while the success rate for plaintiffs was slightly higher for PHK cases than for the second leading category (contracts/*Hak*), it was not very significantly higher (43 percent vs. 40 percent). Fourth, very few cases are actually appealed. This last finding is somewhat odd, given the streamlined appellate procedure for PHI cases.

Gathering qualitative data from case files was in some ways easier, but more hit-and-miss than perusing the registers. I was given full access to any available files I requested from the court's archive. My strategy was to select cases from the register pretty much at random within each frequently occurring category (PHK, *Hak*, and *Kepentingan*), with an aim of broadly representing each. Labor union disputes were adjudicated so seldom that I simply requested every file I could identify as such. I also deliberately overselected and requested files of cases that had been appealed to the Supreme Court. Many files turned out to be missing or in use by the court (and thus not available for viewing). Others were nearly empty or otherwise obviously not complete. Finally, many for cases in which appeals had been filed with the Supreme Court did not contain all the appellate filing documents or the Supreme Court's decision (as they should have). I got the sense, though, that this was due to anything other than insufficient staffing and poor archival skills on the part of the court clerks. That is, never did it appear that anyone was seeking to conceal or withhold files or portions of files from me.

In all, I was able to review nineteen case files thoroughly, twelve from cases involving PHK, one *Hak* and PHK, four *Hak*, and two *Kepentingan*. Rather than simply reviewing these by issue involved, it is more useful to discuss cases that illuminate aspects of Indonesia's nascent judicialization of labor rights. In these cases, we see the PHI acting as seems to have been intended under Law 2.2004 – acting as an impartial arbiter of last recourse in labor disputes, taking into consideration both employer and trade unionist perspectives, and adjudicating cases according to rules and procedures formalized in Law 2.2004 and Law 13.2003.

Some cases are very simple and straightforward, for example Case 127.2007. In this case, a group of metal workers easily persuaded the PHI to enforce provisions of Law 13.2003 upon their intransigent former employer:

> 27 metal workers from Malang sued their foundry in Gempok. The plaintiffs all lost their jobs in August 2006, after 2 years or so of employment. They sued for severance and back wages in accordance with what they took to be the provisions of Law 13.2003.
>
> The defendant argued that its contracts with the plaintiffs superseded the labor law's provisions and that the firm had already paid generous end-of-contract bonuses to all the aggrieved workers. The defendant then presented a variety of documents related to the contracts in question. The plaintiffs called witnesses, who testified that contract provisions were either unclear, invalid, or not performed upon.

> The court ruled in November 2007 that the plaintiffs should be given severance and back pay in accordance with Law 13.2003, which meant they should receive about 75% more than the defendant had offered in their contracts. The defendant appealed to the Supreme Court, but no result of that petition was in the file as of March 2009 [when it was last updated].

In another case (Case 24.2008), the PHI dutifully protected the labor rights of union activists who had been wrongfully fired in the industrial suburb of Sidoarjo:

> 3 workers filed suit against their old employer – a printing company in Sidoarjo – for firing them without severance. All three hired lawyers. The plaintiffs were all labor union leaders and activists (pengurus Komisariat Serikat Buruh Sejahtera Indonesia) at the defendant's plant. In May 2007, the defendant decided to pay workers via a Bank Mandriri ATM, but told them nothing about it. In June, the defendant invited the plaintiffs and others to a meeting to explain the policy. When the plaintiffs then returned to work, workers stopped production for 30 minutes to ask for details of the new system. Eventually, management said the ATM plan would be cancelled. Then, later in June, union leaders and management had two days of talks. At these talks, some issues came up, especially relating to union activities being hindered or blocked by managers, management's alleged use of guards in the factory to suppress legitimate worker activities, and some issues related to pay and bonuses, as well as the ATM incident. The day after these talks concluded, the three plaintiffs received letters saying they were being terminated. They claimed that this happened because of their union activities and asked for severance packages in line with their reading of Law 13.2003, but refrained from requesting back pay during processing.
>
> The defendant argued that plaintiffs never asked for severance or other solutions. They also never asked to continue in their posts (so, they actually resigned de facto). The defendant also said that plaintiffs had been given formal suspensions, "skorsing," (as specified in their termination letters) and that these were part of the basis for their dismissal. Also, because of ongoing mediation, disputes, and other settlements with the union, the plaintiffs' representatives are not valid. Therefore, the defendant said the suit was baseless.
>
> The court found for the plaintiffs and awarded them severance plus back wages for 9 months between their time of dismissal and the court decision [even though they had not asked for the latter].
>
> The defendant appealed to the Supreme Court, which ruled that the basic ruling from the PHI Surabaya was sound and upheld the decision. But, it also found that the plaintiffs' salaries were overestimated in the original proceedings such that they were really Rp.747,000/month, rather than the Rp.802,000/month claimed.[26] Thus, severance packages and back pay amounts were reduced accordingly.

One of the earliest cases heard in Surabaya's PHI (Case 36.2006) was actually also a good example of how judicialization of labor rights was intended to work. Five workers

[26] In the late 2000s, $1.00 was equal to about Rp.9500.

sued one of Indonesia's largest manufacturers of *kretek* (clove cigarettes), claiming that they had been hired in 2005 but denied a contract and unlawfully deprived of protection as formal employees from being wrongly dismissed. In this case:

> 5 workers at the Gudang Garam Cigarette Company in Kediri sued the plant director. Plaintiffs claimed that the defendant had hired them in March 2006 and that they have labor/work relations (*hubungan kerja*) with Gudang Garam since then. They alleged that the defendant never wanted to issue a contract. The plaintiffs said they asked the defendant for a contract in March 2006, but to no avail. The plaintiffs then got a letter issued by the Kediri Manpower Bureau asking the defendant to resolve the problem.
>
> The defendant chose mediation rather than conciliation/capitulation [a form of arbitration]. The defendant was called to meetings with the mediator on April 26 and May 1 (with letters issued on April 21 and April 26), but never showed up or sent a representative. The mediator then issued a letter for the plaintiffs attesting to the meetings missed by the defendant. The mediator also found against the defendant and in favor of the plaintiffs, saying their claims were valid. At this point, the plaintiffs decided to take their case to court.
>
> In June 2006, Gudang Garam was asked by the court to provide – and did provide – a letter detailing the tasks that had been given to each of the plaintiffs when they worked there. They were all labor managers or activists and 4 of the 5 had law degrees (B.A. in Law – Sarjana Hukum). One had been named head of Gudang Garam's Industrial Relations Division, another was his deputy, a third was assistant head of human resources, and the two others worked as employment eligibility examiners in the Industrial Relations Division. The letter states explicitly that it is being provided to comply with a court order.
>
> The court ruled in August 2006 that the plaintiffs' case was solid, agreeing with their interpretation of the facts, and finding that the plaintiffs did indeed have labor relations with the defendant since March 2006. The court also expressed displeasure with the defendant because he never showed up to court, despite being called multiple times. This caused several delays in the case. The plaintiffs won without contest, therefore, and the court ruled that they should be paid proper severance packages and damaged by the defendant.
>
> The case file had no documents related to any appeals or to whether or how the judgment was enforced.

Another case (Case 75.2006) involved clear deception by an employer seeking to dismiss a bus driver, who had been plying a route on which service was being cut. The PHI was able to identify this problem, pass judgment against the bus company despite the presence on the court of an employer association ad hoc judge, and impose a remedy appropriately grounded in Law 13.2003. In this case:

> A driver (the plaintiff) worked for 14 years for a company (the defendant) as a "day laborer" (*kerja harian*) for wages of Rp.1,500,000/month. In 1995, he became a "national driver" (*sopir teladon tingkat nasional*) and went back to being a "provincial driver" (*sopir teladon tingkat propinsi*) in 2005. He always drove the same

> Patas bus and had never had a problem. He was sent home, however, on March 13, 2005, for the supposed reason that his bus needed repairs. The defendant promised the plaintiff he could return to work when repairs were complete. Repairs took 8 months to finish, so the plaintiff was idle the entire time. Once repairs were finished, however, the defendant gave the plaintiff's job to someone else and refused to hire him back. The plaintiff sought mediation from the Pasuruan Manpower Bureau, but the defendant didn't show up for hearings in November or December 2005. In February and early March 2006, he tried again to set up 3-way mediation, but the Manpower Bureau failed to send a letter to the defendant. In late March, all proper procedures were followed, and letters were sent, but the defendant still failed to show up. The plaintiff then got a Manpower Bureau judgment in his favor, ordering the defendant to take him back. The plaintiff rejected this solution, so the mediator ordered the defendant to pay a severance package of Rp.48,375,000 (15 million for 15 months back wages + 33,375,000 for severance) to the plaintiff. The defendant disputed all of these basic facts with scanty documentary evidence.
>
> The court found, after investigating, that the defendant, in fact, had cut scheduled service on the routes driven by the plaintiff from March 1, 2005. Thus, the defendant never intended to hire the plaintiff back, but had lied to him about his bus needing repairs and about the 8-month duration of those repairs. This deception had kept the plaintiff idle for 8 months (March–October 2005), during which he lost wages. The defendant then did offer to hire the plaintiff back in October 2005, though for a different job, and the plaintiff rejected the offer. Therefore, the plaintiff was found not to be entitled to any severance package. But he was ordered to be paid 8 months of back wages (for the idle period of March–October 2005) at a rate of Rp.1.5 million/month, for a total of Rp.12,000,000. The rest of the suit was rejected. The defendant appealed to the Supreme Court, but this appeal was rejected

In all these cases, workers used the PHI to seek formal adjudication of their rights. Before the new court existed, such cases would have been handled by manpower bureaus (often through the so-called P4 system), informally within firms, or in rare instances by the *Pengadilan Negeri*, leaving workers with fewer options and weaker protections. Though different dynamics can also be at work in the PHI,[27] these new institutions clearly have enabled Indonesia to take at least some timid initial steps toward judicialization of labor rights. It is less clear, however, that the creation of new courts is the most expedient means to judicialization, especially without the simultaneous enactment of more comprehensive and clearer rules.[28]

[27] William Hurst, "Judicialization, Venue Shopping, or Bureaucratic Competition? Assessing the Work of Indonesia's Courts of Industrial Relations," paper presented at the Canadian Council for Southeast Asian Studies Conference, Toronto, Ontario, October 2011.

[28] Andrew Harding and Penelope (Pip) Nicholson, "New Courts in Asia: Law, Development, and Judicialization," in *New Courts in Asia*, ed. Andrew Harding and Penelope Nicholson (Routledge, 2010), 1–27.

NEW RULES IN CHINA

Labor Law Reform since 1994

In 1994, China passed its first labor law. This legislation for the first time enumerated workers' rights and protections. Workers were not slow to pick up on their newfound empowerment. Mary Gallagher and Ching Kwan Lee have documented the myriad ways in which at least some categories of workers – especially those in private and foreign-owned firms – "used the law as their weapon" to force concessions from their employers and assert the rights guaranteed them under the law.[29] Most provocatively, Yang Su and Xin He detailed how contentious workers in Southern China managed to press their own agenda of judicialization through extrajudicial – and even often extralegal – direct action, spurring the state apparatus to help bolster legal protections and institutions.[30]

A watershed year for labor legislation in China was 2007. At least two landmark laws were enacted – on labor contracts and on the handling of labor disputes – and myriad other regulations were adopted by the National People's Congress. Of these, the Labor Contract Law (LCL) was the most sweeping and consequential.[31] Key new protections of the LCL include a guarantee of stable employment to workers already at an employer for ten years, close to retirement (especially if at a recently "restructured" state-owned firm), or on their third contract with the same employer (Article 14); other protections against unreasonable or wrongful dismissal (Article 42); enumeration of conditions under which workers are due compensation from employers and specification of how such compensation should be calculated (Articles 46 and 47); specification of required and proscribed contents for labor contracts (Articles 17 and 26); and explicit statements of workers' rights to court adjudication in cases involving nonpayment of wages or benefits (Article 30), and affirming a general right to seek redress through lawsuits for infringement of any labor rights (Article 77). It is this last provision – the right to sue as affirmed in Article 77 – that is most consequential for judicialization of labor rights in China.

But how did firms and workers actually respond to these rule changes? If workers did not file suits, would Article 77 of the LCL have any impact? Rules are only as effective as the institutions that enforce them and the actors who utilize them. If political actors did breathe life into the 2007 rules, however, the form and substance

[29] Mary E. Gallagher, "'Use the Law as your Weapon!': Institutional Change and Legal Mobilization in China," in *Engaging the Law in China: State, Society, and Possibilities for Justice*, ed. Neil J. Diamant, Stanley B. Lubman, and Kevin J. O'Brien (Stanford University Press, 2005), 31–53; Ching Kwan Lee, *Against the Law: Labor Protests in China's Rustbelt and Sunbelt* (University of California Press, 2007).

[30] Su and He, "Street as Courtroom."

[31] Kay-Wah Chan, "China's Labour Laws in Transition," in *Law, Wealth and Power in China: Commercial Law Reforms in Context*, ed. John Garrick (Routledge, 2011), 163–81.

of their actions would exert a powerful influence on just how these legislative changes might advance the cause of judicialization.

How Workers, Firms, and Government Agencies Apply the New Rules

While it is not as yet clear what precise effect the LCL had on workers' proactive use of judicial institutions, there is evidence that labor-related lawsuits across the board increased markedly in number as soon as the LCL took effect, with nearly twice as many being accepted by courts in 2008 as in 2007.[32] It appears anecdotally, however, that most of these suits have been filed by workers in private firms in export sectors, especially in Southern China, sustaining a well-documented pattern from the 1994–2007 era.[33] The new labor protection rules thus seem likely to have contributed to a further segmentation of workers' politics by ownership sector. Workers in state firms enjoy relatively better working conditions and privileges, but fewer rights and less access to judicial or other formal means of recourse than their counterparts in private or foreign-invested firms.

Still, in certain areas at least, workers appear to have taken up the new law as grounds to file numerous suits and complaints. More labor arbitration cases were filed in Guangdong during the first six months of 2008 (before the world economic crisis could have complicated things) than in all of 2007. Similarly, local courts in Dongguan, Shenzhen, and elsewhere in the Pearl River Delta accepted well more than twice as many labor-related cases in the first half of 2008 than in the same period of 2007.[34] Still, lacking much knowledge of the law or clear understanding of their rights,[35] workers often pursue cases of "passive rights defense" (*beidong weiquan*, i.e., pressing claims only when they have been so badly treated that they have no other viable option), especially related to workplace injury. In one city in Henan Province, workplace injury suits represented more than 70 percent of such passive rights defense cases filed in 2011.[36] Such cases often end poorly for workers, as many struggle to pay lawyers' fees or even to support themselves while waiting for their cases to work their way through the courts, where they do not always obtain their hoped-for outcomes.[37] Across the board, migrants have greater difficulty engaging the law in general, as well as the LCL specifically, on their behalf.[38]

32 Ibid., 176.

33 Lee, "Against the Law."

34 Hou Lingling, "Laodong Hetong Fa Quyu Shishi de Kunjing yu Yingdui" [Difficulties and Remedies in the Regional Implementation of the Labor Contract Law], *Fazhi Luntan* 2 (2011): 24–33, at 26.

35 Chan, "China's Labour Laws in Transition," 176.

36 Yu Tan and Ling Jiang, "'Laodong Hetong Fa' Shishizhong de Wenti, Yunyin ji Duice: Jiyu Henan Sheng X Shi de Shizheng Diaocha" [Problems, Reasons, and Countermeasures in the Implementation of the Labor Contract Law: Empirical Research in Henan Province's City X], *Beijing Laodong Baozhang Zhiye Xueyuan Xuebao* 6 (2012): 18–23, at 21.

37 Ibid., 21–2.

38 Chen Cheng, "Nongmin Gong Gai Zeyang Weihu Ming yu Quan?" [How Should Rural-Urban Migrant Workers Protect Their Reputation and Rights?], *Nongcun Kexue Shiyan* 8 (2012): 42–3.

Workers are also not always confident in the ability of courts (or other government agencies) to enforce decisions or judgments.[39]

There has been considerable variation in how firms have approached the new rules. Some differences stem from the different structural positions of state-owned enterprises, private firms, and foreign firms, as well as those of firms in relatively higher- or lower-technology sectors. State-owned firms, by and large, seem to have been relatively less affected. One significant provision of the LCL for state firms is imposition of obstacles to further layoffs under Article 14. Because most layoffs had slowed by 2005[40] and the trend actually reversed (at least temporarily) in response to the world economic crisis of 2008,[41] state-owned enterprises were mostly able to adapt to the new rules without undue burden.

There do seem to have been many misunderstandings around Article 14,[42] however, especially over its concept of "continuous" employment[43] as well as the circumstances under which labor relations can be severed. For example, a worker in Heilongjiang surnamed Zhang alleged that, because he had worked for the same company for twelve years and had signed an indefinite labor contract, he had been improperly dismissed from his job as a driver after an accident he had driving a company truck while drunk caused losses to his employer. Experts and officials disagreed, however, pointing out that his misdeeds allowed the company to unilaterally sever labor relations with him.[44] Other cases, such as one brought by a worker in Dongguan in 2010, revolve around the reason why labor relations were severed and the responsibilities of each party. In the Dongguan worker's case, the court ruled that he had to prove that his former employer had not purchased social insurance on

39 Wang Changcheng, "Laodong Hetong Fa Shishi yilai Woguo Laodong Guanxi Mianling de Wenti yu Duice: Zhendui Hubei Sheng San Shi de Diaocha Yanjiu" [Labor Relations Problems Faced by Our Country and Countermeasures since Implementation of the Labor Contract Law: Investigative Research on Three Cities in Hubei Province], *Zhongguo Renli Ziyuan Kaifa* 8 (2011): 83–7, at 85–6.

40 William Hurst, *The Chinese Worker after Socialism* (Cambridge University Press, 2009).

41 William Hurst and Christian Sorace, "Recession and the Politics of Class and Production in China," *New Political Science: A Journal of Politics and Culture* 33 (2011): 509–24.

42 Ma Liyan, "'Laodong Hetong Fa' zai Minying Qiyezhong de Shishi Xiangzhuang yu Duice: yi Xiningshi wei Li" [The Current Situation of Implementation of "The Labor Contract Law" and Countermeasures in Private Enterprises: A Case Study of Xining City], *Changsha Daxue Xuebao* 26 (2012): 75–7, at 76.

43 Wu Chunming, "Ruhe Lijie Laodong Hetong Fa di Shisi Tiaozhong de 'Lianxu'" [How to Understand "Continuous" in Article 14 of the Labor Contract Law], *Zhongguo Laodong* 4 (2012): 47–9; Xiao Shengfang, Liu Jicheng, and Gao Pengfei, "'Laodong Hetong Fa' zhongwu Guding Qixian Laodong Hetong yu Yongren Danwei Danfang Jiegu Zhidu Xianghu Guanxi Yanjiu" [Research into the Mutual Relationship between the System of Labor Contracts of Indefinite Term and the System of Unilateral Work Unit Dismissals under the Labor Contract Law], *Fazhi Luntan* 2 (2012): 115–27.

44 Ma Shu, "Dengqing Mohu Wenti: Laodong Hetong Fa Geng Caozuoxing, Zhuanjia Bang Nin Jiedu 'Zhongghu Renmin Gongheguo Laodong Hetong Fa Shishi Tiaoli'" [Clarifying Confusing Issues: The Labor Contract Law's Greater Practicality, Experts Help You Decipher the Implementation Regulations of the Labor Contract Law of the People's Republic of China], *Heilongjiang Bao*, October 6, 2008, 11.

his behalf in order to collect any severance subsidy.[45] Similar issues have arisen in other cases elsewhere, such as in Zhejiang,[46] though others have argued that firms are often saddled with undue burdens of providing evidence on the specific circumstances of dismissals, particularly in cases involving rural-urban migrant workers.[47] In such an uncertain environment, firms and employees must both take risks and feel their ways forward should a claim be brought to court.

Even if the bulk of the LCL's impact has focused on private firms, state firms have still faced increasingly complex suits and other claims, brought by workers making more savvy use of the legal system, including the provisions of the LCL, some of which courts and labor bureaus have found more challenging to adjudicate.[48] As the legal and rights consciousness of State-Owned Enterprise (SOE) workers have increased, they are especially apt to bring collective suits based on articles of the LCL. In one such suit, 532 workers from a sugar refinery in Hainan, which had been converted from an SOE to a private company in 1998, brought a suit in 2010 for more than 13 million Renminbi (RMB) in severance and subsidy payments related to their transfer from permanent SOE employees to contract workers, as well as the company's performance on their collective contracts.[49] Still, according to one study, more than 90 percent of SOE workers look to petitioning and protest to resolve labor disputes, while 80 percent of courts place restrictions on accepting SOE labor cases, and judges, concerned about social and economic effects of collective disputes, frequently use less public channels (such as communication with Party Committees or government bureaus, rather than necessarily issuing formal legal decisions or rulings on cases) to improve labor standards and conditions.[50] Progress toward judicializing SOE workers' labor rights thus has been limited.

Foreign-owned and domestic private firms seem to have split in their responses to the LCL depending on the relative skill levels of their workforces.[51] Transitioning

45 Li Yinglan, "Lun Jiechu Laodong Guanxi Liyou de Zhengming Zeren: cong 'Laodong Hetong Fa' di 38 Tiao Tanqi" [On the Burden of Proof for the Reasons for Severing Labor Relations: Discussing Article 38 of the Labor Contract Law], *Zhongbei Daxue Xuebao (Shehui Kexue Ban)* 28 (2012): 27–30, at 29.

46 Wang Boyong, "'Laodong Hetong Fa' de Jingji Butie Jin Wenti Yanjiu" [Research into Problems of Economic Subsidy Payments under the Labor Contract Law], *Fazhi yu Shehui* 3 (2012): 104–5.

47 Pan Mingming, "Chengshi Nongmin Gong Tao Xin Nan Xianxiang de Tansuo yu Sikao" [Exploration and Thoughts on the Difficult Phenomenon of Rural-Urban Migrant Workers Salary Demands], *Wuhan Shangye Fuwu Xueyuan Xuebao* 24 (2010): 35–9, at 37; Yu Na, "Miandui Xin 'Laodong Hetong Fa', Qiye Ruhe 'Ziwo Baohu'?" [Facing a New Labor Contract Law, How Do Enterprises Protect Themselves?], *Minying Jingji Bao*, March 13, 2008, A8.

48 Wu Hui, Su Duiyu, Cao Rong'gang, and Huang Xinyu, "Guanyu Guoyou Qiye Gaizhihou Laodong Zhengyi Anjian de Diaoyan Baogao" [Research Report on Labor Dispute Cases in State-Owned Enterprises after Structural Reform], *Fazhi yu Shehui* 1 (2012): 253–7.

49 Ibid., 254.

50 Ibid., 256.

51 William Hurst, Jonathan Kinkel, and Alexandra Sowash, "Implementing China's Labor Law Reforms: Interests and Obligations at the Firm-Level," in *Law and Policy for China's Market Socialism*, ed. John Garrick (Routledge, 2012), 118–30.

China away from low-end manufacturing and toward higher-tech and higher-skilled sectors with better labor protections is arguably among the motivations for enacting the LCL.[52] Firms specializing in low-end retail, services, or manufacturing – such as Walmart and myriad Chinese contract manufacturers – resisted implementation of the LCL out of concern for their fragile margins and potentially increased costs, even if the new rules did not induce them to lay off workers or close up shop.[53] Others in mid-range sectors – like Toyota – were ambivalent but not resistant to the new rules. While those in high-tech sectors – like Huawei and Lenovo – welcomed the LCL as validation of their existing practices and a tool for leveling the competitive field.[54]

Firms of all ownership types grappled with economic and social implications of compliance with the letter of the LCL. This was especially true for small and medium-sized enterprises. The managers of one firm in Henan Province complained to researchers that after spending roughly 30,000 RMB to recruit and train a technical worker (*jishu gong*), if that worker were to simply abscond without resigning (*bu ci er bie*) the company could be later held liable for payment of generous severance subsidies and back wages, even if managers could not locate the worker in question.[55] While judicialization had been stunted in some areas, in others it had advanced perhaps too quickly and with mixed and problematic implications.

Local governments and courts were hard-pressed to implement the labor law's many complex provisions in ways that promoted local economic development, preserved social stability, and complied with the central state's intentions in the midst of the global economic crisis. Many provisions of the new law were unclear, especially in relation to existing statutes and regulations.[56] Eventually, provincial-level higher courts had to step in. Guangdong's high court issued a document (document thirteen of 2008) giving lower courts guidance on how to interpret and adjudicate key provisions. This was followed in 2009 by similar directives from the Shanghai high court (document seventy-three of 2009), the high courts of Jiangsu and Zhejiang, and the intermediate courts of Guangzhou and Shenzhen.[57] Thus, within eighteen months of the LCL taking effect, nearly every key regional hub of private and export-oriented industry had devised at least semiformal norms and procedures for its implementation. These directives, especially the Guangdong

[52] Fu Yu Chen and Michael Funke, "China's New Labor Law: No Harm to Employment?," *China Economic Review* 20 (2009): 558–72, at 570.

[53] Chan, "China's Labour Laws in Transition," 178.

[54] Hurst, et al., "Implementing China's Labor Law Reforms."

[55] Tan and Jiang, "Laodong Hetong Fa," 21.

[56] Chen Yining, "'Laodong Hetong Fa' Zhong Guanyu Laodong Hetong Jiechu Wenti de Qianlun" [Basic Theories on Problems in the Labor Contract Law Regarding the Severing of Contracts], *Fazhi yu Shehui* 7 (2011): 36–7; Du Qiaoling, "Laodong Zhongcai Zhidu Ruogan Wenti Tantao" [Probing Various Problems in the Labor Arbitration System], *Hezuo Jingji yu Keji* 4 (2012): 127–8.

[57] Hou, "Laodong Hetong Fa Quyu Shishi de Kunjing yu Yingdui," 27.

and Shanghai high courts which served as a basis for the others, specified more clearly which workers had standing to file suit over what types of claims; how courts should handle cases based on oral contracts and contracts of indefinite term; and established standard rates for severance payments and back overtime.[58]

Still, courts in rural areas and smaller cities struggle with shortages of both human and fiscal resources in the face of mounting caseloads – "the cases are numerous, but the personnel are few" (*an duo ren shao*) has become an oft-repeated phrase.[59] As in other areas of the legal system – and Chinese politics in general – smaller and poorer localities are likely to present a picture quite distinct from that of China's gleaming metropolises for some years to come. As judicialization of labor rights lags in rural areas and smaller cities, just as these areas are dominated by SOEs and small low-end private firms that lag behind their larger, higher-end globalized counterparts, the segmentation China's economy and society seems destined only to worsen with the further progress of labor law reform.

CONCLUSIONS

Despite cross-cutting pressures on firms, workers, and state agencies alike, both China and Indonesia have managed to take significant steps toward the judicialization of labor rights and protections over the past decade. That said, neither country moved decisively to enact a comprehensive set of meaningful legal protections and establish institutions capable of enforcing such rules. China's 2007 LCL made admirable progress in enumerating and elucidating workers' rights. But the court system remains tightly bound to the Communist Party and political system, as well as to an economic order that does not privilege labor protections – and that tends to see the reduction of transaction costs as the primary purpose of economic law.[60] There has also been highly uneven implementation by courts in different regions and localities. Indonesia's new PHI system is impressive and potentially an important venue for the adjudication of labor cases, but in their haste to reform the institutions of New Order, DPR members and cabinet ministers perhaps neglected to provide sufficiently clear or comprehensive new rules for the PHI to act upon. Both China and Indonesia, then, risk settling into a type of partial legal reform equilibrium,[61] in which powerful state and private interests benefit from the creation of a "rule by law" or the enabling of new forms of wealth defense.[62]

58 Ibid.

59 Tan and Jiang, "Laodong Hetong Fa," 22.

60 William Hurst, "Politics, Society, and the Legal System," in Garrick, *Law, Wealth and Power in China*, 72–88, at 73–6.

61 Joel S. Hellman, "Winners Take All: The Politics of Partial Reform in Post-communist Transitions," *World Politics* 50 (1998): 203–34.

62 Ginsburg and Moustafa, *Rule by Law*; Jeffrey A. Winters, *Oligarchy* (Cambridge University Press, 2011).

Lurking in the background is a broader question of whether judicialization is the most expedient way to expand and shore up labor rights in authoritarian or newly democratic MICs. There may be obstacles to creating comprehensive rules and effective institutions at the same time. If so, it is not clear whether it is better to enact rules or establish institutions first. It does appear, though, that authoritarian states and countries with relatively stronger or more stable state institutions should be more apt to enact new rules, while democratic ones (or, crucially, those in the midst of regime change or transition) or those with weaker institutions generally ought to opt for new institutions more frequently. In both cases, governments are likely to make choices largely for reasons of political expediency. Authoritarian governments are based on the control of institutions. The more new institutions proliferate, the harder it is for the party or leaders to maintain control of them. Newly democratizing countries may assume that rules are likely to be in flux for some time, but that fresh institutions are needed to wrest control over processes and outcomes away from entrenched holdovers of the old regime. Similarly, countries with strong institutions can be more confident that they will implement new rules effectively and may be fearful of diluting state capacity by creating new ones, while countries with weaker institutions may see the establishment of new ones as an opportunity to shore up weak spots of state capacity.

More importantly, one must wonder whether at the critical middle-income phase of economic and social development, when millions of citizens are moving off the land and into urban industry, labor rights might be best protected through non-judicial means (difficult as these may be for developmentalist states to countenance). Vigorous enforcement of provisions such as minimum wages, workplace safety rules, and maximum working hours by competent and proactive state agencies may be more effective than enabling adjudication of disputes over these matters in courts. Enacting welfare, health care, and pension programs may do more to improve working-class living standards than legal rights. Finally, permitting and nurturing strong independent unions or other worker organizations with at least some collective bargaining and strike rights may do more to improve the quality and enforcement of contracts than new laws or dispute-resolution venues.

14

Environmental Challenges in Middle-Income Countries

A Comparison of Enforcement in Brazil, China, Indonesia, and Mexico

Benjamin van Rooij and Lesley K. McAllister

INTRODUCTION

Regulating environmental pollution in industrializing middle income countries (IMICs) is more challenging than in either high income countries (HICs) or low income countries (LICs). With their limited industrialization and relatively minor industrial pollution problems, LICs generally require less regulation and regulatory capacity. HICs, for their part, often have high levels of regulatory capacity supported by widespread environmental awareness. In many HICs, years of combined social and state pressures have helped internalize the costs of pollution prevention into market prices.[1]

In IMICs, significant industrial pollution problems are often accompanied by low levels of regulatory capacity and environmental awareness. As a national economy industrializes, economic interests greatly overwhelm environmental interests, undermining various forms of legal, political, and social action against polluting firms. A combination of weak enforcement and pervasive noncompliance tend to create a vicious circle that works against pollution mitigation and control. The prevalence of noncompliance creates a situation in which norm violation is the rule and the costs of pollution are not internalized into market prices.

Enforcement is a key weak link in the chain of possible social, market, and state regulatory forces that could help mitigate pollution. Enforcement is weak chiefly because administrative enforcement agencies (or bureaus) have limited regulatory capacity and autonomy. These regulatory agencies are delegated key enforcement responsibilities but they lack the staff, materials, internal management structures, and effective leadership to enable them to do a good job. Furthermore, strong structural and personal relationships between the state and private enterprises lead regulators to be more influenced by probusiness politics or corruptive influences. Deficiencies in capacity and autonomy can, moreover, be mutually reinforcing as limited capacity makes enforcement agencies depend more on external actors as

[1] Neil Gunningham, Robert A. Kagan, and Dorothy Thornton, *Shades of Green, Business Regulation and Environment* (Stanford University Press, 2003).

sources of income, information, or political support. This can cause a form of goal displacement in which environmental enforcement may become subordinate to organizational survival.

This chapter describes and analyzes five recent innovations that selected IMICs (China, Brazil, Indonesia, and Mexico) have undertaken to improve environmental law enforcement. The innovations all seek to enhance the regulatory capacity of the primary agency responsible for enforcing pollution law through involving other actors – other governmental entities; citizens or citizen groups; or the regulated entities. Depending on the type of actor, different advantages and disadvantages obtain. Perhaps most interestingly, in some cases, the innovation enhanced not only regulatory capacity but also regulatory autonomy, which we would expect to have further positive implications for enforcement in the IMIC context. Overall, the innovations offer hope that regulatory experimentation involving multiple governmental, society, and market actors may work well to overcome structural obstacles to environmental enforcement in IMICs.

The remainder of this chapter consists of seven sections. The first five discuss cases of enforcement innovation in China, Brazil, Indonesia, and Mexico. The sixth section discusses how regulatory capacity was enhanced through the observed enforcement alliances as well as the implications of involving different actors. The conclusion draws out some final comparative lessons.

CASE 1: CHINA'S ENFORCEMENT CAMPAIGNS

In 1996, China suddenly closed more than sixty thousand enterprises because of their pollution problems. In December 2000, China's national media reported that nearly 100 percent of the largest polluting enterprises now met pollution standards.[2] These changes were not the result of changes in regular enforcement, but rather of a new national State Council[3] policy. Just months after the 4th conference on environmental protection law and in line with the 1996 9th five-year plan and China's long-term plan for environmental protection, the State Council issued a decision on strengthening the implementation of environmental protection.[4] This decision brought a landmark change in the enforcement of environmental protection law in China, in particular, the promotion of the severest administrative sanction to counter industrial pollution: abatement deadlines, to be followed by the forced closure of polluting industries.

This 1996 campaign marked the start of consecutive campaigns organized yearly from 2000 until the present. The campaigns have been launched in the context of political concern over the failure of regulatory enforcement to curb worsening levels

[2] See *China Environmental Newspaper* (Internet Edition), December 30, 2000.

[3] China's highest executive body, comparable to a cabinet.

[4] State Council, "State Council Decision on Several Problems concerning Environmental Protection," *Environmental Work News Report (Huanjing Gongzuo Tongxun)* 8 (1996): 10.

of pollution. The 1996 campaigns, for instance, followed the 1994 media attention and reports on major pollution at the Huaihe River. Each campaign was initiated at the national level by the State Council and led by the national environmental regulator, the State Environmental Protection Agency, which was upgraded to the Ministry of Environmental Protection in 2008.

Campaigns have been launched through national-level speeches and conferences, which were studied and replicated at various lower levels of administration. By involving different national-level bureaucracies, including the State Council, the national environmental regulators, as well as the civil service oversight and judicial departments and at times specialized agencies in charge of health, water, or construction, an ad hoc coalition was forged at the national level to work jointly on implementing the campaigns. Such coalitions were then broadened even further to include local-level institutions of the same bureaucracies, such as local governments, environmental protection bureaus (EPBs), justice bureaus, supervision bureaus, and local specialized agencies who formed local "small group" organizations to study the speeches and develop local targets and working plans to meet the national targets and deadlines. Local authorities were asked to make reports, which were to be checked during the campaign by higher-level small groups, as well as through the usage of information from the general public in hotlines and hearings. Campaigns led to a short period of targeted, cooperative, and stringent enforcement work, during which local EPBs were supported by their local governments to carry out extra and more intensive (and nighttime) inspections at targeted firms and to issue much stronger sanctions than during regular enforcement. In terms of effects, the campaigns have been somewhat of a mixed bag. There are clear short-term results: each campaign leads to more inspections, extra sanctions, and even the closing down of major polluters. The campaigns are able to achieve something that regular enforcement by the EPBs alone cannot.

However, the short-term results could not always be sustained once the campaigns ended, and many of the successive campaigns were organized to deal with companies that had relapsed into pollution-related violations.[5] Campaigns were unable to offer a structural solution to the lack of capacity and autonomy of regular regulators. By contrast, the campaigns could be seen pragmatically as the only incremental way to at least do something about the worst violators, even if only on an ad hoc basis.

Second campaigns have had a communicative effect as they brought the enforcement problems to the public and actually increased public involvement and awareness in enforcement and perhaps also support for enforcement. And finally, the campaigns seemed to serve a political function,[6] as national-level authorities could use the campaigns not only to signal their commitment, real or not, to

[5] See Benjamin van Rooij, *Regulating Land and Pollution in China, Lawmaking, Compliance, and Enforcement; Theory and Cases* (Leiden University Press, 2006), 345–51, 355–6.

[6] Cf. Murray Edelman, *The Symbolic Uses of Politics* (University of Illinois Press, 1967).

environmental protection, but also enhance their vertical reach by forcing local governments to enforce national environmental law.

CASE 2: STIMULATING CITIZEN AGENTS AND ENFORCEMENT SUPPORTERS IN CHINA

Campaigns were not the only Chinese enforcement innovation. Chinese regulators also started to experiment with ways to involve the general public in environmental enforcement. The first way that some local environmental regulators sought to involve citizens in their enforcement work was through cultivating an environmentally aware community that could provide extra support for environmental enforcement work and counterbalance unsupportive local governments. The best documented case is that of Guangzhou, which has been studied in depth by Carlos Wing Hung Lo and Sai Wing Leung.[7]

Since the late 1980s and throughout the 1990s, the Guangzhou EPB sought to increase public involvement in environmental protection and improve its knowledge about local environmental governance. The objective was, as Lo and Leung summarize, "to foster public sentiment, to support government authorities in implementing green policies and to enforce environmental rules and regulations."[8] By initiating the Guangzhou Environmental Education and Publicity Centre, the EPB enhanced general awareness through publishing a newspaper, providing environmental publicity programs, stimulating environmental education, and providing environmental training. It developed a mechanism that according to Lo and Leung reassembles the mass mobilization mechanisms developed under Mao to allow its activities to reach the broadest range of citizens in its jurisdiction.

The Guangzhou method of combining enforcement with public education and propaganda work is now a normal part of most EPBs. It was at least present in all EPBs in which Benjamin van Rooij conducted research in less-developed southwestern China between 2000 and 2006.[9] The method has much appeal. If an EPB actually wants to enforce environmental law, but sees itself obstructed by the local government that appoints its leaders and pays for its budget, why not try to put pressure on such government for a better environment and better environmental enforcement? This might help overcome weaknesses in capacity and autonomy.

The second way through which regulators have sought to gain support from the public is by stimulating citizens to report pollution and violations of environmental law. Again Guangzhou presents an early model, in which the local EPB established

7 Carlos Wing Hung Lo and Sai Wing Leung, "Environmental Agency and Public Opinion in Guangzhou: The Limits of a Popular Approach to Environmental Governance," *China Quarterly* 163 (2000): 677–704.

8 Ibid., 691–2.

9 van Rooij, *Regulating Land and Pollution in China, Lawmaking, Compliance, and Enforcement.*

a special hotline and a petition unit. In the early 2000s, local EPBs in Jiangsu, Shanghai, and Zhejiang started to experiment with offering rewards of up to 5,000 RMB (about U.S.$700) for accurate complaints about pollution violations.[10] In this way, EPBs supplemented their inspection capacity by tapping into the potential of local amateur inspection agents. In some cases, local people have driven on motorcycles around factories at night in the hope they would catch violations and get rewards. Later these local experiments – the hotlines, public participation meetings, and rewards – were made part of national enforcement campaigns and thus spread throughout the country.

Like the enforcement campaigns, the enforcement innovation of stimulating public support in China arose in a context of challenges in administrative enforcement. The difference is that here it arose from within the local administrative agencies that viewed it as a way of increasing both governmental support by bringing public pressure to bear and inspection capacity by stimulating citizens to detect violations. This practice of stimulating public support spread nationally, most likely through horizontal copying as well as through the campaigns.

An additional factor shaping this innovation was external to the enforcement agencies and the government: the rise of civil society and social unrest. Since the late 1990s, China has witnessed a rapid rise of green civic organizations, citizens complaining about pollution, and pollution related social unrest. This has been part of a wider development of society and societal unrest in China that has led the government to try a combination of both greater responsiveness to social grievances and incentive mechanisms that evaluate civil servants on the basis of controlling the number of complaints and instances of social unrest.[11]

There has been a nationwide growth in complaints.[12] Also, the provincial aggregate data from 2001, 2003, and 2006 show that in this period there is a significant correlation between complaints and the number of sanctions (Pearsons correlation 0.316, Sig. 0.017) and the average fine per case (Pearsons correlation 0.305, Sig 0.012).[13] This can serve as a very general indication that complaints matter but should be used with care given the nature of the governmental statistics and the fact that only a correlation and not a causal relationship can be measured.

Survey data and qualitative data show a richer but also more complex picture. First enforcement officials in EPBs both in southern and southwestern China rely on complaints as a main way to detect violations of the law. This is especially so for EPBs that lack resources and are unable to develop a successful proactive detection strategy. Moreover enforcement agencies that rely chiefly on citizen complaints for

[10] Ibid., 341.

[11] Benjamin van Rooij, "The People's Regulation, Citizens and Implementation of Law in China," *Columbia Journal of Asian Law* 25 (2012): 116–79.

[12] Benjamin van Rooij and Carlos H. W. Lo, "A Fragile Convergence, Understanding Variation in the Enforcement of China's Industrial Pollution Law," *Law & Policy* 32 (2010): 14–37.

[13] Ibid.

detection can be dangerous. It creates a bias both toward pollution affecting richer citizens and pollution that is easier to observe by citizens.[14] For EPBs that have already shifted to proactive detection mechanisms involving prioritized inspections, being forced to respond to citizen complaints may undermine a successful prioritization strategy and steer them away from the worst polluters or violators.

The strategy of garnering public support for local EPBs also has mixed results. Surveys carried out by Lo and his colleagues in 2000 show that there is variation in how public support affects enforcement. While in western Chengdu public support had a slightly positive impact on enforcement, in northeastern Dalian and southeastern Guangzhou, the impact was negative.[15] In another two surveys conducted both in Guangzhou, first in 2000 and then in 2006, Lo and his colleagues sought to understand changes in how perceived public and governmental support influence enforcement.[16] The data show that although in 2000 a combination of high perceived government and public support improved (self-reported[17]) enforcement effectiveness, high public support and low governmental support had a negative effect on enforcement effectiveness. By 2006 this situation had largely reversed and high public support could improve enforcement when there was low governmental support, but had a negative impact when governmental support was high.[18]

Thus in a relatively short time, the force of public support has grown to form a successful counterbalance against limited governmental support. But at the same time, when the government already supported enforcement, it was not perceived by the enforcement agents as an extra stimulus. Most likely, the double support from government and society became a double pressure that they were unable to meet given their persistent constraints in capacity and autonomy.

CASE 3: BRAZIL'S PROSECUTORS AS ENVIRONMENTAL ENFORCEMENT CATALYSTS

Beginning in the 1980s, Brazilian public prosecutors at the state and federal levels became active in environmental enforcement.[19] Traditionally, the prosecutors of

[14] van Rooij, "The People vs. Pollution," *The Journal of Contemporary China* 19 (2010): 55–77.

[15] Carlos W. H. Lo, Gerald E. Fryxell, and Wilson Wai-Ho Wong, "Effective Regulations with Little Effect? The Antecedents of the Perceptions of Environmental Officials on Enforcement Effectiveness in China," *Environmental Management* 38 (2006): 388–410.

[16] B. van Rooij, G. E. Fryxell, Carlos Wing-Hung Lo, and Wei Wang, "Decentered Authoritarian Regulation in China: Changes in Social and Political Influences on the Effectiveness of Environmental Law Enforcement in Guangzhou City," SSRN Working Paper (2012), available at http://ssrn.com/abstract=2111965.

[17] Enforcement effectiveness was measured by asking enforcement agents to report on their own work.

[18] The authors explain that by 2006 the combined support of local governments and the general public put an unreasonable amount of pressure on local environmental regulators that they could not match and negatively affected their enforcement work.

[19] Lesley K. McAllister, *Making Law Matter: Environmental Protection and Legal Institutions in Brazil* (Stanford University Press, 2008).

Brazil's Ministério Público were most involved in criminal law enforcement. However, in 1985, the Public Civil Action Law was passed, creating a new type of civil lawsuit to impose liability for environmental damages. Brazilian prosecutors in the state of Sao Paulo played an important role in drafting and passing the new law, which also gave environmental groups and a variety of other governmental actors authority to file environmental public civil actions. In 1986, the São Paulo's Ministério Público and an environmental group filed the first environmental public civil action. The case drew national and international attention as the defendants comprised the twenty-four petrochemical and steel companies that constituted the country's most important industrial district, Cubatão.

The Ministério Público in many ways supplements the traditional enforcement work of the state regulatory agencies. Between 1990 and 2003, for example, the São Paulo state environmental agency CETESB issued about sixty-eight thousand warnings and thirty-eight thousand fines for environmental violations.[20] Over the same period of years, the prosecutors of the Ministério Público of São Paulo conducted about thirty-one thousand investigations and filed 3,400 public civil actions regarding possible environmental law violations and damages.[21] Importantly, the involvement of prosecutors has made environmental agencies more accountable. Using their investigative instruments, prosecutors may monitor, find facts, and generate evidence regarding the legality of agency decisions and actions in particular environmental cases. Using their civil and criminal enforcement processes, they may even file legal action against the agency and its officials if they have evidence of illegal behavior.

The Ministério Público's enforcement work is often supported by civil society organizations.[22] Most environmental investigations are opened on the basis of a public complaint or a notification by another governmental entity about an actual or potential harm to the environment.[23] While public complaints may also be made to environmental agencies, environmental group representatives consider the Ministério Público to be more responsive. As one activist states, "If the Ministério Público didn't exist, we wouldn't achieve a third of what we do. . . . We pressure the Ministério Público, and the Ministério Público pressures the environmental agency or goes after the problem itself – this is how stuff gets done."[24] In some cases, civil society organizations become coplaintiffs when a public civil action is filed.

The environmental enforcement work of the Ministério Público helped change a climate of impunity that prevailed in Brazilian environmental law. Prosecutorial

[20] Ibid., 49.

[21] Ibid., 99.

[22] Rosangela Batista Cavalcanti, "The Effectiveness of Law: Civil Society and the Public Prosecution in Brazil," in *Enforcing the Rule of Law: Social Accountability in the New Latin American Democracies*, ed. Enrique Peruzzoti and Catalina Smulovitz (University of Pittsburgh Press, 2006), 34–54.

[23] McAllister, *Making Law Matter*, 155–6.

[24] Interview conducted by McAllister, São Paulo, Brazil, 2002.

enforcement is a particularly communicative way of enforcing environmental laws. Prosecution is a "public act" that makes a statement: it is a "formal and newsworthy means of announcing the enforcement of the law and the defence of public interests."[25] Prosecutors wield harsh civil and criminal sanctions, deal with many types of environmental problems, and challenge a wide variety of actors, including powerful economic and political ones.

However, there are several weaknesses and counterproductive consequences of involving prosecutors so extensively in environmental law enforcement. Because individual prosecutors pursue violations on a case-by-case basis, the resulting enforcement activity is generally not well coordinated or prioritized. Also, when filing public civil actions, prosecutors must rely on often-overburdened courts for final resolution. Finally, questions have arisen regarding the accountability of Brazilian prosecutors. Prosecutors are tenured and the constitution guarantees a high degree of independence to both the individual prosecutor and the Ministério Público as an institution. Environmental agency officials have sometimes accused prosecutors of interfering in enforcement decisions committed to agency discretion and otherwise overstepping their authority.

CASE 4: PUBLIC DISCLOSURE TO IMPROVE COMPLIANCE IN INDONESIA

In 1995, Indonesia's national pollution regulator, Bapedal, launched a new initiative called Program for Pollution Control Evaluation and Rating (PROPER). The first phase of the program (which ran until 1998) produced a rating system for the water pollution performance of 187 industrial firms, including medium- and large-scale polluters from Sumatra, Java, and Kalimantan. According to Bapedal data, two-thirds of these factories were not in compliance at the time. Under the rating system, five categories were used to classify the performance of these firms, each with their own color: Black (no pollution-control effort and serious pollution), Red (efforts but do not meet standards), Blue (efforts meet the standards), Green (above standards and good maintenance), and Gold (clean technology, waste minimization, and pollution prevention).

The first phase ended in 1998 amidst the fall of the Suharto government, and the second phase was initiated in 2002. During the second phase, the program had to restart and expand from eighty-five firms in 2002, to 627 firms in 2009.[26] The original rating system was amended to introduce two new colors, Blue Minus and Red Minus, in order to provide a positive stimulus for firms that had invested in abatement but still were unable to fully meet the appropriate standards. Also, the second PROPER was a more ambitious version of the first program, including not just rating

[25] Keith Hawkins, *Law as Last Resort: Prosecution Decision-Making in a Regulatory Agency*. Oxford Socio-Legal Studies (Oxford University Press, 2002).

[26] Eungkyoon Lee, "Information Disclosure and Environmental Regulation: Green Lights and Gray Areas," *Regulation & Governance* 4 (2010): 303–28.

and disclosing compliance, but also disclosing information about pollution emissions and implementation of environmental impact assessments. The program no longer sought to just enhance compliance but also to move firms beyond compliance.

The PROPER program originated in a context again of disappointing administrative enforcement and persistent noncompliance.[27] Indonesian regulatory capacity seemed to decrease after Suharto's fall, and the second PROPER program sought an innovative way to deal with it. The enforcement innovation here was twofold. First, the compliance data were gathered by a combination of inspections and self-reporting by industries.[28] Second, compliance status was disclosed in a simplified form that was readily accessible to civil society, consumers, and shareholders who could then act upon it. The combination of self-reporting and inspection has the potential to reduce the detection burden and thus administrative agency capacity issues, while disclosing compliance data broadens the number of actors that can impose sanctions or other negative repercussions upon violators. The program was attractive not just to the government and regulators who point to its positive results, but also to international organizations such as the World Bank[29] and even the participating firms who applaud its positive effect in teaching them about environmental management.[30]

There is some debate about the effects of PROPER. According to the data released by the PROPER authorities, the program has had a positive effect on enhancing compliance. The official data from the first phase showed that the worst compliers in the Black group had decreased by 83 percent, while 24 percent of the Red firms also showed improvement and were awarded Blue compliant status. According to this data, in total a 53 percent increase in compliance was thus achieved. All of this was done with a minimum of costs: the entire cost of PROPER was about $300,000 over eighteen months. Official data from the second phase show that after an initial drop in compliance from 69 percent to 52 percent, in the period between 2002–3 to 2004–5, compliance grew from 52 percent in 2004–5 to 76 percent in 2006–7 and back to 70 percent in 2007–8.[31]

However, one can raise questions about the success of the program as it has been portrayed. Most critical, and difficult to ascertain, is whether the data used to measure compliance are sufficiently trustworthy, especially in a context of self-reporting with limited inspection capacity. In his study of the second phase of

[27] S. Afsah, J. H. García and T. Sterner, "The Institutional History of Indonesia's Environmental Rating and Public Disclosure Program (Proper) (Draft Paper on File with the Author)" (2011), 10, 17.

[28] Shakeb Afsah, Benoit Laplante, and David Wheeler, "Regulation in the Information Age: Indonesian Public Information Program for Environmental Management," available at http://web.worldbank.org/servlets/ECR?contentMDK=20798617&sitePK=1909405.

[29] World Bank, *Greening Industry, New Roles for Communities, Markets and Governments* (Oxford University Press, 2000).

[30] Lee, "Information Disclosure and Environmental Regulation," 317.

[31] Ibid., 310.

PROPER, E. Lee concludes that the introduction of the new colors in 2006 obscured verification of the success of the program.[32] He shows that the second-phase increase in compliance rates would actually be reversed if the Blue Minus firms were not included in the compliance category as they were by Bapedal, but strictly speaking should not have been.[33] Also, Lee has developed the most detailed data available to date about what two different key stakeholders think of the program: program participants and nongovernmental organizations (NGOs). His data show that there is a great disparity with how they view PROPER. Participating firms see it as highly effective and see NGOs as ineffective. They agree, however, that PROPER did not stimulate either market forces or communities to exert extra pressure on the participating firms, as was the original goal of the program. Instead the participating firms stressed the internal learning that was gained through the program.[34]

CASE 5: TAPPING INTO THE MARKET, MEXICO'S PRIVATE AUDITORS AS DEPUTIZED INSPECTORS

In the early 1990s, the Mexican federal government innovated in the area of environmental enforcement in response to external and internal pressure. North American environmentalists opposed to the ratification of the North American Free Trade Agreement argued that lax enforcement of environmental laws would be used by Mexico as a comparative advantage to attract investment and Mexico would become a "pollution haven."[35] Moreover, a 1992 explosion in the sewers of Guadalajara that killed or injured more than a thousand people provoked a national outcry for environmental protection.

In response, the Mexican government created an agency dedicated to environmental enforcement, the Federal Attorney General for Environmental Protection (PROFEPA, *Procuraduría Federal de Protección al Medio Ambiente*). PROFEPA soon instituted an aggressive enforcement campaign for industrial facilities that resulted in highly publicized facility closures and fines. PROFEPA also created a voluntary compliance program, the National Environmental Audit Program, under which companies could opt out of the agency's traditional enforcement program of inspections and possible penalties by committing to conduct an environmental audit to identify and correct environmental risks.

The Audit Program has been maintained and expanded over the course of twenty years, and it has attracted a significant level of participation. By the year 2000, the

[32] Ibid., 311.
[33] Ibid., 312–13.
[34] Ibid., 314.
[35] Antonio Azuela and Javier Warman, "From 'the Mexican Problem' to a Regional Experience: Environmental Enforcement and Compliance in North America," paper presented at the Sixth International Conference on Environmental Compliance and Enforcement, San Jose, Costa Rica, 2002.

Audit Program had grown to include a majority of the country's large industrial establishments.[36] The program expanded through the 2000s, and by 2010, a total of more than nine thousand facilities had registered to participate.[37] Importantly, however, not all met the requirements for certification, and over the years, approximately 2,500 left the program before completing it.

The Audit Program works as follows.[38] Once a facility registers for the program, the facility selects an auditor approved by PROFEPA to perform a comprehensive environmental audit in accordance with PROFEPA's "terms of reference," which specify the methods to be used in environmental audits.[39] Based on the results of the audit, the auditor proposes a plan of action listing all the actions necessary to come into compliance with the law and otherwise fulfill the expectations of the program. The agency and the facility then negotiate a written agreement under which the facility commits to carrying out the plan of action over a predetermined time period and submitting progress reports to the agency. When the actions required by the agreement have been completed, the company receives an environmental certificate from the agency.

Aside from the ultimate certificate, the agency provides several incentives for a company to join the Audit Program. First, the agency assures the facility that it will not sanction the company for violations identified in the audit. Second, the agency agrees not to conduct regular enforcement inspections as long as the company diligently progresses in fulfilling the conditions of its agreement.[40] Finally, PROFEPA agrees not to inspect the facility for two years after the issuance of the certificate unless it receives a public complaint or an accident occurs.[41]

The types of environmental certificates awarded by the program have grown over the lifetime of the program. The program began with a focus on the largest pollution sources that presented the greatest risk of industrial accidents. Facilities that completed the program received the Clean Industry certificate (*Industria Limpia*).[42] In the late 1990s, the program expanded to include more medium-sized industrial facilities.[43] In the 2000s, the program expanded again to include many nonindustrial facilities in the commercial and service sectors, and two new certificates were

[36] By the end of 2000, the number of facilities that had joined the program stood at 1,749. PROFEPA, *Informe Anual* 2002 (Procuraduría Federal de Protección al Ambiente, 2003), 59.

[37] PROFEPA, *Informe Anual* 2010 (Procuraduría Federal de Protección al Ambiente, 2011), 106.

[38] Allen Blackman, Bidisha Lahiri, William Pizer, Marisol Rivera Planter, and Carlos Munoz Pina, "Voluntary Environmental Regulation in Developing Countries: Mexico's Clean Industry Program," *Journal of Environmental Economics and Management* 60 (2010): 183–4.

[39] PROFEPA, *Informe* 1995–2000 (Procuraduría Federal de Protección al Ambiente, 2000), 63.

[40] Ibid., 65; Harvard University School of Public Health, "Evaluation of Programa Nacional de Auditoria Ambiental," 2000, 5. This is a consultants' report prepared by Harvard University School of Public Health for Procuraduría Federal de Protección al Ambiente (PROFEPA),

[41] Blackman, et al., "Voluntary Environmental Regulation," 184.

[42] Harvard University School of Public Health, "Evaluation of Programa Nacional de Auditoria Ambiental," 4–5.

[43] Ibid., 3.

developed, the Environmental Quality certificate (*Calidad Ambiental*) and the Tourism Environmental Quality certificate (*Calidad Ambiental Turística*).

Several studies have sought to evaluate the outcomes of the Mexican Audit Program. One study of the program using data through the early 2000s found that the program succeeded in attracting relatively dirty plants rather than already-clean firms that would have had to do little to satisfy the program's requirements.[44] The same study showed that facilities that exported products, imported inputs, or sold to the Mexican government were significantly more likely to participate in the program.[45] Also, the larger the facility in terms of sales and/or capitalization, the more likely it was to participate.

Another study analyzed the investments of participating companies in environmental improvements.[46] It found that companies participating in the years from 1993 to 2003 had pledged to invest about U.S.$2.15 billion to come into compliance and become certified. Most of these pledged investments were not verified, but the authors of the study made extrapolations based on those that were and concluded that the environmentally related expenditures of participating companies was actually likely to be even greater at about U.S. $3.32 billion.

In 2010, PROFEPA required the 1,250 companies that were certified or recertified to provide quantitative information about the environmental improvements they made for certification.[47] In total, they reported having reduced water usage by 333 million cubic meters of water, CO_2 emissions by thirteen million tons, electricity consumption by 8,905 kilowatt-hours, and waste generation by five million tons. While the data are unverified, they do suggest that the Audit Program has motivated environmental improvements.

Finally, it is worth noting that the Audit Program has enabled PROFEPA to extend its jurisdictions reach in several ways.[48] For example, PROFEPA does not formally have the authority to enforce water-pollution laws, but companies participating in the Audit Program must show compliance with them.[49] Similarly, compliance with state and local environmental laws is evaluated as part of the audit, and violations must be corrected before certification. Finally, PROFEPA has used the program to encourage beyond-compliance behaviors such as the adoption of environmental management systems or the use of life-cycle analysis.[50]

44 Blackman, et al., "Voluntary Environmental Regulation," 183.

45 Ibid., 188.

46 Ramon Alvarez-Larrauri and Ira Fogel, "Environmental Audits as a Policy of State: 10 Years of Experience in Mexico," *Journal of Cleaner Production* 16 (2008): 66–74.

47 PROFEPA, "Beneficios Ambientales 2011," available at http://www.profepa.gob.mx/innovaportal/v/4098/1/mx/beneficios_ambientales_2011.html.

48 Cf. Lesley K. McAllister, "Co-Regulation in Mexican Environmental Law," *Utah Environmental Law Review* 32 (2012): 181–210.

49 See, e.g., PROFEPA, "Terminos de referencia," available at http://www.profepa.gob.mx/innovaportal/file/534/1/PFPA-SAA-152-DTR-01.pdf.

50 Interview conducted by McAllister, Mexico City, Mexico, 2008.

A variety of factors may limit the Audit Program's effectiveness. It is difficult to determine whether participating facilities come into compliance sooner than nonparticipants and whether they maintain compliance after program participation. In relation to the latter question, one empirical analysis found that when graduates of the program were later inspected, they were not fined at a substantially lower rate than matched nonparticipants.[51] This finding suggests that the program "did not have a large, lasting impact on their environmental performance."[52] Also, problems may arise from the Mexican Audit Program's reliance on private third-party auditors as substitutes for governmental inspectors.[53] The quality of the audit report, and of the program generally, depends on having private auditors that are both competent and independent of the companies they audit.[54]

COMPARATIVE FINDINGS: ENHANCING CAPACITY IN DIFFERENT WAYS

Comparing the five cases of regulatory innovations reveals a key similarity in why they emerged as well as many differences in their outcomes. The innovations in China, Brazil, Indonesia, and Mexico all have the same basic aim: to enhance or augment regulatory capacity, particularly the local pollution agency's capacity to detect and respond to noncompliance. The regulatory agencies that have primary responsibility for enforcing pollution laws in IMICs habitually suffer from deficiencies in the availability of staff and resources to conduct inspections and respond to violations. The innovations discussed in this chapter can all be viewed as ways to bring more people and resources to the task of identifying instances of noncompliance and generating incentives for improvements.

Based on these cases, as shown in Table 14.1, three different types of actors can be incorporated into the regulatory enforcement process to enhance detection and response capacity. First, enforcement innovations may incorporate governmental actors outside the primary regulatory agency. In the case of the campaigns in China (case 1), higher-level officials and local officials from other agencies were brought into strengthen and expand inspection activity. In the case of Brazil, state prosecutors supplemented the enforcement activity of the state environmental agencies.

Second, innovations may directly incorporate citizens and civil society organizations who might be concerned about pollution in their communities. In China (case 2), EPBs stimulated citizens to report possible violations and otherwise support their enforcement work. In the case of Brazil, the Ministério Público's prosecutors often received

[51] Blackman, et al., "Voluntary Environmental Regulation," 183.

[52] Ibid.

[53] Cf. Lesley K. McAllister, "Regulation by Third-Party Verification," *Boston College Law Review* 53 (2012): 1.

[54] Keith A. Houghton and Christine A. Jubb, "The Market for Financial Report Audits: Regulation of and Competition for Auditor Independence," *Law & Policy* 25 (2003): 308–9.

TABLE 14.1. *Sources of Enhanced Capacity and Capacity Enhancements*

	Country	Source of Enhanced Capacity	How Capacity Was Enhanced
Case 1	China	Government: participation of higher-level government and other agencies at same level of government	More targeted inspections, more publicity, stronger sanctions, and increased public awareness and support
Case 2	China	Citizens: citizen complaints	Increase in citizen complaints, more public participation, and more sanctions
Case 3	Brazil	Government: prosecutorial institutions Civil society: environmental NGOs	Increase in prosecutorial investigations and civil actions, and increased public awareness and participation
Case 4	Indonesia	Regulated companies: self-reporting requirements and labeling system	Provided more information on compliance, and mixed evidence of increased compliance especially through better knowledge and awareness
Case 5	Mexico	Regulated companies: companies hire third-party auditors to inspect and propose a compliance plan, as well as labeling system	Provided more information on compliance, increased jurisdictional reach of federal agency regulators, and attracted dirty facilities and probably increased their compliance

information about possible violations from citizens and environmental groups and sometimes collaborated with environmental groups in filing public interest litigation.

Finally, enforcement innovations may incorporate the polluters into processes of violation detection. The reporting and labeling schemes in Indonesia and Mexico took this approach. In Indonesia, the PROPER system introduced environmental self-reporting mechanisms for participants combined with a labeling system that would induce better performance through enhanced awareness and the label's effects through corporate reputation and consumer preferences. In Mexico, companies become responsible for contracting with a third-party auditor to detect violations and propose a plan to reach compliance. Moreover, similar to Indonesia, a labeling scheme was introduced.

The final column of Table 14.1 provides an overview of how capacity was enhanced in each case. In all cases, the enforcement innovation served to supplement or improve the agency's ability to detect violations. This sometimes occurred through better use of existing resources with prioritization (case 1, China) or through the help of community complaints (cases 1 and 2, both China, and case 3, Brazil). In two cases, detection was facilitated by relying on enterprise self-reports that were verified by the administrative enforcement agents (case 4, Indonesia) or by a private firm (case 5, Mexico).

Moreover, in several cases, capacity to respond to detected violations improved. The likelihood of effective sanctions for violations increased through extra vertical pressure (case 1, China), community participation (case 2, China, and case 3, Brazil), or civil investigations and actions led by prosecutors (case 3, Brazil). In Indonesia (case 4) and Mexico (case 5), sanctions may not have become more likely but the enforcement innovation aided companies in learning about environmental risks and their mitigation, while in China (cases 1 and 2) and in Brazil (case 3), it enhanced public environmental awareness. These are important and impressive results. They show that in the diverse circumstances of the four MICs studied, different enforcement innovations were able to create positive results despite the structural challenges that exist. It shows that experimental forms of governance can help counteract a status quo of nonenforcement and noncompliance.

While all the innovations in some way enhanced regulatory capacity, their other implications depend in many ways on which type of actor was incorporated into the enforcement process. Depending on the actor, different advantages and disadvantages were observed. Table 14.2 provides a summary of these observations.

In China (case 1) and Brazil (case 3), where governmental actors outside the primary local enforcement agency became involved, two primary advantages were evident. First, their involvement enabled the enforcement agency to become more independent of the regulated entities. The innovation enhanced not just regulatory capacity but also regulatory autonomy, which is a measure of the regulatory agency's ability to formulate and pursue goals that are not primarily reflective of the interests of the regulated entities.[55] In the Chinese enforcement campaigns, the enforcement agency was able to operate more independently of local government, which tended to reflect the interests of local industry. In Brazil, the involvement of prosecutors often compelled enforcement to adopt more aggressive enforcement actions. Prosecutors in essence became a sort of oversight agent that was likely to make agencies more careful about responding appropriately to violations.

Second, the involvement of additional governmental actors in both cases was accompanied by a push toward higher public awareness and participation. The Chinese campaigns experimented with involving public participation to secure better data about local environmental problems and the impact of the campaigns on solving such issues. In Brazil, the investigations and legal actions by prosecutors against polluters were often well publicized by the press. They communicated to the public that environmental laws mattered and were being enforced. Also, prosecutors in Brazil were very open to receiving public complaints and became

[55] Lesley K. McAllister, "Dimensions of Enforcement Style: Factoring in Regulatory Capacity and Autonomy," *Law & Policy* 32 (2010): 61.

TABLE 14.2. *Advantages and Disadvantages of Involving Different Actors*

Source of Capacity	Advantages	Disadvantages
Government	Greater autonomy and capacity of enforcement agency; can be accompanied by higher public awareness and participation	Unless other agency is structurally committed (i.e., not ad hoc), the enhanced capacity is likely to be temporary. If permanent, other concerns arise; coordination, potential conflicts with primary enforcement agency; and accountability of additional enforcement actors.
Citizens	Enhances autonomy of enforcement agency, countervails internal pressures to go easy on polluters, and higher public awareness and participation	Requires organizational capacity, outreach to often unaware parties with limited resources; hard to sustain; causes bias in reporting and then enforcement; ultimately depends on same enforcement agency with limited resources for follow-up; and can cause unrealistic public expectations.
Regulated Companies	Stimulates corporate environmental learning, more efficient collection of environmental performance data, and can put pressure to pollute less through corporate reputation and customer preferences	Can undermine agency autonomy from regulated firm, company-provided information may not be reliable, lacks public participation/confidence, audit quality depends on the competence and autonomy of auditors, and labeling only works if companies care about their reputation and customers have environmental preferences.

channels for citizens to communicate with the government regarding their environmental concerns.

Potential disadvantages to incorporating governmental actors outside the primary agency into enforcement can also be observed. As in the case of China, this involvement may be short-lived in many cases. The campaigns were in their very nature ad hoc and a form of experimentalist governance. They have been unable to change the fundamental nature of power relations in China. As such, enforcement agents remain mostly dependent on local governments, which in turn retain close ties with local enterprises. Moreover, the campaigns have also not been able to overcome structural enforcement capacity shortages. In Brazil, by contrast, the involvement of prosecutors has been sustained over the long term due to structural legal changes in the institution's authority and mission. However, when another government agency becomes structurally incorporated into enforcement in this way, a different set of issues arises about how to align the work of various governmental agencies and prevent conflicts. In Brazil, prosecutors sometimes worked at counter-purposes with enforcement agencies and the two institutions generally lacked mechanisms to communicate and coordinate their efforts. Also, while the involvement of prosecutors tended to increase the accountability of agencies, prosecutors have been perceived as insufficiently accountable.

A second type of actor that can be incorporated into enforcement is the citizen. The most illustrative case is that of China (case 2), where the enforcement agency sought to enable a high degree of citizen reporting. Again, this innovation has the important advantage of enhancing the autonomy of the regulatory agency. To the extent that citizens and citizen groups place pressure on agencies, they are less able to accommodate the likely preference of regulated entities for less surveillance and lighter sanctions. Also, this involvement has the important advantage of directly raising public awareness and participation.

However, bringing citizens in to improve enforcement has disadvantages as well. First, it requires public outreach and education, which may be costly for the agency. Also, a bias in reporting and enforcement may occur if the agency relies heavily on citizens to detect violations. Violations that are visible to citizens or bothersome to citizens with the resources and organization to detect and report them are likely to be ones that agencies learn about and pursue. These violations, however, may not be the largest or most important in terms of damage to the environment or health. Finally, as in China, a large number of citizen complaints may ultimately overwhelm the agency. While this innovation may help the agency detect violations, it does little to enhance the agency's capacity to respond.

A third type of actor that can be incorporated into enforcement to a greater degree is the regulated company. Indonesia and Mexico provide examples of an enforcement innovation in which regulated companies contribute in a greater way to detecting violations. In the Indonesian case, companies were required to conduct more self-monitoring and self-reporting. In the Mexico case, companies contracted with a private third-party auditor to detect and report violations on their behalf. Besides the additional detection of violations, a major advantage of innovations of this type is that they promote learning within regulated entities. As companies dedicate attention and resources to detection and abatement, there are many corporate learning opportunities that may have lasting impacts that favor compliance.

Several disadvantages may also accompany this approach. Although the Indonesian and Mexican innovations appear designed to inform citizens and consumers of compliance status and thereby put pressure on companies through corporate reputation and consumer preferences, evidence suggests that such pressures do not always materialize. In Indonesia, Lee found that PROPER had not triggered environmentally oriented market forces nor empowered communities in the way that information disclosure regulation is often purported to do.[56] A similar study has not been conducted for the Mexican Audit Program, but available interview data suggests that companies that participate are more motivated by the regulatory relief they receive than by the reputational or market value of the label. The most significant pressure related to the label is probably exerted on facilities that sell their products to the Mexican government and to overseas buyers. Allen Blackman and colleagues found that these facilities are significantly more likely to participate, implying that these buyers recognize the label and possibly even require it of their Mexican suppliers.[57]

Another disadvantage of incorporating regulated entities to enhance capacity is that agencies become more dependent on polluters and their agents for compliance information and determinations. Instead of promoting regulatory autonomy, it may work against it. Programs of this type are often viewed by the agency as a sort of "partnership" with industry, and industry is likely to have a great deal of influence on how information is conveyed to the agency and made available to the public. In Indonesia, citizen group leaders viewed PROPER as a form of "greenwashing" and complained that the program was used as a shield against real enforcement actions.[58] In Mexico, the director of one of the country's most well-known environmental groups had a similar reaction to the Audit Program and distrusted its ability to force compliance.[59] Notably, companies that participate in the program can review and suggest changes to the audit report before it is submitted to the agency, and the audit report is considered confidential information protected from public disclosure.

CONCLUSION

IMICs are important arenas for regulatory practice and study. In IMICs, economic growth and industrialization cause risks that challenge regulation due to close state-enterprise relations, pervasive noncompliance, and structurally weak enforcement. Through the experimental governance practices in the five cases studied, some enforcement improvement was achieved. We saw that in each case, enforcement capacity was expanded when existing and new enforcement actors forged alliances with civic, market, and/or state actors. This shows that as in HICs, IMICs require a broad approach to regulation that makes the implementation of regulation not just a matter of specialized administrative agencies, but one of a broader coalition of governmental, societal, and market forces.

56 Lee, "Information Disclosure and Environmental Regulation," 314–17.
57 Blackman, et al., "Voluntary Environmental Regulation."
58 Lee, "Information Disclosure and Environmental Regulation," 313.
59 Interview conducted by McAllister, Mexico City, Mexico, 2008.

Julia Black has summarized such approaches using the term "decentered regulation."[60] Decentered regulation in IMICs is, however, of a very different nature than that in HICs. In HICs, regulation and its implementation moved beyond dedicated administrative agencies largely because of discontent about the cost and inefficiency of what was deemed to be overregulation. Decentering was aimed at decreasing the regulatory burden for businesses, and instituting a more flexible and efficient system through a combination of market and state actors. In IMICs, by contrast, similar moves to decenter regulation have occurred in response to discontent about the effectiveness of regulatory enforcement, due broadly to inadequacies in regulatory capacity and autonomy.

Our comparative analysis of these five case studies shows that the type of actor brought into the regulatory enforcement mix in IMICs is important. While each had its own positive and negative sides, the involvement of regulated companies is especially noteworthy. In the context of HICs, forms of self- or coregulation that transform companies from mere regulatees to regulators have been a core element of decentered regulation and make sense as they are likely to increase efficiency and reasonableness, and occur against the backdrop of a fall-back mechanism of relatively well-developed state administrative enforcement capacity. In IMICs, however, one of the core original problems was lack of enforcement agency autonomy vis-à-vis the regulated firms, and enforcement capacity has been too limited to function as a fall-back mechanism for failed self-regulation. Thus it seems that in IMICs, as a matter of sequencing, decentered regulation should first seek to tackle issues of regulatory enforcement capacity as much as possible without reducing regulatory autonomy vis-à-vis the regulated firms. A first step in IMICs is then to enhance both regulatory capacity and autonomy by alliances with state and societal actors. Only when this yields a basic level of inspection and sanction quality should attempts be made to involve the regulated firms in enforcement work as a second step.

In sum, the study of regulation and regulatory enforcement would benefit from a much better understanding of IMIC contexts. Risks in IMICs are substantial and require effective regulation, but regulation and governance operate in a rather different socioeconomic, political, and legal context than in HICs. Greater attention to regulation in IMICs may well have a broad impact on how we identify and explain effective regulatory enforcement. Responsive regulation in IMICs, for example, may mean less responsiveness to industry as it is generally understood in HICs[61] and more responsiveness to the citizens that suffer from industrial risks, who can become regulatory partners aiding its enforcement. Regulatory scholars and practitioners in IMICs can learn from the large existing body of knowledge about regulation in HICs, but theories and practices must be reoriented to encompass IMIC conditions.

[60] Julia Black, "Critical Reflections on Regulation," *LSE, CARR Discussion Paper Series* (2002): 1–27.

[61] I. Ayres and J. Braithwaite, *Responsive Regulation, Transcending the Deregulation Debate* (Oxford University Press, 1992).

PART V

International Donor Strategies for Middle-Income Countries

15

The United Nations and Governance in Middle-Income Countries

A Vietnam Case Study

Nicholas Booth

THE UNITED NATIONS AND MIDDLE-INCOME COUNTRIES

For the United Nations, middle-income countries (MICs) matter as never before. The number of developing countries that are MICs has increased from sixty-eight in 1999[1] to 104 in 2011,[2] representing about 75 percent of the world's poor,[3] so that addressing poverty reduction in MICs has become a high development priority.

It is also one for which the United Nations bears a special responsibility, because it is mandated to maintain an engagement[4] with all developing countries (universality) even while allocating more aid toward the least-developed countries (progressivity).[5] By contrast, bilateral aid donors traditionally phase out aid programming

I am grateful Vu Tuan Minh for research assistance and to the many colleagues who provided useful feedback on an earlier draft of the paper, but the views expressed remain mine and do not necessarily represent the views of the United Nations or UNDP.

1 See the table at Annex B of the Report of the Task Force on the World Bank Group and Middle Income Countries April 2001, available at http://siteresources.worldbank.org/COUNTRIES/Resources/mictf.pdf.

2 See Report of the UN Secretary-General on Development Cooperation with Middle Income Countries, August 1, 2011, A/66/220 (hereafter referred to as "SG 2011 report"), para. 3

3 Ibid., para. 4. Within MICs, levels of poverty vary widely: from 0 percent in Belarus to 77 percent in Angola, see Oxford Poverty and Human Development Initiative, *Multi-Dimensional Poverty Index* 2011, available at http://www.ophi.org.uk/wp-content/uploads/OPHI-MPI-Brief-2011.pdf?cda6c1.

4 This engagement does not necessarily imply a physical presence. However, UN country teams do maintain presences in almost all developing countries. UNDP, e.g., is currently present in 177 countries and territories.

5 Remarkably, however, the growth in the number of MICs and the percentage of the world's poor that live in them has not been mirrored by an increase in the United Nations' development resources allocated to them. For instance, in the 2008–11 period about 86 to 87 percent of core funding for UNDP/UNFPA was allocated for LICs, only slightly lower than the 88 percent allocated in 2004–7. See UNDP/UNFPA Executive Board Proposal for Programming Arrangements, 2008–2011, available at http://www.undp.org/content/dam/undp/library/corporate/Executive%20Board/dp07-44.pdf, a proportion that has remained constant since at least 1995 (see Executive Board decision 95/23 at para. 24), available at http://web.undp.org/execbrd/pdf/e95-34e.pdf. The question of resources for MICs will be revisited in the following text.

once a country "graduates" to MIC status. The need for the United Nations to remain engaged with MICs was highlighted for the first time in the 2008 Triennial Comprehensive Policy Review[6] and has figured prominently on the United Nations' agenda since then.[7]

The main engine for the United Nations' development cooperation since 2000, the Millennium Development Goals (MDGs), has proved a useful framework for the least developed countries (LDCs) and lower-income countries (LICs), but less relevant for MICs, many of which have achieved all or most of the MDGs. As the 2015 deadline for achieving the MDGs approaches, the United Nations and other development partners are increasingly focused on ensuring that the post-2015 framework addresses key development challenges, in particular rising levels of income inequality. Average country-level inequality increased 20 percent between 1992 and 2005,[8] and this is particularly true of MICs, in which income inequality is greater than in either LICs or upper-income countries.[9] This emphasizes the importance for the United Nations to focus on human development rather than merely economic development,[10] and to do so in MICs where the poor are increasingly being left behind.

Governance issues, which were not specifically addressed by the MDGs, are also emerging as a stronger priority for the post-2015 development framework, strongly emphasized in the recent report of the High-Level Panel on Global Sustainability,[11] which was commissioned in preparation for the 2012 UN Conference on Sustainable Development ("Rio+20").

A greater focus on governance is well aligned with the development agenda of MICs. A survey of UN country and regional teams in MICs commissioned in 2009 showed governance was ranked as a "top priority" for policy advice in 87 percent of

6 See UN General Assembly Resolution A/62/208 at para. 27.

7 Following three UN-sponsored International Conferences on Development Cooperation with Middle-Income Countries in Madrid, El Salvador, and Windhoek in 2007–8, the GA in December 2008 passed its first resolution focusing on development cooperation and MICs (A/RES/63/223), calling on the Secretary-General to submit a report, which he did in August 2009 (A/64/253). This was followed by a second report in August 2011 (A/66/220, see note 4), and by other discussions, papers, and conferences within UN agencies too numerous to list here.

8 See UN Secretary-General's High-Level Panel on Global Sustainability, *Resilient People, Resilient Planet: A Future Worth Choosing* (United Nations, 2012), 16.

9 "SG 2011 report," para. 14.

10 On the concept of human development, which emerged from the pioneering work of Amartya Sen and Mahbub el-Haq refocusing development on the quality of life and the real choices available to citizens, and which has been at the core of UNDP's development work since 1990, as well as the Human Development Index (hereafter referred to as HDI), which applies a multidimensional approach, see http://hdr.undp.org/en/. In the same vein, more recent work in developing the Multi-Dimensional Poverty Index reflects the current approach to poverty, which goes beyond income and enables a better focus on the persistent poverty within MICs, see http://www.ophi.org.uk/policy/multidimensional-poverty-index/.

11 See note 9. The importance of good governance and the rule of law was affirmed at the outset of the Rio +20 Outcome Document (see para. 10 of A/RES/66/288), although received little elaboration in the body of the text. It remains to be seen whether the Sustainable Development Goals that will follow the MDGs after 2015 incorporate a stronger focus on governance than did the MDGs.

countries and a "top priority" for capacity development in 89 percent of countries. In contrast, only one of the MDGs (MDG6 on HIV/AIDS) was considered to be a top priority in a majority of countries.[12]

Addressing the development needs of MICs needs a new strategy, but the United Nations has not yet developed it. In his 2011 report, the secretary-general went so far as to describe the lack of a well-defined, coherent strategic framework for providing advocacy and policy advice[13] to MICs as "the principal strategic constraint facing the United Nations system."[14]

The United Nations is therefore now actively debating how it should achieve this greater focus on advocacy and upstream policy advice in MICs. A recent joint discussion paper by the executive boards of the UN Development Programme (UNDP), UN Populations Fund, UN Office for Project Services, UNICEF, UN-Women, and UN World Food Programme reveals a large measure of consensus on the key principles that should guide the United Nations:[15]

Comparative advantage:	Building on the UN's strengths, which include a global perspective; a large network of offices and institutes around the world; access to world-class expertise, data and knowledge; wide recognition and credibility; neutrality/impartiality and convening power.
UN role:	Based on the United Nations' normative role, consistent with universality and neutrality of the United Nations operations, with support to policies and programs that reach the poorest and most deprived groups at the centre of this role.
Country context:	Perhaps most importantly, greater responsiveness to the specific demands related to national development challenges, avoiding a "straitjacket" of one set of United Nations policies and procedures.[16]

12 See Report of the UN Secretary-General on Development Cooperation with Middle Income Countries, August 5, 2009 A/63/253 (hereafter referred to as "SG 2009 report"), Annex Table 1.

13 The move "upstream" to focus on policy advocacy and advice is part of a more general repositioning of the United Nations' role, not only in its work with MICs, but it is considered particularly relevant in MICs: cf. UN Development Group Strategic Priorities for 2010–12 include "Engage 'Upstream' in Policy and Program Dialogue and Technical Advice, Especially in MICs and NCCs [net contributor countries]." For a recent study commissioned by the UN Development Operations Coordination Office, see CBI "UNCTs Engaging in National Policy Dialogue: Lessons from the Field," December 2011.

14 A/66/220 at para. 33.

15 The following bullet points are taken from the background paper prepared for a Joint Meeting of the Executive Boards of UNDP/UNFPA/UNOPS, UNICEF, UN-Women, and WFP held in January 2012, *Middle-Income Countries: The Role and Presence of the United Nations for the Achievement of the Internationally Agreed Development Goals*, available at http://www.unicef.org/about/execboard/files/Final_version-MICs_background_paper.pdf.

16 This last point deserves special emphasis. The club of MICs is not only now huge but highly diverse, not only in terms of income (the richest MICs having a gross domestic product more

However, we have made less progress in translating these agreed principles into concrete terms. We still need to understand more clearly: how does the United Nations need to change the way it works in MICs? What are the implications for its programming, its staffing, and the way it organizes its operations?

This chapter seeks to make a contribution to the ongoing debate about how the United Nations can deliver effective, coherent, and strategic support to MICs, through a particular lens: the initiative to establish a Policy Advisory Team within UNDP Vietnam since 2007 addressing governance, economics, and climate change. As a recently graduated MIC, I will argue that Vietnam presents a useful example on the challenges facing the United Nations in policy advice in MICs, and some strategies to overcome them.

In the second section of this chapter I will therefore set out a short account of the context for governance in Vietnam, the challenges facing development partners in the sector, and the circumstances which led UNDP Vietnam to establish a new policy advisory capacity in 2007 to strengthen and complement its program portfolio. I will argue that this initiative has given UNDP a greater flexibility and effectiveness in Vietnam, as well as illustrating its benefits in the context of Vietnam's participation in the "One UN" or "Delivering as One" initiative, which aims to improve UN systemwide coherence.

In the third and final section of this chapter I will provide some reflections on the implications of this initiative for the wider strategic objectives of UN reform, in particular for MICs.

A VIETNAM CASE STUDY

The Early đổi mới *Period*, 1986–2000

Vietnam is a socialist republic under the leadership of the Communist Party of Vietnam. Ho Chi Minh's declaration of independence in 1945 was followed by three decades of devastating conflict, and then a further decade of extreme poverty with a failing economy under Soviet-style central planning,[17] until the beginning of economic reforms from the 1980s, and in particular since the VIth Party Congress in 1986 launched a comprehensive program of "renovation" or *đổi mới* in Vietnamese.

During those first forty years of the Democratic and later the Socialist Republic of Vietnam, the country was run administratively through the party system. The legal

than twelve times those of the poorest) but also in terms of human development, ranging from very-high-human-development Lithuania (ranked 40th in the 2011 index with an HDI of 0.810) to low-human-development Côte d'Ivoire (ranked 170th in the 2011 index with an HDI of 0.400). It is surely fruitless to try to identify common substantive approaches for MICs as a whole: we live in a Post Washington Consensus world and understand that there are no "universal best practices" and that "no size fits all."

[17] Further exacerbated by an embargo on development aid from most Western countries lifted only in the early 1990s.

profession was effectively dormant in the north, and dismantled in the south after reunification. But shortly after beginning economic reforms, from the beginning of the 1990s Vietnam also began governance reforms, based on the principle of a "socialist rule-of-law-based state" (*nhà nước pháp quyền xã hội chủ nghĩa*), and at the same time began a diplomatic engagement with the outside world that also opened the door to wider development cooperation.

Donors were quick to respond. Specifically in the field of legal and judicial reform, 1992 UNDP began its first project with the Ministry of Justice, followed in 1995 by the first projects with the Supreme People's Court and the Supreme People's Procuracy,[18] while the first parliamentary development project with the National Assembly was launched in 1995; other projects over the same period began to support economic governance and public administration reforms. Bilateral development partners soon followed, and since that time governance has continued to be well supported by bilateral and multilateral donors.

From a standing start, the governance landscape transformed dramatically throughout the 1990s. A comprehensive legal framework was quickly enacted, including the progressive development of a legal framework for a "socialist-oriented market economy"; the legal profession was revived; law universities and faculties were established; courts and prosecution offices were fundamentally restructured, and their personnel professionalized; legal aid offices were established; a regulatory framework allowing the establishment of "scientific and technical" associations supported the growth of a nascent civil society, while "grassroots democracy initiatives" and public administration reforms aimed to make local governance more responsive to the needs of citizens.

Throughout this process, the international donors remained strongly engaged, especially in supporting law-drafting processes, introducing Vietnam to experiences around the world through study tours and international workshops, technical assistance including training of personnel, and infrastructure support (e.g., in areas like information technology).

Developing National Strategies for Governance

Throughout the 1990s Vietnam still lacked a clear strategic direction to these reforms, but from the late 1990s onward there was an increasing focus on developing clear national governance strategies. A government review of PAR launched in 1999 led to the adoption in September 2001 of a PAR Master Plan 2001–2010;[19] a

[18] The Supreme People's Procuracy was established in Vietnam in 1960 under Soviet influence. Originally holding wide responsibilities for "ensuring legality" including public prosecution, supervising judicial activities, and supervising compliance of executive agencies with the law, since 2001 the procuracy has been responsible only for public prosecution and supervision of judicial activities.

[19] For details on the 2001–2010 PAR Master Plan see http://caicachhanhchinh.gov.vn. A new PAR Master Plan is now in force, see Resolution 30c/2011/NQCP of November 2011, available in English translation at http://asemconnectvietnam.gov.vn/lawdetail.aspx?lawid=2032.

government review of legal and judicial reform in 2001 was followed by the first Politburo resolution on judicial reform in 2002 and then in 2005 by comprehensive legal[20] and judicial reform strategies.[21] In 2003 Vietnam signed the UN Convention against Corruption and in 2005 a new Anti-Corruption Law was passed,[22] establishing a Steering Committee on Anti-Corruption inside the Communist Party to oversee an overall strategic program to fight corruption; Vietnam signed and, in due course, ratified the UN Convention on Anti-Corruption; and in 2009 promulgated an Anti-Corruption Strategy to 2020.[23] The United Nations and UNDP (together with other donors) consistently played a strong role in supporting these reviews and the adoption of these strategies.

The adoption of national strategies in all these key dimensions of governance was greeted enthusiastically in many quarters, not least among the development partners, who looked forward to supporting real policy change by aligning their donor support to the new strategies.

However, the implementation of the new strategies in practice has generally failed to meet these expectations. A similar pattern can be observed across all of them: while some useful reforms were implemented (e.g., establishment of a national bar association and introduction of local government "one-stop shops"), progress on most of the major reforms necessary for an efficient and responsive public service, rule of law, and judicial reform has been slow, and the problem of corruption has not yet been effectively addressed.

In this changing climate, UNDP's own performance came under increasing scrutiny. In the 1990s it had been a pioneer of legal reform and PAR projects, but now its projects no longer appeared effective to catalyze reforms. Increasingly donors called on the UNDP to leverage its comparative advantage – above all, the political neutrality that enables it to address sensitive issues from the standpoint of international norms; access to global expertise and knowledge; and the convening power to bring governments, civil society, and the international community around the table – in the politically sensitive areas of governance.

At the same time, Vietnam was on the threshold of middle-income status, with donors increasingly preparing to phase out bilateral aid, while the United Nations in Vietnam prepared to implement the "One UN" or "Delivering as One (DaO)" initiative,[24] billed as enabling the United Nations to deliver more effective system-wide policy advisory services and advocacy. This intensified the spotlight on UNDP's ability to deliver in governance, on which it traditionally leads within the UN system and which clearly remained a priority development issue.

[20] Politburo Resolution No. 48-NQ/TW of May 24, 2005 on the strategy for development and improvement of Vietnam's legal system to the year 2010 with direction to the period up to 2020.

[21] Politburo Resolution No. 49-NQ/TW of June 2, 2005 on the judicial reform strategy to 2020.

[22] Law no. 55/2005/QH11 available at http://www.oecd.org/dataoecd/37/50/46817414.pdf.

[23] Government Resolution 21/2009 NQ-CP of May 12, 2009

[24] DaO is discussed in more detail in the following text.

UN DEVELOPMENT PROGRAMME'S INTERNAL REVIEW OF GOVERNANCE, 2006

Accordingly, in 2006 UNDP reviewed the way it was supporting governance in Vietnam. Its conclusions aligned with those of the donors: despite a portfolio of governance programs aligned to national strategies, implemented by appropriate government agencies, these key governance policy reforms appeared stalled, and UNDP's projects were playing no clear role in catalyzing them. Nor did UNDP appear to be providing leadership within the donor community or using its convening power or normative role to lead a policy dialogue on key reform issues.

In contrast, UNDP had over the same period earned a reputation for leadership on economic governance and equity issues, generating evidence-based policy research papers that were seen as major contributions to debates on economic policy, while presenting a distinct and complementary focus to the World Bank's engagement.

At the heart of this success was the resident (international) country economist, with excellent connections both within Vietnam and to the international academic community, who was free to create new partnerships with national counterparts and to stimulate debates through independent policy research.

To examine the underlying reasons for this failure and this success, I will digress for a moment to explain in a little more detail the history of reforms in Vietnam, and the special characteristics of the "basically cooperative way of processing change" that had enabled Vietnam to achieve the economic reforms of the 1980s,[25] and that can provide some useful lessons on the complexities of policy change and the strategies for success.

THE DYNAMICS OF REFORM IN VIETNAM

Despite the clear failures of central planning in Vietnam in the 1980s and the widespread poverty and hunger that resulted, achieving agreement on the policy change to market reforms was anything but straightforward. A political system ideologically built on socialist principles had achieved a decisive military victory and reunified the country: challenging those principles by introducing market reforms was not only highly controversial, it was politically and personally dangerous. As a result, those reforms were pioneered, at first, through highly localized (and

[25] The following account borrows heavily from Rama, "Making Difficult Choices: Vietnam in Transition," Commission on Growth and Development Working Paper No. 40, 2008, available at http://www.growthcommission.org/storage/cgdev/documents/gcwp040bilingualweb.pdf. This paper, authored by a former World Bank Resident Economist in Vietnam, was drawn from extensive discussions in 2007 and 2008 with former Vietnamese Prime Minister Võ Văn Kiệt, who came to play a key role in pioneering the reforms of the 1980s and 1990s. On the "basically cooperative way of processing change" see ibid., 28–31.

technically illegal) experiments, known as "fence-breaking,"[26] that were covertly supported by influential politicians who then – after they had proved successful in practice – discreetly introduced them more widely within political circles. At the same time, the politicians who were to play a key role in introducing reforms drew around them a circle of handpicked expert advisors, rather than relying on state research institutions, because the latter would be bound to be politically restrained in the kind of advice they could give.[27]

Achieving change in this way required considerable negotiation, persuasion, and compromise. There was no political space for the adoption of a radical change in state ideology, because of the potential risk to the political establishment as well as from a well-founded skepticism based on the results of radical reforms of all colors elsewhere, whether Mao's land reforms in 1950s China or the creation of oligarchies through the "shock therapy" of 1990s Russia. Change came about by cautious experimentation that, in turn, gradually gained wider acceptance, changing the minds of key policy makers in the process. Importantly, this was not a story of "reformers" winning over "conservatives": some key figures who were clearly identified with "conservative" positions later became key agents in promoting the reforms.[28]

Similarly, the formulas chosen to express the new state direction – a "market economy with socialist orientation" and a "socialist rule of law state" – reflect these compromises and are underpinned by fundamental ambiguities.[29] In a sense these ambiguities are "constructive" in that they enabled change to take place, but one consequence is that they also left in place ways of thinking, and bureaucratic systems to support them, that were – and are – not yet aligned with the new policy directions.

[26] On fence breaking, see ibid., 13–18.

[27] On the use of informal networks of advisors rather than state research institutions, see ibid., 35–6. Interestingly, shortly before his death in 2008, Võ Văn Kiệt had formed a small team of independent experts to consider how to strengthen judicial independence in Vietnam, suggesting that such independent research and thinking outside state agencies and even the research institutes and universities may still be a relevant strategy for Vietnam today.

[28] See Rama, "Making Difficult Choices," 24–6. The fallacy of attributing change in Vietnam to the work of "reformers" is also a central theme in Martin Gainsborough, *Vietnam: Rethinking the State* (Zed, 2010), 5–7 and passim.

[29] The ambiguity of the concept of "socialist rule of law state" – enshrined in Article 2 of the 1992 Constitution (as amended in 2001) is further underlined by the continued reference in Article 12 to the state "managing society through law and ceaselessly strengthening socialist legality," a instrumentalist concept of law and state introduced in the high socialist period under the 1980 Constitution. For the tensions between these concepts see John Gillespie, "Changing Concepts of Socialist Law in Vietnam," in *Asian Socialism & Legal Change: The Dynamics of Vietnamese and Chinese Reform*, ed. John Gillespie and Pip Nicholson (Canberra, 2005), 45–75. The instrumentalist concept of law is still the only version authorized to be taught in law schools, see Bui Thi Bich Lien, "Legal Education and the Legal Profession in Contemporary Vietnam: Tradition and Modification," in *Legal Reforms in China and Vietnam: A Comparison of Asian Communist Regimes*, ed. John Gillespie and Albert Chen (Routledge, 2010), 303–4.

The "second wave" of governance and legal reforms[30] is in some respects even more challenging than the initial economic reforms. In the 1980s, with the country in economic crisis, the economic reforms increased the prosperity both of cadres in charge of state-owned enterprises and ordinary farmers alike, while the first wave of governance reforms gave all the institutions – including parliament, courts, procuracy, the legal profession, and the government ministries – an opportunity for professional development and institutional strengthening. Building a basic legal and institutional framework in the first stage empowered all of the agencies involved and resulted in a large measure of shared interest between donors and state agencies alike.

Now, after two decades of institutional reforms and economic growth, Vietnamese society is more diverse and more unequal, the economic stakes have become higher, and the challenges are fundamentally political in nature. The different institutions of state – government ministries, court, procuracy, parliament, and the legal profession – have stronger capacities to articulate and defend their own interests. State-owned enterprises remain powerful and well funded; substantial private economic interests have grown alongside them, often well connected to state interests; and civil society and the media have become stronger and more assertive as well.

Governance reforms, whether in the field of economic governance, rule of law, anticorruption, or public administration reform, are no longer "win-wins." Reining-in public investment and access to state credit, introducing a merit-based public service, ensuring accountability to law, requiring state officials to declare their assets publicly: such reforms may enjoy widespread support, and they may be necessary to ensure continued economic and human development through middle-income status and beyond, but they also increase the power of some institutions (e.g., parliament, courts, and lawyers) at the expense of others and limit access to money and patronage for some.

How should donors engage in such a complex environment? Many donor projects – including those of UNDP – are implemented by national agencies, essentially in order to maximize national ownership, which is – rightly – the fundamental tenet of aid effectiveness. However, at least in the context of governance reforms in an environment like middle-income Vietnam, this kind of project has a number of inherent limitations, which I shall now consider.

THE SHORTCOMINGS OF THE TRADITIONAL UN DEVELOPMENT PROGRAMME MODEL

UNDP development projects typically follow a model that is essentially premised upon the political will and capacity of a state agency to achieve the objectives of the project, and upon the feasibility of achieving those objectives in a given time frame.

[30] Viz. those set out in the PAR Master Plan, Legal, Judicial and Anti-Corruption strategies, etc., for which see the preceding discussion.

The state agency may lack the financial and technical resources to do the job: that is where the donor comes in. A simple example could be a project to build a road or a bridge: the government agency may know exactly where it wants the road to go, and can take care of acquiring the land and materials to build it, but may need technical expertise and financial resources from a donor to get there. The objectives and time frame can be easily ascertained; the mandate of the government agency to do the work is clear; and there is a shared commitment between government and donor to get the job done.

Following this model, the government agency is in charge of the project and defining its objectives, outcomes, and time frame. The donor assists the government to hire project staff and to contract technical expertise to do the job. Funds and work planning are under the government's control, subject to quality and financial assurance and audit by the donor.

UNDP's business model is essentially driven by this kind of project. While it is well understood that building the rule of law is quite different from building a road, still UNDP and other donors seek a similar clarity of structure in their projects when supporting governance reforms. They look for a clear national strategy with agreed activities, outcomes, and time lines, and reward it with projects aligned to that strategy, and technical and financial resources to support its implementation.

This is a good strategy when the assumptions stated previously – political will, time frames, and feasibility – hold good. However, as the discussion of Vietnam's reforms illustrated, the path ahead is not usually so clear. Commitments to reforms are negotiated pragmatically between groups with different views, and contain fundamental compromises if not inconsistencies. Different agencies pursue different and sometimes conflicting agendas. At other times, issues need to be discussed and mediated informally before they can be placed openly on the reform agenda.

This goes some way to explaining how UNDP's governance projects became stalled. Sometimes the executing agency's own political commitment to carrying out reforms was weak, so that projects would tend to favor politically safe (but ineffective) activities that did not threaten the status quo; on other occasions the executing agency was powerless to move reforms forward because of the opposition of other agencies. "Agency capture" was standing in the way of both the national reform program and UNDP's ability to support it.

UNDP experts, international and national, were quite aware of the gap between expectations and results, but the project mechanism gave them little opportunity to address it. National execution places the choice of activities and the control of funds under the direction of the project, and ultimately the National Project Director who is a senior decision maker in the implementing agency.

In such a case, the usefulness of the international and national technical experts who are contracted under (and paid by) the project is, like the project, limited by the political will and feasibility of the project. They can and should advocate for more strategic activities with a higher policy content and relevance to the agenda of transforming governance, as well as for methodologies (objective in-country research, appropriate and in-depth comparative expertise), but the implementing partner will ultimately decide. They have no access to other partners or to other funding.

Nor are the program officers within UNDP's country office in a stronger position. Although the project activities and their implementation need to be agreed with UNDP, this power of veto has to be judiciously used, because a project that does nothing and spends nothing is a failure for UNDP just as much as for the implementing agency.

Furthermore, the transaction costs of project management favor multiyear, high-value projects. A program officer with a portfolio of two or three projects has only two or three partners to work with (unless she can persuade her implementing partners to engage with other partners – something they have financial and institutional incentives not to do); she can work on only those issues that those partners agree to address; and outside that framework, she has no money or mechanisms at her disposal.

In contrast, the Country Economics Unit had the benefit of a well-informed expert reporting directly to UNDP outside the project portfolio. The Country Economist helped to put issues of economic governance "on the table," addressing them through new research partnerships and catalyzing policy debates on emerging questions, thus bringing civil society and academics around the table with government agencies. These discussions still remained nationally owned, because the research was driven and supported by key Vietnamese actors (in civil society, in research institutes, or even within ministries).

Because the quality of the research products was high, they readily found high-level audiences with policy makers and could be addressed and taken forward through the projects. It even turned out that projects could be persuaded to host discussions of research that those same projects would not have agreed to commission (or to conduct in the same way), and where the research was good enough, the projects helped bring it to the attention of policy makers. No doubt the ability to obtain press coverage for the findings of the research also helped place an incentive on the government agencies to take the research seriously. And by linking these issues to the United Nations' international norms and standards, as well as international research, UNDP gave added credibility and weight to the positions of national stakeholders.

The result was a powerful and effective synergy between national actors, with their understanding of the national context and their connections to policy makers, and the authority that the United Nations derives from its international standards and its connection to international expertise.

UN DEVELOPMENT PROGRAMME DREW TWO LESSONS FROM THIS EXPERIENCE

First, national reform strategies supported with donor-funded projects, while very important, may not of themselves be sufficient to ensure success in a MIC environment. Giving the state agency in charge of the strategy a development project to "support implementation of the strategy" yielded poor results in practice. The diversity of vested interests and views, and the tensions between the policy commitments in the strategies and other elements in the governance structure, themselves supported by long-standing bureaucratic systems and practices, often require a broader, more tactical, and flexible approach.

Second, as Vietnam's own experience of economic reforms demonstrated, the ability to generate independent advice and evidence to support reforms, especially if coupled with practical demonstrations of success through pilots, can succeed in catalyzing change that may not have come about through the mechanisms of the state system on its own (and would certainly not have emerged from traditional projects on their own). The resulting process is nationally owned, and depends critically upon the role and voice of national actors who are themselves or are connected to key policy makers, but is strengthened through the United Nations' authority and normative foundations as well as the United Nations' ability to connect local and international expertise.

THE POLICY ADVISORY EXPERIENCE, 2007–PRESENT

UNDP's internal review concluded that if it was to reestablish leadership in governance, it needed to replicate its success in the economic governance field and to hire full-time governance policy advisors, working for and accountable to UNDP, and with their own budget resources, while also working closely with and through the project portfolio. With support from the United Kingdom and Spain, in 2007 UNDP Vietnam hired three new international policy advisors: one to address rule of law and access to justice, another responsible for anticorruption and public administrative reform, and the third to work on local governance,[31] each supported by budget funding to support policy research and similar activities.

As an experimental reform, the policy advisory capacity was kept under regular review and by 2010 was established in the form which it retains today: a Policy Advisory Team (PAT) comprising four international policy advisors (rule of law/access to justice, anticorruption/public administrative reform, climate change, and economics) each supported by a dedicated national policy support officer, and with budgetary funds under UNDP's direct control to support policy research and other activities. At the same time, from the beginning the policy advisors were situated within their thematic program clusters, working closely with the project portfolio to maximize the engagement with national counterparts in policy dialogues, the discussion of policy research commissioned by advisors, and follow-up actions to turn research recommendations into policy change through capacity development initiatives.

[31] Subsequently it was decided to formally rename the Country Economist as Policy Advisor for Economics, add a Policy Advisor on Climate Change, and discontinue the policy advisory post on local governance, subsuming this issue within the AC/PAR portfolio.

How has the United Nations used this access to independent expertise and funds to strengthen its policy engagement? Some illustrations:

- Policy advisors contribute substantively in their own right as experts, writing articles in national and international publications, and presenting papers at conferences (many of them organized through the project portfolio). In so doing they directly contribute to policy debates, dialogues and advocacy. At the same time, they establish UNDP's reputation as a knowledge leader both among Vietnamese counterparts (whether state officials, academics or civil society), enhancing national demands for UNDP's engagement on policy issues, and among the international donor community, demonstrating the kind of leadership the UN is expected to show in areas like governance and climate change;
- Closely related to this, policy advisors support the UN's convening role, commissioning and presenting independent research and advocacy on emerging (and often sensitive) issues in donor/government policy dialogue fora, and informally convening technical working groups and meetings in climate change, PAR, legal reform and civil society development;
- Policy advisors establish new partnerships both through and outside projects, such as a research cooperation with the Judicial Reform Steering Committee inside the Communist Party focusing on key cross-cutting questions of judicial reform;
- A partnership with the Vietnamese Fatherland Front (the Party's channel for engagement with the grassroots) to conduct the Public Administration Performance Index, Vietnam's first citizen-survey-based instrument to measure grassroots-level perceptions of public services and public participation in local decision-making, with province-level rankings to provide incentives to improve performance;
- Advising and accompanying the Vietnamese delegation to the annual Conference of Parties under the UN Framework Convention for Climate Change; supporting Vietnam's first independent civil society policy advisory network to engage in research and advocacy for constitutional reforms from the perspective of civil society and focused on the needs of the poor and disadvantaged;
- Working with Vietnamese media to develop online fora to solicit public opinions on salary reform, public services and other issues of public administration reform.
- Policy advisors connect Vietnam's leadership with leading international experts on key policy issues, for instance: a UNDP-Harvard partnership under which analyses of Vietnam's development trajectory, higher education system and land policy were produced and discussed with high-level Vietnamese officials;
- Arranging a visit of high level experts, such as Yvo De Boer, former UNFCCC [UN Framework Convention on Climate Change] Executive Secretary, and IPCC [International Panel on Climate Change] chair and Nobel laureate Rajendra Pachauri, to discuss the implications of climate change on Vietnamese development policies;
- A research cooperation with University of Sydney analyzing the justice systems of Russia, China, Korea, Japan and Indonesia to support the Judicial Reform

Steering Committee in its recommendations to the Politburo on the directions for future judicial reform;

- An analysis of the Trans-Pacific Partnership (TPP) trade agreement, conducted in cooperation with ODI at the direct request of the Ministry of Foreign Affairs, which directly informed Vietnam's decision to join the Agreement.

POLICY ADVISORS AND "DELIVERING AS ONE"

An important dimension of the policy advisory team has been its support to the delivery of coordinated "One UN" systemwide policy advice. Since the 2006 report of the Secretary-General's High-Level Panel on UN System Wide Coherence,[32] eight countries have been piloting a "One UN" approach with one leader, one program, one budget, and, where appropriate, one office, known as the "Delivering as One" (DaO) initiative.[33]

Initially only one of the eight pilot countries (Uruguay) was a MIC, but that number has risen to four with the graduation since 2007 of Albania, Pakistan, and Vietnam, and the relationship between DaO and development cooperation with MICs has become one of the key dimensions of the pilot, and was also stressed in the Secretary-General's 2009 report.[34]

The access to resident expertise on governance and climate change issues has enabled UNDP to act as a resource to other agencies to forge cross-agency coalitions on strategic policy issues and enhance the coherence and voice of the UN system in Vietnam. The climate change advisor, for instance, works extensively with the UN Resident Coordinator to support a UN-wide engagement on climate change; while the rule-of-law advisor convened a cross-agency coalition to advocate for UN standards and norms related to due process, child rights, HIV/AIDS policy, and the right to human health in relation to legal reforms to the administrative detention regime in Vietnam.

Another example is provided by the cooperation between UNDP and UNAIDS on legal empowerment of People Living with HIV. UNAIDS in Vietnam has policy specialists on HIV/AIDS but does not have legal specialists. UNDP policy advisors have helped UNAIDS design and implement programs furthering the objectives of the Global Commission on HIV/AIDS and the Law, meeting UNDP's strategic policy commitments on HIV/AIDS response without requiring both agencies to engage in parallel programming.

32 The report is available at http://www.undg.org/archive_docs/9021-High_Level_Panel_Report.pdf.

33 The eight pilot counties are Albania, Cape Verde, Mozambique, Pakistan, Rwanda, Tanzania, Uruguay, and Vietnam. Five high-level conferences have been held to assess the pilots, and a comprehensive independent evaluation of the pilot initiative was submitted as an input to the Quadrennial Comprehensive Policy Review, which was completed in 2012. For further information on DaO, see http://www.undg.org/?P=7.

34 See "SG 2009 report," at paras. 55–6.

ASSESSING THE RESULTS SO FAR

No external evaluation has yet been conducted specifically to assess the results of the policy advisory innovation. However, its impact has already been noted in a number of other evaluations, for instance:

> The independent country-led evaluation of the DaO pilot in Vietnam noted that "when stakeholders outside the UN were asked about examples of policy engagement the most frequently cited example is the work of four policy advisors in UNDP dealing with economics, climate change, and governance including the legal sector, public administration reform and anti-corruption."[35]

A recent evaluation of donor anticorruption programs in Vietnam commissioned by the Norwegian aid agency noted that "although this evaluation is not directly concerned with the work of UNDP, it emerges as an influential participant in the AC interaction with government,"[36] adding that "UNDP has . . . managed to turn around [its] performance. A team of policy advisers was recruited. Working relationships have been established. . . . New ways of working with Government – with policy advisers building personal relationships with key decision-makers – have been developed in the process,"[37] concluding that "historically, bilateral donors have been more influential than the multilaterals at governance reform, but bilateral donor support to both the World Bank and UNDP has started to change that relationship."[38]

At any rate, within the UN Country Team in Vietnam it is viewed as an integral part of our ability to meet our mandate to deliver high-quality policy advice and advocacy in Vietnam, and to support the continuation of DaO; and donors strongly confirmed their support during the process of negotiating the new One Plan 2012–2016 and the supporting One Plan Fund, which will drive the United Nations' work for the next five years. However, it cannot sustainably remain forever in its current project-based status. If its value is truly recognized then it should be institutionalized within the United Nations' country office structure for addressing governance.

Our own internal reflections highlight three critical success factors:

Linking international and national expertise. A policy advisory team relies heavily on national experts whose networks and understanding of the emerging issues will usually be superior to those of even well-informed foreigners; and to ensure knowledge management over time because the turnover of international experts is likely to

[35] See Derek Poate, Dang Ngoc Dung, and Nguyen Hang: "Country-led Evaluation, Delivering as One: UN Pilot initiative in Vietnam," May 2010, at para. 4.16, available at http://www.dao4conference.org/ckfinder/userfiles/files/CLE_VietNam.pdf.

[36] See Norad (Norwegian Agency for Development Cooperation), "Joint Evaluation of Support to Anti-Corruption Efforts 2002–2009" (2011), available at http://www.norad.no/en/tools-and-publications/publications/evaluations/publication?key=384730, 27.

[37] Ibid., 34.

[38] Ibid., 52.

be higher. Conversely, international experts should bring an objective perspective, the ability to articulate messages that may be too sensitive for national staff, and an awareness of emerging scholarship and new approaches from other countries that can enrich the national debate.

Integration between policy and program work. Projects remain essential as vehicles to engage state policy makers and as the main channel for turning policy recommendations into actual reforms on the ground. At the same time, the freedom of policy advisors to respond to emerging priorities, commission independent research, engage multiple channels (including media, civil society, and academia alongside national agencies), and use the United Nations' convening role to bring them together has proved an essential "added value" to enrich the policy component of work done under projects. Advisors recruited under single-agency–executed projects were not able to play this catalytic role.

Sustainability and scope. The policy advisory team is funded on an annual basis by locally mobilized resources under the One Plan. Policy advisors work on one-year contracts whose renewal is subject to availability of funding for the next year. This was fully appropriate at the start given the experimental "pilot" nature of the initiative, but the time has come to address sustainability and the role of policy advisors in the future. At the same time, it is timely to consider whether the model can be usefully applied in other policy areas and by other UN agencies.

OTHER DONOR APPROACHES TO SUPPORTING GOVERNANCE IN VIETNAM

The United Nations is only one of many development partners supporting governance in Vietnam, and I will briefly attempt to contrast other donors' approaches, although an adequate treatment of that subject would require a separate chapter.

A number of bilateral donors have – individually or jointly – programmed in a similar manner to the traditional UNDP approach, through nationally executed projects with technical expertise contracted at project level. This approach, as with UNDP, worked well in the early phase of governance reforms when the main objective was to build basic capacities and get laws passed. Some projects have continued to focus on technical aspects of reforms, and to that extent have also proved successful. For instance, in the last few years a Japanese-funded technical assistance program has worked intensively with judges and prosecutors at the local level, looking at the practical difficulties they have raised in applying provisions of criminal, civil, and administrative procedure laws, and helping to draft manuals such as a judgment drafting manual. Australian support, with strong engagement of the Australian Supreme Court, for the judiciary to draft a benchbook for the judiciary has also been successful, as has a U.S.-funded project to support a court website and publication of the highest-level Supreme Court judgments.

Where, however, the aim has been to work on more political issues of governance touching on reform of the court system, independence of judiciary and similar issues, projects under this modality seem to have faced similar problems to those UNDP encountered in the first years of the last decade.

For UNDP, however, these structural and political issues are precisely those that the United Nations is supposed to address. The United Nations' mandate and comparative advantage does not lie in strengthening the legal framework for investors, or in skills training, but in advancing a rights-based agenda by reference to principles such as the right of access to counsel and the right to a fair hearing before an independent tribunal. It is supposed to leverage its political neutrality and the adherence of member states to these international norms to engage effectively on such sensitive topics. Without interventions raising these issues, or objective research identifying the human rights gaps in the legal and judicial system, UNDP found it increasingly hard to justify its comparative advantage, and bilateral donors began to question the added value of funding projects through UNDP rather than engaging directly with national partners.

Some other aid modalities have also sought to address governance reforms. For instance, from 2001 to 2011 the World Bank led a multidonor budget support program known as the "Poverty Reduction Support Credit," under which annual budget support commitments were negotiated together with a "policy matrix," a set of benchmarks related to policies that the government agreed to implement as a condition of granting the loan. Public governance reforms came to form a separate pillar of the policy matrix, and UNDP took a leading role in coordinating the policy advice on governance aspects such as rule of law, anticorruption, and public administrative reform.

While the Poverty Reduction Support Credit (PRSC) program as a whole has been positively evaluated from a number of aspects,[39] the impact in relation to specific governance reforms is hard to assess. This is perhaps because "Bank adjustment operations ... demonstrated a degree of flexibility in interpreting policy conditionality, relying on a bottom-line assessment of whether overall progress on reform measures was satisfactory."[40] Accordingly, the nonfulfillment of specific policy actions under the PRSC process did not have negative impacts on the grant of budget support.

[39] See Roger Grawe, "Poverty Reduction Support Credits: A Vietnam Case Study," World Bank Independent Evaluation Group Working Paper 2010/9, available at http://lnweb90.worldbank.org/oed/oeddoclib.nsf/DocUNIDViewForJavaSearch/9F267B71F0A833AE8525779D006A9E3D/$file/prsc_vietnam_cs.pdf. In 2011 a further independent evaluation was conducted by the European Union that assessed PRSC to have been one of the most successful budget support operations conducted to date, but the evaluation was not published and detailed findings on its impact on specific policies were not released. See http://eeas.europa.eu/delegations/vietnam/press_corner/all_news/news/2011/20110706_01_en.htm.

[40] Grawe, "Poverty Reduction Support Credits," op. cit.

By way of example, a policy action was designed to address the need for an improved policy framework for the registration and operations of civil society organizations. However, in the event, the proposed Law on Associations was dropped from the legislative agenda and replaced with a government decree which, if anything, tightened the restrictions on registration of nongovernmental organizations even further. In response, the relevant policy action was first deferred through successive PRSC rounds and then ultimately dropped altogether.

In contrast with these "top-down" approaches, which work directly with state agencies, a number of donors (mainly nongovernmental donors such as grant foundations) focus more on "bottom-up" strategies to strengthen the capacities and support the advocacy of civil society organizations, media, research institutions, and academia, supporting activities such as research on strategically important topics and legal empowerment of vulnerable groups. Donors in this category include the Asia Foundation and the Justice Initiatives Facilitation Fund, which is the grant-making component of the joint European Union/Swedish/Danish Justice Partnership Programme, the various German political foundations (Konrad Adenauer Stiftung, Friedrich Naumann Stiftung, Friedrich Ebert Stiftung, and Rosa Luxemburg Stiftung), and some human rights institutions that support universities and research institutions on human-rights related issues (the Danish and Norwegian Institutes for Human Rights).

The approach of the grant foundations has a great deal in common with that of the UNDP PAT. They also seek to put strategic governance issues "on the table" through partnerships with those stakeholders in-country who are able and willing to take them forward, and are supported with international expertise. They support direct work with grassroots communities (such as legal empowerment initiatives) and independent research on strategic governance issues. Conversely, unlike UNDP, they tend not to work with state agencies, and in comparison they generally enjoy a less trusted relationship with the government.

In contrast, PAT tries to be both "top-down" and "bottom-up" at the same time, and to find a way to synergize both approaches: to work directly with government agencies, the party, and parliament, as well as supporting universities, researchers, and CSOs and engaging the media. The aim is to combine UNDP's structural advantages (political neutrality, UN standards, trusted by governments and with access to them, and a convening role) with the more flexible approach of grant foundations (proactive, multiple partners including academia and civil society) and to bring researchers and CSOs to the same table as the state agencies.

SUPPORTING GOVERNANCE IN MIDDLE-INCOME COUNTRIES: REFLECTIONS ON THE VIETNAM EXPERIENCE AND BEYOND

The PAT was developed in the specific context of Vietnam. Can its success be replicated elsewhere, or should it be regarded as a unique response to a particular political economy at a particular moment in its history?

It is a key question that deserves further analysis and discussion, but the key features of the Vietnam context that gave rise to the creation of the PAT can typically be expected to be present in MIC environments:

Complex, context-specific governance problems. By the time a country reaches MIC status, the most basic – and easily resolved – issues of governance are likely to have been addressed. Basic institutions have been built; a fundamental legal framework is in place. State budgetary resources are adequate to fund the ordinary business of government. However, the number of new entrants to the MIC club continues to outstrip the modest number of graduates to "developed country" status; most seem to remain mired in the "middle income trap." Those countries that escaped it within the last fifty years, including Japan, South Korea, Singapore, and Taiwan, did so in very different ways, and all of them defying the neat prescriptions of the Washington Consensus or any other "model."

This suggests that it is easier to realize the gains from basic elements of governance, such as a legal framework and core institutions of governance, than to develop these institutions to support a high-performing and inclusive governance culture. The challenges are twofold:

At the highest level of policy making, governing elites need to be convinced of the necessity of prioritizing governance reforms, and to be convinced that such reforms – including those that lessen inequalities and may harm the interests of the richest and most powerful – are a necessary path to graduating from MIC status. While it is easy to show that stronger rule of law and other aspects of good governance tend to be present in developed countries, the direction of causality remains unproven, despite a continuing vigorous debate;[41] and even if so convinced, given that such reforms are deeply embedded in political, cultural, and institutional contexts, concrete advice needs to be based both in a sound understanding of the national context and in a perceptive analysis of the success factors in other country contexts.

The PAT model, with long-term in-country experts (international and national), linked to emerging international scholarship as well as the United Nations' own experience base, and directly advising UNDP (and not one specific government implementing agency) on the key issues to be addressed and how to address them, presents clear advantages in such contexts, although it needs to be supported by more analysis and research at headquarters level and a much better basis of comparative knowledge and expertise than is available at present. I will return to this theme in the following text.

[41] For recent examples see, e.g., Daron Acemoglu and James Robinson, *Why Nations Fail: The Origins of Power, Prosperity and Poverty* (Crown Publishers, 2012), arguing that "inclusive" political systems are essential for sustainable long-term growth, while "extractive" political systems as in China and many Latin American countries cannot bring countries to high levels of development: Joseph Stiglitz, *The Price of Inequality* (W. W. Norton and Company, 2012) arguing that at every level of development, political/governance systems that reduce income inequality produce higher levels of growth.

Conflicting interests of key players. MICs have a wider range of stakeholders able to articulate their own, different interests. They have increasingly well-educated middle classes; increasingly articulate civil society organizations, mass media, and academia; powerful businesses interests; and a range of state institutions with diverse and sometimes conflicting interests and the capacity to advance and defend them. In such environments and in contexts of growing inequality there is a strong risk of alignment between power and money, so that those arguing for more participatory and transparent governance are more likely to include journalists, civil society, and scholars rather than officials in the most powerful branches of state institutions.

The PAT model provides the necessary flexibility to work with and fund civil society and academia (strengthening their capacities and enabling them to conduct in-country research) and then bring them to the same table as government (using the United Nations' convening role), as well as strategic engagement with the media. By contrast, projects controlled by selected government agencies are unlikely to be successful vehicles for advocating change that disempowers elites at the expense of the people.

Growing financial autonomy. As countries become richer, Official Development Assistance (ODA) becomes financially less significant. ODA accounted for more than 10 percent of gross national income in thirty-five countries in 2010; in Vietnam, at the bottom end of the MIC club, the figure is 2.9 percent.[42] Many MICs can afford to ignore donors' advice, but they remain interested in getting good advice that actually helps them achieve their objectives, and they are sophisticated enough to distinguish good advice from bad.

In such contexts, donors can influence governments only through the quality of advice they give. If they are not perceived as being able to solve governments' problems, then they risk being manipulated to fund study tours and workshops that provide additional income streams for civil servants, without contributing to policy change. A PAT, locally embedded but globally connected, can be well placed to provide this, but this is critically dependent not only on the knowledge and skills of the local PAT but also on the strength of the intellectual network supporting it within the organization. Again, I will return to this in the following text.

Long-term engagement. Governance reforms take time, and are rarely accomplished in neatly defined time frames. In Vietnam, for instance, the notion of constitutionalism has been discussed by scholars since the beginning of reforms in the 1990s; more concrete discussions on issues such as constitutional review began to take place from 2001, with periods of intense discussion alternating with longer periods when the debate fell silent. A decision to amend the constitution in 2011, likely to include the establishment of a Constitutional Council after 2013, will just be one step in a much longer journey.

[42] See chart at http://data.worldbank.org/indicator/DT.ODA.ODAT.GN.ZS.

The PAT model has the necessary flexibility to address strategic issues when their time is ripe, or to disengage if political circumstances dictate. It can and does strategically use projects and partnerships as a vehicle for these issues, but is not limited by their scope (either in terms of substance or timing).

Political context. Although I argue that Vietnam has many typical features of MICs in its country context, in other ways it is unusual. It is one of only a handful of remaining one-party socialist republics. It may be argued that perhaps a PAT approach is needed as a corrective to the one-party environment, with its more restricted space for open debate and no separation of powers. In a multiparty environment with a free press and an unmuzzled civil society, a culture of free debate will put pressure on governments. With the necessary political will secured, traditional projects will be adequate to help the government get the job done.

However, it is doubtful whether too much should be made of the form of the political system rather than the reality of its governance. Even in systems that have the form of multiparty democracies with separation of powers, the political agenda may be controlled by powerful elites and alliances, to the exclusion of the poor and disadvantaged groups. Occupy Wall Street and similar protest movements have recently reminded us that this danger exists even in the richest and most "developed" countries. Where such imbalances exist, development processes risk being captured and restricted by elites, and the PAT model has the virtue of providing the means to let the United Nations do its job of strengthening and supporting other voices, perspectives, and evidence (even within the elites, as well as outside them) to those processes.

Conversely, it may be argued that the PAT model requires a minimum of responsiveness from the government. The story of Vietnam's own trajectory from central planning to market and rule-of-law reforms is one of openness to change from within, willingness to experiment, and a concern to retain the Communist Party's legitimacy, which has provided the entry points for reform that the PAT was designed to exploit. Without those characteristics, PAT would surely have failed.

To this argument it must be conceded, with regret, that political contexts can arise where no meaningful engagement with the government is possible, and where governance issues cannot meaningfully be addressed or advanced, however persuasive the evidence or skillful the advisor. In those contexts, policy advisory capacity would be a wasted investment, but then it is hardly supposed that a more traditional model would fare better, and the real question is whether to invest in democratic governance at all. There are countries in which UNDP has no democratic governance program for precisely such reasons. Happily, they are few, and none of them are MICs. This is not to underestimate the very real challenges facing democratic governance in many countries; but where there is some kind of scope for working with the government, parliament, and courts at the same time as strengthening media, civil society, and academia, I argue that a PAT approach should be considered as a worthwhile investment.

IMPLICATIONS FOR UN ENGAGEMENT IN MIDDLE-INCOME COUNTRIES

This chapter therefore argues that the Vietnamese experiment with the PAT model in UNDP should be considered for wider introduction in UNDP at country-office level, especially to address governance in MICs, including international and national technical experts in each policy field to be recruited directly in, and accountable to, the country office; and, a directly implemented program with its own funds (both for salaries and for research, etc.) in addition to the nationally executed projects, so that the policy advisors can directly support research and independent national and international expertise. As discussed, this does not mean that the policy advisors work exclusively through such a program. Nationally implemented projects remain essential for securing the involvement of senior policy makers. A remarkable feature of the PAT initiative in Vietnam has been that emerging and sensitive issues have been discussed through such projects at high-level policy dialog fora, even though those projects had proved unable to address those issues proactively without the "push" from the policy advisors and the research and expertise they bring to bear.

However, I believe that a number of other elements of UNDP's business model will need to be considered in order to provide a truly sustainable basis for providing effective policy advice in MICs, including its strategy for human resources and what is known within UNDP as "knowledge management."

KNOWLEDGE

As discussed previously, getting the right issues raised at the right time is only one aspect of successful policy advice: the quality of the advice is just as important.

This is not a simple question, especially in the field of governance. Governance issues, although addressed in the Millennium Declaration, were passed over entirely when the MDGs were formulated, and no one should underestimate the political challenges to getting governments to take governance seriously.

UN officials do not need to be persuaded of the virtues of rule of law and good governance, but as Juvenal once said, who would ever embrace virtue if you took away her rewards?[43] The United Nations needs, therefore, not only to preach these virtues, but also to provide sound empirical evidence that the governments that practice them will be rewarded with higher growth and an escape from the middle-income trap. As mentioned previously, although more academic research and discussion is being devoted to this, there is a long way to go, and the case has not yet been convincingly made to governments: it remains to be seen whether this time the governance agenda will make it onto the post-2015 "Sustainable Development Goals."

[43] Juvenal, *Satires* X, 140: "Quis enim virtutem ipsam amplectitur, praemia si tollas?"

At global level, therefore, the United Nations needs to engage more with this research and provide a stronger empirical framework to get MICs more interested in what it has to say on governance.

At the country level, the United Nations' claim to comparative advantage as a knowledge organization is based upon its global reach, and the breadth of the United Nations' presence gives it access to an unrivaled source of data and experience of development practice.

However, extracting really useful data and concrete advice from UNDP's myriad governance projects around the world to generate useful solutions in a concrete country context is a far from trivial task. With a PAT model in place, the country office is well placed to understand the country context and the problem to be solved, but how to access the evidence around the world and find solutions?

Although UNDP assigns a high priority to its knowledge management strategy, it is not yet clear that we have found a satisfactory answer to this challenging issue. In order to better connect country offices, UNDP's priority in recent years has been to establish a "social network" solution, Teamworks (which has been described as "Facebook for UNDP"), with the aim of providing a platform for discussions and sharing of experiences between practitioners in country offices, regional centers, and headquarters.

However, at least in my experience, the value of what is shared is not yet meeting the – admittedly challenging – needs. In our new Post Washington Consensus world, we are still struggling to develop an adequate concept of knowledge about rule-of-law development, to know how to interpret and analyze the data from rule-of-law development projects[44] – let alone to carry out serious empirical research into those projects. We therefore have a "problem of knowledge" at the microlevel that mirrors that at the macrolevel. It is one thing to share what has been done in each country, but much harder to have a rigorous analysis of its impact and results, and the factors that would enable it to be adapted successfully to other contexts. We do not know enough about what really works and does not, and why; and although we know that governance reforms are contextual and path dependent, we do not know enough to identify the critical features of those contexts and paths.

No doubt UNDP, with a presence in most countries of the world and with governance projects in more than 130 of them, has the potential to access a fantastic store of data and experience and to advance the cause of knowledge considerably. However, it will likely take much more than a user-driven exchange across a social-network platform to realize that potential.

[44] See Thomas Carothers, ed., *Promoting the Rule of Law Abroad: In Search of Knowledge* (Carnegie Endowment for International Peace, 2006); David M. Trubek and Alvaro Santos, eds., *The New Law and Economic Development* (Cambridge University Press, 2006); Michael J. Trebilcock and Ronald J. Daniels, *Rule of Law Reform and Development: Charting the Fragile Path of Progress* (Edward Elgar Publishing, 2006).

Engaging policy advisory expertise directly in country offices would seem a good first step. At present, as each project ends, so too do the contracts of the technical experts engaged under them, and there is a real risk that much of the knowledge about the project goes with them. There is no UNDP-wide policy to capture and retain that knowledge within the country office, and without the necessary expertise in the country office it is hard to know how that could be done.

But even this is not likely to be enough. UNDP needs a stronger partnership with professional academic researchers, engaging with its work and helping it to conduct more research and analysis, more case studies, so that it can produce a much richer knowledge base for its work – and contribute this richer knowledge base for the discipline of governance and rule-of-law development as a whole. A long-term cooperation with an academic institution similar, for instance, to that between the Human Development office and the Oxford Poverty and Human Development Initiative would be highly beneficial.

Establishing good networks between offices has certainly been an important first step toward effective knowledge management in UNDP. But to really achieve the strategic lift in UNDP's knowledge base, in the next phase the focus needs to shift to the substance and quality of the knowledge being shared, with all levels – headquarters, regional, and country level – having an important role to play, and with much more, and more proactive, engagement outside UNDP with academics, researchers, and other development practitioners. Evidently, a strong component of in-house policy advisors at the country level could play a significant role in that task as well.

HUMAN RESOURCES

The strategy that this chapter is proposing for UN governance support to MICs places considerable demands on the skills and expertise of the policy advisors, in terms of their technical knowledge about governance and rule of law, the emerging body of research on rule-of-law development, and the different techniques of engagement that have proved successful in supporting reform.

An important question, therefore, is whether UNDP's business model is fit for the purpose of attracting policy advisors of sufficient quality and retaining them in the system.

Historically, the long-term international career path within UNDP starts with the Junior Professional Officers who learn to manage individual projects, and who then graduate to manage wider portfolios of projects as Assistant Resident Representatives, before assuming senior management functions in charge of the country office's entire program. By contrast, as previously mentioned, technical expertise is contracted under short-term project-based contracts, with only a small number of policy advisory posts established on a long-term basis in headquarters and regional centers.

Providing a longer-term career perspective to policy advisors would appear to have a number of advantages. First, it would help attract the best applicants for positions where the skills and knowledge of the advisors plays a critical role. Quite obviously, the PAT model cannot work effectively unless highly knowledgeable, imaginative, and experienced policy advisors can be recruited at country level.

Second, given that the technology of effective governance support is an emerging field of scholarship (as noted previously), and given the importance of the United Nations' role in this area, the United Nations should seek to retain its policy advisors, rotating them to new policy advisory assignments elsewhere, continuously building their capacity, and helping ensure that the emerging expertise remains within the UN system.[45]

PROGRAMMING ARRANGEMENTS

The flexibility that policy advisors can bring needs to be matched with maximum operational flexibility, to commission leading expertise, experiment with new models, and form innovative partnerships (nationally and internationally, short and long term), and this requires a flexible range of project modalities, which can be deployed quickly through light procedures that provide transparency and accountability without unnecessary bureaucracy. This has proved an ongoing challenge in Vietnam, and needs to remain a priority for reform at the highest levels.

DELIVERING AS ONE

Although the Quadrennial Comprehensive Policy Review in 2012 will deliver a more considered reflection on the experiences of the DaO pilot, the Secretary-General has already committed to launch a second generation of DaO.[46] The Vietnam experience demonstrated that policy advisory capacity can play a critical role in the success of DaO, enabling agencies to focus on their area of comparative advantage and within that area to act as a resource to other agencies, catalyzing cross-agency engagement and reducing overlapping programming.

CONCLUSION

There is a broad consensus about the United Nations' comparative advantages, which should enable the United Nations to play a leading role in supporting development in MICs: a global perspective; a large network of offices and institutes

[45] Although, in line with the theme of this conference, this paper focuses on governance, the same case should be made for a "policy career track" within the United Nations across a number of key policy areas. Similar considerations led the UN Department of Peacekeeping Operations in 2008 to create long-term career perspectives for civilian advisors in peacekeeping missions rather than, as previously, hiring them on short-term mission-specific assignments.

[46] See Secretary-General's Five-Year Action Agenda, January 25, 2012, Section II.4, available at http://www.un.org/sg/priorities/sg_agenda_2012.pdf.

around the world; access to world-class expertise, data, and knowledge; wide recognition and credibility; neutrality/impartiality; and convening power. But there is also some skepticism outside (and perhaps even within) the United Nations about the degree to which they are successfully exploited in practice. I have argued that, in Vietnam, the initiative to place policy advisory expertise outside – but working with – nationally executed projects, accountable to UNDP, and with its own source of funding has demonstrated its ability to leverage these comparative advantages, and deserves consideration for wider adoption – at least in relation to governance in UNDP, and at least in MICs.

But I also argue that a number of further reforms are equally necessary, requiring a more proactive approach to knowledge management; more engagement outside UNDP and more investment in research; more flexible programming and procurement modalities; and a real career track for policy expertise within UNDP.

My recommendations have financial implications: taking governance seriously in MICs will, I accept, require more than the resources that are currently allocated. No doubt, the bulk of development aid will and should go to the poorest countries. But as more of the world's countries reach MIC status, and the percentage of the world's poor living within them continues to rise, it is surely time to reconsider the funding balance between LICs and MICs, which (at least for UNDP) has not evolved to reflect these changes. In 1995, 88 percent of core funding was allocated to LICs, and this has fallen to about 86 percent now, with no significant change contemplated for the future.[47]

As bilateral donors withdraw from MICs, it is vital that – in line with the principles of progressivity and universality – the United Nations commits sufficient resources to enable high-quality support to governance reforms. Building a sustainable policy advisory capacity in UN country offices, linked strongly to international thinking within and outside the United Nations, is an effective way to catalyze change across a diverse base of stakeholders and mitigate the risks of "agency capture" within individual projects, thus supporting MICs' governance strategies as well as donors' strategic aims, and enabling the United Nations to fulfill the role that the international community – donors and recipient countries alike – expect of it.

[47] See note 6.

16

Law and Development in Middle-Income Countries

Conclusion

Randall Peerenboom

This chapter summarizes the key findings of this volume; locates these findings within the existing literatures on law and development and related fields; highlights areas for further research; and develops policy recommendations for middle-income country (MIC) governments and development agencies. The discussion is organized around the eight issue areas set forth in the introduction: (1) Is "middle-income country" an analytically useful category? (2) Is there a middle-income trap, are there various traps, or is it a myth? (3) What if anything do successful MICs share? (4) Why have East Asian states been so successful, and does the recent success of Central and Eastern European (CEE) states provide an alternative model? (5) What is the relationship between politics, or political-economy, and development in MICs? (6) How have MICs been influenced by and adapted to the new international economic order? (7) What approaches are available to MICs to address pressing socioeconomic issues? And finally, (8) what lessons are there for policy makers and development agencies in promoting rule of law and good governance in MICs? We conclude with some recommendations for future research.

IS "MIDDLE-INCOME COUNTRY" AN ANALYTICALLY USEFUL CATEGORY?

There are both quantitative and qualitative arguments in favor of MICs as a useful analytical category or concept. There is a well-established correlation between wealth, good governance, rule of law, the protection of human rights, and other indicators of human well-being.[1] Nevertheless, sorting countries by levels of wealth provides additional insights because the relationship is not uniform at all levels of the income scale. Table 16.1 provides correlations between per capita income, the Governance Indicators of the World Bank, along with the Human Development

I thank Michael Dowdle for his comments on the conclusion. Special thanks to Taimoor Aziz, who prepared Table 16.1.

[1] See, e.g., Randall Peerenboom, *China Modernizes: Threat to the West or Model for the Rest?* (Oxford University Press, 2007), 40–1.

TABLE 16.1. *Correlations between Wealth and Governance*

	All countries	HICs (n = 67)	All MICs (n = 108)	UMICs only (n = 54)	LMICs only (n = 54)	LICs (n = 36)
Voice and accountability	.49[b]	0.2	.34[b]	.31[a]	.38[b]	0.19
Government effectiveness	.66[b]	.38[b]	.49[b]	.28[a]	.30[a]	0.21
Regulatory quality	.65[b]	.37[b]	.43[b]	.30[a]	.32[a]	0.34[a]
Rule of law	.60[b]	.31[a]	.44[b]	.29[a]	.34[a]	0.02
Corruption	.64[b]	.46[b]	.40[b]	0.26	.34[a]	0
Human Development Index	.65[b]	.45[b]	.75[b]	.53[b]	.75[b]	0.68[a]
Gini Coefficient	−0.31[b]	0.16	−0.15	−0.22	0.04	−0.27
Environmental quality	.45[b]	0.25	.44[b]	0.22	.59[b]	−0.03

[a] Indicates significant at 90 percent confidence level.
[b] Indicates significant at 95 percent confidence level.

Index and selected other indicators. Consistent with other work, we see strong overall correlations when all countries are included in the analysis (column 1). When one breaks down the correlations by income class, however, one sees differential links at different levels of income. The correlation coefficients are highest at the middle-income level, and the relationships are more significant. Dividing the MIC category into upper middle-income countries (UMICs) and lower middle-income countries (LMICs) provides further dividends. Again the correlation coefficients are higher at the lower level of wealth, that is, for LMICs than for UMICs, with equal or greater levels of significance. The basic story that emerges is that greater wealth makes a significant difference at the LMIC stage, but after that, although wealth matters for both UMICs and high-income countries (HICs), policies matter more for producing governance outcomes. What matters most is how wealth is distributed, and what measures are adopted to deal with environmental issues, alleviate poverty, reduce inequality, raise literacy rates, decrease child mortality, curb corruption, enhance administrative efficiency, and promote the rule of law. This is consistent with Juan Botero's data (Chapter 10) showing that the gap between HICs and MICs in delivering justice is greater than the gap between MICs and LICs. The major point of the table is that the issues related to law and development are posed most starkly in the MIC context.

There are also a number of qualitative reasons in support of viewing the development process through the lens of MICs. Simply put, MICs are structurally different than LICs and HICs: they face different development issues and challenges, and differ in the amount of resources and institutional capacity available to address the challenges.

First, by definition, MICs have more resources than LICs, but fewer than HICs. Moreover, institutions are generally stronger in MICs than in LICs, but weaker than in HICs, in keeping with the high correlation between wealth and institutional strength. In LICs, the main obstacles to effective governance are the lack of resources and even weaker, and in some extreme cases nonexistent, institutions. Many LICs are failed states or wracked by civil war. The demand for rule of law may also be low in LICs given the nature of the economy, which is often heavily agricultural and not well integrated into the global economy. Nevertheless, as the economy develops and diversifies, and LICs become MICs, there is generally an increase in the demand for rule of law and good governance. For LICs, then, the main tasks are to pass laws and establish basic institutions. For MICs, the main task is to strengthen the capacity of existing institutions so that they can implement the laws on the books justly, fairly, and efficiently, while simultaneously building out the regulatory architecture.

At the other end of the scale, MICs differ in significant ways from HICs. MICs confront a wide range of challenges at once: economic, legal, social, political, and geopolitical. They must adopt, from a range of conflicting options, the correct economic policies and create a business environment that is supportive and effective; establish and strengthen economic institutions needed for a market economy; promote research and development and adopt policies to stimulate innovation; react in a timely fashion to external crises; build an efficient administrative system; root out corruption; train thousands, and in some cases, hundreds of thousands of civil servants, judges, lawyers, notaries, accountants, and police; create a welfare system; improve education and the health care systems; oversee the urbanization process; deal with increased pollution; and manage tensions with other countries that may arise as they become more powerful and begin to assert themselves on the international stage. Many MICs are simply overwhelmed by the sheer number and scale of the challenges, which exceed the capacity of MIC governments. When they turn to external sources for help, they are inundated with policy advice, much of it highly technical and out of step with local conditions. Eastern European MICs, for example, were required to adopt and comply with more than eighty thousand pages of highly specific requirements to join the European Union (EU). Adoption as a formal matter was surely easier than ensuring effective implementation of this massive volume of regulation.

Second, given all the challenges, MICs must set priorities and sequence reforms.[2] They simply cannot deal with all issues at once, or fully implement the ambitious

[2] Sequencing, in particular prioritizing legal reforms aimed at strengthening rule of law before democratization, has recently come under attack. See, e.g., Thomas Carothers, "How Democracies Emerge: The 'Sequencing' Fallacy," *Journal of Democracy* (January 2007): 12–27. For a contrary view on that issue as well as a discussion of other sequencing issues, see Randall Peerenboom, "The East Asian

programs set out by development agencies based on the institutions, rules, and regulatory structures in HICs that took decades, if not centuries, to develop. Unfortunately, the plethora of tool kits on offer from development agencies contain precious little advice on how to prioritize and sequence reforms. Most advice is heavy on the content and substance of reforms and light on the process and methodology of reform, laying out the end state but not shedding much light on how to get there.

Third, demands on government institutions rise more quickly than does capacity. Consider the courts, by way of example. The judicial system is often expected to play a major role in supervising government and protecting citizens. But, as illustrated in a recent International Foundation for Electoral Systems/US Agency for International Development report, the courts often lack the capacity to do so.[3] The many problems confronting judiciaries in MICs include the fact that courts are often asked to handle controversial cases involving economic and social rights; a rise in crime, including complicated white collar and cross-border crime, as a country moves to a market economy and urbanizes; corruption; and the changing relationship of the courts to other organs of state power. The report concludes, "It would be unrealistic to think that the judiciaries can carry the full burden for resolving these complex problems."[4] There is then a need to rethink the role of institutions in MICs. The global trends toward juridification and judicialization may be more suitable in HICs than in MICs.[5] Moreover, rather than emphasizing judicial independence and a strict separation of powers, as the rule-of-law promotion industry has emphasized for MICs, there appears to be greater need for a more collaborative approach at least on some issues, particularly socioeconomic issues.[6]

Fourth, political stability is often fragile in MICs. Given limited resources and weak institutions, many citizens will be unhappy with the government and state institutions when they fail to satisfy their legitimate demands. As a result, there is likely to be a sharp increase in mass protests. In China, for example, the number of mass demonstrations has risen from 8,700 in 1993 to almost two hundred thousand a year, by some estimates. Similarly, Vietnam has witnessed an explosion in mass protests in recent years.[7] Meanwhile, social unrest fueled the Jasmine Revolutions

Model and the Sequencing Debate: Lessons from China and Vietnam," in *Legal Reforms in China and Vietnam*, ed. John Gillespie and Albert Chen (Taylor and Francis, 2010), 29–50.

3 IFES/USAID, "Guidance for Promoting Judicial Independence and Impartiality," 2002, 6, available at http://www.usaid.gov/our_work/democracy_and_governance/publications/pdfs/pnacm007.pdf.

4 Ibid.

5 Juridification refers to an expansion of legal discourse and modes of analysis into other spheres (e.g., economics and politics), whereas judicialization refers to an expanded role for the courts in deciding a wider range of social, political, and economic issues.

6 Perhaps the most challenging approach to socioeconomic issues from the perspective of separation of power and the traditional role of the courts is grand mediation in China. Keith Hand, "Resolving Constitutional Disputes in Contemporary China," *University of Pennsylvania East Asia Law Review* 7, no. 1 (2011): 51–159.

7 See Carlyle A. Thayer, "Vietnam and the Challenge of Political Civil Society," *Contemporary Southeast Asia: A Journal of International and Strategic Affairs* 31, no. 1 (April 2009): 1–27; Benedict

that toppled governments throughout the Middle East and North Africa. To be sure, satisfaction polls show that many people are not happy with public institutions in HICs, including parliament or congress, the judiciary, and police.[8] But the nature of the discontent is different. Institutions in HICs are generally stronger. They may be subject to political capture or influenced by money or politics, but they generally work better on a daily operational level. They are more technically efficient. Moreover, there is a larger middle class in HICs than in MICs. Fewer people are ready to risk jail or personal injury trying to overthrow the government or demonstrating in the street. There are also more opportunities for peaceful political participation in HICs. In contrast, discontent in MICs is potentially much more destabilizing. Regimes, whether authoritarian or democratic, are regularly overthrown. The stakes are therefore higher for the government, and there is accordingly more repression.

Fifth, political economy issues become more salient in MICs than in LICs because there are more interest groups, more resources to fight over, and more venues to pursue one's interests. Moreover, the low-hanging fruit has already been picked in MICs. There are few if any win-win solutions remaining. Reforms produce winners and losers. In addition, there is more consensus on the character of the very basic reforms needed in LICs, relative to the range of different opinions about what is needed in MICs. Even when there is general agreement about some basic principles, the wide variation in institutions, rules, and practices leads to controversy, and provides stakeholders ample opportunity to pursue their own interests. As Dani Rodrik observes, "[F]irst-order economic principles – protection of property rights, market-based competition, appropriate incentives, sound money, and so on – do not map into unique policy packages."[9] The same can be said for basic rule-of-law principles. Take, for example, the current debates over judicial reforms in China. Among the issues being debated are: What will the role of the judiciary be in policy making? Over what types of cases will courts exercise jurisdiction? What will the judiciary's relations be with other political organs? Will the court be able to determine its own budget? How much say will the judiciary have in promotions and appointments? Invoking the mantras of rule of law or just and efficient courts does not get one very far toward answering specific questions. How similar issues are resolved varies tremendously even in HICs known for the rule of law.

Sixth, as the chapters in this volume on World Trade Organization (WTO) and intellectual property (IP) illustrate, the role of MICs in global governance and the international trade regime differs from the role of both HICs and LICs. Large MICs have now become an influential, if fragile, bloc, capable of not only resisting policies

J. Tria Kerkvliet, *Government Repression and Toleration in Contemporary Vietnam* Southeast Asia Research Centre, Working Paper Series No. 119, 2012, 5–8.

8 See Randall Peerenboom, *China Modernizes*, 250–6, for various polls from developed and developing countries in Europe, Asia, and Latin America..

9 Dani Rodrik, *One Economics, Many Recipes* (Princeton University Press, 2007), 6.

advocated by HICs but also of promoting an agenda that better serves their own interests. They are forming their own organizations and holding their own events, such as the BRICS summit and the India–Brazil–South Africa Dialogue Forum. The G7 has now given way to the G20. Large MICs are demanding more say in the World Bank and International Monetary Fund. Their influence is also being felt in the security area. Rising MIC powers are clamoring for greater representation and voice in the UN Security Council and forming new security organizations, such as the China-Russia–led Shanghai Cooperation Organization.

In sum, there are quantitative and qualitative reasons for focusing on MICs as an analytical concept. Nevertheless, caution is in order. We are not claiming that the particular World Bank divisions are "correct" or the most useful way to categorize countries by wealth. The number of LICs is small and getting smaller, in part because the bottom threshold for MICs is a mere $1,026 per capita. The twelvefold difference in gross domestic product (GDP) per capita for MICs is large, and encompasses very significant differences in the quality of life and strength of institutions in MICs. Similarly, per capita income in HICs ranges from $12,400 to more than $183,000 per capita, with twenty-six countries falling between $12,400 and $30,000, twenty-three between $30,000 and $50,000, and ten more than $50,000 (see Appendix). Further quantitative analysis and qualitative studies may find that there are more useful ways to define the categories or that more subcategories are necessary. Researchers may also find that, as in many other studies, it makes sense to eliminate countries with small populations or to control for economies based on oil or other natural resources. As the chapters on WTO and IP show, for some issues, what matters most is not the gross national income (GNI) per capita of MICs but their aggregate GNI.

Several authors have found it useful to draw further distinctions among MICs. Yu draws on six factors to identify a subcategory of MICs – middle-income intellectual property powers (MIPPs) – to explain the political economy of policy making in the IP area. In addressing the role of courts in providing health care, César Rodríguez-Garavito distinguishes between democratic upper middle-income countries (DUMICs) and authoritarian or LMICs. Benjamin van Rooij and Lesley McAllister observe that environmental challenges in industrialized middle-income countries (IMICs) are more severe than in HICs, LICs, or MICs that rely on nonindustrial sources of revenue such as tourism. Linn Hammergren, as discussed in the following text, distinguishes between four types of MICs, and argues that international development agencies need to tailor their policies for each type. Other taxonomies – such as the threefold corruption taxonomy presented by Kevin Davis can also be overlaid against the MIC category to produce more nuanced insights in certain issue areas.

Nor are we claiming that GNI per capita is the only or best standard for measuring development or that wealth is all that matters. Two of the important lessons that emerge from this volume are, first, that it is not sufficient to focus exclusively on aggregate economic growth – growth must be sustainable, and there may be normatively desirable trade-offs between efficiency and equity, aggregate growth, and higher quality growth. And second, wealth is clearly not the only factor in determining institutional strength or human well-being. The causality between wealth and institutions is bidirectional. And how resources are allocated is as important as how much wealth there is to distribute in improving governance and raising standards of living in MICs. Finally, we are not claiming that there is *a* middle-income trap – if anything, there are various traps – or perhaps more accurately, challenges, for MICs.

IS THERE "A MIDDLE-INCOME TRAP"?

Many MICs face a number of difficulties, and appear to be stuck. Some have experienced decades of slow growth, or cycles of growth followed by declines. Many suffer from governance malfeasance, rampant corruption, and shortcomings in the rule of law. Often, the rapid improvements in poverty alleviation, longevity, and literacy rates have slowed, and in some parts of the country and for some groups there may even be reversals. Environmental conditions generally deteriorate as manufacturing increases. Rapid urbanization gives rise to shanty towns and an increase in crime. Inevitably, some people claim a bigger share of the newly created wealth than others, leading to higher inequality. The policy-making arena is increasingly crowded and contested, with economically powerful groups competing with, and generally outcompeting, socially disadvantaged groups of laborers, migrant workers, pensioners, and the urban and rural poor.

Yet it bears recalling that all HICs were at one point MICs, and faced many of the same challenges. Moreover, despite all of the problems, a number of countries have managed to overcome the obstacles and join the ranks of HICs in recent decades. And many LICs have become MICs. Longer term, there is reason for hope. Notwithstanding the setback caused by the financial crisis in developing countries, growth in developing countries is occurring across the globe, even if not as fast as we might wish. It is, therefore, perhaps more accurate to speak of the "middle-income blues" rather than the middle-income trap, which seems unduly pessimistic and suggests that MICs face virtually insurmountable obstacles.

But even deferring to more established metaphors, it is more accurate to refer to middle-income traps than to "the middle-income trap." Different disciplines have emphasized different types of traps.

Given that economists have dominated discussions about MICs, it is no surprise that economic versions of the middle-income trap are most well-known. The World Bank, for instance, succinctly summarizes the problem:[10]

> The factors and advantages that propelled high growth in . . . countries during their rapid development phases – low-cost labor and easy technology adoption – disappeared

[10] World Bank, *China 2030*, 12.

> when they reached middle- and upper-middle-income levels, forcing them to find new sources of growth.... Large productivity gains occur through a reallocation of labor and capital from low-productivity agriculture to high-productivity manufacturing. As countries reach middle-income levels, the underemployed rural labor force dwindles and wages rise, eroding competitiveness. Productivity growth from sectoral reallocation and technology catch-up are eventually exhausted, while rising wages make labor-intensive exports less competitive internationally. If countries cannot increase productivity through innovation (rather than continuing to rely on foreign technology), they find themselves trapped.

In short, poorer countries are able to take advantage of their backwardness to catch up by combining foreign technology with cheap labor to produce inexpensive clothes, toys, and electronics consumed by people in rich countries. But once wages increase, they need to move up the value added chain and increase efficiency and productivity:

> To get to that next level – that high-income level – an economy needs to do more than just make stuff by throwing people and money into factories. The economy has to innovate and use labor and capital more productively. That requires an entirely different way of doing business. Instead of just assembling products designed by others, with imported technology, companies must invest more heavily in R&D on their own and employ highly educated and skilled workers to turn those investments into new products and profits. It is a very, very hard shift to achieve. Thus the "trap."[11]

Political scientists see the problem more in terms of capture, corruption and preservation of power by the elites, entrenched interests, and the ruling regime. Thus, in Chapter 2 Tom Ginsburg argues:

> Middle-income countries face a particular set of challenges that are, ultimately, political rather than technical or purely economic in nature. The basic problem is one of path dependency. Institutions that are suitable for growth at the early stages of development may not be able to work for later stages. Instead, the regime that gets the country to middle-income status may stick with the strategies and institutions that have worked to date. After all, early stage economic growth underpins regime legitimacy, and may generate increasing political returns that lock in particular structures. The challenge for the political leadership in middle income countries is how to reform the political and institutional bases of growth at the right time to avoid what the economists call a "local maximum." It is an extraordinarily difficult challenge, but one that is essential to overcoming development barriers. It is also helpful, in some cases at least, for political survival. Developmental regimes that manage to transform their political bases and economic institutions to fit the changing environment may survive. Those that do not may be cast aside in favor

[11] Available at http://curiouscapitalist.blogs.time.com/2010/08/10/escaping-the-middle-income-trap/?xid=rss-topstories.

of a new coalition. Alternatively, the regime may survive but keep the country stuck in middle-income status, or even witness dedevelopment or stagnation.

Malaysia's inability to claw back preferential quotas for ethnic Malays is a good example, as are the difficulties China's leaders face in making the transition from a state-investment and export-led model of growth to a more consumption-based economy given opposition from powerful interest groups that have benefitted from the current model.

Ginsburg also sketches a legal version of the middle-income trap in which courts lack autonomy and have limited jurisdiction to decide key types of cases. To overcome this trap, the ruling regime must be willing to empower the courts. But ruling regimes in MICs are often reluctant to do so for fear that the courts will undermine their power. Such fears may be justified when one considers the key role courts have played in triggering some democratic transitions. Even if leaders are willing to empower courts, the courts must have the capacity to shoulder the additional responsibility. In many MICs, either the political will to empower autonomous courts is lacking or the judiciary simply lacks the professional skills and capacity to handle the responsibility.

Moreover, powerful political or economic interests can capture the legal system and undermine rule of law. Many commentators have suggested the concentration of wealth in CEE has given rise to a form of political capitalism in which powerful economic actors have usurped the courts and undermined rule of law. In contrast to the more favorable opinions about constitutional courts, the regular courts are seen as chronically dysfunctional and strikingly inefficient:

> The evidence is undisputable – and the picture is abysmal. Survey after survey, opinion poll after opinion poll confirm that in Eastern Europe judges (as opposed to Justices) have a reputation as self-interested actors whose moral and professional integrity has been compromised, and courts are perceived as under-performing institutions that basically fail to deliver what is expected of them. In 2005 – i.e. *after* the first round of EU's eastward expansion as a result of which most former Soviet satellites gained full membership – Estonia was the *only* country where more than 50% of firm managers assessed the courts as "honest and uncorrupted." Since the late 1990s, the number of East Europeans who believed that their courts are "honest" has been *declining*, and only one in four businessmen expressed the view that judges can be trusted. Levels of dissatisfaction with the way ordinary judiciaries operate are astonishingly high in the EU's newest members. A stunning 100% of those polled in countries like Bulgaria, Romania and Slovakia complained that they find it difficult to ensure a reliable access to transcripts of court proceedings; 90% reported problems with obtaining judicial decisions, on both trial and appellate level. Less than half of firm managers believe that courts are "able to enforce their decisions" in countries like Hungary, Slovenia, Estonia, Czech Republic; the percentage is less than a third in Lithuania and Poland.[12]

[12] Venelin Ganev, "The Rule of Law as an Institutionalized Wager: Constitutions, Courts and Transformative Social Dynamics in Eastern Europe," *Hague Journal on Rule of Law* 1, no. 2 (2009): 263–83.

The dominant view attributes the disappointing performance of regular courts to political economy factors. Privatization created a powerful class that saw rule of law and strong independent regular courts as either unhelpful for, or a threat to, their economic activities and interests. Former communist *apparatchiks* turned *entrepreneurchiks* as a result of privatization "stood to benefit if courts were marginalized, legal norms were not implemented, and the reach of law-enforcement agencies is curtailed."[13]

For all versions of the middle-income trap, the basic problem is the same. What worked in the past no longer works. Countries need to change and adopt new strategies, but they do not or cannot, often because they cannot overcome political economy barriers to reform.[14] Fortunately, some countries have been able to overcome the various versions of the middle-income trap. What lessons can be learned from their experiences?

WHAT, IF ANYTHING, DO SUCCESSFUL MIDDLE-INCOME COUNTRIES SHARE?

At first glance, the most salient feature shared by MICs that have achieved HIC status relatively recently is their diversity. They are located in Europe, the Middle East, and Asia. Some are tiny states with populations between fifty thousand and five hundred thousand, others are large states. Some are democratic, some are authoritarian, and some are theocratic. The nature of the economy and the development model varies: some depend on tourism, tax haven status or gaming; others on oil; still others on advanced manufacturing, services, and the knowledge economy.

Nevertheless, a closer look reveals some interesting patterns and perhaps some lessons for MICs. First, development tends to cluster by region. The early risers to HIC status congregated in Europe and North America. Several other European countries – Spain, Greece, Portugal, and Ireland – later joined the group, followed more recently by CEE countries Slovenia, Croatia, Slovak Republic, Czech Republic, Poland, and Hungary. Similarly, there are now several East Asia HICs, with several East Asian MICs poised to join the mix. There is also a congregation of HICs in the Middle East. Conversely, Latin America remains dominated by MICs, except for some small island states in the region, and Africa is primarily low income, although there is an increasing number of MICs in Africa as well. This is not to claim that geography is destiny. After all, Australia and New Zealand were also early HICs. Nevertheless, there are likely to be regional effects that are worth exploring in more detail, including the impact of intraregional trade and the types of epistemic

13 Ibid.

14 Another possibility is that MICs are not so much trapped as floundering – they are willing to change and trying to change but what they are doing just isn't working, or enough, to get them to the next stage.

networks and learning processes explored by John Gillespie (Chapter 6). East Asian countries, for instance, clearly learned from Japan and each other, and followed a different development model than early or more recent risers in Europe. The success of several Middle East countries may be attributable to oil. But many countries have failed to leverage rich natural resources to climb the ladder to HICs. It is certainly more likely that Middle East HICs learned as much if not more from each other than from the radically different development paths of either European or Asian countries. The sources of regional clustering in institutional design are not totally clear, and cannot be exclusively attributed to colonial legacies.

Second, to return to a dominant theme, HICs generally do much better in terms of good governance and rule of law than MICs and LICs. Whether wealth leads to better institutions, or vice versa, or both, development is associated with institutional capacity, and institutions become more efficient and effective at delivering the kinds of services expected by businesses and citizens alike. Longevity and literacy also rise, reflecting investments in human capital, the medical system, and a social safety net. Environmental pollution abates as a result of shifting social priorities, higher institutional capacity for enforcement agencies, and investment in new, cleaner technologies. Those MICs that fail to invest in human capital and new technologies or to upgrade governance institutions are likely to find themselves trapped.

Third, MICs also face rising inequality. Although some HICs including the United States, Singapore, and Qatar have relatively high levels of inequality, in general inequality is lower in HICs than in MICs.[15] The economist Joseph Stiglitz argues that countries that reduce income inequality produce higher levels of growth at every level of development.[16] Inequality also has negative consequences for the quality of democracy. At some point, the pursuit of aggregate growth must give way to a more equitable development and a higher-quality sustainable growth.

Fourth, and perhaps most importantly, today's HICs all had to overcome a series of difficult challenges, external shocks, and political-economic barriers along the way. To do so required not just political will but also flexibility. East Asian countries in particular are known for their nonideological, pragmatic approach to reforms. MIC governments must be adaptive and responsive. They must also be willing to take stock of local conditions, adapt international standards to fit their circumstances, and develop their own strategies for development. As Bojan Bugaric (Chapter 8) concludes in assessing both the failures and the more recent successes in CEE countries, "there is no development without an indigenously created developmental strategy by developing countries."

[15] See Appendix, and Peerenboom, *China Modernizes*, 50.

[16] Joseph Stiglitz, *The Price of Inequality* (W. W. Norton and Company, 2012)

WHY HAVE EAST ASIAN STATES BEEN SO SUCCESSFUL, AND DOES THE RECENT SUCCESS OF CENTRAL AND EASTERN EUROPEAN STATES PROVIDE AN ALTERNATIVE MODEL?

In the 1970s many Latin American countries were at least as wealthy, and enjoyed comparable or higher growth rates, to East Asian countries. But now Japan, Singapore, South Korea, Hong Kong, and Taiwan are all HICs. What explains their surprising success? Many attribute their meteoric rise to the developmental state (Surain Subramaniam, Chapter 3) or more broadly to the East Asian Model (EAM). The EAM model involves the sequencing of economic growth, legal reforms, democratization, and constitutionalism, with different rights being taken seriously at different times in the process. More specifically, the EAM involves:[17]

(i) an emphasis on economic growth rather than civil and especially political rights during the initial stages of development, with a period of rapid economic growth occurring under authoritarian regimes;
(ii) a pragmatic approach to reforms, with governments following some aspects of the Washington Consensus and rejecting or modifying others; in particular, with governments adopting most of the basic macroeconomic principles of the Washington Consensus for the domestic economy; rejecting or modifying the neoliberal aspects that would greatly reduce the role of the state through rapid privatization and deregulation, with the state also more active in reducing poverty and in ensuring minimal material standards to compete in a more competitive global economy; and modifying the prescribed Washington Consensus relationship between the domestic and global economy by gradually exposing the domestic economy to international competition while offering some protection to key sectors and some support to infant industries;
(iii) as the economy grows and wealth is generated, the government invests in human capital and institutions, including reforms to establish a legal system that meets the basic requirements of a procedural rule of law; over time, as the legal system becomes more efficient, professional and autonomous, it comes to play a greater role in the economy and society more generally;
(iii) democratization in the sense of freely contested multiple party elections for the highest level of office is postponed until a relatively high level of wealth is attained;
(iv) constitutionalism begins to emerge during the authoritarian period, including the development of constitutional norms and the strengthening of institutions; social organizations start to proliferate and "civil society" begins to develop, albeit often a civil society with a different nature and political orientation than in Western liberal democracies, and with organizations

[17] Peerenboom, *China Modernizes*, 31–2.

with a political agenda subject to limitations; citizens enjoy economic liberties, rising living standards for the vast majority, and some civil and political rights although with limitations especially on rights that involve political issues and affect the control of the regime; judicial independence remains limited, with the protection of the full range of human rights and in particular civil and political rights suffering accordingly;

(v) there is greater protection of civil and political rights after democratization, including rights that involve sensitive political issues, although with ongoing abuses of rights in some cases and with rights frequently given a communitarian or collectivist interpretation rather than a liberal interpretation.

This very roughly describes the arc of several Asian states, including MICs such as China and Vietnam, albeit with countries at various levels of economic wealth and legal system development, and with political regimes ranging from democracies to semidemocracies to socialist states.

CEE provides an interesting contrast to China and the EAM of development. In CEE, political reforms proceeded economic reforms, or occurred rapidly with democratization; in general, economic reforms reflected a neoliberal, "big bang" approach rather the pragmatic, gradualist approach of China and other East Asian states; after democratization, there was rapid dismantling or modification of socialist institutions and their replacement, or attempted replacement, by liberal democratic ones; and whereas the regional effects for China and Vietnam pushed in the direction of the EAM, Eastern European countries were significantly influenced by the EU accession process, including efforts to establish a rule of law modeled on the legal systems found in European HICs.

So, which path is best? At least until recently, the big bang approach has generally been considered to be less successful than the gradual approach of China and other East Asian states. The initial result of the big bang approach was much lower GDP per capita, increased poverty, rising inequality, a decline in life expectancy of up to six years, and higher rates of social alienation, depression, and alcoholism. Whereas in 1988, only 2 percent of the population in the socialist countries of Europe lived in absolute poverty, ten years later more than 20 percent did, with the rapid transition estimated to have led to between three and ten million premature deaths.[18]

By the mid-1990s, however, many CEE economies had regained lost ground. During the next decade, the region outperformed Latin America by a vast margin, although growth rates and GDP per capita still lagged East Asia.[19]

[18] Jan Drahokoupil and Martin Myant, "The Political Economy of Welfare Reforms in Eastern Europe and Central Asia," 2009, available at http://ssrn.com/abstract=1396736.

[19] Mody, et al. argue in favor of the more open model recently adopted in Eastern Europe, including financial sector liberalization, in contrast to the EAM, with more gradual financial liberalization. However, East Asian countries have weathered the global crisis much better than Eastern Europe and Latin American countries. Although most countries in Latin America and Eastern Europe experienced deep recessions, the downturn was less severe, and the recovery quicker, in Latin America. Ashoka

Accordingly, the economic and governance data is now more mixed. While many CEE countries are now HICs, compared to MIC China, high-income CEE countries have yet to catch up to the income levels of Japan, Singapore, Hong Kong, Taiwan, and South Korea. Moreover, in keeping with the general correlation of wealth, HICs, whether in Asia or CEE, outperform MICs on most governance indicators. Thus, CEE HICs generally outperform China on most governance indicators, but fall short in comparison to the high-income Asian Tigers on the same indicators. Even more worryingly, not only do CEE countries face many governance challenges, as Bugaric notes, in some respects there is evidence of reversals and a growing antidemocratic trend.

To be sure, Asian countries face their own challenges. There is an emerging consensus that although the EAM is useful during the catch-up phase, it is not so effective later. This view draws support from the "lost decade" in Japan during the 1990s, the diminished role for technocrat administrators in the new economy, and the many legal and political reforms that have occurred in Japan and Korea. In both countries, there has been deregulation and greater reliance on market forces, as well as a shift in the nature of regulation toward heavier reliance on "new governance" regulatory mechanisms that provide a greater role to consumer advocates, nongovernmental organizations, lawyers, prudential regulators, and shareholder activists.[20] As Subrahainam points out, Malaysia's development has been hindered by the inability to deal with the political economy issue of ethnic quotas for Malays, while the ruling People's Action Party in Singapore is now facing greater pressure for political liberalization. Moreover, there are serious doubts in the wake of the financial crisis about whether emerging MICs, particularly large ones, will be able to pursue the EAM, maintaining access to robust economies in developed countries while being allowed to suppress the value of their currencies to promote exports.

Of particular interest is China, where growth has slowed from double digits to close to 7 percent, although some economists argue the growth rate is much lower. Economists are divided about whether growth is likely to continue in the 6–8 percent range, and if so for how long, or slow to 3–4 percent or even less at some

Mody, et al., "The Second Transition: Eastern Europe in Perspective," IMF Working Papers, 2009, 1–33, available at http://ssrn.com/abstract=1366173. Herrero, et al. attribute the better performance of Latin America to improved economic policies which "played a significant role in containing macro-financial vulnerabilities before the crisis.... The authorities had learned the lessons from past crises and paid substantial policy and regulatory attention to signs of excessive short term capital flows, credit booms and the formation of potential asset price bubbles." In contrast, Eastern Europe was subject to financial vulnerabilities as a result of growth policies in which "large capital inflows and rapid credit growth were perceived as manageable and supportive to the catching-up process, while downside risks were seen as being contained." Gallego Herrero, et al., "The Impact of the Global Economic and Financial Crisis on Central Eastern and Southeastern Europe (CESEE) and Latin America," Banco de Espana Occasional Paper No. 1002, 2010, available at http://ssrn.com/abstract=1635773.

20 For Japan, see Veronica Taylor, "Globalization and Japanese Regulation," in *Regulation in Asia: Pushing Back on Globalization*, ed. John Gillespie and Randall Peerenboom (Routledge, 2009), 226–56.

point.[21] A 2012 World Bank report, written with significant participation from Development Research Center of the State Council, emphasized that China is now in danger of falling into the middle-income trap as wages have increased and China has reached the limits of gains from the exploitation of foreign technologies. To avoid the trap, new growth drivers are required, including "increased efficiency in input use, higher human capital investments, increased innovation, and a shift to high-value services."[22] The report lays out six strategic directions for China's future:

- Completing the transition to a market economy;
- Accelerating the pace of open innovation;
- Going "green" to transform environmental stresses into green growth as a driver for development;
- Expanding opportunities and services such as health, education and access to jobs for all people;
- Modernizing and strengthening its domestic fiscal system;
- Seeking mutually beneficial relations with the world by connecting China's structural reforms to the changing international economy.

Equally important, the report envisages a fundamental change in the role of government:

> It is imperative that China adjusts its development strategy as it embarks on its next phase of economic growth. At its core, this adjustment requires changing the role of government and its relations with the market, the private sector, and society at large. While the government needs to withdraw from direct involvement in production, distribution, and resource allocation, it will need to focus greater attention on designing and implementing the policy and regulatory framework that empowers others to participate in economic decision making so that the desired outcome of rapid, inclusive, and sustainable growth is achieved. To play this role, the government will need to transform itself into a lean, clean, transparent, and highly efficient modern government that operates under the rule of law. In redefining its role, the government will need to accelerate reforms in the state-owned sector and combine it with further development of the private sector. It will also need to advance reforms in factor markets (capital, land, and labor) to help strengthen the foundations of a market economy and promote greater competition and innovation. At the same time, society's role will need to change significantly, with the middle class becoming a major force in promoting harmonious development through greater participation of the people in the development process.[23]

21 For a more bullish view, see Nicholas Lardy. For a bearish view, see Michael Pettis, "Lardy v. Pettis: Debating China's Economic Future," November 2, 2012, available at http://blogs.wsj.com/chinarealtime/2012/11/02/lardy-vs-pettis-debating-chinas-economic-future/; "Lardy v. Pettis: Debating China's Future, Round 2," November 7, 2012, available at http://blogs.wsj.com/chinarealtime/2012/11/07/lardy-vs-pettis-debating-chinas-economic-future-round-2/.

22 World Bank, *China 2030*, 11.

23 Ibid., 18.

Three points merit comment. First, the new role for government is very similar to that advocated by Bugaric for CEE countries as part of the New Developmental State, albeit approached from the other direction: that is, in China, the problem has been too visible a hand and too much government intervention, while in the neoliberal-driven CEE the problem has been an invisible hand and too little government intervention. This suggests that there may be some convergence on a Post Washington Consensus (PWC).[24]

Second, these changes, while simple to state, are politically very difficult to implement. There continue to be ongoing debates about these basic principles and the direction of the economy in China, with some groups steadfastly opposing the rebalancing of the economy away from state-investment and export-led growth toward a more consumption-oriented economy with a greater role for the private sector and small and medium enterprises. Moreover, there will be even more disagreement when it comes time to develop specific policies to flesh out and implement these broad principles. As the report notes, "the close links between the government, big banks, and state enterprises have created vested interests that inhibit reforms and contribute to continued ad hoc state interventions in the economy."[25] There are many with reason to oppose many of the reforms considered essential if China is to avoid the middle-income trap: the large state-owned banks that have benefitted from restrictions on foreign competition; the large state-owned enterprises that have benefitted from subsidized energy and electricity, easier access to loans and the security markets, and preferential policies that aim to create domestic champions to compete with foreign multinational companies; the princelings, that is the offspring and relatives of top party and government officials, who have been granted oligopolies in key sectors such as telecommunications, mining, and energy production; and the provinces in the eastern region that have benefitted from preferential tax and investment policies and the buildup of new infrastructure. Once again, the ability to overcome vested interests and political economy obstacles is likely to determine success or failure.[26]

24 The global financial crisis, particularly the crisis in the Eurozone, led to conflicting views in HICs between those who favored austerity and believed the most pressing task was to rein in debt, and those who believed that the immediate task was to stimulate the economy and get people back to work, with the debt problem to be dealt with later. While the jury remains out on what will happen in Europe, the victory of Obama over Romney suggests that most Americans favored the latter approach. Obama also ran on an economic platform that was much closer to the PWC, with the government playing a more active role in sponsoring research and development, supporting new technologies and infant industries, and coordinating long-term development projects between the state, private sector, and academic institutions. In contrast, Romney favored a neoliberal agenda of tax cuts, a roll back on entitlements, and a minimalist role for the state.

25 World Bank, *China 2030*, 18.

26 Michael Pettis argues that China must rebalance the economy in the next few years, shifting from investment-driven, export-led model that suppressed consumption to a more consumption-based economy in which household income and wealth become a larger share of the GDP. The only questions are when and how. He sketches five possible scenarios:

Third, the report implicitly endorses a strong version of modernization theory: economic growth leads to a rising middle class that will demand greater political freedom and participation, more transparency, and the rule of law. East Asia generally lends support to that model, with two caveats: the transition to democracy has occurred at much higher levels of wealth in East Asia than other countries; and, even after democratizing, East Asian states remain less liberal than their counterparts in Euro-America. However, development patterns in other regions have cast doubt on modernization theory. In Latin America, South Asia, and elsewhere, many countries democratized at low levels of wealth, while in the Middle East, at least until recently, economic growth has produced high levels of wealth but limited political reform.

To sum up, there is no simple answer to whether the EAM or CEE approach is best. Much depends on the time frame for assessment. It may very well be too early to deliver a final assessment. Much will depend on what happens in China and CEE in the coming decades. Moreover, the assessment also depends on contested normative assumptions. The big bang in the CCE undeniably caused a great deal of pain. By contrast, many would reject the East Asian trade-off of limits on political freedoms for high growth with improved standards of living.

Nor is the question necessarily a useful one. For China, CEE countries, and other MICs, it is never a matter of choosing carte blanche from a menu of options. CEE countries had little choice but to engage in across-the-board reforms when the Soviet Union disintegrated in such an unexpected and dramatic fashion. China was able to proceed at a more measured pace because the CCP remained in power, and perhaps more importantly, China had the benefit of several millennia of a highly centralized, reasonably meritocratic, and relatively technocratic bureaucracy, which made state direction of the economy a more feasible option. Conversely, CEE countries have had other advantages: they started at a higher level of wealth than China, were

1. Beijing can slowly reverse the transfers from households to the state, for example by gradually raising real interest rates, the foreign exchange value of the currency, and wages, or by lowering income and consumption taxes.
2. Beijing can quickly reverse the transfers in the same way.
3. Beijing can directly transfer wealth from the state sector to the private sector by privatizing assets and using the proceeds directly or indirectly to boost household wealth.
4. Beijing can transfer wealth from the state sector to the private sector by absorbing private sector debt.
5. Beijing can cut investment sharply, resulting in a collapse in growth, but it can mitigate the employment impact of this collapse by hiring unemployed workers for various make-work programs and paying their salaries out of state resources.

Which path is taken, and whether China comes crashing back to earth after decades of high growth or manages a soft landing, depends on overcoming entrenched interests. As he notes, all options accomplish the same end of decreasing the state share of GDP and increasing the household share, but their impact on the household and state sector differs. He then considers the political economy obstacles to each option, and who wins and loses as a result, although he points out that some combination of the various options is possible. Michael Pettis, "The Ways China Can Rebalance," April 9, 2012, available at http://www.mpettis.com/2012/04/09/the-ways-china-can-rebalance/.

more industrialized, and benefited from financial and technical assistance from Western Europe and the proximity of European markets. In short, each region had idiosyncratic elements.

MICs may learn from both China and CEE. But they will not be able to slavishly follow their paths because they all have different endowments and starting conditions. The experience of East Asian and CEE countries demonstrates that market forces alone are insufficient to ensure growth. As the PWC suggests, the government has a role in setting policies, coordinating investment, developing regulatory structures, and enhancing institutional capacity. But the precise nature of that role depends much on local circumstances, and requires a government that is pragmatic rather than dogmatic, leadership that is committed to reform, and policy makers who are flexible and willing to experiment. Feedback mechanisms that help identify which reforms work and which do not are of crucial importance.

WHAT IS THE RELATIONSHIP BETWEEN POLITICS, OR THE POLITICAL ECONOMY, AND DEVELOPMENT IN MIDDLE-INCOME COUNTRIES?

Empirical studies demonstrate that regime type alone is a poor predictor of economic success.[27] Moreover, while rule of law and democracy tend to be mutually reinforcing,[28] good governance and rule of law need not necessarily march in lockstep with democracy. In Asia and the Middle East several of the legal systems that score highest in terms of good governance and rule of law are not democracies or are illiberal democracies. Within Asia, Hong Kong and Singapore and, within Arab countries, Oman, Qatar, Bahrain, Kuwait, and the United Arab Emirates are in

[27] For yet another overview piece that reaches this conclusion, see Daniel Kaufmann, "On Democracy and Development: Rejecting the Extremes," June 2008, available at http://www.america.gov/st/democracy-english/2008/June/20080605094537ebyessedoo.3466913.html. As with most of these studies, Kaufmann does not attempt to sort by levels of wealth but simply provides aggregates. Not surprisingly, he finds that "in the long term," freedom of expression and other civil and political rights (aggregated in the "voice and accountability" variable) are correlated with higher levels of development. Richer countries tend to be democratic and more liberal. Another study found that the long-term causality is from income to democracy. However, the political system can become a drag on the economy and thus in some cases democratization may stimulate growth, although usually with a significant time lag. Conversely, however, there may be a poor fit between democracy and economic, political, and cultural traditions, which will also impede development. Thus they conclude that imposing "high-income style democracy" on some countries is unlikely to succeed. Marin Paldam and Erich Gundlach, "The Democratic Transition: A Study of the Causality between Income and the Gastil Democracy Index," October 21, 2008, available at http://ssrn.com/abstract=1287582. While Rodrik did not find evidence that democracy promotes growth, he did find that democracies have more predictable growth rates and economic performance, handle adverse shocks better, pay higher wages, and deliver better distributional outcomes. However, as the success of East Asian states on these issues shows, much depends on the nature of the authoritarian regime. Dani Rodrik, *One Economics, Many Recipes* (Princeton University Press, 2007).

[28] Rigobon and Rodrik found that greater rule of law produces more democracy and vice versa but the effects are not strong. Roberto Rigobon and Dani Rodrik, "Rule of Law, Democracy, Openness, and Income: Estimating the Interrelationships," *Economics of Transition* 13 (2005): 533.

the top quartile on the World Bank rule-of-law index but have a 0 to 2 ranking on the 0–10 point Polity IV Index. Conversely, just as nondemocracies may have strong legal systems, democracies may have legal systems that fall far short of rule of law. Guatemala, Kenya, and Papua New Guinea, for example, all score (or recently scored) highly on democracy (8–10 on the Polity IV Index) and yet poorly on rule of law (below the 25th percentile on World Bank rule-of-law index). Moreover, as the example of Kenya shows, having a high score on the democracy scale does not mean that the country is well governed or politically stable.

The emphasis on regime type in political science has hindered the development of a useful research agenda that begins with a nonideological, pragmatic assessment of the actual political, governance, and legal problems in the country. There is a need to distinguish among different types of democratic regimes and different types of authoritarian regimes; evaluate them objectively and fairly across a wide range of indicators; and then draw lessons why some fail and some succeed.[29] This is beginning to happen, as evidenced in the shift in focus from the consolidation of democracy to the quality of democracy, and the booming literature on varieties of authoritarianism.[30]

Not surprisingly, successful democratic regimes and successful authoritarian regimes tend to share certain features. They adopt market economies; invest in human capital and institutions; develop mechanisms for sharing power and peacefully transferring power from one generation to the next; and limit military involvement in politics. Arguably, authoritarian regimes are better suited to lower levels of development because they can force through tough economic decisions and maintain social stability, albeit by restricting civil and political rights, during a volatile period when resources are insufficient to satisfy rising citizen demands and institutions are weak. In contrast, democracies are more subject to public and interest group pressures, and less able to repress without undermining the legitimacy of, and support for, the regime. However, as society becomes more pluralistic and the market economy develops, some decisions are arguably better made by a more democratic and open process. Furthermore, maintaining flows of accurate information, essential for feedback loops to guide policy, can be a challenge for

[29] Much of the support for democracy in empirical studies results from (1) classifying illiberal democracies or failed states as authoritarian or nondemocratic states and counting only consolidated or high-scoring democracies as democracies; (2) failing to distinguish between different types of authoritarian regimes; (3) including high-income democracies or excluding high-income authoritarian regimes; and (4) failing to sort by levels of wealth. As a result, they shed little light on the implications for development of authoritarian regimes following the EAM.

[30] See David Epstein, et al., "Democratic Transitions," *American Journal of Political Science* 50 (2006): 551–69, (classifying countries into autocracies, democracies, and partial democracies, they find that higher incomes per capita significantly increased the likelihood of both the transition to and the consolidation of democracy, thus supporting the modernization thesis); Steven Levitsky and Lucan Way, *Competitive Authoritarianism: Hybrid Regimes after the Cold War* (Cambridge University Press, 2010).

authoritarians. Thus, much will depend on the particular conditions of each country, and the particular types of issues they face.

To be sure, different regime types may give rise to different paths or approaches to resolving some of these issues. As Ginsburg notes, both democratic and authoritarian MICs can fall into a legal middle-income trap. But how they get out of it differs:

> In democracies, the central condition for judicial empowerment is sufficient political uncertainty that various forces believe they may be out of power in a future period. In such an instance, all will prefer to have a set of independent courts that can protect their policies from reversal and persons from retaliation. In the authoritarian path, the ruling regime decides to invest in neutral, insulated judicial (and bureaucratic) institutions for a variety of reasons, economic growth being one of the most prominent. By insulating property from expropriation, and economic activity from arbitrary action, authoritarian empowerment of insulated courts can facilitate growth.

Despite different pathways, most reform recommendations would be the same for democratic and authoritarian regimes. These would include efforts to strengthen rule of law; foster good governance; combat corruption; increase transparency and accountability; promote access to information and justice; reduce poverty and support education; increase the capacity and role of civil society; carry out banking system and tax reforms; adopt sound macroeconomic policies; and so on. In the end, the main obstacles to reform are political economy obstacles. The countries that succeed are the ones that are able to overcome entrenched interests to implement reforms that strengthen institutions and enhance the public good.

HOW HAVE MIDDLE-INCOME COUNTRIES BEEN INFLUENCED BY AND ADAPTED TO THE NEW INTERNATIONAL ECONOMIC ORDER?

We are witnessing a tectonic shift in the global economic order, with the global GDP share of Euro-America falling and the share of MICs, particularly China and the other larger MICs, rising. The "rise of the rest" will require, and be reflected in, a change in existing institutions and how they operate, as well as the creation of new institutions. Gregory Shaffer and Charles Sutton's chapter (Chapter 4) documents the impact of larger MICs on the WTO. They attribute the failure of the Doha Round in part to the rise of Brazil, Russia, India, China, and South Africa (the BRICS). They emphasize that the G20's proposed framework for agricultural negotiations was a critical step in that it "set forth proactive demands and an alternative framework for negotiations, rather than limiting itself to blocking the U.S.-EU proposal." Some of the larger MICs have also been more aggressive in using the WTO to settle disputes with HICs. They have overcome limits in knowledge and resources. MICs are now able to create their own transnational networks; acquire and provide technical assistance; do the necessary research and run sophisticated economic models to determine policy positions; and share expertise. Similarly, Peter Yu's chapter (Chapter 5) highlights the growing importance of MIPPs and their potential impact across a range of controversial IP issues.

However, there are doubts whether MICs will form a stable voting bloc. First, large and rapidly growing MICs share much in common with HICs – if all goes according to plan, they will soon be HICs. Accordingly, they often side with HICs on many development issues.

Second, MICs are divided among themselves: they are often economic competitors, have different competitive advantages, and have conflicting interests reflected in different policy goals. As Shaffer and Sutton note:

> So far Brazil and India have downplayed economic challenges rising from China as part of their political commitment to the BRIC bloc and G20 in order to present a unified front in multilateral economic policy against the United States and EU. Yet there are very real economic conflicts. For example, one of the biggest concerns of Brazil in the last years is the lack of competitiveness of Brazilian manufacturing goods in light of the appreciation of the Brazilian real against the Chinese renminbi. In 2011, Brazil called for the WTO Working Group on Trade, Debt and Finance to organize meetings to discuss the challenges and implications of currency misalignments. The Brazilian leadership has publicly critiqued the "quantitative easing" of the United States as of great concern, but it is generally known that Brazilian industry pressures the government because of cheap Chinese goods, facilitated by the undervaluation of China's currency and China's massive interventions in the currency markets. The BRICS have so far been able to manage these tensions in public, but the underlying pressure will remain.

At the moment, the alliance appears to be holding, but shaky. No BRICS country has brought a WTO suit against another BRICS country since 2001. There have been surprisingly few suits by MICs against China, given China's role in the global economy and the number of suits by HICs against China. And there has been only a modest increase in the number of claims by one MIC against another. However, tensions have been evident in the wake of the financial crisis in an increase in protectionism in MICs, with China hardest hit.

In the IP area, Yu argues that MIPP positions are internally incoherent and inconsistent, and predicts that there will be convergence and divergence, depending on issue areas. In summarizing possible outcomes, he suggests the relation among MIPPs could be that of bonded siblings or rival siblings; the relationship between MIPPs and HICs could be convergence on goals, and thus one big happy family, or divergence, and thus a feuding family; while MIPPs could either become the big brother of smaller MICs or the new bullies.

There is no doubt that the rise of MICs has produced considerable "system friction" in the multilateral global trade regime, and contributed to increased reliance on regional and bilateral agreements. Shaffer and Sutton argue that while there are many potential benefits to MICs to such agreements, larger MICs are likely to benefit more than smaller MICs. Smaller MICs may be able to piggyback on some of the work of their larger MIC counterparts in using the WTO settlement process or in multilateral agreements, but they will need to take care that they do not end up being bullied by their big brothers when negotiating regional and bilateral agreements.

WHAT APPROACHES ARE AVAILABLE TO MIDDLE-INCOME COUNTRIES TO ADDRESS PRESSING SOCIOECONOMIC ISSUES?

MICs face a series of pressing socioeconomic issues from education to health care to labor rights to the environment. MICs must decide how to allocate responsibility for providing social welfare among government, the private sector, nongovernmental organizations (NGOs) and social organizations, and individuals and families. They must also decide whether to funnel disputes and grievances to political, administrative, or judicial channels. The rule-of-law promotion industry has pushed a court-centric dispute-resolution model, and human rights organizations including the Committee on Economic, Social and Cultural Rights have encouraged the judicialization of economic and social rights (ESR) cases.

Supporters of a judicialization point to a number of positive benefits: (1) the provision of a safety value for disgruntled citizens to channel their anger in a peaceful way; (2) an increase in social justice, the provision of some relief to the socially disadvantaged, and a closer relationship between the judiciary and the socially vulnerable; (3) an increase in the stature and legitimacy of the judiciary; (4) an expansion of the jurisprudence of fundamental rights, and the creation of new rights; (5) the promotion of good governance and rule of law; (6) the filling of gaps in the legislative framework and the stimulation of new legislation by the legislature; (7) the facilitation of a dialogue between the judiciary and other state organs; and (8) the creation of another venue for democratic deliberation, arguably one less affected by the interest group bargaining that typically prevails in legislatures.[31]

Critics, however, argue that (1) the courts lack the competence to handle disputes over ESR;[32] (2) judicializing ESR leads to separation of power issues, an overly activist judiciary, and tyranny by unelected "men in robes"; (3) courts will decide

[31] Surya Deva, "Public Interest Litigation in India: A Critical Review," *Civil Justice Quarterly* 28 (2009): 19–40.

[32] Nolan, et al. provide a useful breakdown, and point-by-point refutation, of competency concerns: "(i) the courts lack the information required to deal with social and economic rights; (ii) the judiciary lacks the necessary expertise, qualification or experience to deal with social and economic rights issues; (iii) the courts are incapable of dealing successfully with 'polycentric' tasks, such as those entailed by adjudication involving social and economic rights; and (iv) the courts lack the necessary tools and remedies to deal effectively with social and economic rights." Aoife Nolan, et al., "The Justiciability of Social and Economic Rights: An Updated Appraisal," CHRGJ Working Paper No. 15, 2009, available at http://ssrn.com/abstract=1434944.

cases without due consideration of their cost and bankrupt the state; (4) conversely, courts will not be able to provide effective and enforceable remedies that satisfy the legitimate claims of citizens; (5) conservative judiciaries or judiciaries captured by powerful political and economic interests will decide cases in ways that benefit the rich and middle class rather than the poor and socially vulnerable; and (6) the emphasis on litigation detracts from the need for social movements and structural reforms.[33]

Proponents and opponents of judicialization of ESRs can each point to evidence in support of their positions. The many controversies that have arisen suggest that courts should adopt a cautious and collaborative approach. There is a risk of judicial overreaching and excessive judicial activism, with negative consequences for individual plaintiffs and the judiciary alike. Remedies that lack popular support or are too costly are likely to be underenforced. Overly ambitious judicial decisions may invite a backlash against the judiciary, and undermine support for judicial reforms, including more independence and decision-making power for the courts. China and Colombia, for instance, have witnessed efforts to dejudicialize ESR cases.[34]

Nevertheless, the ever-accumulating body of experience with domestic courts implementing ESR demonstrates that the preceding concerns need not preclude some constructive role for domestic courts in implementing ESR.[35] The courts have the ability to mitigate the risks by adopting a restrained approach and carefully selecting their remedies. The key is to adopt a cautious and collaborative approach along the lines of the dialogic approach discussed by Daniel Brinks and William Forbath and Rodríguez-Garavito in their chapters (Chapters 11 and 12). Similarly, courts should explore opportunities to develop enforcement alliances with other government branches, administrative agencies, and private-sector organizations, as discussed by van Rooij and McCallister (Chapter 14).

MIC governments should experiment with political, administrative, and public-private mechanisms for dealing with socioeconomic issues and resolving disputes. In the end, many problems are economic in nature, and require sustained growth to resolve. Even then there will be debates about how best to proceed, as there are in HICs. Along the way, MICs need to explore various mechanisms and assess their

33 See, generally, Deva, "Public Interest Litigation in India"; Raju Ramachandran, "The Supreme Court and the Basic Structure Doctrine," in *Supreme but Not Infallible*, ed. B. N. Kirpal, et al. (Oxford University Press, 2000), 107, ("unelected judges have assumed vast political power not given to them by the Constitution"); Brinks and Forbath, Chapter 11 in this volume.

34 For Colombia, see Rodríguez-Garavito, Chapter 12. For China, see Randall Peerenboom, "More Law, Less Courts: Legalized Governance, Judicialization and Dejudicialization in China," in *Administrative Law and Governance in Asia*, ed. Tom Ginsburg and Albert Chen (RoutledgeCurzon, 2008), 175–202.

35 Even in countries where courts have limited authority and confront a challenging political environment, there are opportunities for courts to play a positive role in addressing ESR. See Randall Peerenboom, "Economic and Social Rights: The Role of Courts in China," *San Diego International Law Review* 12 (2011): 303–25 (comparing the much less favorable environment in China to that in South Africa).

advantages and disadvantages in the particular context, much as van Rooij and McCallister have done in examining the five different mechanisms adopted to enhance environmental in China, Indonesia, Mexico, and Brazil.

WHAT LESSONS ARE THERE FOR POLICY MAKERS AND DEVELOPMENT AGENCIES IN PROMOTING RULE OF LAW AND GOVERNANCE IN MIDDLE-INCOME COUNTRIES?

The individual chapters contain many detailed lessons for policy makers seeking to avoid the various middle-income traps, improve governance, and implement rule of law. In many cases, the lessons will be highly context specific. Here we highlight several key themes of general applicability to MICs. Some of the themes are well-known to those who study law and development, and hold true for efforts to promote rule of law in LICs as well as MICs. Others are if not specific to MICs, more crucial in MICs.

First, rather than a single model of development, there are various paths to HIC status, and wide institutional variance among MICs and HICs. Different regions, and countries within these regions, are likely to pursue different paths. Countries will need to adopt models that fit their general circumstances, and then adapt them further to meet their specific needs. In Europe, EU accession requirements will ensure that states continue to follow the Euro-American model of markets + democracy + liberal civil and political rights. In Arab states and Russia, where resource-dependent growth has stymied political reforms by allowing leaders to buy off the populace in exchange for rising living standards, escaping the "natural resources curse" will require a more diversified economy, with broader investment in human capital and institutions, and deep political reforms. Turkey and Indonesia may become modern democracies in which Islam, rather than secular liberalism, shapes the national identity. In Latin America, some states are likely to continue to embrace populism because of ethnic and demographic patterns, a history of widespread inequality, and the temptation of quick fixes made possible by the availability of revenues from the sale of oil and other natural resources. The vast majority of Latin American states, however, are likely to continue on their winding path to become consolidated democracies, led in many cases by pragmatic, moderate, or center-left parties, though left-right vacillations are still likely in some cases. In any event, most Latin America countries must overcome the historical legacies of colonialism, slavery, and commodity-dependent economies that have led to a high concentration of economic and political power and some of the world's highest levels of inequality, while hindering the state investment in poverty reduction, education, infrastructure, and institutions that provided the foundation for more sustainable growth in East Asia.[36]

[36] See, generally, Michael Reid, *Forgotten Continent: The Battle for Latin America's Soul* (Yale University Press, 2007); Francis Fukuyama, ed., *Falling Behind: Explaining the Development Gap between Latin America and the United States* (Oxford University Press, 2008).

Second, successful MIC governments tend to be pragmatic rather than dogmatic. Ideologically driven development agendas tend to fail, whether the right-leaning neoliberal Washington Consensus or radical left populism. Policy makers should be wary about the latest magic bullet on offer, whether the PWC, New Development State, EAM, or Beijing Consensus.

Third, and related, successful MIC governments are those most willing to experiment free from ideology and the latest consensus in the development community. While much of the policy advice of international donor agencies focuses on content, successful MICs such as China have put methodology first. Much of the success of China can be attributed to the approach of "feeling the stones as you cross the river": that is, the multistage methodology of theoretical and empirical analysis of the problem; followed by debate over various policy options, with input from non-government experts, academics, and increasingly citizens; semicontrolled testing of various policy options in different localities; close monitoring of results; local benchmarking, or the identifying of the best results for the particular circumstances of China; and then the ramping up to national scale of promising experiments, often with policies that acknowledge and accommodate local differences and provide local officials the discretion and incentives to adapt national policies.

Fourth, successful MIC governments need to overcome many political-economy obstacles. To do that, they need to prioritize reforms based on a political as well as economic cost-benefit analysis of which reforms are easiest or, if difficult, likely to deliver the biggest impact. There will not be many quick wins left at this stage. Reforms will encounter resistance from state organs, market actors, and citizens. Given the many challenges, policy makers need to develop, coordinate, and continually adjust short-term, medium-term, and long-term plans with an eye to addressing the structural issues required to lay a foundation for sustainable growth.

Fifth, successful MICs require strong, flexible, and proactive leadership. Strong leadership will be necessary to forge the alliances required to overcome resistance from entrenched interest groups. Flexibility is essential as new challenges, internal and external, arise constantly. Governments that are nimble and quick to adjust in light of global crises or when policies fail to deliver the expected results are the ones that come on top. Those that hesitate miss the opportunity and fall behind. All too often governments, whether in LICs, MICs, or HICs, are too reactive rather than proactive. They are able to muster the political will to undertake the structural changes needed to get ahead only when forced to do so by crises. Internal or external shocks may provide the incentive to break through barriers, but, as the World Bank report on China observes, government then often adopts policies without adequate reflection. Policy makers with their backs to the wall may also have to choose from a more limited range of options that are less than optimal. Moreover, if reforms are delayed, the costs in the end may be much higher.

Most importantly, and related to the need for strong leadership, MIC governments must seize control over their own destiny. They must not let major powers and international development agencies set the agenda. Major powers have their own interests, are inevitably biased to some extent by their own histories and experiences, and generally have limited knowledge of the situation in other countries.[37] International agencies may offer good advice, but their knowledge of local affairs is also likely to be limited. In addition, they face their own institutional restraints and limitations, which have been much discussed in analyzing the poor results of rule-of-law promotion efforts to date.[38]

Finally, MIC governments should remember that at the end of the day, to use a popular phrase from American political campaigns, "it's the economy, stupid." What separates MICs from HICs is wealth! The only way MICs are ever going to join the ranks of HICs is by growing the economy. There is a reason that so much of the development literature is by economists. Nevertheless, it is *not only* the economy, as the U.S. election results also demonstrate. MICs must strive for sustainable high-quality growth. They must strengthen governance institutions, build up social welfare systems and meet the demands of citizens for a higher-quality life.

These lessons for MIC governments necessarily entail a different approach on the part of international development agencies in dealing with MICs. It is now clear from decades of failed law and development projects that MICs cannot simply transplant or mimic the institutions, rules, and practices of HICs. Exhorting developing countries to adopt international best practices is like telling a ten-year-old with a stick in his hand for a golf club and rock for a ball that if he wants to win the Masters he should watch Tiger Woods videos. MICs will need to get by with second-best solutions and "good enough" institutions.[39] International agencies will need to research which institutions work at lower levels of wealth and develop a menu of LIC and MIC options. These options will need to be cost-effective and deliver enough bang for the buck to persuade financially stressed MIC governments that the returns to investing in good governance and rule of law outweigh the opportunity costs.

One of the criticisms of the rule-of-law promotion industry has been the heavy reliance on one-size-fits-all solutions that fail to distinguish between postconflict situations and stable environments, or among different stages of development. The diversity among MICs mandates that development agencies come up with more

[37] Fank Schimmelfennig, "A Comparison of the Rule of Law Promotion Policies of Major Western Powers," in *The Dynamics of Rule of Law in an Era of International and Transnational Governance*, ed. Michael Zurn, Andre Noelkamper, and Randall Peerenboom (Cambridge University Press, 2012).

[38] See, e.g., Thomas Carothers, ed., *Promoting the Rule of Law Abroad: In Search of Knowledge* (Carnegie Endowment for International Peace, 2006); Alvaro Santos, "The World Bank's Uses of the 'Rule of Law' Promise in Economic Development," in *The New Law and Economic Development: A Critical Appraisal*, ed. David Trubek and Alvaro Santos (Cambridge University Press, 2006); Veronica Taylor, "Frequently Asked Questions about Rule of Law Assistance (And Why Better Answers Matter)," *Hague Journal on Rule of Law* 1, no. 1 (2009): 46–52.

[39] Dani Rodrik, "Second-Best Institutions," *American Economic Review: Papers & Proceedings* 98, no. 2 (2008): 100–4.

tailored policies to address the complex governance issues in MICs. It is highly unlikely that MICs as currently defined (i.e., countries with per capita income from $1,026 to $12,000) will emerge as a useful category for rule-of-law programming. Further disaggregation is required, not only by levels of wealth but along other dimensions as well. Linn Hammergren, formerly of the World Bank, has begun that process by distinguishing on functional grounds between four different types of MICs and then offering more tailored reform proposals for each:

1. Countries (either low end MICs or MICs by virtue of a rich primary resource endowment) with dysfunctional systems largely because of internal disorganization, few curbs on external interference of all types, low budgets and small size, and a mass of citizens physically far removed from the reaches of the state system.
2. Countries (usually low to mid-range MICs) with larger, but still dysfunctional systems because of systematic political penetration, rampant but often more organized corruption, and inaccessibility to most citizens owing to costs, cultural factors, and simple distrust.
3. Countries (usually mid-level MICs) with more orderly and usually larger state systems that are nonetheless unsatisfactory performers because of lingering, but more targeted political interference, significant but not rampant corruption, often overly complex but poorly engineered organizations, or ... an independence-accountability gap (courts and other sector actors have achieved sufficient independence to function in relative disregard of user needs and sometimes to strike their own bargains with political authorities).
4. Higher end MICs characterized by inefficiency, some outmoded practices, and a rising supply-demand gap for sector services.[40]

She notes that at all four levels, tailoring programs to different needs requires more sophisticated donor skills – both in recognizing what is required and being able to point counterparts toward appropriate sources of technical expertise – as well as an ability to recognize a political issue for what it is and thus avoid imposing answers. Traditionally donor programs have relied on well-meaning generalists, sometimes entrusting program development and management to individuals with only a rudimentary knowledge of the justice sector.[41]

UNDP representative Nicholas Booth also argues that a dedicated in-house policy advisory is better able to respond to the more political and multistakeholder governance challenges that confront MICs.

[40] Linn Hammergren, "Rule of Law Challenges in Middle-Income Countries and Donor Approaches to Them," in *The Dynamics of Rule of Law in an Era of International and Transnational Governance*, ed. Michael Zurn, Andre Noelkamper, and Randall Peerenboom (Cambridge University Press 2012), 199–200.

[41] Ibid., at 201.

Even with such changes, international donor agencies face challenges and decreased influence. Because many of the most pressing problems are political economy obstacles, they require local knowledge of who benefits and loses from reform, and ultimately a political solution. Unfortunately, as Hammergren notes, the World Bank and other international donors are not well positioned to address these types of local political contests, in some cases, because of limited mandates, in other cases because of the lack of local knowledge and other financial and institutional limitations.

Moreover, the World Bank has acknowledged that development in general and in MICs in particular requires a comprehensive and interdisciplinary approach. Yet the World Bank remains dominated by economists, and its research and recommendations focus on economic reforms and policies. Similarly, the Ford Foundation and other NGOs focus on human rights issues, while a number of single-issue NGOs focus on their own area of concern be it judicial reforms, gender issues, the welfare of children or the environment. So far there has been very little collaborative programming by development agencies or attempts to pool internal and external resources to develop a comprehensive, interdisciplinary plan for development.

Finally, most MICs are now sufficiently wealthy, and international capital flows sufficiently fluid, that MICs will not accept conditionalities or allow external actors to impose their agenda. International and bilateral donors will need to play a more facilitative role. The reform process must genuinely be country owned and country led. To date, MICs have had little input into the policy-making process of the World Bank and other international donor agencies.[42]

CONCLUSION

Research into MICs by noneconomists is only just beginning. Accordingly, we conclude with some areas for further research. The following list is illustrative but by no means exhaustive. Some of the issues were touched on in this volume, others break new ground.

There is a need for more quantitative studies that break countries down by HIC, MIC, LIC; that explore alternative measures of governance outcomes and wealth; and that control for factors besides GNI per capita, such as aggregate size of economy, regional effects, growth rates, legal families, and so on. Many of the quantitative studies on the relationship of economic growth, regime type, democratization, rule of law, good governance, and human rights could be redone distinguishing between LICs, MICs, and HICs. The results might be clearer and shed

[42] Independent Evaluation Group, "Development Results in Middle-Income Countries: An Evaluation of World Bank Support," 2007, available at http://siteresources.worldbank.org/EXTMIDINCCOU/Resources/MIC_evaluation.pdf.

light on the distinct challenges at different levels of wealth and the different pathways to success.

In a related vein, there is a pressing need to better understand sequencing issues, whether through large-N quantitative studies or qualitative studies. Most of the attention has been on the sequencing of political reforms and rule of law, and whether it is best to democratize at an early stage when rule of law is weak, or whether there are benefits to democratizing at a later stage after reforms have strengthened the legal system, as in the case of East Asian countries. But MICs face countless other sequencing issues: whether in postconflict situations to prioritize peacekeeping and security relative to promulgation of new laws and institution building; whether to engage in financial liberalization, including capital account convertibility at an early stage, or to slowly open the financial sector to foreign competition with current account convertibility preceding capital account convertibility; whether to prioritize judicial independence or to seek a balance between judicial independence and judicial accountability; and whether to emphasize aggregate development or promote rights-based sustainable development.

Much remains to be done to develop measures of sustainable development. China began work on creating a green GDP index, but the project has become mired in contested normative issues and complex technical challenges. Attempts to develop a happiness index have met a similar fate. While wealth is highly correlated with most good things in life, including longer life, more literacy, better governance, rule of law, more personal security, and more political freedom, wealth alone does not ensure happiness. Surveys indicate that many reasonably well-off citizens in rich countries are deeply unhappy, oftentimes less happy than their counterparts in poorer countries. While citizens of MICs may suffer from the middle-income blues, citizens in rich countries may suffer from postmodern blues.[43]

We also need to better understand the geography of development. There appear to be significant regional effects. But how do regulatory changes occur and spread across a region? How transferrable are different regulatory regimes? What are the comparative advantages and disadvantages of the Euro-American and Asian transnational production regimes identified by John Gillespie (Chapter 6)? More generally, we need to better understand the specific challenges and opportunities in different regions, including the Middle East and Africa as more countries become MICs. There is a need for more systematic study of what determines success or failure among MICs globally, but particularly within regions or among countries with similar natural endowments and starting points. Broadly defined regions like Latin America, Africa, CEE, the Middle East, Asia, or even South and East Asia contain within them wide diversity, presenting challenges and opportunities for further research.

[43] Ronald Ingleheart, *Modernization and Postmodernization: Cultural, Economic and Political Change in 43 Societies* (Princeton University Press, 1997).

There are many issues in need of further investigation regarding good governance and rule of law. While all acknowledge the need for more tailored advice, international and bilateral donors are still very far from being able to provide such advice. It remains to be seen whether they will rise to the occasion and restructure their operations to meet the challenges of MICs, and whether their responses will work.

How to handle socioeconomic issues remains a serious challenge for MICs. Further work needs to be done exploring, creating, and testing innovative policies, and comparing the advantages and disadvantages of different mechanisms and approaches. The relative advantages and disadvantages of the courts versus political, administrative, public-private, or market mechanisms also needs to be further analyzed across a range of issue areas and in countries with different political, legal, and social traditions and at different levels of development.[44]

In this volume, we were only able to begin to address the impact of MICs on the international economic order. We will need to wait and see how the multilateral system reacts to the system friction caused by MICs with diverse political and economic systems more aggressively pursuing their own interests and agendas. We will also need to see which of the scenarios sketched by Yu pan out across a range of issue areas.

Much remains to be said about the influence of MICs beyond the international trade regime. The rise of MICs from different regions with different normative traditions could have an impact on the human rights regime and undermine claims of universality. For instance, critics contend that China is taking advantage of its growing economic and geopolitical influence to defend and advocate rights policies and a normative vision of the world at odds with the current rights policies based on secular liberalism. They point to China's attempts to restructure the UN Human Rights Commission and its support of authoritarian regimes in North Korea, Myanmar, and Africa as evidence.

MICs will also exercise increasing geopolitical influence. They are already altering existing military alliances, forming new alliances and affecting the balance of power regionally and globally. The rise of China has increased tensions in the region and the possibility of military conflict whether with Taiwan over independence or

[44] Different issues will arise in different countries. In some countries, background conditions will favor a broader role for the courts in ESR cases: ESR will be incorporated into the constitution; standing rules will encourage individuals and NGOs to act as private attorney generals and engage in public interest litigation; procedural laws will permit class-action suits; and there will be a tradition of judicial independence. In other countries, these conditions might not prevail. In traditional civil law systems, the judiciary may have limited powers to make law or engage in broad policy making through deciding individual cases. The lack of a precedent system may also lead to numerous cases being litigated over similar issues, resulting in reforms that push such cases to administrative channels or the development of structural injunctions, as described by Rodríguez-Garavito. Public interest litigation may also be discouraged through strict standing requirements. In many countries, there are limits on class-action suits, sometimes because of concerns about social stability as in China, or complementary structures such as contingency fees or a private market to finance class action suits are lacking. More generally, the relative capacity of legislatures, administrative agencies, and the courts varies.

with other countries over disputed islands whose location is linked to rights over oil. In addition, MICs are likely to exert increasing influence over the UN Security Council. There is also the growing risk of nuclear proliferation as rising MICs like Iran develop nuclear capabilities.

There are then many possible avenues for further research. A more comprehensive and holistic understanding of how MICs become mired in or break out of middle-income traps will require an interdisciplinary approach that brings together economists, political scientists, sociologists, anthropologists, historians, legal scholars, rural planners, health care, and welfare specialists. We hope this volume will provide the stimulus for the development of the kind of interdisciplinary epistemic and professional networks needed to address the many challenges confronting the 70 percent of the world's population living in MICs.

Appendix: Selected Country Data as of 2011

Country	GNI per capita (Atlas method)	Voice/ Accountability	Government effectiveness	Regulatory Quality	Rule of Law	Corruption	Human Development Index (UNDP)	Gini Coefficient	Environmental Performance
High Income Countries									
Monaco	183150	78.9			79.3				
Liechtenstein	137070	97.7	95.7	92.4	92	93.8	0.905		
Bermuda	125287	80.8	80.6	90	85	88.2			
Qatar	80440	21.6	75.8	66.4	73.7	80.6	0.831	41.1	48.9
Luxembourg	78130	98.1	94.8	98.6	96.7	98.1	0.867		67.8
Switzerland	76380	100	97.6	94.8	95.3	95.7	0.903	33.7	89.1
Cayman Islands	60526	65.3	85.8	83.9	75.6	88.6			
Denmark	60390	99.1	99.5	100	99.1	100	0.895		69.2
Sweden	53230	98.6	98.6	97.6	99.5	99.1	0.904	25	86
San Marino	50400	87.3			79.3				
Netherlands	49730	96.2	96.7	98.1	97.7	97.6	0.91		66.4
Isle of Man	48910								
Kuwait	48900	30.5	53.1	54.5	65.7	60.2	0.76		51.1
United States	48450	85.9	88.6	91.9	91.1	85.8	0.91	40.8	63.5
Finland	48420	97.2	100	96.2	100	98.6	0.882	26.9	74.7
Austria	48300	94.4	93.4	91.5	97.2	89.6	0.885	29.1	78.1
Australia	46200	95.3	95.3	96.7	96.2	96.7	0.929		65.7
Belgium	46160	93.9	93.8	86.7	89.7	92.4	0.886	33	58.1
Canada	45560	94.8	97.2	95.7	94.8	95.3	0.908	32.6	66.4
Macao	45460	66.7	87.2	87.7	70	70.6			
Japan	45180	77.9	87.7	78.2	86.9	90.5	0.901		72.5
Germany	43980	92.5	91.9	92.9	91.5	92.9	0.905	28.3	73.2
Singapore	42930	42.7	99.1	97.2	93.4	96.2	0.866		69.6
France	42420	88.7	88.2	82.5	90.1	91	0.884	32.7	78.2

Andorra	41750	93.4	91	93.8	89.2	88.2	0.838		
United Arab Emirates	40760	20.2	77.7	63	65.3	82.5	0.846		40.7
Ireland	38580	93	89.1	95.3	95.8	90	0.908	34.3	67.1
United Kingdom	37780	92	92.4	94.3	92.5	91.5	0.863		74.2
Italy	35330	74.6	66.4	75.4	63.4	57.3	0.874	36	73.1
Hong Kong	35160	64.8	94.3	99.1	90.6	94.3	0.898		
Iceland	35020	95.8	92.9	80.6	93	94.8	0.898	93.5	
Brunei Darussalam	31800	29.1	77.3	84.8	77.9	77.3	0.838		60.8
Spain	30990	84	82	82	85.9	81	0.878	34.7	70.6
Cyprus	29450	82.2	91.5	85.3	83.1	79.6	0.84		56.3
Israel	28930	67.7	84.4	88.6	80.3	73	0.888		62.4
Greenland	26020	90.6	79.1	88.2	94.4	84.8			
Greece	25030	71.4	66.8	69.7	66.7	55.9	0.861	34.3	60.9
Slovenia	23610	78.4	79.6	73	83.6	79.1	0.884		65
Aruba	23148	91.1	85.8	89.1	87.3	83.9			
Bahamas	21970	76.1	78.2	68.2	68.1	89.1	0.771		
Portugal	21250	85	78.7	73.9	81.7	82.9	0.809		73
Korea, Republic of	20870	68.5	86.3	79.1	80.8	70.1	0.897		57
French Polynesia	19953								
Oman	19260	18.8	65.9	62.6	67.6	60.7	0.705		45.9
Malta	18620	85.4	82.9	87.2	87.8	78.2	0.832		76.3
Czech Republic	18520	76.5	81.5	86.3	81.2	66.8	0.865		71.6
Saudi Arabia	17820	3.3	40.8	52.6	56.8	48.3	0.77		55.3
Puerto Rico	16560	69	64.5	76.3	72.3	71.1			
Slovak Republic	16070	75.1	76.3	81	69	66.4	0.834		74.5
Bahrain	15920	14.1	71.1	75.8	62.4	64.9	0.806		42
Estonia	15200	83.6	84.8	90.5	85.4	78.7	0.835	30.1	63.8
Trinidad and Tobago	15040	62.9	63	63.5	49.8	49.3	0.76		54.2

Country	GNI per capita (Atlas method)	Voice/ Accountability	Government effectiveness	Regulatory Quality	Rule of Law	Corruption	Human Development Index (UNDP)	Gini Coefficient	Environmental Performance
Equatorial Guinea	14540	2.8	3.3	7.6	10.8	1.9	0.537		41.9
Croatia	13850	60.1	69.2	70.1	60.6	59.2	0.796	33.7	68.7
Hungary	12730	73.2	73	81.5	73.2	67.3	0.816	31.2	69.1
Barbados	12660	89.2	90	71.1	82.2	93.4	0.793		
Poland	12480	79.3	71.6	80.1	71.4	71.6	0.813	34.2	63.1
St Kitts and Nevis	12480	87.8	75.4	64	70.4	82			
Middle Income Countries									
Latvia	12350	69.5	72.5	79.6	74.2	63.5	0.805	35.7	72.5
Libya	12320	6.1	4.7	5.2	12.2	4.7	0.76		50.1
Lithuania	12280	72.8	72	78.7	72.8	65.9	0.81	37.6	68.3
Chile	12280	81.2	83.9	93.4	88.3	91.9	0.805	22.6	73.3
Antigua and Barbuda	12060	64.3	67.8	72.5	79.8	88.2	0.764		69.8
Venezuela	11920	24.4	13.3	6.2	1.4	7.6	0.735	43.5	62.9
Uruguay	11860	84.5	69.7	64.5	70.9	86.3	0.783	42.4	59.1
Seychelles	11130	52.6	62.1	36	54.9	65.4	0.773	19	
Brazil	10720	63.8	55.5	55.9	55.4	63	0.718	53.9	63.4
Turkey	10410	43.7	65.4	65.4	57.7	61.1	0.699	39.7	60.4
Russian Federation	10400	22.5	42.2	38.9	25.4	13.3	0.755	42.3	61.2
Argentina	9740	57.7	48.8	25.1	33.3	42.2	0.797	45.8	61
Mexico	9240	53.5	63.5	60.7	39	45.5	0.77	51.7	67.3
Lebanon	9110	34.3	43.6	53.6	30	19.4	0.739		57.9
Malaysia	8420	33.8	81	74.4	66.2	57.8	0.761	46.2	65
Mauritius	8240	70.4	74.4	76.8	75.1	72.5	0.728		80.6
Kazakhstan	8220	13.6	45.5	42.7	31.5	15.2	0.745	30.9	57.3

American Samoa	8000	80.8	67.8	62.1	85	68.2			
Gabon	7980	23.9	19.4	30.8	38	24.2	0.674	41.5	56.4
Romania	7910	59.6	47.4	74.9	56.3	55	0.781	31.2	67
Panama	7910	63.4	58.8	64.9	53.5	46	0.768	52.3	71.4
Costa Rica	7660	77.5	64	66.8	64.8	72	0.744	50.3	86.4
Suriname	7630	57.3	51.7	31.3	52.1	45	0.68		68.2
Botswana	7480	60.6	68.2	69.2	69.5	80.1	0.633		41.3
Palau	7250	88.3	33.2	21.3	74.6	39.3	0.782		
Grenada	7220	70.9	61.6	57.8	59.2	68.7	0.748		
Dominica	7090	77	70.1	56.9	67.1	73.5	0.724		
Montenegro	7060	55.9	59.2	51.7	55.9	52.6	0.771	30	
South Africa	6960	65.7	64.9	65.9	58.7	59.7	0.619	57.8	50.8
St. Lucia	6680	89.7	76.8	67.3	71.8	85.3	0.723	42.6	
Bulgaria	6550	61.5	56.4	70.6	51.6	55.5	0.771	45.3	62.5
Maldives	6530	41.8	44.1	37.4	44.1	30.3	0.661	37.4	65.9
Colombia	6110	44.6	62.6	61.1	47.9	46.4	0.71	58.5	76.8
St. Vincent and the Grenadines	6100	86.4	75.4	61.6	78.4	82	0.717		
Belarus	5830	5.2	13.7	9.5	14.1	25.1	0.756	27.2	65.4
Serbia	5680	56.3	49.8	53.1	46	54.5	0.766	28.2	
Peru	5500	51.6	49.3	68.7	32.4	54	0.725	48	69.3
Cuba	5460	7	46	4.3	35.2	69.2	0.776		78.1
Azerbaijan	5290	11.7	23.2	37.9	21.6	9.5	0.7	33.7	59.1
Dominican Republic	5240	50.7	34.6	46	26.3	22.3	0.689	48.4	68.4
Tuvalu	5010	70	23.7	9	64.3	38.4		31.9	
Jamaica	4980	61	61.1	60.2	41.8	43.6	0.727	42.2	58
China	4940	4.7	60.7	45.5	40.4	28.9	0.687	41.5	49
Bosnia and Herzegovina	4780	41.3	25.1	52.1	46.5	49.8	0.733	36.2	55.9
Macedonia	4730	49.8	50.7	59.7	48.8	56.9	0.728	44.2	60.6

Country	GNI per capita (Atlas method)	Voice/ Accountability	Government effectiveness	Regulatory Quality	Rule of Law	Corruption	Human Development Index (UNDP)	Gini Coefficient	Environmental Performance
Namibia	4700	56.8	57.8	55	61	64	0.625	63.9	59.3
Iran	4520	6.6	38.9	2.8	20.2	19	0.707	38.3	60
Algeria	4470	18.3	29.4	11.4	24.9	34.6	0.698	35.3	67.4
Thailand	4420	33.3	59.7	56.4	48.4	44.5	0.682	53.6	62.2
Jordan	4380	25.4	57.3	57.3	62	58.8	0.698	37.7	56.1
Ecuador	4140	37.6	35.1	15.6	13.6	21.3	0.72	49	69.3
Turkmenistan	4110	0.9	4.3	1.9	4.7	2.4	0.686		38.4
Tunisia	4070	35.7	56.9	46.4	51.2	53.1	0.698	40.8	60.6
Angola	4060	14.6	11.4	12.3	10.3	3.8	0.486	58.6	36.3
Albania	3980	53.1	48.3	58.8	37.6	32.7	0.739	34.5	71.4
Marshall Islands	3910	87.3	3.8	19.9	60.1	51.7			
Belize	3690	68.1	43.1	32.7	36.2	51.2	0.699	59.6	69.9
Fiji	3680	19.2	27	34.6	19.7	37.9	0.688	46.8	65.9
Tonga	3580	58.2	42.7	28.9	57.3	47.9	0.704		
Cape Verde	3540	75.6	60.2	54	63.8	74.4	0.568	50.5	
Kosovo	3520	39.9	37.9	48.8	32.9	30.8			
El Salvador	3480	52.1	51.2	67.8	27.7	52.1	0.674	46.9	69.1
Armenia	3360	27.7	52.1	58.3	43.7	33.6	0.716	30.9	60.4
Swaziland	3300	12.7	28.4	28.4	42.3	50.2	0.522	60.7	54.4
Samoa	3190	62	55	42.2	68.5	61.6	0.688		
Ukraine	3120	46.5	21.8	31.8	23	17.1	0.729	27.5	58.2
Morocco	2970	28.6	47.9	50.2	49.3	50.7	0.582	40.9	65.6
Paraguay	2970	46	20.9	39.8	22.5	25.6	0.665	52	63.5
Indonesia	2940	46.9	46.9	41.7	31	27.5	0.617	36.8	44.6
Micronesia	2900	81.7	26.5	20.9	54	46.9	0.636		

Guyana	2890	50.2	50.2	28	39.4	33.2	0.633		59.2
Guatemala	2870	36.2	28	47.9	15	36.5	0.574	53.7	54
Vanuatu	2870	66.2	46.4	27	61.5	67.8	0.617		
Georgia	2860	43.2	68.7	73.5	50.7	56.4	0.733	41.3	63.6
Syrian Arab Republic	2750	3.8	39.3	18.5	30.5	17.5	0.632	35.8	64.6
Timor-Leste	2730	54	12.3	14.7	11.7	14.7	0.495	31.9	
West Bank and Gaza	2710	20.7	30.3	59.2	41.3	20.9			
Iraq	2640	15	10.4	12.8	2.3	7.1	0.573		41
Egypt	2600	16	32.2	41.2	42.7	28	0.644	32.1	62
Sri Lanka	2580	31	52.6	50.7	53.1	40.8	0.691	40.3	63.7
Mongolia	2320	49.3	31.3	44.5	45.5	27	0.653	36.5	42.8
Congo, Republic of	2270	17.8	9	8.5	12.7	11.8	0.533	47.3	54
South Sudan	2267	16.9	0.9	3.3	2.8	0.9			
Philippines	2210	48.8	55.9	43.6	34.7	22.7	0.644	44	65.7
Kiribati	2110	73.7	24.2	6.6	58.2	62.6	0.624		
Bhutan	2070	32.4	70.6	10.9	59.6	73.9	0.522	46.8	68
Bolivia	2040	47.4	41.2	24.2	16.9	38.9	0.663	57.3	44.3
Moldova	1980	48.4	33.6	51.2	45.1	31.3	0.649	38	58.8
Honduras	1970	31.9	34.1	49.3	19.2	21.8	0.625	57.7	49.9
Uzbekistan	1510	1.9	24.6	3.8	5.2	4.3	0.641	36.7	42.3
Papua New Guinea	1480	47.9	26.1	33.6	24.4	11.4	0.466		44.3
Ghana	1410	62.4	53.6	55.5	54.5	62.1	0.541	42.8	51.3
India	1410	59.2	54.5	40.3	52.6	35.1	0.547	33.4	48.3
Sao Tomé and Principe	1360	54.5	27.5	24.6	28.2	44.1	0.509	50.8	57.3
Sudan	1300	4.2	7.1	8.1	8.5	5.7	0.408		47.1

Country	GNI per capita (Atlas method)	Voice/ Accountability	Government effectiveness	Regulatory Quality	Rule of Law	Corruption	Human Development Index (UNDP)	Gini Coefficient	Environmental Performance
Djibouti	1270	11.3	16.1	33.2	26.8	47.4	0.43	40	60.5
Vietnam	1260	8.5	45	29.4	38.5	29.9	0.593	37.6	59
Lesotho	1220	45.1	44.5	30.3	47.4	64.5	0.45	63.2	
Cameroon	1210	17.4	18.5	22.7	14.6	18	0.482	32.6	44.6
Nigeria	1200	26.8	12.8	27.5	9.9	10	0.459	43.9	40.2
Nicaragua	1170	29.6	18	39.3	29.6	24.6	0.589	52.3	57.1
Zambia	1160	42.3	29.9	36.5	39.9	37	0.43	54.6	47
Lao PDR	1130	5.6	17.1	19.4	18.3	13.7	0.524	36.7	59.6
Pakistan	1120	26.3	22.3	29.9	20.7	15.6	0.504	32.7	48
Solomon Islands	1110	51.2	20.4	13.7	31.9	40.3	0.51		51.1
Côte d'Ivoire	1100	15.5	9.5	21.8	8	12.3	0.4	46.1	54.3
Senegal	1070	39	39.8	44.1	40.8	31.8	0.459	39.2	42.3
Yemen	1070	9.9	11.8	23.2	8.9	8.1	0.462	37.7	48.3
Lower Income Countries									
Mauritania	1000	22.1	17.5	23.7	21.1	34.1	0.453	39	33.7
Kyrgyz Republic	920	27.2	30.8	45	9.4	10.4	0.615	33.4	59.7
Tajikistan	870	9.4	16.6	19	11.3	9	0.607	29.4	51.3
Cambodia	830	24.9	25.6	35.1	15.5	12.8	0.523	44.4	41.7
Kenya	820	40.4	36	46.9	16.4	18.5	0.509	47.7	51.4
Benin	780	55.4	38.4	40.8	27.2	28.4	0.427		39.6
Bangladesh	770	37.1	19.9	22.3	28.6	16.1	0.5	31	44
Comoros	770	32.9	1.4	7.1	16	26.1	0.433		
Haiti	700	28.1	2.8	14.2	5.6	6.2	0.454		39.5
Chad	690	10.3	6.6	15.2	3.8	6.6	0.328		40.8
Zimbabwe	640	8.9	6.2	2.4	0.9	5.2	0.376	50.1	47.8

Gambia	610	13.1	31.8	43.1	36.6	37.4	0.42		50.3
Mali	610	54.9	21.3	38.4	35.7	32.2	0.359	39	39.4
Guinea-Bisau	600	21.1	14.7	11.8	6.1	14.2	0.353		44.7
Burkina Faso	570	36.6	37	47.4	44.6	43.1	0.331		47.3
Rwanda	570	12.2	58.3	48.3	46.9	69.7	0.429	53.1	44.6
Togo	560	23	7.6	17.5	23.5	16.6	0.435	34.4	36.4
Nepal	540	31.5	22.7	25.6	17.4	23.7	0.458		68.2
Tanzania	540	45.5	36.5	35.5	34.3	36	0.466	37.6	47.9
Uganda	510	30	37.4	49.8	43.2	19.9	0.446	44.3	49.8
Korea, Democratic Republic	503	0	0.5	0	6.6	2.8			41.8
Central African Republic	470	16.4	8.1	10	7	20.4	0.343		33.3
Mozambique	470	44.1	35.5	37	33.8	41.7	0.322	45.6	51.2
Guinea	440	23.5	10.9	16.6	3.3	8.5	0.344	39.4	44.4
Eritrea	430	0.5	5.7	0.9	7.5	35.5	0.349		54.6
Madagascar	430	25.8	19	32.2	23.9	48.8	0.48	47.2	49.2
Afghanistan	410	7.5	5.2	4.7	0.5	1.4	0.398		
Ethiopia	400	10.8	41.7	18	29.1	26.5	0.363	29.8	43.1
Myanmar	380	2.3	2.4	1.4	4.2	0.5	0.483		51.3
Niger	360	38.5	28.9	34.1	37.1	29.4	0.295	34	37.6
Malawi	340	39.4	40.3	26.5	50.2	42.7	0.4		51.4
Sierra Leone	340	40.8	10	26.1	22.1	23.2	0.336	62.9	32.1
Burundi	250	19.7	14.2	17.1	13.1	10.9	0.316	33.3	43.9
Liberia	240	38	8.5	16.1	17.8	39.8	0.329	52.6	
Somalia	211	1.4	0	0.5	0	0			
Congo, Democratic Republic	190	8	1.9	5.7	1.9	3.3	0.286	44.4	51.6

(*Source:* World Bank unless noted)

Index

www.ingramcontent.com/pod-product-compliance
Lightning Source LLC
LaVergne TN
LVHW011530200926
848484LV00001B/213
9781107028159